POVERTY
EXCLUSION IN BRITAIN

The millennium survey

Chr

First published in Great Britain in January 2006 by

The Policy Press
University of Bristol
Fourth Floor
Beacon House
Queen's Road
Bristol BS8 1QU
UK

Tel +44 (0)117 331 4054
Fax +44 (0)117 331 4093
e-mail tpp-info@bristol.ac.uk
www.policypress.co.uk

North American office:
The Policy Press
c/o International Specialized Books Services (ISBS)
920 NE 58th Avenue, Suite 300
Portland, OR 97213-3786, USA
Tel +1 503 287 3093
Fax +1 503 280 8832
e-mail info@isbs.com

© Christina Pantazis, David Gordon and Ruth Levitas 2006

Reprinted 2006, 2010

British Library Cataloguing in Publication Data
A catalogue record for this book is available from the British Library.

Library of Congress Cataloging-in-Publication Data
A catalog record for this book has been requested.

ISBN 978 1 86134 373 4 paperback
ISBN 978 1 86134 374 1 hardcover

Cover design by Qube Design Associates, Bristol.
Front cover: photograph supplied by kind permission of Mary Shaw.
Printed and bound in Great Britain by Hobbs, Southampton.

This book is dedicated to the inventors of
the consensual poverty method,
Joanna Mack, Stewart Lansley, Harold Frayman and Brian Gosschalk

Contents

List of figures

List of tables

Acknowledgements

The Poverty and Social Exclusion Survey of Britain (PSE) questionnaire contains both modified and new questions as well as questions which have been asked in the best social surveys from around the world. It builds on over one hundred years of experience in the social sciences in Britain in the scientific study of poverty. The authors acknowledge the contribution made to this research from the following sources and surveys: Breadline Britain in the 1990s, British Crime Survey, British Household Panel Survey, British Social Attitudes, Canadian General Social Survey, Disability Discrimination Act Baseline Survey, Eurobarometer, European Community Household Panel Survey, EuroQol 5D, General Household Survey, GHQ12, Harmonised Question Set, Health Survey of England, Living in Ireland Survey, Living in Britain Survey, Lorraine Panel Survey, MORI Omnibus, Poor Wales, Poverty in the United Kingdom, Small Fortunes: National Survey of the Lifestyles and Living Standards of Children, Survey of English Housing and the Swedish Living Conditions Survey.

The Breadline Britain in the 1990s survey was funded by London Weekend Television (LWT) with additional funding from the Joseph Rowntree Foundation and was carried out by Marketing and Opinion Research International (MORI). It was conceived and designed by Joanna Mack and Stewart Lansley for Domino Films, with the help of Brian Gosschalk of MORI. We would also like to thank Brian Gosschalk, Mark Speed and Sarah Birtles from MORI for their helpful comments and advice on the preparatory stages of this research.

The PSE Survey was carried out by the Office for National Statistics, Omnibus and General Household Survey (GHS) teams. We would particularly like to thank Ann Bridgewood, Jo Maher and Olwen Rowlands for all their sound professional advice and help. We would also like to thank Björn Halleröd of the University of Umeå, Tony Manners, Dave Elliot, Linda Murgatroyd and June Bowman at the Office for National Statistics, Richard Berthoud and Jonathan Gershuny at the University of Essex, Rick Davies of Swansea University, John Veit-Wilson, University of Newcastle upon Tyne and Michael Bitman at the University of New South Wales for their helpful advice.

We would like to thank Barbara Ballard, David Darton, David Utting, Lynne Spence, Alison Elks, Dominic Hurley, Mark Hinman and Peter Barclay from the Joseph Rowntree Foundation for their advice, encouragement and support throughout this project and Donald Hirsch for his editing work on the JRF report. We would like to thank all the members of the JRF advisory committee for their helpful support, including Martin Barnes, Fran Bennett, Ann Bowtell, Ann Bridgwood, Gillian Dollamore, Rebecca Endean, Phillip Edwards, John Hills, Will Hutton, Joanna Mack, Tim Marsh, Jane Millar, Linda Nicolson, John Pullinger and Tom Taylor. The Joseph Rowntree Foundation funded the PSE Survey.

Thanks are due to Helen and May Gordon, Tom Hore, Jean Corston and Robert Hunter for their unfailing support during this research.

Dawn Rushen, Alison Shaw, Laura Greaves and Julia Mortimer deserve our thanks for their patience, professionalism and support in editing, producing and marketing this book.

Finally we would like to thank all our colleagues at the Universities of York and Loughborough who worked on the PSE Survey, particularly, Jonathan Bradshaw, Julie Williams, Naomi Finch, Sue Middleton, Laura Adelman and Karl Ashworth. Without their generous help and expertise this research would not have been possible.

List of acronyms

ABS	Australian Bureau of Statistics
AHC	After Housing Costs
ALSPAC	Avon Longitudinal Study of Pregnancy and Childhood
ASBO	anti-social behaviour order
BCS	British Crime Survey
BHC	Before Housing Costs
BHPS	British Household Panel Survey
CASE	Centre for the Analysis of Social Exclusion
CIS-R	Clinical Interview Schedule – Revised
DALYs	Disability-Adjusted Life Years
DSS	Department of Social Security
DWP	Department for Work and Pensions
ECHP	European Community Household Panel
EYF	European Youth Forum
FACS	Families and Children Survey
FES	Family Expenditure Survey
FRS	Family Resources Survey
GC	Guarantee Credit
GHQ	General Health Questionnaire
GHS	General Household Survey
HBAI	Households Below Average Income
JSA	Jobseeker's Allowance
LCA	low cost but acceptable
MIG	Minimum Income Guarantee
MUD	moral underclass discourse
NDLP	New Deal for Lone Parents
OECD	Organisation for Economic Co-operation and Development
ONS	Office for National Statistics
OPCS	Office for Population Censuses and Surveys
PAT12	Policy Action Team
PRILIF	Programme of Research on Low Income Families
PSA	Public Service Agreement
PSE Survey	Poverty and Social Exclusion Survey
PSI	Policy Studies Institute
RED	redistributive discourse

SC	Savings Credit
SDS	social deprivation scale
SEU	Social Exclusion Unit
SID	social integration discourse
SOLIF	Survey of Low Income Families

Notes on contributors

Nick Bailey is a senior lecturer in the Department of Urban Studies, University of Glasgow and Acting Director of the Scottish Centre for Research on Social Justice. His interests include: labour markets, economic restructuring and welfare reform; area deprivation and neighbourhood policy; and housing policy.

Glen Bramley is Professor of Urban Studies and Director of the Centre for Research into Socially Inclusive Services (CRSIS) at Heriot-Watt University in Edinburgh, where he leads a substantial research programme in housing and urban studies. Recent research is focused particularly on poverty, deprivation and local services (including education), flows of funds to local areas, housing need and affordability, low cost home ownership, planning for new housing and the impact of planning and infrastructure on city competitiveness. His publications include *Key issues in housing*; *Planning, the market and private housebuilding*; *Equalization grants and local expenditure needs*; and *Analysing social policy*.

Sharon Collard is a research fellow at the Personal Finance Research Centre, based at the University of Bristol. Since joining the Centre in 1998, she has worked on a wide range of research projects, exploring topics such as the use of credit and other financial services by low-income consumers, the provision of money advice and debt counselling services, and financial capability. In a personal capacity, Sharon is on the management committee of Bristol Debt Advice Centre.

Eldin Fahmy is a research fellow in the Centre for the Study of Poverty and Social Justice at the School for Policy Studies, University of Bristol. His research interests include: youth, poverty and social exclusion; poverty, area-based initiatives and anti-poverty strategy; rural poverty; and inequality and social and civic participation.

Naomi Finch is a research fellow at the Social Policy Research Unit at the University of York. She has undertaken research, including comparative research, focusing on issues of poverty, living standards, and family policy. Her current research interests focus on pensioner poverty.

Tania Fisher is a research fellow in the Health Policy and Economic Research Unit at the British Medical Association. Her current research focuses on health policy. Other research interests include urban change and development, population change and social inclusion.

David Gordon is Professor of Social Justice and Director of the university-wide Townsend Centre for International Poverty Research at the University of Bristol. His main research and publications are in the fields of the scientific measurement of poverty, social justice and social harm, area-based anti-poverty measures, childhood disability, the causal effects of poverty on ill health, housing policy and rural poverty.

Emma Head is a research fellow in the School of Sociology and Social Policy, University of Leeds, UK. Her research interests are broadly in the areas of family policy and family sociology; and she has particular interest in issues of lone parenthood, care and poverty.

Ruth Levitas is Professor of Sociology and Head of Department elect at the University of Bristol. She writes on contemporary politics and policy, inequality, and social indicators, as well as on social theory and utopianism. Her books include *The ideology of the New Right* (1986), *The concept of utopia* (1990), *Interpreting official statistics* (ed with Will Guy, 1996) and *The inclusive society? Social exclusion and New Labour* (1998, second edition 2005).

Eva Lloyd is Senior Lecturer in Early Childhood Studies in the Centre for the Study of Poverty and Social Justice at the School for Policy Studies, at the University of Bristol. Prior to joining Bristol University, she spent 15 years with children's NGOs. She is also an associate of the Centre for Family Research at the University of Cambridge and an honorary research fellow at the Centre for Childcare Research at the Queen's University Belfast, UK. Her research interests include early childhood policies and programmes, anti-poverty strategies and evidence-based policy and practice in the social sciences.

Steve McKay is Deputy Director of the Personal Finance Research Centre, based at the University of Bristol. His research interests include low-income families, the effects of benefits and tax credits on incentives and behaviour, pensions and retirement, and measuring poverty. He recently completed work on a new survey of attitudes to inheritance.

Christina Pantazis is Head of the Centre for the Study of Poverty and Social Justice at the University of Bristol. Her main research interests are in poverty, social exclusion and inequality, and crime, criminalisation and social harm. Previous publications include: *Breadline Britain in the 1990s* (with David Gordon), *Tackling inequalities: Where are we now and what can be done?* (with David Gordon) and *Beyond criminology: Taking harm seriously* (with Paddy Hillyard, Steve Tombs, and David Gordon).

Demi Patsios is a research fellow in the Centre for Health and Social Care, within the University of Bristol's School for Policy Studies. He was previously a research fellow for three years within the University's International Institute on Health and Aging. His main areas of research include the health and social care of older people, long-term and community care, cross-national comparisons of ageing policy and poverty and social exclusion of older populations in the UK.

Sarah Payne is a senior lecturer and the Head of the Centre for Health and Social Care Research at the School for Policy Studies at the University of Bristol. Her main research in recent years has focused on poverty and social exclusion, sex and gender influences on health, and policy issues including the care of women in secure psychiatric hospitals, preventing suicide, and gender equity in mental health services.

Elisabetta Ruspini is Associate Professor in Sociology, Faculty of Sociology, University of Milano-Bicocca, Milan, Italy. Her research interests include: the gender dimension of poverty and social exclusion; single motherhood and fatherhood; the social construction of gender identities; changing femininities, masculinities and sexual minorities; and within the methodological field: gender issues in social research; the analysis of social change; longitudinal research and analysis. Her recent publications include: *Introduction to longitudinal research*; *The gender dimension of social change: The contribution of dynamic research to the study of women's life courses* (with Angela Dale); and *Le identità di genere* (*Gender identities*).

Peter Townsend is Centennial Professor of International Social Policy at the London School of Economics, where he continues to teach postgraduate students about human rights, development and social policy. He is AcSS and FBA. In 1963 he was appointed Professor of Sociology at the University of Essex upon its foundation and in 1982 moved to the University of Bristol, where he is now also Emeritus Professor. He has worked lately with UNICEF, DFID and the ILO and was consultant to the UN at the time of the World Summit for Social Development at Copenhagen in 1995.

His latest books are *Poverty and social exclusion in Britain* (with David Gordon and others, 2000); *Breadline Europe: The measurement of poverty* (co-editor, 2001); *Targeting poor health* (2001); *World poverty: New policies to defeat an old enemy* (co-editor with David Gordon, 2002); *Child poverty in the developing world* (with others, 2003); *Inequalities of health: The Welsh dimension* (2005); and *The right to social security and national development: Lessons of OECD experience for low income countries* (2006).

ONE

Introduction

The Poverty and Social Exclusion (PSE) Survey is the only comprehensive source of information on the extent and nature of deprivation in contemporary Britain. At the turn of the millennium, there were more people living in or on the margins of poverty than at any time in British history. According to this most rigorous survey of poverty and social exclusion ever undertaken, by the end of 1999 approximately 14 million people in Britain, or 25% of the population, were objectively living in poverty. In previous centuries, higher proportions of the British population have been poor and their poverty has often been more severe. But rapid population growth in the 20th century means that there are now more people experiencing poverty than at any previous time. However, the growth in poverty is not only the result of population increase. In the 1980s, economic restructuring coupled with changes in the tax and benefit systems led to both widening inequality and rapid rises in poverty and social exclusion (Pantazis and Gordon, 2000). Between 1983 and 1990, the number of households who could scientifically be described as living in poverty increased by almost 50%. In 1983, 14% of households were living in poverty and, by 1990, this figure had risen to 21% (Gordon and Pantazis, 1997). Poverty continued to increase during the 1990s and, by 1999, the proportion of households living in poverty had reached almost one in four.

The main results of the PSE Survey are that:

- Roughly nine million people in Britain cannot afford adequate housing. For example, their home is unheated or damp, or they cannot afford to keep it in a decent state of decoration.
- Around 10.5 million adults cannot afford one or more essential household goods, such as carpets for living areas or a telephone, or to repair or replace electrical goods or furniture when they break or wear out.
- A third of British children are forced to go without at least one of the things they need, such as three meals a day, toys, out-of-school activities or adequate clothing. Eighteen per cent of children go without two or more necessities.

- Around five million adults and three quarters of a million children go without essential clothing, such as a warm waterproof coat or new, properly fitted shoes, because of lack of money.
- Around three million adults and 400,000 children are not properly fed by today's standards. For example, they do not have enough fresh fruit and vegetables, or two meals a day for adults or three meals for children.
- More than 12 million people are financially insecure. They cannot afford to save, insure their house contents or spend money on themselves[1].

Besides the material deprivation revealed by the survey, many people also suffer the effects of different forms of social exclusion:

- Almost 10 million adults and one million children are too poor to engage in common social activities such as visiting friends and family, having celebrations on special occasions or attending weddings and funerals.
- A third of the population does not have a week's annual holiday away from home.
- Nine per cent of the population have no family member outside the household whom they see or speak to at least weekly. More than half a million people, mainly men, have neither a family member nor a friend with whom they are in contact at least weekly.
- Nine per cent of the population, and 16% of those over 65, have poor support in times of practical or emotional need.

These shocking findings illustrate the scale of the task faced by the Labour government, which made a commitment to abolish child poverty in 1999, the same year that the PSE Survey was carried out. The Prime Minister's Beveridge lecture on 18 March 1999 gave a clear pledge to end child poverty forever within a generation (Walker, 1999), while the Chancellor of the Exchequer announced, in his 1999 Pre-Budget Report, the ambitious aim to halve child poverty within 10 years. If the government is to succeed with its objectives, then reliable and valid research on poverty and social exclusion, as well as more exact measures of trends and causes, is needed. Unfortunately, in the past 30 years, there has been only limited research of this type.

Poverty research in Britain

Since the foundation of the welfare state in 1948, successive governments have neither undertaken nor funded any nationally representative surveys on poverty. In 1948, the National Assistance Act began with deliberately dramatic words: "the existing Poor Law shall cease to have effect" (quoted in Briggs, 1994, p 309). The welfare state was meant to end poverty. But, unlike other countries, Britain had never undertaken an official national survey, or even had an official definition, of poverty.

There have been only four nationally representative scientific surveys of poverty in the past 50 years, listed below – all were funded by the Joseph Rowntree Foundation, and two received additional funding from London Weekend Television; all were undertaken by academics.

- Poverty in the United Kingdom, 1967-69, 2,052 households (Townsend, 1979);
- Living in Britain, 1983, 1,174 households, published as *Poor Britain* (Mack and Lansley, 1985);
- Breadline Britain, 1990, 1,831 households (Gordon and Pantazis, 1997);
- Poverty and Social Exclusion, 1999, 1,534 households (Gordon et al, 2000a).

For the past 50 years, those concerned with poverty and inequality at a national level have had to rely either on the results from these small surveys or on the less than ideal Low Income Families series and its successor, the Households Below Average Income (HBAI) series, produced previously by the Department of Social Security and more recently by the Department for Work and Pensions (DWP). These government statistics have generated useful data on the size and characteristics of the low-income population over time but, being based exclusively on the Family Expenditure Survey (or more recently on the Family Resources Survey), have been restricted to *indirect* measures of poverty in terms of household income. For example, a threshold of low income such as half average household equivalised income or incomes below the supplementary benefit threshold are indirect measures of poverty. The government has also funded a number of surveys on specific population groups that look at poverty among other issues, such as the Office of Population, Censuses and Surveys' Disability Surveys (Martin and White, 1988; Smyth and Robus, 1989; Gordon et al, 2000b) in the 1980s and the more recent Families and

Children Survey (see Marsh et al, 2001; Vegeris and McKay, 2002; Vegeris and Perry, 2003; Berthoud et al, 2004).

The HBAI series demonstrates that, on the basis of *indirect* measures of poverty, the levels of both adult and childhood poverty grew during the 1980s and 1990s, reflecting the growth of inequality of income that was "exceptional compared with international trends" (Hills, 1998, p 5). By the time Labour came to power, there were 14 million people in Britain living in households with less than half average household income. This represented a threefold increase in both the number and the proportion of people in relative poverty between 1979 and 1997-98 (Gordon, 2000). Figure 1.1 shows this huge increase in inequality. It shows the numbers living on low incomes and how this changed between 1961 and 2002.

During the 1960s, just over 10% of the population lived in a low-income household. This rose slightly under the Conservative administration and following the oil shock in the early 1970s, and then declined to about 8% during the mid-1970s. In 1979, when Margaret Thatcher was elected Prime Minister, changes in economic and social policy resulted in a trebling of the proportion of people living in low-income households from 8% to 25% – clearly showing that governments do have an effect on the amount of poverty in a country and that social policy does make a difference. Poverty levels remained at around 25% throughout the 1990s and have fallen only slightly since the turn of the millennium. Child poverty also increased dramatically in the 1980s. The number of children in households with below half average income rose from 1.4 million to 4.4 million. By the mid-1990s, the UK's child poverty rate was the third highest of the 25 nations for which information was available (see, for example, Bradshaw, 1999, 2000; Bradbury and Jantii, 1999, 2001; Piachaud and Sutherland, 2000; UNICEF Innocenti Research Centre, 2000, 2005).

Increases in poverty were part of a wider increase in inequality, with changes pronounced at the top as well as at the bottom of the income scale. Between 1979 and 1996, the incomes of the richest tenth of the population grew by 68% after allowing for inflation and housing costs, while those of the poorest fell by 12% (Gordon, 2000, p 34). The share of total national income taken by the bottom 10% dropped from 4% to 2%, while the share taken by the top 10% rose from 21% to 28%. Thus, by the time Labour came to power in 1997, "the distribution of incomes in Britain was more unequal than at any time in recent history" (Sefton and Sutherland, 2005, p 231). This remains true. Between 1997 and 2002/03, there was essentially no change in the income distribution. The redistributive effects of successive Budgets

Figure 1.1: Low income in Britain, 1961-2002

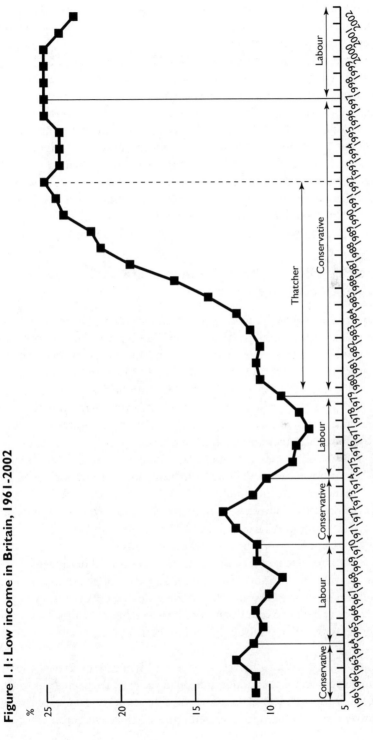

Source: Goodman and Webb (1994) and Households Below Average Income series

under two Labour administrations have only halted the overall growth in inequality, not reversed it. Indeed, the share taken by the top 10% of households rose to 29% of total income, while the top 1% hugely increased their share between 1997 and 2002 (Paxton and Dixon, 2004; Levitas, 2005, pp 231-3). Both the Institute for Public Policy Research and the Institute for Fiscal Studies issued reports in 2004 suggesting that this was a permanent and irreversible shift (Goodman and Oldfield, 2004; Paxton and Dixon, 2004). In this context, the welcome recent reductions in income poverty nevertheless look small compared to the very large rises in the 1980s, and sustained falls will require concerted and strategic action. These changes have also been accompanied by continually widening inequalities in health (Shaw et al, 1999, 2005) and falls in social mobility (Aldridge, 2001), showing that rising inequality also diminishes equality of opportunity.

The Breadline Britain Surveys: the PSE Survey's forerunner studies[2]

The 1983 *Living in Britain* or *Poor Britain* Survey pioneered what has been termed the 'consensual' or 'perceived deprivation' approach to measuring poverty – a methodology that has since been widely adopted by other studies both in Britain and abroad (Mack and Lansley, 1985; Veit-Wilson, 1987; Walker, 1987). This methodology investigates whether there are some people whose standard of living is below the minimum acceptable to society. It defines 'poverty' from the viewpoint of the public's perception of minimum need:

> This study tackles the questions 'how poor is too poor?' by identifying the minimum acceptable way of life for Britain in the 1980s. Those who have no choice but to fall below this minimum level can be said to be 'in poverty'. This concept is developed in terms of those who have an enforced lack of *socially perceived* necessities. This means that the 'necessities' of life are identified by public opinion and not by, on the one hand, the views of experts or, on the other hand, the norms of behaviour *per se*. (Mack and Lansley, 1985, p 45; emphasis in original)

Thus it is the *population's* perception of what is necessary and affordable that provides an independent criterion in the construction of a poverty line; it does not rely on opinions of elite 'experts' or use officially approved sets of income and expenditure statistics with arbitrary cut-off points. By then enquiring about the possession or otherwise of socially perceived necessities, rather than inferring deprivation from levels of income, it offers a *direct* measure of poverty based on this consensual definition of minimum need. The Breadline Britain Surveys (Mack and Lansley, 1985; Gordon and Pantazis, 1997) were able to provide *direct* evidence of poverty and trends in poverty during the Thatcher years by measuring the number of people who were poor in terms of being unable to afford items that the majority of the general public considered to be basic necessities of life.

The 1999 Poverty and Social Exclusion (PSE) Survey

The PSE Survey attempts to build on and extend the pioneering methodology developed by Mack and Lansley and to provide comprehensive information on poverty and social exclusion. The survey has four main objectives.

First, it seeks to re-establish the long national tradition of investigating and measuring the scale and severity of poverty among adults and children, and in different social groups. By using a range of measures of poverty in addition to income, including the lack of socially perceived 'necessities' and subjective measures, it provides unparalleled detail about the material and social deprivation and exclusion among the British population at the end of the 20th century. The PSE Survey uses comparable methods to the previous surveys, based on identifying the items that a majority of the population perceive as necessary, so that the trends spanning nearly two decades can be described and analysed. Thus, it provides the first independent *direct* evidence of trends in poverty in 1983, 1990 and 1999 on a consistent basis.

Second, the PSE Survey attempts to extend this tradition to the modern investigation of social exclusion, so that for the first time the relationship between poverty and social exclusion can be examined in depth. Townsend's survey of poverty emphasised the relationship between resources and people's capacity to meet social expectations as full members of society: "[Poor] People are deprived of the conditions of life which ordinarily define membership of society. If they lack or are denied resources to obtain access to these conditions of life and so fulfil membership of society, they are in poverty" (Townsend, 1979, p 915). This membership involves both participation in widely expected social activities, and meeting socially determined norms in relation to such things as "standards of child care, the practices of marriage and family relationships, [and] reciprocity between neighbours" (Townsend, 1979, p 922). Elements of this were included in Townsend's survey, and in the Breadline Britain Surveys: all incorporated some social necessities such as being able to have family or friends round for a meal, being able to visit family members and attend weddings and funerals, and being able to afford a holiday.

In the 1980s and 1990s, the concept of 'social exclusion' became increasingly central to discussions of social policy and politics. It does not have the obvious resonance with public understanding that 'poverty' has, and its definition and measurement is equally problematic. As Chapter Five shows, both UK and European indicators of social exclusion have been heavily weighted towards labour market participation and poverty. Most analyses of social exclusion have focused on poverty, lack of work and area deprivation, rather than the questions of social membership addressed in the Breadline Britain Surveys. This is partly the result of how social exclusion is understood, and partly an inevitable outcome of the absence of data on social relations. Employment and household income thus often serve as *indirect* measures of social exclusion. At the request of the Joseph Rowntree Foundation, the PSE Survey set out to investigate this aspect of social deprivation more fully and more systematically than the earlier surveys. In consequence, the PSE Survey is able to offer *direct* measurement of social exclusion across four dimensions: impoverishment, labour market exclusion, service exclusion and exclusion from social relations. Uniquely, the PSE Survey treats exclusion from social relations as a constitutive aspect of social exclusion. This is not, of course, to reduce social exclusion to this dimension. Rather, the assessment of this alongside other aspects of social exclusion provides an unparalleled opportunity to both *describe* exclusion from social participation, and to consider how far social isolation and lack of participation may correlate with or be caused by low income, non-engagement in the labour market and service exclusion.

Third, the survey seeks to contribute to the cross-national investigation of poverty, as Britain agreed to do at the World Summit for Social Development in 1995 (UN, 1995). Building on previous work undertaken by some of the authors (Townsend et al, 1997), the survey operationalised the notions of *absolute* and *overall* poverty accepted by 117 countries after the 1995 World Summit. Our hope is that this method might become a model to apply in industrialised countries as well as in the developing world.

Fourth, the survey attempts to understand the relationships between poverty and social exclusion and other social phenomena, such as crime, social harm, unemployment and poor health. There is a large evidence base demonstrating that living in poverty is associated with experiencing other social problems. The PSE Survey provides the opportunity for these relationships to be explored more fully and also, for the first time, to explore the impact of social exclusion in Britain.

Data collection

Funded by the Joseph Rowntree Foundation, the PSE Survey was developed and analysed by researchers at the Universities of Bristol, Loughborough, York and Heriot-Watt, with the fieldwork undertaken in 1999 by the Office for National Statistics (ONS) (Gordon et al, 2000a). The research was completed in two stages (see ibid).

The first stage of the research was to ask members of the general public about what items and activities they considered defined the living standards that everyone in Britain ought to be able to reach. The ONS Omnibus Survey, in June 1999, asked a representative sample of people aged 16 and over to classify various items and activities as either necessities or desirable. They had to sort cards containing 39 items and 15 activities relating to households, and 23 items and seven activities relating to children, into one of two categories. They were asked:

> I would like you to indicate the living standards you feel all adults (and children) should have in Britain today.... BOX A is for items which you think are necessary; which all adults should be able to afford and which they should not have to do without. BOX B is for items which may be desirable but are not necessary.

This approach extended the methodology of the Breadline Britain Surveys by adding items to the list of indicators of necessities based on the results from focus-group research and a comprehensive survey of similar studies in industrialised countries (see Bradshaw et al, 1998; Gordon et al, 2000a for details). The additional questions mainly address two areas: goods and activities that are particularly relevant to children (see Chapter Eleven in this volume); and social activities, which, although included as a minor aspect of the earlier studies, were extended to properly address the question of social exclusion (see Chapters Four and Five in this volume).

The Omnibus Survey established which items 50% or more of the population considered necessary. The main PSE Survey, carried out later in 1999, sought to establish which sections of the population had these necessities and which sections could afford them, and also looked at both poverty and social exclusion in greater depth. The PSE Survey was administered to a follow-up sample of the General Household Survey of 1998-99, consisting of 1,534 respondents (see www.bris.ac.uk/poverty/pse/welcome.htm). In developing the survey, some of the new and revised questions were also piloted in a regular Omnibus Survey carried out by the Market and Opinion Research Institute in July 1998 (for further details, see Bradshaw et al, 1998).

Respondents were asked:

> Now I'd like to show you a list of items and activities that relate to our standard of living. Please tell me which item you have or do not have by placing the cards on ... Pile A for the items you have, Pile B is for items you don't have but don't want and Pile C is for items you do not have and can't afford.

Academic and policy impact

The four post-Second World War British poverty surveys have had a large academic and policy impact considering their relative modest size and cost. The 1967-69 Poverty in the UK Survey provided the empirical evidence for Peter Townsend's relative deprivation theory of poverty. The relative definition of poverty has now been adopted as the official definition of poverty among the 25 member states of the European Union (see Chapter Two in this volume). Townsend's definition has also influenced the 'overall' poverty definition adopted by the governments of 117 countries at the World Summit for Social Development in 1995 (see Chapter Three in this volume). Even Townsend's critics concede that the Poverty in the UK Survey "ranks alongside the surveys of Booth and Rowntree" in its impact and importance (Piachaud, 1981, p 419).

The Breadline Britain Surveys formed an integral part of two award-winning television series; Breadline Britain, four 30-minute programmes first broadcast on ITV in 1983 and Breadline Britain in the 1990s, six 30-minute programmes broadcast on ITV in spring 1991 and repeated in the London area in summer 1991. These 10 television programmes were watched by millions of people and raised the issue of poverty in Britain, which the Conservative governments at the time were trying to ignore. Indeed, a senior civil servant, the Assistant Secretary for Policy on Family Benefits and Low Incomes at the Department of Health and Social Security, had given evidence to the Select Committee on Social Services on 15 June 1988 and stated:

"The word poor is one the government actually disputes": the policy seemed to be to end poverty by removing the word from the dictionaries. The government's strategy was explained by ex-government minister Ian Gilmour thus:

> Measuring poverty in the Thatcher era is difficult because of the inadequacy, and sometimes deliberate obfuscation, of Government statistics. That, in itself, is revealing. Just as a Government will only find it necessary to fiddle the unemployment figures when unemployment is rising fast, it will only fudge and conceal the figures on poverty when it knows that poverty is spreading. (Gilmour, 1992, p 137)[3]

The Breadline Britain Surveys provided independent and detailed information on the extent and nature of poverty that was not available from government surveys and statistics. They had little policy impact on the 'hostile' governments of the era but they received support from a young Labour MP (Tony Blair) and had considerable academic impact. In particular, Björn Halleröd, in Sweden, produced a shortened list of deprivation questions adapted from the 1983 survey that was included in the Swedish Level of Living Surveys and subsequently in the EUROMODULE surveys in 19 European countries (Delhey et al, 2002). A subset of this shortened question list was then included in the European Community Household Panel Survey used in every European Union member state. Similarly, the Irish government incorporated the consensual poverty method with a revised set of questions into the National Anti-Poverty Strategy in 1997. It is ironic that the Breadline Britain Surveys had a greater policy impact on the Irish government than on the UK government.

Versions of the consensual method for measuring poverty were first used by academics in Australia (Travers and Richardson, 1993) and then incorporated into that government's Household Expenditure Survey in 1998/99 (see Bray, 2001). The Australian Social Security Ministry (Commonwealth Department of Family and Community Services) recently gave evidence to a parliamentary inquiry into poverty and argued that "approaches such as deprivation as well as longitudinal analyses of household incomes, offer much greater potential" than the current low-income threshold methods (CDFCS, 2003, p 107). Similarly, the New Zealand government has used an updated version of the consensual poverty method to measure standard of living in a number of official surveys (Jensen et al, 2002; Krishnan et al, 2002). The consensual method has also been used in academic studies in a large number of countries in both the industrialised and developing world (see Chapter Two in this volume).

The PSE Survey results were first released in 2000 in a political atmosphere that was much more favourable than that surrounding the previous poverty surveys. Despite the relatively short time that has elapsed since the PSE Survey was completed, it has already had a significant academic and policy impact. The PSE Survey provides both the scientific credibility and also the raw data that have helped persuade the government to modify the way it measures child poverty and adopt a tiered approach (DWP, 2003). The new measures of child poverty will in future consist of:

- *Absolute low income*: To measure whether the very poorest families are seeing their incomes rise in real terms, the DWP will monitor the number of children living in families with incomes below a particular threshold that is adjusted for inflation – set for a couple with one child at £210 a week in the baseline year 1998/99.
- *Relative low income*: To measure whether the poorest families are keeping pace with the growth of incomes in the economy as a whole, the DWP will monitor the number of children living in households below 60% of contemporary median equivalised household income.
- *Material deprivation and low income combined*: To provide a wider measure of people's living standards, the DWP will monitor the number of children living in households that are both materially deprived and have an income below 70% of contemporary median equivalised household income.

The government has also set targets in the Public Service Agreements (PSA) to halve child poverty by 2010 and eradicate it by 2020. Specifically, the current PSA target is to:

> Halve the number of children in relative low-income households between 1998-99 and 2010-11, on the way to eradicating child poverty by 2020.... The Government will also set a target as part of the next Spending Review to halve by 2010-11 the numbers of children suffering a combination of material deprivation and relative low income. The target will be met if there is an equivalent proportionate reduction to that required on relative low income between 2004-05 and 2010-11. (Treasury, 2004, p 37)

In order to monitor this new PSA target, direct questions about deprivation will be included in the Family Resources Survey from 2004 and will be used in deriving the material deprivation element of the tiered approach (see McKay and Collard, 2004). In relation to a series of items, families will be asked:

> Do you and your family have ...?/Are you and your family able to afford ...?

Possible responses will be:

> 1. We have this;
> 2. We would like to have this, but cannot afford it at the moment;
> 3. We do not want/need this at the moment.

The items used for assessing adult deprivation are:

1. Keep your home adequately warm
2. Two pairs of all-weather shoes for each adult
3. Enough money to keep your home in a decent state of repair
4. A holiday away from home for one week a year, not staying with relatives
5. Replace any worn-out furniture
6. A small amount of money to spend each week on yourself, not on your family
7. Regular savings (of £10 a month) for rainy days or retirement
8. Insurance of contents of dwelling
9. Have friends or family for a drink or meal at least once a month
10. A hobby or leisure activity
11. Replace or repair broken electrical goods such as refrigerator or washing machine.

For child deprivation, the items are:

1. A holiday away from home at least one week a year with his or her family
2. Swimming at least once a month
3. A hobby or leisure activity
4. Friends round for tea or a snack once a fortnight
5. Enough bedrooms for every child over 10 of different sex to have his or her own bedroom

6. Leisure equipment (for example, sports equipment or a bicycle)
7. Celebrations on special occasions such as birthdays, Christmas or other religious festivals
8. Play group/nursery/toddler group at least once a week for children of preschool age
9. Going on a school trip at least once a term for school-aged children.

Notably, these criteria incorporate some 'necessities' that are properly seen as pertaining to social exclusion as well as to poverty. Indeed, as Chapter Five suggests, the dividing line between poverty and social exclusion is not easy to draw.

Academically, the PSE method has so far been used in the first poverty survey of Northern Ireland (Hillyard et al, 2003), to measure poverty and social exclusion in Wales (Malcolm Fisk, personal communication) and to measure poverty and social exclusion among the elderly in deprived areas of England (Scharf et al, 2003). The PSE data are currently being used in a number of comparative studies with other countries (Australia, Finland, Germany, Israel, Ireland, New Zealand, Mexico and Sweden), and have been reanalysed by British academics (see, for example, Burrows, 2003).

Outline of the book

The book is divided into three parts: 'Principles', 'Processes', and 'People'. The chapters in Part One discuss the main theoretical and conceptual debates on poverty and social exclusion and draw on the general findings from the PSE Survey. Chapters in Part Two focus on some of the key processes that relate to poverty and social exclusion, such as work, service provision, crime and mental health. The chapters in Part Three look at the extent of poverty and social exclusion among social groups differentiated on the basis of age, gender and household type.

Principles

In Chapter Two, David Gordon discusses the concept and measurement of poverty. Poverty is a universal and meaningful concept in all countries in the world. However, the definition of poverty is often contested and the concept has evolved and changed over time. Townsend has argued that poverty can be defined scientifically and measured objectively in terms of the concept of relative deprivation. David Gordon shows step by step how this can be done using low-income and deprivation indicators. He also addresses some of the conceptual controversies of poverty measurement, including the debates about absolute versus relative poverty and direct versus indirect measures. The new theoretical framework developed explains why there often appears to be a relatively low correlation between low income and deprivation.

In 1995, the governments of 117 countries agreed at the World Summit for Social Development in Copenhagen to produce national anti-poverty plans based on measures of 'absolute' and 'overall' poverty. In Chapter Three, Peter Townsend, David Gordon and Christina Pantazis show how both absolute and overall poverty can be measured in Britain using a range of scientific methods. The results show that the two definitions are viable in rich countries like Britain. They also have an important bearing on the rates approved by government for means-tested and universal benefits.

One of the main building blocks of the PSE Survey was establishing what possessions and activities the public perceive as necessary, and that no adult or child should have to go without because of lack of money. In Chapter Four, Christina Pantazis, David Gordon and Peter Townsend demonstrate that the public's perception of the necessities of life is wide-ranging, incorporating both material and social elements. The perception of what is necessary is remarkably stable across society, with generally few variations in opinion among different social groups. It does, however, seem that in 1999 younger people were less likely to view certain items and activities as essential compared to older respondents. Besides comparing the PSE Survey results with the previous two Breadline Britain Surveys, this chapter considers why young people's responses have become harsher – an issue further discussed by Eldin Fahmy in Chapter Twelve. Some recent critiques of the consensual approach to poverty are also summarised and addressed.

In Chapter Five, Ruth Levitas discusses the development of definitions and indicators of social exclusion in the UK and in the European Union. She draws attention to the excessive focus on paid work, and the lack of attention to distinctively *social* aspects of social exclusion and inclusion in both indicators and policy. The unique feature of the PSE Survey is, then, its direct attention to *exclusion from social relations* and patterns of sociability – and consequently the possible exploration of the interaction between this facet of exclusion and other dimensions such as impoverishment, lack of access to services and non-participation in paid work. The chapter shows that poverty has a profound effect on some, though not all, aspects of social participation. This is an objective relation, raising questions about the significance of choice. It also suggests, in ways that are further endorsed by Chapter Six, that while paid work is broadly associated with increased participation, this is an indirect effect mediated by the relief of poverty. In itself, participation in paid work may inhibit rather than facilitate social inclusion. The relationship between the different dimensions of social exclusion is not straightforward, suggesting that the concept itself has to be used with caution.

Processes[4]

Part Three begins with Chapter Six, where Nick Bailey takes further some of the issues about the impact of paid work raised in Chapter Five. Within the general focus of whether those who are in work are actually better off than those who are unemployed or 'economically inactive', Bailey explores whether the benefits of work are continuous. Does working longer hours, or full-time rather than part-time work, progressively deliver greater freedom from poverty and increased social participation? Are the answers to these questions the same for men and for women? Bailey shows that the benefits of work are greater for men in terms of objective measures of poverty and for women when the general (or subjective) poverty measure is used. This is explicable in terms of the unequal intra-household distribution of earnings (see further Pantazis and Ruspini in Chapter Thirteen). A further implication is that objective measures tend to underrepresent both the poverty of women and therefore the financial benefits of work. However, the impacts of employment on poverty are far stronger than on exclusion from social relations. More work is not always better: part-time employment is associated with lower levels of exclusion from social relations than either full-time paid work or no paid work.

Chapter Seven, by Stephen McKay and Sharon Collard, looks at debt and financial exclusion – issues that, they remind us, may be related but should not be conflated. Debt is much less common among older groups, while financial exclusion is concentrated on young and old alike. Again, the scope of the PSE Survey unusually permits the exploration of the interaction between financial exclusion, debt, low income and lack of socially perceived necessities. One in three respondents have no savings, over a quarter are worried about debt and almost half indicate some degree of exclusion or indebtedness over a range of seven separate indicators. Each of these factors is more common among those in poverty: both financial exclusion and debt are associated with low income, perceived deprivations and subjective indicators of poverty. Moreover, debt is strongly associated with a range of psychiatric problems, and the authors conclude that 'one must suspect either that debt is creating or exacerbating such problems, or that a particular group of people does not receive adequate support in making financial decisions' (p 212).

Chapter Eight looks at the use and provision of, and exclusion from, local services. Tania Fisher and Glen Bramley's analysis both sets out the data from the PSE Survey and uses them to explore whether local services are an effective mechanism of redistribution in favour of the 'poor'. Many public services show a pro-rich bias in terms of usage, and this bias increased during the 1990s, although services for the elderly do show a pro-poor bias (see also Chapter Fifteen by Demi Patsios). The PSE Survey identifies problems with availability, quality and cost of services. Gordon et al (2000a) distinguish between collective exclusion (when a service is unavailable or inadequate) and individual exclusion (when it is too expensive). Both forms of exclusion are here discussed together as a broad index of constraint, with collective exclusion being a greater barrier to use than affordability. Multivariate modelling is used to explore the impact of different factors on service use. Poor households face poorer quality services and deprivation reinforces constraints on service use. However, local service usage, quality and satisfaction are driven more by household than by area characteristics, raising questions about the current policy emphasis on area deprivation.

Chapters Six, Seven and Eight look at issues that are treated as aspects of social exclusion either within the PSE Survey or elsewhere: labour market activity, financial exclusion and debt as well as local service exclusion. Chapter Nine turns to crime, linked in much public discussion to social exclusion. Here, Christina Pantazis looks at crime, disorder and insecurity, and their relationships with social exclusion. For the government, crime and disorder are both products and aspects of social exclusion, and are related to other problems, such as unemployment and poor housing. Crime is seen as a cause of social exclusion because it prevents people from going about their daily business through fear. Pantazis examines the extent of crime and insecurity among people living in poverty and those affected by social exclusion. However, by adopting a social harm perspective, the chapter also allows these experiences to be contextualised in a broader framework. Consequently, it shows that although crime risks are higher for people living in circumstances of poverty, the risks of experiencing other social harms, such as debt or problems with social relationships, are far greater compared with other groups. In this sense, crime should be seen as one aspect of social harm of which poor people experience a greater share.

In Chapter Ten, Sarah Payne examines the relationship between mental health, poverty and social exclusion. Using the GHQ-12 questionnaire, Payne shows that nearly one in five respondents in the PSE Survey report mental health problems. However, rates of poor mental health are much higher for people in poverty, and for those reporting social exclusion across a range of indicators including labour market inactivity. While this lends support to the idea that getting people into work may have positive public health impacts, Payne, like Levitas and Bailey in Chapters Five and Six, discusses the potential negative impacts of paid work where it involves long hours or anti-social hours that constrain people's social relationships.

People

The government's commitment to ending child poverty within a generation is dependent on research to identify whether anti-poverty policies are correctly targeted and effective. Put simply, without appropriate quantitative evidence, the government will not know if its policies are working or failing to deliver. Government low-income statistics, such as the HBAI series, assume that families with young children are likely to be better off if they have the same level of income as families with older children (babies need less food than teenagers). These statistics also assume that all members of the household share their income equally. Both these assumptions are questionable: Chapter Two discusses the problems of equivalence scales and the imputed costs of children of different ages relative to adults; and Chapters Six and Thirteen address, in different ways, the problem of intra-household resource distribution. In Chapter Eleven, Eva Lloyd examines critical issues about child poverty and social exclusion, using the measures offered by the PSE Survey. This chapter provides hard direct evidence about levels of poverty among children of different ages, and the extent to which parents sacrifice their own standard of living to try to protect their children from poverty and social exclusion.

Child poverty is at the top of the policy agenda. However, policy makers often ignore the poverty and social exclusion of young men and women aged 16-25, especially that of young single people. During the 2005 General Election campaign, there were suggestions that this was because young people were among the least likely to vote. A less cynical explanation is that this age group falls into a gap between policies designed to meet the needs of children, and those aimed at working-age adults. Such policies as do exist, such as the New Deal for Young People, are almost exclusively oriented to the labour market. Chapter Twelve, by Eldin Fahmy, looks at the poverty and social exclusion of this too-often neglected group. There is increasing evidence that youth transitions in Britain are becoming more protracted, complex and often more hazardous than for previous generations. However, excluded young people are often perceived as the 'undeserving poor' who should 'help themselves' rather than expect help from policy makers. Most 16- to 17-year-olds were excluded from eligibility for benefits by the previous Conservative administration, and this exclusion has not been reversed under Labour. Fahmy documents the consequences for this vulnerable section of society.

Gender, as well as age, shapes people's experience of poverty and social exclusion, as Christina Pantazis and Elisabetta Ruspini demonstrate in Chapter Thirteen. Taking a lifecourse approach, they reveal how critical life events shape men's and women's experiences of poverty and social exclusion – and how these critical events tend to be work-centred for men and family-centred for women. They argue that the multidimensional approach of the PSE Survey, going beyond a focus on income or access to resources, offers a better way to understand – and therefore to tackle – the different problems of poverty and social exclusion faced by men and women. In particular, the stress on exclusion from social relations allows a much wider framework of analysis. The authors conclude that anti-poverty strategies need to incorporate gendered perspectives that reflect the realities of both men's *and* women's lives.

Lone mothers are widely known to be among the poorest groups in society, and are frequently the target of government interventions, most recently of the New Deal for Lone Parents, which aims to increase their participation in paid work. Chapter Fourteen, by Ruth Levitas, Emma Head and Naomi Finch, looks at the situation of lone mothers, compared with that of partnered mothers and of women of working age living alone ('solo women'). All three groups have a relatively high risk of poverty. All three have higher rates of exclusion from common social activities. The poverty of lone mothers constrains their lives and social participation, and also, of course, constrains the opportunities that they are able to offer their children. But paid work does not necessarily solve their problems. Lone mothers in employment are likely to remain materially deprived as well as being subject to intense time pressure. However, the original analytical approach of this chapter, combined with the PSE Survey data, shows that solo women are also likely to remain poor and suffer social exclusion even when in paid work. This endorses the view that the poverty of lone mothers is driven by gender and class, rather than by lone parenthood itself.

In the final substantive chapter in Part Three, Demi Patsios offers evidence from the PSE Survey on the extent of poverty and social exclusion among pensioner groups. Chapter Fifteen shows how poverty and social exclusion are differentially experienced by 'younger' and 'older' pensioners (those under and over 80 respectively) as well as by single and couple pensioner households. Patsios highlights the complexity of studying pensioner poverty. If only low income is examined, then older pensioners are much more likely to be 'poor' than younger pensioners – reported income decreases with age. However, almost all other measures of poverty, deprivation and exclusion show that the older the pensioner the less likely they are to be poor – reported deprivation also decreases with age. Younger single women pensioners are the poorest and most excluded group. Being widowed young has a profound impact on poverty, exclusion and well-being. Many pensioners are excluded from social relations in that they are unable to afford to engage in common social activities and are socially isolated, or lack potential social support.

Chapter Sixteen, the final chapter in the book, draws out the main theoretical and empirical threads of the book, and their implications for social policy. Perhaps the strongest implications are these:

• We cannot understand the full extent or impact of poverty and social exclusion unless we use direct rather than indirect measures of both.

• The government's commitment to ending child poverty is commendable, and accompanied now by clear targets as well as revised measures incorporating direct measures of deprivation. This is wholly welcome.

• However, similar commitments, indicators and targets are needed for the population as a whole, and especially for vulnerable groups within it, such as young people, lone mothers and the elderly. These indicators need to be sensitive to both age and gender, and to cover both poverty and social exclusion, especially exclusion from social relations.

• There is an over-emphasis on paid work as a panacea for poverty and social exclusion. The PSE Survey suggests that paid work, though clearly important in relieving poverty, does not always do so; and the impact on social exclusion, especially exclusion from social relations, is at the very least ambiguous.

• The ending of poverty cannot be divorced from the wider picture of social inequality. The widening chasm between rich and poor that opened up between 1979 and 1997 needs to begin to close. The project of eliminating poverty and social exclusion in Britain in the 21st century will require more dramatic, and more dramatically redistributive, policies than have been contemplated by the first two Labour governments of this time.

Notes

[1] These findings differ somewhat from those reported in Gordon et al, 2000, p 68. The release of the 2001 Census results made it possible to recalculate the numbers and percentages of adults and children suffering the effects of different kinds of deprivation after allowing for intra-household deprivation (the fact that parents often go without necessities but manage to provide for their children) and for age-specific deprivations, for example, lack of 'all required school uniform' should only apply to children of school age.

[2] The first of these surveys was called Poor Britain, the second Breadline Britain, but their similarity has led to them being referred to collectively as the Breadline Britain Surveys.

[3] Ian Gilmour was a minister in both the Thatcher and the Heath governments serving as Defence Secretary and Lord Privy Seal. He also served as a Shadow Home Secretary and Shadow Defence Secretary.

[4] The book does not include a separate chapter on housing as this analysis has been undertaken by Roger Burrows (see Burrows, 2003).

References

Aldridge, S. (2001) 'Social mobility: a discussion paper', Performance and Innovation Unit (www.strategy.gov.uk/downloads/files/socialmobility.pdf).

Berthoud,R., Bryan, M. and Bardasi, E. (2004) *The dynamics of deprivation: The relationship between income and material deprivation over time*. Department for Work and Pensions Research Report No 219, Leeds: Corporate Document Services (www.dwp.gov.uk/asd/asd5/rports2003-2004/rrep219.asp).

Bradbury B. and Jantii, M. (1999), *Child poverty across industrialised nations*, Innocenti Occasional Papers, EPS 1971, Florence: UNICEF.

Bradbury B. and Jantii, M. (2001) 'Child poverty across the industrialized world: evidence from the Luxembourg Income Study', in K.Vleminckx and T.M. Smeeding (eds) *Child well-being, child poverty and child policy in modern nations*, Bristol: The Policy Press, pp 11–32.

Bradshaw, J. (1999) 'Child poverty in comparative perspective', *European Journal of Social Security*, vol 1, no 4, pp 383-404.

Bradshaw, J. (2000) 'Child poverty in comparative perspectives', in D. Gordon and P. Townsend (eds), *Breadline Europe: The measurement of poverty*, Bristol: The Policy Press, pp 223-50.

Bradshaw, J., Gordon, D., Levitas, R., Middleton, S., Pantazis, C., Payne, S. and Townsend, P. (1998) *Report on preparatory research*, Bristol: Centre for International Poverty Research, University of Bristol.

Bray, J.R. (2001) *Hardship in Australia: An analysis of financial stress indicators in the 1998–99 Australian Bureau of Statistics Household Expenditure Survey*, Occasional Paper No 4, Department of Family and Community Services, Canberra. (www.facs.gov.au/internet/ facsinternet.nsf/vIA/occasional_papers/$file/No.4.pdf).

Briggs, A. (1994) *A social history of England*, London: Weidenfield and Nicolson.

Burrows, R. (2003) *Poverty and home ownership in contemporary Britain*, Bristol: The Policy Press.

CDFCS (Commonwealth Department of Family and Community Services) (2003) *Inquiry into poverty and financial hardship*, Occasional Paper 9, CDFCS submission to the Senate Community Affairs References Committee, Canberra (www.facs.gov.au/research/op09/ OP_No_09.pdf).

Delhey, J., Boehnke, P., Habich, R. and Zap, W. (2002) 'Quality of life in a European perspective. The EUROMODULE as a new instrument for comparative welfare research', *Social Indicators Research*, vol 58, no 1, pp 161-76.

Department for Work and Pensions (DWP) (2003) *Measuring child poverty: Final conclusions*, London: DWP (www.dwp.gov.uk/ consultations/consult/2003/childpov/final.asp).

Gilmour, I. (1992) *Dancing with dogma*, London: Simon and Schuster Ltd.

Goodman, A. and Oldfield, Z. (2004) *Permanent differences? Income and expenditure inequality*, London: Institute of Fiscal Studies.

Gordon, D. (2000) 'Inequalities in income, wealth and standard of living', in C. Pantazis, and D. Gordon (eds) *Tackling inequalities: Where are we now and what can be done?* Bristol: The Policy Press, pp 25-58.

Gordon, D. and Pantazis, C. (eds) (1997) *Breadline Britain in the 1990s*, Aldershot: Ashgate.

Gordon, D., Adelman, A., Ashworth, K., Bradshaw, J., Levitas, R., Middleton, S., Pantazis, C., Patsios, D., Payne, S., Townsend, P. and Williams, J. (2000a), *Poverty and social exclusion in Britain*, York: Joseph Rowntree Foundation (see also www.bris.ac.uk/poverty/pse/welcome.htm for details).

Gordon, D., Parker, R. and Loughran, F., with Heslop, P. (2000b) *Disabled children in Britain: A reanalysis of the OPCS Disability Surveys*, London: The Stationery Office.

Hills, J. (1998) *Income and wealth: The latest evidence*, York: Joseph Rowntree Foundation.

Hillyard, P., Kelly, G., McLaughlin, E., Patsios, D. and Tomlinson, M. (2003) *Bare necessities: Poverty and social exclusion in Northern Ireland: Key findings*, Democratic Dialogue, Belfast (www.democraticdialogue.org/PSEtsvqxf.pdf.pdf).

HM Treasury (2004) *Spending Review Public Service Agreements 2005–2008*. London: HM Treasury (www.hm-treasury.gov.uk/media/658/F3/sr04_psa_ch15.pdf).

Jensen, J., Spittal, M., Crichton, S., Sathiyandra, S. and Krishnan, V. (2002) *Direct measurement of living standards: The New Zealand ELSI scale*, Wellington: Ministry of Social Development.

Krishnan, V., Jensen, J. and Ballantyne, S. (2002) *New Zealand living standards 2000*, Centre for Social Research and Evaluation, Wellington: Ministry of Social Development.

Levitas, R. (2005) *The inclusive society? Social exclusion and New Labour* (2nd edn), Basingstoke: Palgrave Macmillan.

Mack, J. and Lansley, S. (1985) *Poor Britain*, London: Allen and Unwin.

Marsh, A., McKay, S., Smith, A. and Stephenson, A. (2001) *Low/moderate income families in Britain: Work, welfare and social security in 1999*, DSS Research Report No 138, Leeds: CDS.

Martin, J. and White, A. (1988) *The financial circumstances of adults living in private households*, Report 2, London: HMSO.

McKay, S. and Collard, S. (2004) *Developing survey deprivation questions for the Family Resources Survey*, DWP Working Paper Series No 13, London: Department for Work and Pensions (www.dwp.gov.uk/asd/asd5/WP13.pdf).

Pantazis, C. and Gordon, D. (2000) *Tackling inequalities: Where are we now and what can be done?*, Bristol: The Policy Press.

Paxton, W. and Dixon, M. (2004) *The state of the nation: An audit of injustice in the UK*, London: Institute for Public Policy Research.

Piachaud, D. (1981) 'Peter Townsend and the Holy Grail', *New Society*, 10 September, pp 419-21.

Piachaud, D. and Sutherland, H. (2000) *How effective is the British government's attempt to reduce child poverty*, CASE Paper 38, London: Centre for Analysis of Social Exclusion.

Scharf, T., Phillipson, C. and Smith, A.E. (2003) 'Older people's perceptions of the neighbourhood: evidence from socially deprived urban areas', Sociological Research Online, vol 8, no 4.

Sefton, T. and Sutherland, H. (2005) 'Inequality and poverty under New Labour', in J. Hills and K. Stewart (eds), *A more equal society*, Bristol: The Policy Press.

Shaw, M., Dorling, D., Gordon, D. and Davey Smith, G. (1999) *The widening gap: Health inequalities and policy in Britain*, Bristol: The Policy Press.

Shaw, M., Davey Smith, G., and Dorling, D. (2005) 'Health inequalities and New Labour: how the promises compare with real progress', *British Medical Journal*, vol 330, pp 1016-21.

Smyth, M. and Robus, N. (1989) *The financial circumstances of families with disabled children living in private households*, OPCS Surveys of Disability Report 5, London: HMSO.

Townsend, P. (1979) *Poverty in the United Kingdom: A survey of household resources and standards of living*, Harmondsworth: Penguin.

Townsend, P., Gordon, D., Bradshaw, J. and Gosschalk, B. (1997) *Absolute and overall poverty in Britain in 1997: What the population themselves say: Bristol Poverty Line Survey. Report of the second MORI Survey*, Statistical Monitoring Unit Report No 8, Bristol: University of Bristol.

Travers, P. and Richardson, S. (1993) *Living decently: Material wellbeing in Australia*, Melbourne: Oxford University Press.

UNICEF Innocenti Research Centre (2000). *Innocenti Report Card No 1, A league table of child poverty in rich nations*, Florence: The United Nations Children's Fund (www.unicef-icdc.org/cgi-bin/unicef/Lunga.sql?ProductID=226).

UNICEF Innocenti Research Centre (2005). *Innocenti Report Card No 6, Child poverty in rich countries 2005*, Florence: The United Nations Children's Fund (www.unicef-icdc.org/cgi-bin/unicef/Lunga.sql?ProductID=371).

UN (United Nations) (1995) *The Copenhagen Declaration and Programme of Action, World Summit for Social Development, 6-12 March 1995*, New York, NY: UN.

Vegeris, S. and McKay, S. (2002) *Low/moderate-income families in Britain: Changes in living standards 1999-2000*, Department for Work and Pensions Research Report No 164, Leeds: CDS.

Vegeris, S. and Perry, J. (2003) *Families and Children Study 2001: Report on living standards and the children*, Department for Work and Pensions Research Report No 190, Leeds: CDS (www.dwp.gov.uk/asd/asd5/rrep190.html).

Veit-Wilson, J.H. (1987) 'Consensual approaches to poverty lines and social security', *Journal of Social Policy*, vol 16, no 2, pp 183-211.

Walker, R. (1987) 'Consensual approaches to the definition of poverty: towards an alternative methodology', *Journal of Social Policy*, vol 16, no 2, pp 213-26.

Walker, R. (ed) (1999) *Ending child poverty: Popular welfare for the 21st century?*, Bristol: The Policy Press.

Part One:
Principles

TWO

The concept and measurement of poverty

David Gordon

Introduction

Poverty is a widely used and meaningful concept in all countries in the world. In September 2000, the governments of 189 countries adopted the United Nations Millennium Declaration and resolved to "spare no effort to free our fellow men, women and children from the abject and dehumanizing conditions of extreme poverty"[1].

Although poverty is a universal concept, its definition is often contested. The term 'poverty' can be considered to have a cluster of different overlapping meanings depending on the subject area or discourse (Gordon and Spicker, 1999). In the Poverty and Social Exclusion (PSE) Survey both poverty and social exclusion have been measured using a range of different definitions and techniques so that the results can be usefully compared with other work and a better scientific consensus developed.

The purpose of this chapter is twofold: first, to describe how the concept of poverty is defined; and second, to show how poverty is measured in the PSE Survey. It is divided into two main sections: (i) the definition of poverty; and (ii) the measurement of poverty in the PSE Survey.

Definitions of poverty

Despite the UK government's repeated commitment to halve child poverty by 2010 and eradicate child poverty by 2020 (see Chapter Eleven in this volume), there is still no official definition of poverty in the UK. Indeed, in the past, ministers have often defined poverty by 'knowing it when they see it'.

The first of the annual *Opportunity for All* (OFA) reports in 1999 on tackling poverty and social exclusion defined poverty as follows:

> Poverty affects different aspects of people's lives, existing
> when people are denied opportunities to work, to learn, to
> live healthy and fulfilling lives, and to live out their
> retirement years in security. Lack of income, access to good-
> quality health, education and housing, and the quality of
> the local environment all affect people's well-being. Our
> view of poverty covers all these aspects.
>
> Low income is an important aspect of poverty. But short
> spells of low income may not damage an individual's well-
> being or their prospects in the longer term. Our strategy
> focuses on those who are, or are at risk of becoming trapped
> on low incomes for long periods, especially those who
> have limited opportunities to escape.
>
> The problem is not restricted to limited income. (DSS,
> 1999, p 23)

This statement is not really a definition of poverty but a discussion of
the problems of poverty. However, it is clear that the UK government
does not consider that short spells of low income constitute poverty
unless they have negative consequences.

However, over the past 30 years, successive governments have signed
a range of international treaties and agreements that have incorporated
definitions of poverty. For example, in 1975, the European Council
adopted a relative definition of poverty as "individuals or families whose
resources are so small as to exclude them from the minimum acceptable
way of life of the Member State in which they live" (Council Decision,
1975). The concept of 'resources' was defined as "goods, cash income,
plus services from public and private resources" (EEC, 1981).

On 19 December 1984, the European Commission extended the
definition as follows:

> the poor shall be taken to mean persons, families and groups
> of persons whose resources (material, cultural and social)
> are so limited as to exclude them from the minimum
> acceptable way of life in the Member State in which they
> live. (EEC, 1985)

This is the 'official' definition of poverty that is used in the European
Union (EU) for all 25 member states.

After the World Summit for Social Development in Copenhagen in 1995, 117 countries (including the UK) adopted a declaration and programme of action that included commitments to eradicate 'absolute' and reduce 'overall' poverty, drawing up national poverty-alleviation plans as a priority (UN, 1995; see also Chapter Three in this volume).

The United Nations (UN) defined absolute poverty as "a condition characterised by severe deprivation of basic human needs, including food, safe drinking water, sanitation facilities, health, shelter, education and information. It depends not only on income but also on access to services" (UN, 1995, p 57).

Overall poverty was considered to take various forms, including "lack of income and productive resources to ensure sustainable livelihoods; hunger and malnutrition; ill health; limited or lack of access to education and other basic services; increased morbidity and mortality from illness; homelessness and inadequate housing; unsafe environments and social discrimination and exclusion. It is also characterised by lack of participation in decision-making and in civil, social and cultural life. It occurs in all countries: as mass poverty in many developing countries, pockets of poverty amid wealth in developed countries, loss of livelihoods as a result of economic recession, sudden poverty as a result of disaster or conflict, the poverty of low-wage workers, and the utter destitution of people who fall outside family support systems, social institutions and safety nets." (UN, 1995, p 57)

These are clearly *relative* definitions of poverty in that they all refer to poverty not as some 'absolute basket of goods' but in terms of the minimum acceptable standard of living applicable to a certain member state and within a person's own society.

They are similar to the relative poverty definition devised by Peter Townsend who has defined poverty as "objectively and applied consistently only in terms of the concept of relative deprivation.... The term is understood objectively rather than subjectively. Individuals, families and groups in the population can be said to be in poverty when they lack the resources to obtain the types of diet, participate in the activities and have the living conditions and amenities which are customary, or at least widely encouraged or approved, in the society to which they belong" (Townsend, 1979, p 31).

However, they differ quite substantially from the definitions of poverty that were being used when the UK welfare state was first established. The 'subsistence' idea, used by Beveridge (1942), was based on the minimum standards to maintain physical efficiency. It developed from the work of researchers such as Rowntree (1901) in his famous study of poverty in York at the turn of the 20th century (see Bradshaw,

1993, and below). A minimum basket of goods was costed, for emergency use over a short period of time, with 6% extra added for inefficiencies in spending patterns, in order to draw up the national assistance rate[2]. Subsistence rates were designed to be an emergency level of income and were never designed to keep a person out of poverty for any length of time. However, these rates became enshrined in the social security legislation.

The 'modern' definitions of poverty are very different to those used when European welfare states were first being established, particularly in that they deliver much higher poverty lines. They are also concerned with participation and membership within a society and not just inadequate income. The meaning of the concept of poverty has changed and evolved over time in Britain.

Poverty controversies

It often seems that if you put five academics (or policy makers) in a room you would get at least six different definitions of poverty. The literature on poverty is full of controversies, implying that there are considerable differences of opinion on how poverty should be defined and measured. Many, possibly most, of these controversies arise from a misunderstanding of the difference between definition and measurement[3].

First, there is general agreement that poverty can be defined as having an 'insufficient command of resources over time'. A consequence of this lack of 'resources' is that a 'poor' person/household will eventually become deprived – they will be forced to live like the 'poor' – that is, they will not be able "to obtain the types of diet, participate in the activities and have the living conditions and amenities which are customary, or at least widely encouraged or approved, in the society to which they belong". Poverty is the lack of resources and deprivation is the consequence of poverty.

A key policy problem when measuring poverty is how to use scientific methods to find the correct level of resources (often measured as an income level) at which to separate the poor from the non-poor. Many poverty measures simply use an arbitrary threshold level of income as the 'poverty line', such as 60% of the median. Townsend and Gordon (1989) have argued that to set a scientific threshold level of income/resources in a cross-sectional (one point in time) survey, you need to measure both resources/income and deprivation/low standard of living. Both low income and low standard of living can only be accurately measured relative to the norms of the person's or household's society.

Poverty surveys are usually measurements at one point in time (not over several points in time) and so the poor will be measured as those people/households that have both a low standard of living and a low income. They are 'not poor' if they have a low income and a reasonable standard of living or if they have a low standard of living but a high income. This does not mean that the definition of poverty has changed: the 'poor' still remain those with an 'inadequate command of resources over time', but cross-sectional scientific measurement of poverty requires that both resources and deprivation/low standard of living are measured in order to identify the 'correct' poverty threshold level. If high-quality longitudinal data were available, then the 'poor' would be those whose income/resources fall below the 'poverty threshold' and remain below it for a sufficient length of time for them to suffer the effects of deprivation as an enforced consequence of this low income. Poverty is and always has been a dynamic concept. Although some authors have sought to differentiate the concepts of 'poverty' and 'social exclusion' by claiming that 'poverty is a static concept and social exclusion a dynamic concept' (for example, see Berghman, 1995), this is a misunderstanding. For example, Townsend (1962, p 219) clearly explained that "poverty is a dynamic, not a static concept.... Our general theory, then, should be that individuals and families whose resources over time fall seriously short of the resources commanded by the average individual or family in the community in which they live ... are in poverty".

The debate between Townsend and Ringen (1988) and Sen (1981) on 'direct' versus 'indirect' measures of poverty is not about the definition of poverty per se but about the ways of measuring poverty. Sen has argued that, in developing countries, poverty is best measured directly using indicators of standard of living rather than indirectly using income or consumption measures.

> In an obvious sense the direct method is superior to the income method ... it could be argued that only in the absence of direct information regarding the satisfaction of the specified needs can there be a case for bringing in the intermediary of income, so that the income method is at most a second best. (Sen, 1981, p 26)

There is little disagreement here. Even in industrialised countries like Britain it is much easier to accurately measure deprivation than income.

For example, it is easier to measure if someone has gone hungry or cannot afford adequate clothing than to calculate how much income should be imputed in lieu of rent among owner occupiers who have paid off their mortgages (see Canberra Group, 2001; Behrendt, 2002). Deprivation questions are generally simpler and easier to answer than questions about income. However, the controversy can be easily sidestepped, since it is clearly preferable and fairly straightforward to measure both income and deprivation. Indeed, Ringen (1988) has argued that poverty can be considered as a 'state of general deprivation [which] is characterised by both a low standard of consumption and a low level of income'.

A second 'poverty' controversy, which is found in many textbooks, is the debate between Townsend and Sen on absolute versus relative poverty. Sen (1983) has argued that "there is ... an irreducible absolutist core in the idea of poverty. If there is starvation and hunger then, no matter what the relative picture looks like – there clearly is poverty" (p 159). Examples of this absolutist core are the need "to meet nutritional requirements, to escape avoidable disease, to be sheltered, to be clothed, to be able to travel, to be educated ... to live without shame"[4] (pp 162-3).

Townsend (1985) responded that this absolutist core is itself relative to society. Nutritional requirements are dependent on the work roles of people at different points of history and in different cultures and on foods available in local markets. Avoidable disease is dependent on the level of medical technology. The idea of shelter is relative, not just to climate but also to what society may use shelter for. Shelter includes notions of privacy, space to cook, work and play and highly cultured notions of warmth, humidity and segregation of particular members of the family, as well as different functions of sleep, cooking, washing and excretion.

Much of this debate is largely a question of semantics. Sen (1985) argued that "the characteristic feature of absoluteness is neither constancy over time nor invariance between societies nor concentration on food and nutrition. It is an approach to judging a person's deprivation in absolute terms (in the case of a poverty study, in terms of certain specified minimum absolute levels), rather than in purely relative terms vis à vis the levels enjoyed by others in society" (p 673). This definition of absoluteness in non-constant terms is different from the notion of absolute poverty adopted by the Organisation for Economic Development (OECD) (OECD, 1976, p 69): "a level of minimum need, below which people are regarded as poor, for the purpose of social and government concern, and which does not change over time".

From an operational point of view, Sen's concept of absolute poverty is effectively identical to the relative poverty concepts of Townsend and others (Townsend and Gordon, 1993). Indeed, Sen (1985) concluded that:

> There is no conflict between the irreducible absolutist element in the notion of poverty ... and the 'thoroughgoing relativity' to which Peter Townsend refers. (p 674)

The notion of absolute poverty as defined by Sen can be considered to be simply a more severe poverty threshold than that defined by Townsend. Both Townsend's 'relative' poverty threshold and Sen's 'absolute' poverty threshold can be measured in the same cross-sectional survey using the same methods of low income and low standard of living measurement – the 'absolute' poor will be those who suffer from worse/deeper poverty than the 'relative' poor. Indeed, the definitions of 'overall' and 'absolute' poverty agreed at the World Summit for Social Development (see above) make this distinction clear. Therefore the issue of absolute versus relative poverty can be considered to have been resolved by the World Summit agreements in 1995.

The scientific measurement of poverty

In the final draft of the major EU report on *Indicators for social inclusion in the European Union*, Atkinson and his colleagues (2001, p 102) argued that since poverty is relative, multi-dimensional and changed over time, "it is scientifically impossible to determine an accurate, uniquely valid poverty line: i.e. a financial threshold below which a person is defined as being poor". A similar argument could be made that it is 'scientifically impossible' to measure the motion of the planets in the solar system as their movement is also relative, multi-dimensional and changes over time. It is not easy to scientifically measure poverty or the motion of the planets, but it is not impossible.

Other commentators have gone even further and claimed that it is not just scientifically impossible to measure poverty but that it is also 'morally' wrong to attempt to do so:

> The term, 'poverty', carries with it an implication and a moral imperative that something should be done about it. The definition by an individual, or by society collectively,

> of what level represents 'poverty', will always be a value
> judgement. Social scientists have no business trying to pre-
> empt such judgements with 'scientific' prescriptions.
> (Piachaud, 1981, p 421)

These arguments misunderstand the nature of science as they imply
that a scientific measurement of poverty would preclude 'value
judgements' and ignore the 'moral imperative that something should
be done'. First, many social phenomena carry 'an implication and a
moral imperative that something should be done', for example, crime,
violence, care of children or the infirm, and so on. A world in which
science could not play a role in providing an evidence base for policy
making would not be a more 'moral' world but one where policy
decisions about people's lives were often made in a state of ignorance.

Second, all scientific observations/measurements are theory-
dependent and all theories incorporate 'value judgements'. All
measurement, whether it is the height of a person, the charge on an
electron or the level of poverty, is dependent on a theory. There can
be no objectively true value to those measurements that are
independent of the theories used to measure them. As Albert Einstein
famously stated, the theory tells you what you can observe (see
Chalmers, 1978; Shapere, 1982; Medwar, 1984).

For a measurement of poverty to be 'scientific', the theory it is
based on must also be 'scientific'. The theory must not only be logically
internally consistent but also fulfil a number of strict criteria:

1. The theory must be falsifiable, that is, it must be capable of being
   shown to be untrue. The existence of a loving God and Freudian
   psychology are unfalsifiable theories and therefore unscientific.
2. The theory must be testable.
3. The theory must have predictive value.
4. The results of the theory must be reproducible. Other people using
   the same methods will reach the same results.

These criteria are known to philosophers as the Falsificationist view
of science and are attributable to the work of Karl Popper (1968,
1972). They contain the idea of a logical asymmetry that a theory can
never be proved only falsified. This work has been extended by Imre
Lakatos (1974), who claimed that scientific research programmes must
also:

5. Possess a degree of coherence that involves the mapping out of a definite programme for future research.
6. Lead to the discovery of novel phenomena, at least occasionally.

For the measurement of poverty to be scientific, the theory on which the measurement is based must fulfil the criteria of Popper and Lakatos. Gordon and Pantazis (1997) and Gordon (2000) have argued that both the relative and the consensual theories of poverty (used in the PSE Survey) meet these criteria and are therefore scientific theories. The 'consensual' measurement of poverty in the PSE survey is therefore a scientific measurement. However, it is important to note that this does not mean that the PSE Survey results are 'correct' or 'true', as at any given point in history, many, possibly most, scientific theories and measurements are 'wrong' and will eventually be superseded by subsequent theories and measures[5].

The pre-history of scientific poverty measurement

Empirical and scientific investigations of poverty have a very long history in Britain, which predate the work of Charles Booth and Seebohm Rowntree by hundreds of years (see Chapter Four for a discussion of Booth and Rowntree's work). The use of scientific evidence to inform policy making about poverty in Britain dates back to the beginning of the 'scientific revolution' in the 17th and 18th centuries. Fisher (1938, p 14) has described the scientific role of statistics in that era:

> In the original sense of the word, 'Statistics' was the science of Statecraft: to the political arithmetician of the eighteenth century, its function was to be the eyes and ears of the central government.

The first detailed statistical research into the incomes and expenditure of both the 'poor' and other groups in English society was based on the analyses of tax records by Gregory King in 1696 and 1697 in his *Natural and political observations upon the state and conditions of England* (see Stone, 1997). Table 2.1 shows the incomes of 'cottagers and paupers' in 1688 compared with the rest of society. Similar analyses from 1803 (for England and Wales) and 1812 (for Britain and Ireland) by Patrick Colquhoun (*Treatise on indigence* and *Treatise on the wealth, power and resources of the British Empire*) are also shown in Table 2.1. These data are not taken from the original texts but from the amended tables

Table 2.1: Paupers' incomes, 1688-1812

| | Population | | Income per year | | |
	Families	People	Total income (£000s)	Income per family (£)	Income of a poor family as a % of average income
1688 – England					
Cottagers and paupers	400,000	1,300,000	1,950	5	16
All people	1,360,586	5,500,520	43,506	32	
1803 – England and Wales					
Paupers	260,179	1,040,716	6,868	26	23
All people	1,905,823	9,343,561	216,944	114	
1812 – Britain and Ireland					
Paupers	387,100	1,548,400	9,871	25	21
All people	3,501,781	17,096,803	425,310	121	

produced by Stone (1997), who corrected some minor errors in the original tables.

Table 2.1 shows that in 1688 there were about 1.3 million people classified as 'paupers' or 'cottagers' (the lowest feudal class of peasant) in England. They had an average family income of £5 per year, which was approximately equivalent to 16% of average family income. By 1803, the number of paupers had fallen to 1.04 million in England and Wales and the incomes of pauper families had increased in both absolute and relative terms – to £26 per family, which was approximately equivalent to 23% of average family income. The relatively comprehensive data for 1812 include Ireland (which had a population of around eight million before the famine of the 1840s) and show that there were 1.5 million people in pauper families with an average family income of £25 per year, which was approximately equivalent to 21% of average family income. Although there have been many advances in social statistics over the past 300 years, the current Households Below Average Income statistics do not provide much greater insight into poverty in the 21st century than the 17th and early 19th century research summarised in Table 2.1. Pre-nineteenth century scientific investigations of poverty in Britain were not just confined to investigations of income and expenditure; in 1797, Fredrick Morton Eden published the *State of the poor*, three immense volumes about the lives of paupers in England. Morton Eden used questionnaire methods to produce a study so detailed that even Karl Marx in *Das Kapital* commented that "Sir F.M. Eden is the only disciple of Adam Smith during the eighteenth century that produced a work of importance" (see Pyatt and Ward, 1999).

These early scientific investigations of poverty provided evidence for the radical republican thinkers of the 18th century that poverty was not inevitable and could be eradicated using universal benefits funded by progressive taxation. The French Enlightenment philosopher Marie Jean Antonine Nicolas de Caritat, Maquis de Condorcet argued in *Sketch for a historical picture of the progress of the human mind* (published in 1794) that poverty was not a result of natural laws or divine will but was caused by 'the present imperfections of the social arts' (quoted in Stedman Jones, 2004). He argued that poverty could be ended by the universal provision of pensions, grants to the young, sickness benefits and state education. Similar 'welfare state' solutions for poverty can also be found in Thomas Paine's *Agrarian justice* (1785) and *Rights of man* (1791), which argued for progressive taxation and death duties to fund child benefits, pensions and education (see Stedman Jones, 2004). The need to end poverty was seen as necessary to reduce social and economic polarisation, which, if allowed to persist, would undermine the stability and unity of the democratic republic.

Scientific poverty measurement in the PSE Survey

In the PSE Survey the scientific measurement of poverty was based on a statistical model first developed by Townsend and Gordon (1989) and Gordon (1997) and a theoretical model developed by Gordon (1998) and Gordon (2000). In scientific terms, a person or household in Britain is 'poor' when they have both a low income *and* a low standard of living. They are 'not poor' if they have a low income and a reasonable standard of living or if they have a low standard of living but a high income. Both low income and low standard of living can only be accurately measured relative to the norms of the person's or household's society.

A low standard of living is often measured by using a deprivation index (high deprivation equals a low standard of living) or by consumption expenditure[6] (low consumption expenditure equals a low standard of living). Of these two methods, deprivation indices are more accurate since consumption expenditure is often only measured over a brief period and is obviously not independent of available income. Deprivation indices are broader measures because they reflect different aspects of living standards, including personal, physical and mental conditions, local and environmental facilities, social activities and customs. Figure 2.1 illustrates these concepts.

The 'objective' poverty line/threshold is shown in Figure 2.1. It can be defined as the point that maximises the differences *between* the two

Figure 2.1: Definition of poverty

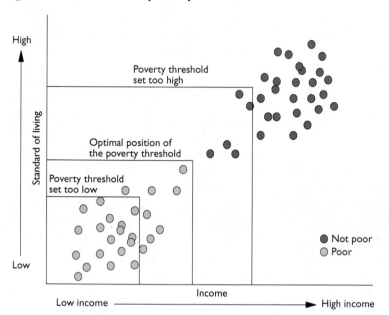

groups ('poor' and 'not poor') and minimises the differences *within* the two groups ('poor' and 'not poor'). For scientific purposes, broad measures of both income and standard of living are desirable. Standard of living includes both the material and social conditions in which people live and their participation in the economic, social, cultural and political life of the country.

Income and standard of living are correlated, they are not orthogonal variables (at right angles – 90° – to each other) as shown in Figure 2.1. It is therefore statistically impossible to establish a perfect ordering for every person in the survey. There will always be some ambiguities near the margins about whether a person should be defined as 'poor' or not. Therefore it is better to conceive the poverty threshold as a band of low income and standard of living rather than as a hard fixed line (as shown in Figure 2.1)[7]. However, it must be stressed that this does not mean that poverty cannot be defined and measured scientifically. There are many scientific problems where the exact boundaries between two groups are hard to identify precisely. As Edmund Burke (1770, p 38) argued, "though no man can draw a stroke between the confines of day and night, yet light and darkness are upon the whole tolerably distinguishable".

There are a variety of scientific approaches that can be used to measure poverty. In this study we have used the consensual method, devised by Joanna Mack and Stewart Lansley during the 1980s (Mack and Lansley, 1985; see also Chapter One in this volume).

Dynamics of poverty

From the definition above, it is clear that people/households with a high income and a high standard of living are not poor, whereas those with a low income and a low standard of living are poor. However, two other groups of people/households that are 'not poor' can also be identified in a cross-sectional (one point in time) survey, such as the PSE Survey.

- *People/households with a low income but a high standard of living.* This group is not currently poor but if their income remains low they will become poor – they are vulnerable to sinking into poverty. This situation often arises when income falls rapidly (due to job loss, for example) but people manage to maintain their lifestyle, for at least a few months, by drawing on their savings and using the assets accumulated when income was higher.
- *People/households with a high income but a low standard of living.* This group is 'not poor' and if their income remains high their standard of living will rise – they will rise out of poverty. This group is in the opposite situation to the previous group. This situation can arise when the income of someone who is poor suddenly increases (due to getting a job, for example). However, it takes time before they are able to buy the things that they need to increase their standard of living. Income can both rise and fall faster than standard of living.

A cross-sectional 'poverty' survey can provide some limited but useful information on the dynamics of poverty since it is possible not only to identify the 'poor' and the 'not poor' but also those likely to be sinking into poverty (that is, people/households with a low income but a high standard of living) and those escaping from poverty (that is, people/households with a high income but a low standard of living).

Living in poverty is, by definition, an extremely unpleasant situation so it is not surprising that people go to considerable lengths to avoid it and try very hard to escape from poverty once they have sunk into it. Therefore, a cross-sectional poverty survey ought to find that the group of households sinking into poverty is larger than the group escaping from poverty, since, when income falls, people will try to delay the descent into poverty but, if the income of a poor person increases, they will quickly try to improve their standard of living.

Figure 2.2 illustrates this concept. Between time 0 and 1 the household has both a high standard of living (dotted line) and a high income (solid line): it is 'not poor'. At time 1, there is a rapid reduction in income (for example, due to job loss, the end of seasonal contract income, divorce or separation and so on). However, the household's standard of living does not fall immediately; it is not until time 2 that the household's standard of living has also fallen below the 'poverty' threshold. Therefore, between time 1 and time 2, the household is 'not poor' but is sinking into poverty (that is, it has a low income but a relatively high standard of living). At time 3, income begins to rise rapidly, although not as fast as it previously fell. This is because rapid income increases usually result from gaining employment but there is often a lag between starting work and getting paid. Standard of living also begins to rise after a brief period as the household spends its way out of poverty. However, this lag means that there is a short period when the household has a high income but a relatively low standard of living. By time 5, the household again has a high income and a high standard of living.

On the basis of this discussion, it is possible to update Figure 2.1 to give a more realistic picture of movements into and out of poverty. Figure 2.3 illustrates this.

Figure 2.2: Dynamics of poverty

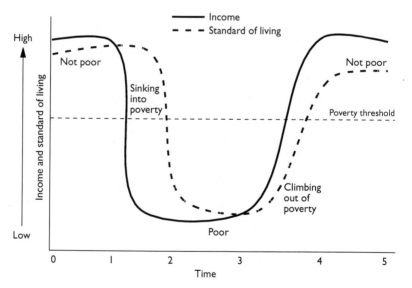

Figure 2.3: Revised definition of poverty

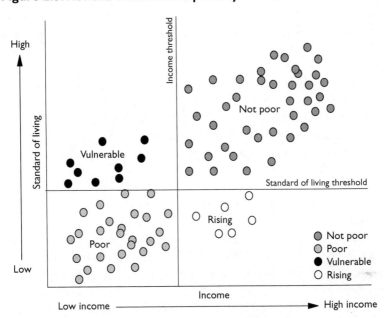

The proportion of the population in these four groups in the PSE Survey is shown in Table 2.2. Approximately a quarter of the population are living in poverty, 2% are rising out of poverty, 13% were potentially vulnerable to poverty because of their low incomes and 60% are relatively well off. These results and the theoretical model described above explain the findings of many authors that in cross-sectional (one point in time) surveys there is a relatively low correlation between low income and deprivation, but in longitudinal surveys the correlation increases (for example, see Tsakloglou and Papadopoulos, 2002; Berthoud et al, 2004).

In the PSE Survey the consensual method of measuring poverty was used to divide the population into the four groups shown in Table 2.2 and involved three steps. First, to establish what the public perceives as social necessities. Second, to identify those who suffer an enforced lack of the socially perceived necessities. Third, to determine at what levels of household income people run a greater risk of not being able to afford the socially defined necessities in a given national context (this identifies the poverty line or band).

Table 2.2: Population groups in the PSE Survey

Group	%
Poor	25
Rising	2
Vulnerable	13
Not poor	60
Total	100

The first step was taken by building up a long list of ordinary household goods and activities. Respondents were asked to indicate which items they thought were necessities that no household or family in Britain should be without (see Chapters One and Four). The second step was to ask people what items they already had or wanted but could not afford. Items defined as necessities by more than 50% of the population but that households lacked because of a shortage of money were then used to construct an initial deprivation index. The use of a democratic threshold (50%) to identify what items and activities are necessities provides both 'political' and face validity[8] for the deprivation index.

The third step, finding the poverty threshold, was taken by using multivariate methods to determine the income for each kind of household that maximised the differences between the 'poor' and 'not poor' and minimised the differences within the two groups ('poor' and 'not poor'). This is the 'objective' poverty line and households that have had to survive on this low level of income for any appreciable length of time are highly likely to suffer the effects of multiple deprivations. A more detailed description of the statistical methods used to determine the scientific poverty line can be can be found in Appendix 2.1.

Mack and Lansley's consensual approach has had a significant impact on modern poverty research (see Chapter One). Their original 1983 study was replicated: in Britain in 1990 (Gordon and Pantazis, 1997) and by the PSE Survey in 1999 (Gordon et al, 2000); in Wales in 1995 (Gordon, 1995); and in Northern Ireland in 2002 (Hillyard et al, 2003). Local authorities in London, Manchester, Liverpool, Greenwich and Kent have conducted similar surveys. The Office of Population, Censuses and Surveys used a similar set of questions to measure the standard of living of disabled adults and families with disabled children in Britain in 1985 (Martin and White, 1988; Smyth and Robus, 1989). Similarly, representative surveys were carried out by the PPRU among disabled people in Northern Ireland in 1990 and 1991 (Zarb and Maher, 1997). The European Statistical Office (Eurostat) has used a similar set of questions to measure standard of living in Britain and the other member states annually since 1994 as part of the European Community Household Panel Survey (Ramprakash, 1994; Vogel, 1997; Eurostat, 2000). This approach to measuring standard of living has also been adopted in Denmark (Mack and Lansley, 1985), Sweden (Halleröd, 1994, 1995a, 1995b, 1998), Ireland (Callan et al, 1993; Nolan and Whelan, 1996a), Belgium (van den Bosch, 1998), Holland (Muffels, 1993; Muffels and Vreins, 1991; Muffels et al, 1992), Finland (Kangas and Ritakillio, 1998) and Germany (Andreß and Lipsmeir, 1995). In the less developed world the adapted versions of the consensual method to measure poverty have been used in Russia (Tchernina, 1996), Tanzania (Kaijage and Tibaijuka, 1996), Vietnam (Davies and Smith, 1998) and Yemen (Hashem, 1996).

Income poverty in the PSE Survey

It is clear from the previous discussion that reliable and valid measures of both 'command of resources over time' and 'standard of living' are needed in order to produce accurate scientific measurements of poverty. Given the relatively small scale and limited budget of the PSE Survey, usual net household income was used as a proxy measure of command of resources over time and deprivation measures were used as indicators of low standard of living.

In addition to the scientific poverty estimates discussed above and in Appendix 2.1, the PSE Survey data were also used to calculate a range of income poverty lines for comparative purposes with other poverty statistics produced by the UK government and the European Union. Table 2.3 shows the number of people living in households below the income poverty lines that have been most frequently used in Britain and Europe.

However, all poverty estimates that are solely based on income are less accurate and reliable than the consensual method estimate of poverty:

1. the income threshold used to define who is poor is arbitrary;
2. the equivalisation of income to adjust for different household sizes and compositions is also arbitrary (see discussion below);
3. the low income poverty thresholds used in Britain are really crude measures of inequality that have a number of undesirable mathematical properties, for example, if every household's income doubles or trebles (or falls by half), the same number of people will be defined as poor;
4. many households in Britain with zero or negative incomes also have high expenditures and do not consider themselves to be poor (Elam et al, 1999). Their very low incomes are often an artefact of the way the incomes of the self employed and students are measured.

The percentage of people defined as poor using low income thresholds ranges from 23.1% to 25.6% (Table 2.3), which is similar to the consensual method estimate of 25% of people living in poverty (see

Table 2.3: Income poverty rates in the PSE Survey

	% poor
HBAI half average income	23.5
HBAI 60% median income	23.1
Eurostat 60% median income	23.7
PSE half average income	25.6
PSE 60% median income	25

HBAI: Households Below Average Income.

Table 2.2). However, it must be stressed that the same people are not always identified as being poor using these different methods (see McCregor and Borooah, 1992; Callan et al, 1993; Kangas and Ritakallio, 1998; Bradshaw and Finch, 2003 for a discussion of the overlap between different methods of measuring poverty). The differences are the result of the different threshold levels of income used (that is, below half average income and below 60% of median income) and the different methods of adjusting income for household size and composition – equivalisation. The HBAI results use the McClements equivalisation scale, the Eurostat results use the modified OECD equivalisation scale and the PSE income poverty results use the PSE equivalisation scale, which is based on budget standards. The definition and measurement of income and equivalisation are explained below.

Definition of income

Income is a key concept in almost all definitions and studies of poverty; however, 'income' is an extremely difficult concept to define and measure. The term is sometimes used loosely to refer only to the main component of monetary income for most households – that is, wages and salaries or business income. Others use the term more widely to include all receipts including lump-sum receipts and receipts that draw on the household's capital. Much of the debate has centred on whether:

- income should include only receipts that are recurrent (that is, exclude large and unexpected, typically one-off, receipts);
- income should only include those components that contribute to current economic well-being, or extend also to those that contribute to future well-being;
- whether the measure of income should allow for the maintenance of the value of net worth (Canberra Group, 2001).

Classically, income has been defined as the sum of consumption and change in net worth (wealth) in a period. This is known as the Haig-

Simons approach (see Atkinson and Stiglitz, 1980, p 260). Unfortunately, this approach fails to distinguish between the day-to-day 'living well' and the broader 'getting rich' aspects of individual or household finances (in technical terms, it fails to distinguish between current and capital receipts).

There are a number of international organisations that have provided guidelines on defining and measuring income. The UN provides two frameworks: the 1993 System of National Accounts (UN, 1992) and guidelines on collecting micro-level data on the economic resources of households (UN, 1977, 1989). The International Labour Organization (ILO) has also produced guidelines on the collection of data on income of households, with particular emphasis on income from employment (ILO, 1971, 1992, 1993). In 1997, the Australian Bureau of Statistics (ABS) tried to get an international agreement on definitions of income, consumption, saving and wealth. It has proposed the following definition:

> income comprises those receipts accruing (in cash and in-kind) that are of a regular and recurring nature, and are received by the household or its members at annual or more frequent intervals. It includes regular receipts from employment, own business and from the lending of assets. It also includes transfer income from government, private institutions and other households. Income also includes the value of services provided from within the household via the use of an owner-occupied dwelling, other consumer durables owned by the household and unpaid household work. Income excludes capital receipts that are considered to be an addition to stocks, and receipts derived from the running down of assets or from the incurrence of a liability. It also excludes intra-household transfers. (ABS, 1995)

This initiative by the ABS led to the establishment of the United Nations Expert Group on Household Income Statistics (Canberra Group), which issued a series of recommendations on the definitions and components of household income in its final report[9] in 2001 (see Table 2.4).

Townsend (1979, 1993) has argued that broad definitions of income should be used, particularly if international comparisons are to be made. It is crucial, when comparing individual or household incomes of people in different countries, that account is taken of the value of government services in, for example, the fields of health, education

Table 2.4: Definitions of income (Canberra Group recommendations)

I   Employee income

Cash or near cash
1.1   Cash wages and salaries
1.2   Tips and bonuses
1.3   Profit sharing including stock options
1.4   Severance and termination pay
1.5   Allowances payable for working in remote locations etc, where part of conditions of employment

Cash value of 'fringe benefits'
1.6   Employers' social insurance contributions
1.7   Goods and services provided to employee as part of employment package

2   Income from self-employment

Cash or near cash
2.1   Profit/loss from unincorporated enterprise
2.2   Royalties

In-kind, imputed
2.3   Goods and services produced for barter, less cost of inputs
2.4   Goods produced for home consumption, less cost of inputs
2.5   Income less expenses from owner-occupied dwellings

3   Rentals
3.1   Income less expenses from rentals, except rent of land

4   Property income
4.1   Interest received, less interest paid
4.2   Dividends
4.3   Rent from land

5   Current transfers received
5.1   Social insurance benefits from employers' schemes
5.2   Social insurance benefits in cash from government schemes
5.3   Universal social assistance benefits in cash from government
5.4   Means-tested social assistance benefits in cash from government
5.5   Regular inter-household cash transfers received
5.6   Regular support received from non-profit making institutions such as charities

6   Total income *(sum of I to 5)*

7   Current transfers paid
7.1   Employers' social insurance contributions
7.2   Employees' social insurance contributions
7.3   Taxes on income
7.4   Regular taxes on wealth
7.5   Regular inter-household cash transfers
7.6   Regular cash transfers to charities

8   Disposable income *(6 less 7)*

9   Social transfers in kind (STIK) received

10   Adjusted disposable income *(8 plus 9)*

and transport (Evandrou et al, 1992). Unfortunately, attempts in Britain to measure income and wealth using broad definitions of these concepts have often ended in failure (Knight, 1980). The concept of resources can be considered to encompass elements of human capital and therefore can be wider than even a broad concept of income. A household's resources can be considered to include both financial resources and the human resources of time, abilities and energy of each household member (Andreß, 1998). However, in practice, most poverty surveys in industrialised nations only analyse poverty in terms of 'usual' income and use an 'arbitrary' threshold of income to identify the 'poor', for example, below half average income or below 60% of median income. Thus, income poverty lines define the 'poor' as those with a low income even if they have a high standard of living.

The income concept used in the PSE Survey is usual net weekly household income and is identical to that used in the General Household Survey (GHS). It is the sum of usual post-tax income for all adults in the household from earnings, benefits, pensions, dividends, interest and other regular payments. If the last pay packet/cheque was unusual, for example in including holiday pay in advance or a tax refund, the respondent is asked for usual pay (Bridgwood et al, 2000). The usual net weekly household incomes recorded in the 1998 GHS were adjusted to take account of household income changes (increases or decreases) between the 1998 GHS and 1999 PSE Survey.

Income equivalisation

Gordon and Pantazis (1997) have argued that equivalisation of income presents one of the major problems when determining the poverty line/threshold. It is self-evident that the larger the household the more income will be needed to maintain the same standard of living. It is also clear that economies of scale exist within a household, that is, it does not cost a family of four twice as much as a family of two to maintain the same standard of living. However, it is not self-evident how much extra larger households need to have the same standard of living as smaller households. Unfortunately, the UK government's calculations at the time of the PSE Survey (McClements equivalisation scale) assumes that, if a household gives birth to (or adopts) six babies under two, this will cost them *less* than if one additional adult joins the household – one additional adult costs more than six babies after allowing for housing costs (McClements, 1977, 1978). This is unlikely to be correct and it leads to perverse and incorrect policy conclusions, since the low-income statistics (HBAI) appear to show that there are comparatively fewer problems of poverty and low income among families with young children than among families with older children. However the scientific evidence indicates that it is families with young children that are often most likely to suffer the effects of poverty as, by the time children have reached their teens, family finances are often more robust (see Chapter Eleven in this volume). Unsurprisingly, the McClements scale has been criticised for making unrealistic allowances for the costs of children (Muellbauer, 1979, 1980). It has also been criticised by Coulter et al (1992, p 1081), who argue that the McClements scale "provides lower estimates of inequality and poverty that do other scales". Banks and Johnson (1994) have argued that even lower poverty and inequality rates are possible with other equivalence scales, but it is clear that the McClements scale produces "lower estimates of poverty and inequality levels than most other scales" (Jenkins and Cowell, 1994, p 899).

Unfortunately, much of the economic theory underlying equivalence scales is adult-orientated and defines 'household welfare' in ways that obscure the needs of children (Nelson, 1993). Nelson argues that "if on the other hand, households (and policy makers?), really do consider the welfare of children directly when making consumption decisions, these models can hardly provide good guidelines" (pp 482-3) and concludes that "the search for one, true, definitive set of scales appears to be a chimera since no completely superior method exists for their estimation" (p 493).

This is problematic because the results obtained from a poverty study are sensitive to the equivalence scale used (Whiteford, 1985; Buhman et al, 1988; Bradbury, 1989; Weir, 1992; de Vos and Zaidi, 1997). Both the household composition of the 'poor' and the position of the poverty line can be influenced by equivalisation. For example, the surprising findings of Jorgenson (1998) that the long-run trend in poverty in the USA since the 1970s has been declining not slightly increasing as in the official Census reports is a result the equivalence scales used in the study (Triest, 1998).

As a result of these problems, one of the innovations introduced in the PSE Survey was the adoption of an equivalisation scale based on the latest available budget standards information to adjust income for household size and composition (the PSE equivalisation scale). This new scale was used to both help select the households for interview (Gordon et al, 2000) and to compare the incomes of households of different sizes and compositions in the study (see Table 2.5).

Equivalisation scales should be based on budget standards results so that they are socially meaningful[10]. In the PSE Survey, the equivalisation

Table 2.5: PSE equivalised income scale

Type of household member	Equivalence value
Head of household	0.70
Partner	0.30
Each additional adult (anyone over 16)	0.45
Add for first child	0.35
Add for each additional child	0.30
If head of household is a lone parent, add	0.10
If there is a person with a disability in the household, add	0.30

scale was based upon the simplified relativities in the low cost but acceptable (LCA) budgets for various 'idealised' household types (Bradshaw, 1993; Parker, 1998, 2000). These relativities were slightly modified to take account of more detailed budget standards results on the cost of children by age and gender (Oldfield and Yu, 1993) and the additional costs of disability (Berthoud et al, 1993; Dobson and Middleton, 1998).

The PSE equivalisation scale has now been used in a number of academic studies (for example, Hillyard et al, 2003; Adam and Brewer, 2004) and the UK government has decided to abandon the use of the McClements scale for measuring child poverty and has adopted the modified OECD scale used by Eurostat to compare poverty rates in European Union member states (DWP, 2003).

Throughout this book, the PSE equivalisation scale has been used to adjust income by household size and type. However, some tables also report income adjusted using the McClements and modified OECD equivalisation scales for comparative purposes. Similarly, a range of income poverty thresholds have been used for comparative purposes, particularly the below 60% median equivalised household income level used by Eurostat and the Department for Work and Pensions to measure poverty (see Table 2.3).

Subjective poverty in the PSE Survey

The final sets of method used to measure poverty in the PSE Survey are subjective measures – asking people if they think they are poor and how much income they would need to avoid poverty. This approach, to identifying poverty thresholds, is also known as the income proxy method (Veit-Wilson, 1987) consensual poverty lines (see Walker, 1987, Halleröd, 1995a) or sociovital minimum income level (SMIL) (Callan et al, 1989). Subjective poverty lines are estimations by populations (obtained through surveys) about the minimum income level at which people find it is still possible to live 'decently'. In the

PSE Survey this methodology has been used to obtain estimates of how much money would be needed to avoid absolute and overall poverty, as defined at the World Summit for Social Development (see Chapter Three in this volume).

The most important advantage of the subjective method is that the level of the poverty line is not fixed by experts but defined by society itself. The subjective method is therefore a socially realistic method.

All methods of estimating a subjective poverty line make use of a minimum income question (MIQ) designed to measure the smallest income required to avoid 'poverty', live 'decently' or 'adequately' or to 'get along'. However, the exact wording of the MIQ varies considerably in different studies (Bradbury, 1989; Callan and Nolan, 1991).

The simplest and arguably most democratic method of producing a 'subjective' poverty line is to use the average response to the MIQ from the population (survey sample) as a whole. This is a procedure that has been used in Britain (Townsend and Gordon, 1991; Townsend et al, 1996, 1997) and Australia (Saunders and Matheson, 1992). However, several other methods have been used in European countries (see Goedhart et al, 1977; van Praag et al, 1980; Deleeck et al, 1988).

Perceptual poverty lines have been measured in the PSE Survey by asking respondents if their income is 'a lot below' the income needed to avoid poverty and 'a lot below' the income needed to avoid 'absolute' and 'overall' poverty. Respondents were also asked if they considered themselves to be 'genuinely poor now – "all the time", "sometime" or "never"'. Table 2.6 shows the percentage of people who consider their household income to be either 'a lot' or 'a little' below the absolute, general and overall poverty threshold. It also shows the percentage of respondents who consider that they are genuinely poor now – 'all the time' or 'sometimes'.

The percentage of people defined as poor in Table 2.6 ranges from 17% to 26% depending on the definition of poverty presented to the respondent (see www.bris.ac.uk/poverty/pse/welcome.htm). The proportion of people who defined themselves as poor in answer to the overall poverty (25%) and genuine poverty (26%) questions are very similar to the scientific consensual poverty rates (25% – Table 2.2). Again, it must be stressed that the same people are not always identified as poor when using these different methods.

Table 2.6: Subjective poverty rates in the PSE Survey

	% poor
Absolute poverty	17
General poverty	20
Overall poverty	25
Genuinely poor	26

Conclusion

The PSE Survey contains a number of significant technical and theoretical advances in poverty measurement. It implemented a new theoretical model for scientific poverty measurement that has the power to explain the relatively low correlation between low income and deprivation in cross-sectional surveys. The PSE income poverty analyses and interview sample selection made use of a new socially realistic (budget standards based) equivalisation scale (the PSE equivalisation scale). The PSE Survey is the first in Britain to provide a comprehensive measurement of poverty using a range of different methods and definitions of poverty.

In summary, poverty has been measured in the PSE Survey using three different methods:

1. the consensual method, which defines people as poor who have both a low income and a low standard of living;
2. the income poverty method, which defines people as poor when their income falls below a relative income poverty threshold;
3. the subjective method, where people define themselves as poor in response to questions using different definitions of poverty.

The consensual method identified a quarter (25%) of the population as poor. An effectively identical poverty rate was also found using the income poverty method (25% and 26%) when the PSE equivalisation scale was used. Finally, effectively identical proportions of people (25% and 26%) said they were poor in answer to the overall and genuine subjective poverty questions. All three sets of poverty measurement methods used in the PSE Survey produce similar poverty rates. It seems clear that approximately a quarter of the population of Britain was living in poverty at the beginning of the millennium.

Notes
[1] http://daccessdds.un.org/doc/UNDOC/GEN/N00/559/51/PDF/N0055951.pdf?OpenElement

[2] Atkinson (1990, p 10) defines a subsistence standard of poverty by the formula:

$$(1 + h) \, p.x^*$$

where:

x^* is a vector denoting a basket of goods,

p is the price of the basket, and

h is a provision for inefficient expenditure or waste.

[3] This is an old and common problem, which was described by Spinoza in the 17th century: "Many errors, in truth, consist merely in the application of the wrong names of things" (Spinoza, *The ethics*, 1677).

[4] This definition of absolute poverty by Sen goes some way beyond the conception of Keith Joseph, who argued that: "An absolute standard means one defined by reference to the actual needs of the poor and not by reference to the expenditure of those who are not poor. A family is poor if it cannot afford to eat" (Joseph and Sumption, 1979, pp 27-8).

[5] The claim that the PSE measurement of poverty is 'scientific' is not a rhetorical device designed to foreclose argument and prove the 'truth' and 'superiority' of our results. It simply means that the measurement and theory of poverty used in the PSE Survey conform to the requirements of the philosophy of science.

[6] The United Nations defines household final consumption expenditure as "the expenditure, including imputed expenditure, incurred by resident households on individual consumption goods and services, including those sold at prices that are not economically significant" (see http://unstats.un.org/unsd/cdb/cdb_dict_xrxx.asp?def_code= 165).

[7] I would like to thank the members of the United Nations Expert Group on Poverty Statistics (Rio Group), and in particular Ruben Suarez of the Pan American Health Organization, for their helpful discussions of this issue.

[8] Face validity is concerned with how likely to be 'true' a measure or procedure appears. Anastasi (1988) describes the concept of face validity as follows: "Content validity should not be confused with face validity. The latter is not validity in the technical sense; it refers, not to what the test actually measures, but to what it appears superficially to measure. Face validity pertains to whether the test 'looks valid' to the examinees who take it, the administrative personnel who decide on its use, and other technically untrained observers" (p 144).

[9] See www.lisproject.org/links/canberra/finalreport.pdf

[10] Budget standards are themselves not unproblematic. Bradshaw et al (1987) argued that: "It would be wrong to claim too much for budget standards methodology. There will be arguments about the components of a modern budget standard just as there were about Rowntree's standards. The quality of people's lives cannot be completely represented by the goods they consume. Budgets cannot represent fringe benefits, wealth and the consumption of unmarketed public and private services. Neither can a budget show how goods are consumed variously within households. However, budget standards are capable of incorporating elements concerned with social participation and can represent a measure of relative deprivation". However, despite these limitations, a budget standards-based income equivalisation scale is still preferable to an arbitrary equivalisation scale such as the modified OECD scale.

References

ABS (Australian Bureau of Statistics) (1995) *A provisional framework for household income, consumption, saving and wealth*, Canberra: Australian Government Publishing Service (http://lisweb.ceps.lu/links/canbaccess.htm).

Adam, S. and Brewer, M. (2004) *Supporting families: The financial costs and benefits of children since 1975*, Bristol: The Policy Press.

Andreß, H.J. (ed) (1998) *Empirical poverty research in a comparative perspective*, Aldershot: Ashgate.

Andreß, H.J. and Lipsmeir, G. (1995) 'Was gehört zum notwendigen Lebensstandard und wer kann ihn sich leisten? Ein neues konzept zur Armutsmessung', *Aus Politik und Zeitgeschichte, Beilage zur Wochenzeitung Das Parlament*, B, 31-32/95 (28 July).

Anastasi, A. (1988) *Psychological testing*. New York, NY: Macmillan.

Atkinson, A.B. (1990) *Comparing poverty rates internationally*, London: London School of Economics Welfare State Programme.

Atkinson, A.B. and Stiglitz, J.E. (1980) *Lectures on public economics*, London: McGraw-Hill.

Atkinson, A.B., Cantillon, B., Marlier, E. and Nolan, B. (2001) *Indicators for social inclusion in the European Union*. Report presented at the Conference on Indicators for Social Inclusion: Making Common EU Objectives Work, Antwerp, 14-15 September. Final version published as Atkinson, A.B., Cantillon, B., Marlier, E. and Nolan, B. (2002) *Indicators for social inclusion in the European Union*, Oxford: Oxford University Press.

Banks, J. and Johnson, P. (1994) 'Equivalence scales relativities revisited', *The Economic Journal*, vol 104, pp 883-90.

Behrendt, C. (2002) 'Do income surveys overestimate poverty in Western Europe? Evidence from a comparison with institutional frameworks', *Social Indicators Research*, vol 58, pp 429-40.

Berghman, J. (1995) 'Social exclusion in Europe', in G. Room (ed), *Beyond the threshold. The measurement and analysis of social exclusion*, Bristol: The Policy Press.

Berthoud R., Lakey, J. and McKay, S. (1993) *The economic problems of disabled people*, London: Policy Studies Institute.

Berthoud, R., Bryan, M. and Bardasi. E. (2004) *The dynamics of deprivation: The relationship between income and material deprivation over time*, Department for Work and Pensions, Research Report No 219, Leeds: CDS (www.dwp.gov.uk/asd/asd5/rports2003-2004/rrep219.asp).

Beveridge Report (1942) *Social insurance and allied services*, Cm 6064, London: HMSO.

Bradbury, B. (1989) 'Family size equivalence scales and survey evaluations of income and well-being', *Journal of Social Policy*, vol 18, no 3, pp 383-408.

Bradshaw, J. (ed) (1993) *Budget standards for the United Kingdom*, Aldershot: Avebury.

Bradshaw, J. and Finch, N. (2003) 'Overlaps in dimensions of poverty', *Journal of Social Policy*, vol 32, no 4, pp 513-25.

Bradshaw, J., Mitchell, D. and Morgan, J. (1987) 'Evaluating adequacy: the potential of budget standards', *Journal of Social Policy*, vol 16, no 2, pp 165-82.

Bradshaw J., Gordon D., Levitas R., Middleton S., Pantazis C., Payne S. and Townsend P. (1998) *Perceptions of poverty and social exclusion 1998*, Report on Preparatory Research, Bristol: Townsend Centre for International Poverty Research, University of Bristol.

Bridgwood, A., Lilly, R., Thomas, M., Bacon, J., Sykes, W. and Morris, S. (2000) *Living in Britain: Results from the 1998 General Household Survey*. London: The Stationery Office.

Buhman, B., Rainwater, L., Schmaus, G. and Smeeding, T. (1988) 'Equivalence scales, well-being, inequality and poverty: sensitivity estimates across ten countries using the Luxembourg Income Study database', *Review of Income and Wealth*, vol 34, pp 115-40.

Burke, E. (1770) *Thoughts on the cause of the present discontents*, London: Printed for J. Dodsley (www.underthesun.cc/Classics/Burke/DiscontentsSpeeches/DiscontentsSpeeches1.htm).

Callan, T. and Nolan, B. (1991) 'Concepts of poverty and the poverty line', *Journal of Economic Surveys*, vol 5, no 3, pp 243-61.

Callan, T., Nolan, B., Whelan, B.J., Hannan, D.F. and Creighton, S. (1989) *Poverty, income and welfare in Ireland*, Dublin: Economic and Social Research Institute.

Callan, T., Nolan, B. and Whelan, C.T. (1993) 'Resources, deprivation and the measurement of poverty', *Journal of Social Policy*, vol 22, no 2, pp 141-72.

Canberra Group (2001) *Expert Group on Household Income Statistics: Final report and recommendations*, Ottawa.

Chalmers, A.F. (1978) *What is this thing called Science?* Milton Keynes: The Open University Press.

Coulter, F., Cowell, F. and Jenkins, S. (1992) 'Equivalence scale relativities and the extent of inequality and poverty', *Economic Journal*, vol 102, pp 1067-82.

Council Decision 75/458/EEC of 22nd July 1975 – *Concerning a programme of pilot schemes and studies to combat poverty* (OLJ 99/3430.7.75.)

Davies, R. and Smith, W. (1998) *The Basic Necessities Survey: The experience of Action Aid Vietnam*, London: Action Aid.

Deleeck, H., de Lathouwer, L. and van den Bosch, K. (1988) *Social indicators of social security. A comparative analysis of five countries*, Antwerp: Centre for Social Policy.

Deleeck, H., van den Bosch, K. and de Lathouwer, L. (eds) (1992) *Poverty and the adequacy of social security in the EC*, EUROPASS Research Consortium, Aldershot: Avebury.

de Vos, K. and Zaidi, M.A. (1997) 'Equivalence scale sensitivity of poverty statistics for member states of the European Community', *Review of Income and Wealth*, vol 43, no 3, pp 319-33.

Dobson, B. and Middleton, S. (1998) *Paying to care: The cost of childhood disability*, York: YPS.

DSS (Department of Social Security) (1999) *Opportunity for All: Tackling poverty and social exclusion*, London: The Stationery Office.

DWP (Department for Work and Pensions) (2003) *Measuring child poverty: Final conclusions*, London: DWP (www.dwp.gov.uk/consultations/consult/2003/childpov/final.asp).

EEC (1981) *Final report from the Commission to the Council on the first programme of pilot schemes and studies to combat poverty*, Brussels: Commission of the European Communities.

EEC (1985) *On Specific Community Action to Combat Poverty* (Council Decision of 19 December 1984) 85/8/EEC, Official Journal of the EEC, 2/24.

Elam, G., Lee, S. and Tadd, E. (1999) *Minimal income households: Circumstances and strategies*, Department for Work and Pensions Research Report No 57, London: DWP.

Eurostat (2000) *European social statistics: Income, poverty and social exclusion*, Luxembourg: Eurostat.

Evandrou, M., Falkingham, J., Hills, J. and Le Grand, J. (1992) *The distribution of welfare benefits in kind*, Welfare State Programme Discussion Paper WSP/68, London: LSE.

Fisher, R.A. (1938) 'First Indian Statistical Conference', *Sankhya*, vol 4, p 14.

Goedhart, T., Halberstadt, V., Kapteyn, A. and Van Praag, B. (1977) 'The poverty line: concept and measurement', *Journal of Human Resources*, vol 12, no 4, pp 503-20.

Gordon, D. (1998) 'Definitions of concepts for the perceptions of poverty and social exclusion', in J. Bradshaw, D. Gordon, R. Levitas, S. Middleton, C. Pantazis, S. Payne and P. Townsend (eds) *Perceptions of poverty and social exclusion 1998*, Report on Preparatory Research, Bristol: Townsend Centre for International Poverty Research, University of Bristol, pp 5-14 (www.bris.ac.uk/poverty/pse/99-Pilot/99-Pilot.doc).

Gordon, D. (2000) 'The scientific measurement of poverty: recent theoretical advances', in J. Bradshaw and R. Sainsbury (eds) *Researching poverty*, Aldershot: Ashgate, pp 37-58.

Gordon, D. and Pantazis, C. (1997) *Breadline Britain in the 1990s*, Aldershot: Ashgate.

Gordon, D. and Spicker, P. (eds) (1999) *The international glossary on poverty*, Cape Town, Dhaka, Bangkok, London and New York: Zed Books.

Gordon, D., Adelman, A., Ashworth, K., Bradshaw, J., Levitas, R., Middleton, S., Pantazis, C., Patsios, D., Payne, S., Townsend, P. and Williams, J. (2000) *Poverty and social exclusion in Britain*, York: Joseph Rowntree Foundation (www.bris.ac.uk/poverty/pse/welcome.htm).

Halleröd, B. (1994) *Poverty in Sweden: A new approach to direct measurement of consensual poverty*, Umeå Studies in Sociology No 10, vol 6, Sweden: University of Umeå.

Halleröd, B. (1995a) 'Perceptions of poverty in Sweden', *Scandinavian Journal of Social Welfare*, vol 4, no 3, pp 174-89.

Halleröd, B. (1995b) 'The truly poor: indirect and direct measurement of consensual poverty in Sweden', *Journal of European Social Policy*, vol 5, no 2, pp 111-29.

Halleröd, B. (1998) 'Poor Swedes, poor Britons: a comparative analysis of relative deprivation', in H.J. Andreß (ed) *Empirical poverty research in a comparative perspective,* Aldershot: Ashgate, pp 283-312.

Hashem, M.H. (1996) *Goals for social integration and realities of social exclusion in the Republic of Yemen,* Research Series No 105, Geneva: IILS.

Hillyard, P., Kelly, G., McLaughlin, E., Patsios, D. and Tomlinson, M. (2003) *Bare necessities: Poverty and social exclusion in Northern Ireland: Key findings,* Democratic Dialogue: Belfast (www.democraticdialogue.org/PSEtsvqxf.pdf.pdf).

ILO (International Labour Organization) (1971) *Scope, methods and users of family expenditure surveys, Report III: Twelfth International Conference of Labour Statisticians,* Geneva: ILO.

ILO (1992) *Report 1: General Report Fifteenth International Conference of Labour Statisticians,* Geneva: ILO.

ILO (1993) *Report of the conference: Fifteenth International Conference of Labour Statisticians,* Geneva: ILO.

Jenkins, S. and Cowell, F. (1994) 'Parametric equivalence scales and scale relativities', *The Economic Journal,* vol 104, pp 891-900.

Joseph, K. and Sumption, J. (1979) *Equality,* London: John Murray.

Jorgenson, D. (1998) 'Did we lose the war on poverty?', *Journal of Economic Perspectives,* vol 12, pp 79-96.

Kaijage, F. and Tibaijuka, A. (1996) *Poverty and social exclusion in Tanzania,* Research Series No 109, Geneva: IILS.

Kangas, O. and Ritakallio, V.M. (1998) 'Different methods – different results? Approaches to multidimensional poverty' in H.J. Andreß (ed) *Empirical poverty research in a comparative perspective,* Aldershot: Ashgate, pp 167-203.

Knight, I. (1980) *The feasibility of conducting a national wealth survey in Great Britain,* New Methodology Series NM6, London: OPCS.

Lakatos, I. (1974) 'Falsification and the methodology of scientific research programmes', in I. Lakatos and A.E. Musgrave (eds) *Criticism and the growth of knowledge,* London: Cambridge University Press, pp 91-196.

Mack, J. and Lansley, S. (1985) *Poor Britain,* London: Allen and Unwin.

Martin, J. and White, A. (1988) *The financial circumstances of adults living in private households,* Report 2, London: HMSO.

McClements, L.D. (1977) 'Equivalence scales for children', *Journal of Public Economics,* vol 8, pp 197-210.

McClements, L.D. (1978) *The economics of social security,* London: Heinemann.

McCregor, P. and Borooah, V. (1992) 'Is low spending or low income a better indicator of whether or not a household is poor: some results from the 1985 Family Expenditure Survey' *Journal of Social Policy*, vol 21, no 1, pp 53-69.

Medwar, P. (1984) *The limits of science*, Oxford: Oxford University Press.

Muellbauer, J. (1979) 'McClements on equivalence scales for children', *Journal of Public Economics*, vol 12, pp 221-31.

Muellbauer, J. (1980) 'The estimation of the Prais-Houthakker model of equivalence scales', *Econometrica*, vol 48, no 1, pp 153-76.

Muffels, R. (1993) 'Deprivation standards and style of living standards', in J. Berghman and B. Cantillon (eds), *The European face of social security,* Aldershot: Avebury.

Muffels, R. and Vreins, M. (1991) 'The elaboration of a deprivation scale and the definition of a subjective deprivation poverty line', Paper presented at the Annual Meeting of the European Society for Population Economic, 6-8 June, Pisa.

Muffels, R., Berghman, J. and Dirven, H. (1992) 'A multi-method approach to monitor the evolution of poverty', *Journal of European Social Policy*, vol 2, no 3, pp 193-213.

Nelson, J. (1993) 'Household equivalence scales: theory versus policy?', *Journal of Labor Economics*, vol 11, no 3, pp 471-93.

Nolan, B.J. and Whelan, C.T. (1996a) *Resources, deprivation and poverty,* Oxford: Clarendon Press.

Nolan, B.J. and Whelan, C.T. (1996b) 'Measuring poverty using income and deprivation indicators: alternative approaches', *Journal of European Social Policy*, vol 6, no 3, pp 225-40.

OECD (Organisation for the Economic Co-operation and Development) (1976) *Public expenditure on income maintenance programmes*, Paris: OECD.

Oldfield, N. and Yu, A.C.S. (1993) *The cost of a child: Living standards for the 1990s*, London: Child Poverty Action Group.

Parker, H. (ed) (1998) *Low cost but acceptable. A minimum income standard for the UK: Families with children*. Bristol: The Policy Press.

Parker, H. (ed) (2000) *Low cost but acceptable: Incomes for older people*, Bristol: The Policy Press.

Piachaud, D. (1981) 'Peter Townsend and the Holy Grail', *New Society*, 10 September, pp 419-21.

Popper, K.R. (1968) *The logic of scientific discovery*, London: Hutchinson.

Popper, K.R. (1972) *Objective knowledge*, Oxford: Oxford University Press.

Pyatt, G. and Ward, M. (eds) (1999) *Identifying the poor: Papers on measuring poverty to celebrate the publication 'The state of the poor' (1797)* by Eden, Amsterdam: IOS Press.

Ramprakash, D. (1994) 'Poverty in the countries of the European Union: a synthesis of Eurostat's research on poverty', *Journal of European Social Policy*, vol 4, no 2, pp 117-128.

Rowntree, S.B. (1901) *Poverty: A study of town life*, Macmillan: London. Republished (2000) *Poverty: A study of town life: Centennial edition*, Bristol: The Policy Press. (www.bris.ac.uk/Publications/TPP/pages/at036.htm).

Ringen, S. (1988) 'Direct and indirect measures of poverty', *Journal of Social Policy*, vol 17, no 3, pp 351-65.

Saunders, P. and Matheson, G. (1992) *Perceptions of poverty, income adequacy and living standards in Australia*, Reports and Proceedings No 99, Sydney: Social Policy Research Centre, University of New South Wales.

Sen, A.K. (1981) *Poverty and famines: An essay on entitlement and deprivation*, Oxford: Clarendon Press.

Sen, A.K. (1983) 'Poor, relatively speaking', *Oxford Economic Papers*, vol 35, pp 135-69.

Sen, A.K. (1985) 'A sociological approach to the measurement of poverty: a reply to Professor Peter Townsend', *Oxford Economic Papers*, vol 37, pp 669-76.

Shapere, D. (1982) 'The concept of observation in science and philosophy', *Philosophy of Science*, vol 49, pp 485-525.

Smyth, M. and Robus, N. (1989) *The financial circumstances of families with disabled children living in private households*, OPCS Surveys of Disability Report 5, London: HMSO.

Stedman-Jones, G. (2004) *An end to poverty: A historical debate*, London: Profile Books.

Stone, R. (1997) *Some British empiricists in the social sciences 1650-1900*, Cambridge: Cambridge University Press.

Tchernina, N. (1996) *Economic transition and social exclusion in Russia*, Research Series No 108, Geneva: IILS.

Townsend, P. (1962) 'The meaning of poverty', *British Journal of Sociology*, vol 13, no 3, pp 210-19.

Townsend, P. (1979) *Poverty in the United Kingdom,* London: Allen Lane and Penguin Books.

Townsend, P. (1985) 'A sociological approach to the measurement of poverty: a rejoinder to Professor Amartya Sen', *Oxford Economic Papers*, vol 37, pp 659-68.

Townsend, P. (1993) *The international analysis of poverty*, New York/London: Wheatsheaf.

Townsend, P. and Gordon, D. (1989) 'What is enough? New evidence on poverty in Greater London allowing the definition of a minimum benefit', *Memorandum of evidence to the House of Commons Social Services Select Committee on Minimum Income 579*, London: HMSO, pp 45-73. Reprinted as Townsend, P. and Gordon, D. (1991) 'What is enough? New evidence on poverty allowing the definition of a minimum benefit', in M. Alder, C. Bell, J. Clasen and A. Sinfield (eds) *The sociology of social security*, Edinburgh: Edinburgh University Press, pp 35-69.

Townsend, P. and Gordon, D. (1993) 'What is enough? The definition of a poverty line, in P. Townsend *The international analysis of poverty*, New York, London: Harvester Wheatsheaf, pp 40-78.

Townsend, P., Gordon, D. and Gosschalk, B. (1996) *The poverty line in Britain today: What the population themselves say*, Statistical Monitoring Unit Report No 7, Bristol: Bristol Statistical Monitoring Unit, University of Bristol.

Townsend, P., Gordon, D., Bradshaw, J. and Gosschalk, B. (1997) *Absolute and overall poverty in Britain in 1997: What the population themselves say*, Report of the second MORI Survey, Bristol: Bristol Statistical Monitoring Unit, University of Bristol.

Triest, R. (1998) 'Has poverty gotten worse?', *Journal of Economic Perspectives*, vol 12, pp 97-114.

Tsakloglou, P. and Papadopoulos. F. (2002) 'Poverty, material deprivation and multi-dimensional disadvantage during four life stages: evidence from the ECHP', in M. Barnes, C. Heady, S. Middleton, J. Millar, F. Papadopoulos, G. Room, and P. Tsakloglou (eds) *Poverty and social exclusion in Europe*, Cheltenham: Edward Elgar Publishing, Inc, pp 24-52.

United Nations (UN) (1977) *Provisional guidelines on statistics of the distribution of income, consumption and accumulation of households, studies in methods*, Series M, No 61, New York, NY: United Nations Department of Publications.

UN (1989) *National Household Survey Capability Program: Household Income and Expenditure Surveys: A technical study*, New York, NY: United Nations Department of Publications.

UN (1992) *Revised system of national accounts (provisional)* August 1992 (to be presented to and adopted at the 27th session of the Statistical Commission, February-March 1993), New York, NY: United Nations Department of Publications.

UN (1995) *The Copenhagen Declaration and Programme of Action: World Summit for Social Development 6-12 March 1995*, New York, NY: United Nations Department of Publications.

van den Bosch, K. (1998) 'Perceptions of the minimum standard of living in Belgium: is there a consensus?', in H.J. Andreß (ed) *Empirical poverty research in a comparative perspective*, Aldershot: Ashgate, pp 135-66.

van den Bosch, K. (2001) *Identifying the poor: Using subjective and consensual measures*, Aldershot: Ashgate.

van Praag, B., Hagenaars, A. and van Weeren, J. (1980) *Poverty in Europe*, Report to the Commission of the EC, Leyden: University of Leyden.

Veit-Wilson, J.H. (1987) 'Consensual approaches to poverty lines and social security', *Journal of Social Policy*, vol 16, no 2, pp 183-211.

Vogel, J. (1997) *Living conditions and inequality in the European Union 1997*, Eurostat Working Papers: Population and Social Conditions E/1997-3, Luxembourg: Eurostat.

Walker, R. (1987) 'Consensual approaches to the definition of poverty: towards an alternative methodology', *Journal of Social Policy*, vol 16, no 2, pp 213-26.

Weir, J. (1992) *Sensitivity testing in HBAI: An examination of the results*, Department of Social Security Analytical Notes, No 1, London: DSS..

Whiteford, P. (1985) *A family's needs: Equivalence scales, poverty and social security*. Research Paper No 27, Canberra: Development Division, Australian Department of Social Security.

Zarb, G. and Maher, L. (1997) *The financial circumstances of disabled people in Northern Ireland*, PPRU Surveys of Disability Report No 6, Belfast: Northern Ireland Statistic and Research Agency.

Appendix 2.1: How to identify the poor: scientific poverty measurement

This appendix describes the statistical methods used to determine the scientific poverty line and divide the population into four groups ('poor', 'rising', 'vulnerable' and 'not poor').

The first step was taken by building up a long list of ordinary household goods and activities. Respondents were asked to indicate which items and activities they thought were necessities that no person should have to do without in Britain (see Chapter One and Chapter Five). The second step was to ask people what items they already had or wanted but could not afford. Items defined as necessities by more than 50% of the population but were lacked because of a shortage of money were then used to construct an initial deprivation index. The use of a democratic threshold (50%) to identify what items and activities are necessities provides both 'political' and face validity for the deprivation index.

The deprivation index was then refined using standard scientific methods to ensure that all the components were valid, reliable and added up. The validity of each item in the index was tested by calculating the correlation (odds ratio) between the item and two health variables ('general health question' and 'limiting long-term illness') and four perception of poverty variables (genuinely poor now 'all the time', income 'a lot below' the poverty line, income 'a lot below' the absolute and overall poverty line). These variables are robust measures of criterion validity as there is considerable evidence that poverty causes ill health (Townsend and Davidson, 1988; Whitehead, 1988; Power et al, 1996; Acheson, 1998; Gordon et al, 1999; Shaw et al, 1999; Davey Smith and Gordon, 2000). It would also be expected that respondents who can objectively be defined as living in poverty are also more likely to perceive themselves as poor than their non-poor peers.

The reliability of each item in the index was then tested using a classical test theory model. A summary table (A2.1) of the reliability and validity results are shown below. Overall, the 35-item index had a Cronbach's Alpha of 0.8853, which is indicative of a highly reliable index.

The items that were not included in the index, as there was little evidence that they were either valid or reliable, were:

Table A2.1: Validity and reliability summary table

	Number of non-significant validity indicators	Level of reliability (bold = unreliable)
A television	5	**0.8859**
Medicines prescribed by doctor	4	0.8851
Refrigerator	3	**0.8859**
Beds and bedding for everyone	2	**0.8856**
A washing machine	2	**0.8854**
Telephone	2	0.8845
Deep freezer/fridge freezer	2	0.8848
Visits to friends or family	1	0.8835
Visits to school, eg sports day	1	**0.8858**
Collect children from school	1	**0.8856**
Appropriate clothes for job interviews	1	0.8814
Carpets in living rooms and bedrooms	1	0.8824
A dictionary	1	0.8843

- a television
- a fridge
- beds and bedding for everyone
- a washing machine.

Additivity and removing outliers

The components of any deprivation index should be additive, for example, a person or household with a deprivation score of 3 should be poorer than a person or household with a deprivation score of 2 (Gordon, 1995). It is necessary to check that all components of a deprivation index are additive[1]. This was done by examining both the main effects and all possible second-order interaction effects between the components of the deprivation index using equivalised income as the dependent variable. Income outliers had first been removed using standard robust exploratory data analysis techniques (for example, Boxplots). This resulted in all households with net incomes above £895 per week, which is the equivalent of an annual income after tax of over £46,500 per year and approximately £77,500 gross annual income, not being included in the final poverty threshold model. Examination of the second-order interactions showed that not being able to afford 'all medicines prescribed by a doctor' was not additive with 18 other deprivation items. Similarly, not being able to afford 'a deep freezer/fridge freezer' was not additive with seven other deprivation items, so both these items were not included in the final valid, reliable and additive deprivation index.

Finding the 'objective' poverty line

General linear models (both ANOVA and logistic regression) were used to determine the scientific poverty threshold, that is, the deprivation score that maximises the between-group differences and minimises the within-group differences (sum of squares). These techniques were applied to a succession of groups created by increasing the number of items that respondents did not have because they could not afford them. Thus, the first analysis was undertaken on groups defined by households lacking no items compared with households lacking one or more items (a deprivation score of 1 or more). Similarly, the second analysis was undertaken on a group comprised of households lacking one or no items against two or more items, and so forth.

The dependent variable in the ANOVA model was net household income and the independent variables were deprivation group (constructed as described above), number of adults in each household and number of children in each household. With the logistic regression models, the dependent variable was the deprivation group and the independent variables were net household income, number of adults and number of children. Both the ANOVA and logistic regression models yielded the same final result – that a score of two or more on the deprivation index was the optimum position for the poverty line. Summary results are shown in Table A2.2 and Figure A2.1.

Identifying the rising and the vulnerable groups

In a cross-sectional survey there will probably be a few people who have recently 'risen out of poverty', that is those with a high deprivation score and a high income. Their incomes and/or 'standard of living' should have increased in the recent past. These few cases were identified

Table A2.2: Brief summary of ANOVA and logistic regression models of optimum position for the poverty threshold

Model	F statistic for corrected ANOVA model	Logistic regression model chi-square
Null model	26	
Deprivation score of 1 or more	45	145
Deprivation score of 2 or more	**51**	**223**
Deprivation score of 3 or more	45	205
Deprivation score of 4 or more	42	192
Deprivation score of 5 or more	36	170
Deprivation score of 6 or more	31	126

**Figure A2.1: Average income by deprivation score
(95% Confidence Intervals)**

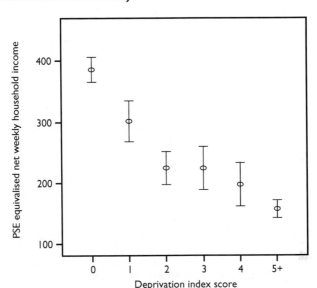

using boxplots of income by 'multiply deprived' group (that is, with a
deprivation score of 2 or more) and controlling for household size/
type. The outliers (with high incomes) in each household type should
be those risen out of poverty.

There should also be a much larger group of households that have
relatively low incomes but are not yet suffering the effects of multiple
deprivation (that is, people in the vulnerable to poverty group who
have incomes equivalent or less than the median incomes of the
multiply deprived – 2 or more – group).

Figure A2.2 shows how the statistical procedure described above
divides the sample into four groups: 'poor', 'rising', 'vulnerable' and
'not poor'. It should be noted that the model produces this division in
multi-dimensional space (income, deprivation, household size and
household composition), whereas the graph shows just two dimensions
– equivalised income (to try to allow for household size and
composition differences) and standard of living (the reciprocal of the
deprivation index score).

Figure A2.2 shows that there appears to be a very clear separation
on the standard of living dimension (y axis) between the 'poor' and
'not poor' groups. The 'vulnerable' and 'not poor' groups have also
been clearly separated. However, the statistical model does not appear
to be so efficient at distinguishing between the 'poor' and the 'rising'

Figure A2.2: Standard of living score by income with population groups

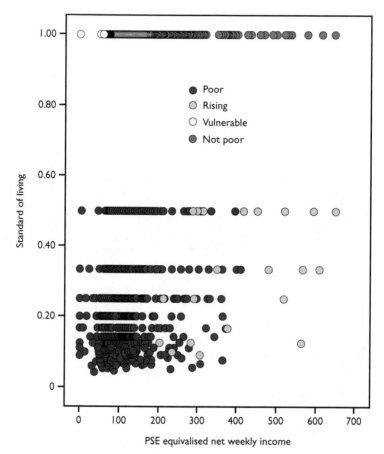

PSE equivalised net weekly income

groups and there is some degree of overlap visible. This may either be a result of the PSE equivalisation scale being incorrect for some household situations (for example, households with a severely disabled member) and/or because of inefficiencies in the statistical model. Further research should be undertaken, ideally with longitudinal data.

Note

[1] Technically a 'good' index should be monotonic, one of the major problems encountered when using income to measure poverty is that in industrialised countries those people/households who have zero or negative incomes are often less 'poor' than those with slightly higher incomes. Income poverty measures can therefore violate the montonicity assumption of many linear statistical methods

References

Acheson, D. (1998) *Independent Inquiry into Inequalities in Health report,* London: Stationery Office (www.archive.official-documents.co.uk/document/doh.ih.ih.htm).

Davey Smith, G. and Gordon, D. (2000) 'Poverty across the life-course and health', in C. Pantazis and D. Gordon (eds) *Tackling inequalities: Where are we now and what can be done?* Bristol: The Policy Press, pp 141-58.

Gordon, D. (1995) 'Census-based deprivation indices: their weighting and validation', *Journal of Epidemiology and Community Health,* vol 49 (Suppl 2), pp S39-S44.

Gordon, D., Davey Smith, G., Dorling, D. and Shaw, M. (eds) (1999) *Inequalities in health: The evidence presented to the Independent Inquiry into Inequalities in Health,* Bristol: The Policy Press.

Power, C., Matthews, S. and Manor, O. (1996) 'Inequalities in self-rated health in the 1958 birth cohort: lifetime social circumstances or social mobility?', *British Medical Journal,* vol 313, pp 449-53.

Shaw, M., Dorling, D., Gordon, D. and Davey Smith, G. (1999) *The widening gap: Health inequalities and policy in Britain,* Bristol: The Policy Press.

Townsend, P. and Davidson, N. (1988) *Inequalities in health: The Black Report* (2nd edn), London: Penguin Books.

Whitehead, M. (1988) *Inequalities in health: The health divide* (2nd edn), London: Penguin Books.

THREE

The international measurement of 'absolute' and 'overall' poverty: applying the 1995 Copenhagen definitions to Britain

Peter Townsend, David Gordon and Christina Pantazis

Introduction

Since the start of the 21st century, there has been increasing public concern about the failure to reduce – still less eradicate – world poverty. In the years from 1960 to the late 1990s, the share of world gross domestic product of the poorest 20% of population actually diminished and the numbers with incomes below the crude 'absolute' formula of $1 per day laid down by the World Bank increased (UNDP, 1997, 1998, 1999, 2000; UNICEF Innocenti Research Centre, 2000). This was during a period of substantial economic growth. In the early years of the new millennium, the same concern has been reiterated (Townsend and Gordon, 2002; Sachs, 2005).

The President of the World Bank had put poverty eradication at the top of the Bank's agenda in 1960. By 1990, the Bank had to admit that progress had been fitful – if not negative – and that a fresh commitment had to be made (for example, see World Bank, 1996). New strategies were duly announced but little evidence emerged of success at either global or national level – at least so far as the majority of countries were concerned. Other international agencies took up the theme strongly. However, although there were useful additions to the analysis, there was little significant departure from the Bank's prescriptions for action[1].This has led to disbelief that the United Nations' (UN) expressed aim of halving world poverty by 2015 will be achieved or even approached[2]. Governments also find themselves with decreasing room for policy manoeuvre at a time when international agencies seem to be expecting them to do yet more to solve the problem.

To a growing number of European social scientists at least, the problem is not just policy prescription and conformity with Bank precepts or edicts. It is also a question of the definition of poverty, measurement of the trends in the problem and analysis of the causes of those trends. By means of authoritative measurement of severe conditions, priorities in policy can be identified more precisely. Poverty has been the subject of intense scrutiny in some countries for decades and many reports on the phenomenon are very sophisticated.

These scientists are also aware that they must join in the struggle to extricate the concept of poverty from political ideology and simultaneously widen scientific perspectives from narrow concern with the physical and nutritional needs of human beings to include all their complex social needs. Part of the struggle has been to find reliable measures to compare conditions in different countries and, especially, conditions in rich *and* poor countries, so that priorities for change might be more securely established and agreed.

Therefore, an internationally comparable meaning of poverty has to be constructed so that a scientific – if not political – consensus might be sought for the threshold of income needed in different countries to escape multiple deprivation, incapacity and premature death. Societies are familiar with thresholds of risk derived from scientific work on radiation, pollution and global warming and 'poverty' can be treated similarly. Although some international organisations have contributed more than others to the sensitive handling of the investigation of poverty, the international community has failed to encourage the formulation of a scientific consensus around definition and measurement and, accordingly, identify precisely which policies have contributed to the worsening or the alleviation of poverty and by how much.

The Copenhagen contribution

Some governments attempted to sidetrack the problem altogether. In 1989, John Moore, as Secretary of State for the Department of Social Security, stated that the problem of poverty did not apply to the UK (Moore, 1989). Only 10 years later, his successor, Alastair Darling, announced a programme to undertake a poverty audit "and so place the problem at the top of the nation's agenda"[3]. This illustrates the changes that can take place in political reactions to accumulating evidence of social problems. Substantial reduction of poverty in the UK became the declared objective of the Prime Minister and the Chancellor of the Exchequer.

Poverty is a recognised evil but has lacked precise international definition and a scientifically constructed remedy. For example, the USA has its own definition and measure, which the international agencies have not hitherto related to their priorities for development. Indeed, the amendments to measurement recommended by the National Academy of Sciences seems to have served the purpose of bolstering a US approach that is highly sophisticated but insular (Citro and Michael, 1995). Root and branch reform on an avowed scientific or international basis has not been considered.

However, the United Nations Children's Fund (UNICEF) has recently taken a novel step in reporting the extent of child poverty in rich nations. In comparing poverty rates across countries, the organisation used the familiar standard of 50% of the national median household income but also used a standard representing 'absolute' child poverty – as depicted by the official US poverty line (UNICEF Innocenti Research Centre, 2000, 2005). The latest report confirms startlingly high rates of child poverty for Mexico (28%), the USA (22%), New Zealand (16%), Portugal (16%) and the UK (15%). Denmark and Finland have the lowest poverty rates, at less than 3%. Rather worryingly, the proportion of children living in poverty has risen in 17 out of 24 OECD (Organization for Economic Cooperation and Development) countries during the 1990s, with increases of more than 4% for the Czech Republic, Luxembourg and Poland. The UK is one of only four countries (with Australia, Norway and the USA) where there have been significant reductions in child poverty rates (UNICEF Innocenti Research Centre, 2005)

The UNICEF initiative approaches the 1995 Copenhagen recommendation for a two-tier measure of poverty, though that is not yet applied to poor countries. It also reintroduces the problem of replacing – or supplementing – the US national standard with a more appropriate international standard of 'absolute' poverty.

The approach of the World Bank and other agencies has been concerned, above all, with the world's poorest. The social customs and relationships of the people in the poorest countries and, especially their social roles and obligations, attracted small interest. What mattered was the acquisition of the 'absolute necessities of life'. These were arbitrarily interpreted as minimal nutrition, warmth and shelter. It was along such lines of argument that the World Bank's $1 a day was originally justified.

Unfortunately, this led to a form of apartheid between the first and third worlds. The problem was defined differently in the two worlds and, as a consequence, comparisons relevant to the construction of priorities of policy were either avoided or were thoroughly confused. One absurd result of this has been the proliferation of different 'standards' for different regions – as in United Nations Development Reports – without any attempt to explore whether there might be, say, an international standard with the topping-up of variable standards conditioned by the particular circumstances of individual countries and regions.

The 1995 World Summit for Social Development was called because, among other things, many governments were becoming restive with the lack of progress in reducing the gap in living standards between rich and the poor countries during the 1980s and early 1990s and, despite the work of the international financial agencies, the persistence and growth of severe poverty (UN, 1995).

The report repeatedly emphasised that the gap between rich and poor *within* both developed and developing societies was widening, just as the gap *between* developed and developing societies was also widening. Calling world attention to this dual structural phenomenon is perhaps the most notable achievement of the summit – whatever might be said in criticism of the attempts in the text to please different governments and satisfy their conflicting objectives.

The intention was to try to promote sustained economic growth within the context of sustainable development and by "formulating or strengthening, preferably by 1996, and implementing national poverty eradication plans to address the structural causes of poverty, encompassing action on the local, national, subregional, and international levels. These plans should establish, within each national context, strategies and affordable, time-bound, goals and targets for the substantial reduction of overall poverty and the eradication of absolute poverty.... Each country should develop a precise definition and assessment of absolute poverty" (UN, 1995, pp 60-1).

After 1995, progress in following up the agreement was slow (Townsend, 1996). Ireland was one of the first Western countries to produce a follow-up report (Irish Government, 1996). Third world governments followed suit in later years, for example, Kenya in 1999 (Ministry of Planning and National Development, 1998a, 1998b). However, many reports seem to be addressed more to the agenda of the international financial agencies than to the 1995 agreement.

The two-level definition of poverty was designed to bridge first and third worlds and to afford a basis for cross-national measurement.

Absolute poverty is defined as "a condition characterised by severe deprivation of basic human needs, including food, safe drinking water, sanitation facilities, health, shelter, education and information. It depends not only on income but also on access to services" (UN, 1995, p 57).

Overall poverty takes various forms, including "lack of income and productive resources to ensure sustainable livelihoods; hunger and malnutrition; ill health; limited or lack of access to education and other basic services; increased morbidity and mortality from illness; homelessness and inadequate housing; unsafe environments and social discrimination and exclusion. It is also characterised by lack of participation in decision-making and in civil, social and cultural life. It occurs in all countries: as mass poverty in many developing countries, pockets of poverty amid wealth in developed countries, loss of livelihoods as a result of economic recession, sudden poverty as a result of disaster or conflict, the poverty of low-wage workers, and the utter destitution of people who fall outside family support systems, social institutions and safety nets" (UN, 1995, p 57).

By recommending a two-tier measure of 'absolute' and 'overall' poverty to be applied to every country, a means was found to bring all governments together in a common purpose. An opportunity was created to explore the severity of poverty according to standards that seemed to be acceptable everywhere. Even countries where it was assumed absolute poverty no longer existed found it easier to accept an international two-tier approach that self-evidently included their own conditions.

Accordingly, all governments were expected to prepare a national poverty eradication plan. In 1997, nearly a hundred European social scientists drew up a statement asking for an international approach to the measurement and explanation of poverty (Townsend et al, 1997, pp 34-5). This statement urged the use of the UN's two-level definition.

Absolute and overall subjective poverty lines

The 1995 Copenhagen definitions of absolute and overall poverty were adapted to conditions in Britain in the Poverty and Social Exclusion (PSE) Survey. This used the MORI survey questions asked by Townsend and his colleagues (1997), which were subsequently modified by the results from focus-group research (Bradshaw et al, 1998). Survey respondents were invited to say what level of income was required by a household of their type to surmount 'absolute' – and what level, 'overall' – poverty and then they were asked to say whether the income, after taxes, of their household was *above* or *below* – or *a lot* above or below, the income given (see www.bristol.ac.uk/poverty/pse/welcome/htm).

In Britain, absolute poverty is perceived as being widespread. As many as 14% of the sample, including 'don't knows', representing over

7.5 million people, say they have less income than the level they identified as being enough to keep a household like theirs out of 'absolute' poverty. If the 'don't knows' are excluded, this figure rises to 17% (Table 3.1).

The income, after tax, said to be needed each week to escape 'absolute' poverty averages £178 for all households. Some respondents give estimates widely different from this average but the great majority, allowing for type of household, are within 20% of this figure.

Perceptions of the poverty line vary by type of family, as would be expected (see Table 3.2). More lone parents (than any other type of family) (46%) say they have an income below that needed to keep out of 'absolute' poverty. Next are single pensioners (22%) and single people without children (21%).

Significantly larger percentages in each case are found to place themselves in 'overall' poverty, as Table 3.2 shows. Although, as expected, the additions applied to each family type, they are disproportionately high for families with children.

In estimating their weekly income needs, many respondents gave a round figure, such as £100, £125 or £150 for small households, and £200, £250 or £300 for larger households. Overall, the pattern of answers by family type carries conviction. Table 3.3 sets out the average incomes specified by people in different types and sizes of families. The average for some types of families, especially when the sample numbers are small, can sometimes be pushed upwards or downwards by, say, only one or two individual estimates that diverge widely from the average. This explains certain quirks in the pattern disclosed in Table 3.3. According to type of family, the income needed to escape 'overall' poverty exceeds that needed to escape 'absolute' poverty by

Table 3.1: Income needed each week to keep a household of your type out of absolute, general and overall poverty

	Absolute poverty	General poverty	Overall poverty
Mean income needed (£)	178	219	239
Actual income a lot above (%)	53	35	40
A little above (%)	23	31	26
About the same (%)	8	14	8
A little below (%)	8	10	11
A lot below (%)	9	10	15
Total	**100**	**100**	**100**
Number	1,334	1,332	1,306
(+ 'Don't knows')	(1,527)	(1,527)	(1,527)
Don't know (%)	13	13	14

Table 3.2: Income is either 'a lot' or 'a little' below level needed each week to keep the household out of absolute, general and overall poverty, by population category

	Absolute poverty (%)	General poverty (%)	Overall poverty (%)
Gender			
Male	13	16	23
Female	20	23	28
Age group			
16-24	17	23	27
25-34	19	23	31
35-44	10	15	21
45-54	16	18	22
55-64	17	18	24
65-74	20	21	28
75+	17	21	30
Family type			
Pensioner couple	14	19	22
Single pensioner	22	25	35
Non-retired couple with children	14	23	29
Non-retired couple without children	12	17	18
Single person with children	46	62	61
Single person without children	21	24	29
Other	16	9	22
Ethnic group			
Majority ethnic group	15	19	24
Minority ethnic group*	52	39	80
Total	**17**	**20**	**26**

Note: * denotes fewer than 50 cases.

Table 3.3: Weekly household income said to be needed to escape different levels of poverty

	Absolute poverty (£)	General poverty (£)	Overall poverty (£)
Pensioner couple	140	185	191
Single pensioner	107	115	136
Couple with children	216	276	295
Couple without children	160	220	245
Single person with children	163	186	211
Single person without children	147	183	207
Other family type	197	239	259
All families	**177**	**219**	**239**

between £29 and £85 per week. Single non-pensioners estimate the weekly income needed to escape absolute poverty at £40 more than the figure quoted by pensioners. This differential applies also to pensioner and non-pensioner couples. The differential is also markedly higher in the case of overall poverty.

Subjective and objective poverty

There were two important subjective questions in the PSE Survey. Those interviewed were invited to:

1. give an estimate of the weekly household income needed to surmount different poverty lines; and
2. say how far above or below that estimate they judged their own income to be.

However, they were also asked how many of the material items and social activities (agreed by a majority of the sample to be necessary in everyday life) they did not have and whether they lacked these items by choice or because they could not afford them. Because of observable conditions at interview, the answers were considered to be acceptably 'objective' (see discussion in Chapters One and Two). The correlation is summed up in Tables 3.4, 3.5 and 3.6. It can be seen that there is a

Table 3.4: Income needed each week to keep household out of absolute poverty, by mean number of unaffordable necessary items and by actual level of equivalised net weekly household income

	Mean number of items don't have because of lack of money	Net weekly household income (£)
Actual income a lot above that	0.4	418
A little above	1.3	258
About the same	3.1	186
A little below	5.3	156
A lot below	6.3	150
Total	**1.7**	**320**

Table 3.5: Income needed each week to keep household out of general poverty, by mean number of unaffordable necessary items and by actual level of equivalised net weekly household income

	Mean number of items don't have because of lack of money	Net weekly household income (£)
Actual income a lot above that	0.3	477
A little above	0.9	293
About the same	2.4	203
A little below	3.3	178
A lot below	7.1	145
Total	**1.8**	**320**

Table 3.6: Income needed each week to keep household out of overall poverty, by mean number of unaffordable necessary items and by actual level of equivalised net weekly household income

	Mean number of items don't have because of lack of money	Net weekly household income (£)
Actual income a lot above that	0.3	455
A little above	0.9	304
About the same	1.7	223
A little below	2.9	187
A lot below	6.3	148
Total	**1.7**	**323**

linear relationship between the average number of necessary items missing from everyday life and net weekly household income.

It was also possible to compare objective multiple deprivation of households (PSE poverty) with answers to two further subjective questions – whether people felt themselves 'never poor', 'sometimes poor' or 'poor all the time'; and whether in their lifetimes they had 'never or rarely been poor', 'occasionally poor' or 'poor often or most of the time'. Table 3.7 shows the result only for those in the sample estimating that their incomes are 'a little' or 'a lot' below the relevant poverty line. The correlation, again, is striking.

A final step in the analysis shows the economic and health status of those falling below the respective poverty lines. Table 3.8 shows the vulnerability to poverty of the unemployed and economically inactive

Table 3.7: Income is either 'a lot' or 'a little' below the level each week to keep the household out of absolute, overall and general poverty, according to objective and subjective poverty variables

	Absolute poverty (%)	General poverty (%)	Overall poverty (%)
PSE poor			
Yes	48	52	69
No	6	8	11
Genuinely poor			
All the time	70	74	83
Sometimes	35	43	57
Never	6	7	11
History of poverty			
Often or mostly	42	48	17
Occasionally	26	30	45
Never or rarely	11	13	17
Total	**17**	**20**	**26**

and also those with long-standing illness. One significant feature of the table is to bring out the substantial number of working households in 'overall' and even 'absolute' poverty.

Table 3.8: Income is either 'a lot' or 'a little' below the level each week to keep the household out of absolute, overall and general poverty, according to health and economic status

	Absolute poverty (%)	General poverty (%)	Overall poverty (%)
Long-standing illness			
No	14	17	22
Yes	21	25	32
Economic status			
Working	9	12	17
Unemployed	35	47	50
Economically inactive	26	28	36
Workers in the household			
No workers	40	48	53
Workers	11	13	20
Retired	18	21	28
Total	**17**	**20**	**26**

Extending the measure in the first and third worlds

In establishing "economies to serve human needs and aspirations" – an ambitious objective built into the 1995 World Summit – the research in Britain shows, beyond reasonable doubt, that the scale of needs in some rich industrial societies are perceived by their populations to be much larger than generally allowed in national and international discourse. When taken with reports from poorer countries, where comparable methods have been piloted, this two-level measure deserves to be extended internationally. It can, of course, take the form of self-perceived poverty but also 'objective' poverty as revealed by sets of indicators of deprivation and low income.

Thus, a series of surveys of poverty and social exclusion sponsored by the International Institute for Labour Studies, affiliated to the International Labour Organization, included three that drew on methods of measuring poverty previously tried in London (Townsend and Gordon, 1989; Gordon and Pantazis, 1997). The three were reports on Tanzania, Yemen and Russia (Kaijage and Tibaijuka, 1996, p 7, pp 118-126, p 182; Hashem, 1996, p 86; Tchernina, 1996; see also Narayan, 1997 and the concluding report by Gore and Figueiredo (1996, p 18). Davies and Smith (1998) used a similar 'standard of living' methodology to measure poverty in Vietnam, also largely based on the categories adopted in Britain in the 1990s.

The World Summit in Copenhagen highlighted the problems in rich and poor countries of poverty and social exclusion. The report called for "the substantial reduction of overall poverty and the eradication of absolute poverty.... Each country should develop a precise definition and assessment of absolute poverty" (UN, 1995, pp 60-1).

In the process of developing comparisons between different countries, it is likely that a cross-national core of questions may be distinguished from country-specific or culture-specific ones. One possibility is to say to those interviewed that the World Bank estimated 'absolute' needs at approximately one dollar a day – though substituting the equivalent in national Purchasing Power Parity rate – and inviting their comments.

In most cases, the subjective method produces poverty lines at a relatively high level. Some European social scientists have argued that, in many cases, the poverty line is at such a level that it would be very difficult to maintain that all households below it are poor, in the sense of being socially excluded (Deeleck et al, 1992). The term 'insecurity of subsistence', meaning a situation in which households encounter financial difficulty in participating in the average or most widely shared lifestyle, would be more appropriate. However, this acknowledges the importance of extending the meaning of poverty to include social as well as 'subsistence' needs and begs the question of the respective precise meanings of social exclusion and poverty.

Empirical studies have shown that estimates of the subjective poverty line usually rise systematically with the actual income of the household/individual (Citro and Michael, 1995). Therefore, subjective poverty lines tend to fluctuate over time depending on changes in the social reference group (for example, due to an increase in the overall living standard of the elderly, they respond with a higher necessary minimum income) and on the period of reference (for example, in a period of crisis, aspirations might decline). Given the wide variations in economic and social circumstances between regions and countries, the subjective poverty lines are less suitable for comparative purposes across time and space.

The problem with subjective measures is that the elucidation of opinion takes precedence over the elucidation of behaviour. Although this is understandable, because of the limited resources made available for research, it does mean that there can be no easy check on the extent to which people's views about need correspond with the behaviour which may be said to be *revelatory* of need. The same point might be made about lists of needs drawn up by those conducting such research. Human priorities have to be ascertained in terms of observed actions and not only expressed views or preferences. People reveal their priorities as well as their needs in the way they act when short of cash as well as in expressions of their opinion. The investigation of individual opinion sits more easily with interpretations of them as consumers than as people obliged collectively and individually to meet, from their resources, obligations imposed by society and the general customs of their culture. The definition of conditions and the identification of the causes of those conditions may often lie outside the perceptions of individuals. The 'consensual judgement of society' may be said to be a necessary but insufficient criterion on which to build a poverty line and interpret conditions in a society.

Nonetheless, much research suggests that, while individuals in the same types of household will sometimes differ to an extreme extent in their opinions of their income needs, the majority are close to the mean. Moreover, for each principal type of household, people's perceptions of their income needs turn out to be quite close to objective measures of those needs. The perceptions therefore represent valuable indicators both of what people experience and how financial hardship can restrict their opportunities and activities.

Summary

Among the innovations agreed for the Copenhagen Declaration and Programme of Action at the World Summit for Social Development in 1995 was the preparation of national anti-poverty plans based on measures of 'absolute' and 'overall' poverty in all countries. The aim was to link – if not reconcile – the difference between first and third world conceptions, allow more reliable comparisons to be made between countries and regions and make easier the identification of acceptable priorities for action. In developing anti-poverty strategies, this international agreement was a breakthrough.

In this chapter, the UN initiative was applied to Britain as it might be to other countries at different levels of development. One of the unique features of the PSE Survey is that the definitions of 'absolute' and 'overall' poverty, agreed at the World Summit, were each operationalised in both 'subjective' and 'objective' terms. Of the sample, 17% of respondents (or 14% if 'don't knows' are included) said their income was 'a lot' or 'a little' below the level they had identified as being just enough to lift a household like theirs out of 'absolute' poverty. A larger number (26% or 22% if 'don't knows' are included) ranked themselves in 'overall' poverty. In each case, lone parents with children had the highest rates of poverty. Single pensioners and couples with one child also had above-average rates.

The results show that the two definitions are viable in wealthy countries like Britain. The definitions also have an important bearing on the rates approved by the government for means-tested and universal benefits and a detailed review of the implications will be the subject of a later report.

The survey also found that, when care is taken to identify multiple deprivation, subjective and objective poverty correspond quite closely. Thus, when all responses are included, 13.6% of the sample were found to have a score of two or more deprivations on an absolute poverty index, that is, they were multiply deprived, a figure that is comparable with the 14.2% who judged their income to be 'a lot' or 'a little' below the absolute poverty line.

Notes

[1] For example, Ravi Kanbur, the prime mover of the World Bank's Development Report on Poverty in 2000, was reported to have resigned because he was "believed to have wanted to emphasise that economic growth alone will not be enough to reduce poverty and that it will also require equal emphasis on redistributive tax and spending policies" (M. Atkinson, *Guardian*, 15 June 2000).

[2] Thus, the Bank admits, "the number of poor people has risen worldwide, and in some regions the proportion of poor people has also increased" (World Bank, 1999). See also the statement of goals, including halving world poverty by 2015 (World Bank, 2000).

[3] The first report was published in late 1999 (see DSS, 1999).

References

Bradshaw, J., Middleton, S., Townsend, P. and Gordon, D. (1998) *Perceptions of poverty and social exclusion: Final report on preparatory stages of research*, York: Social Policy Research Unit, University of York.

Citro, C. and Michael, R. (1995) *Measuring poverty: A new approach*, Panel on Poverty, National Research Council, Washington DC: National Academy Press.

Davies, R. and Smith, W. (1998) *The Basic Necessities Survey: The experience of Action Aid Vietnam*, London: Action Aid.

Deeleck, H., van den Bosch, K. and de Lathouwer, L. (1992) *Poverty and the adequacy of social security in the EC: A comparative analysis*, Aldershot: Avebury.

DSS (Department of Social Security) (1999) *Opportunity for All: Tackling poverty and social exclusion*, Cm 4445, London: The Stationery Office.

Gordon, D. and Pantazis, C. (1997) *Breadline Britain in the 1990s*, Aldershot: Ashgate.

Gordon, D., Adelman, L., Ashworth, K., Bradshaw, J., Levitas, R., Middleton, S., Pantazis, C., Patsios, D., Payne, S., Townsend, P. and Williams, J. (2000) *Poverty and social exclusion in Britain*, York: Joseph Rowntree Foundation.

Gore, C. and Figueiredo, J. (1996) *Social exclusion and anti-poverty strategies*, Geneva: International Institute for Labour Studies.

Hashem, M. (1996) *Goals for social integration and realities of social exclusion in the Republic of Yemen*, Research Series No 105, Geneva: International Institute for Labour Studies.

Irish Government (1996) *Sharing in progress: National anti-poverty strategy*, Dublin: The Stationery Office.

Kaijage, F. and Tibaijuka, A. (1996) *Poverty and social exclusion in Tanzania*, Research Series No. 109, Geneva: International Institute for Labour Studies.

Ministry of Planning and National Development (1998a) *First report on poverty in Kenya, vol I: Incidence and depth of poverty*, Report presented by the Central Bureau of Statistics and the Human Resources and Social Services Department, Nairobi: Government of Kenya.

Ministry of Planning and National Development (1998b) *First report on poverty in Kenya, vol II: Poverty and social indicators*, Report presented by the Central Bureau of Statistics and the Human Resources and Social Services Department, Nairobi: Government of Kenya.

Moore, J. (1989) *The end of poverty*, London: Conservative Political Centre.

Narayan, D. (1997) *Voices of the poor: Poverty and social capital in Tanzania*, Environmentally and Socially Sustainable Development Studies and Monographs Series 20, Washington DC: World Bank.

Sachs, J. (2005) *The end of poverty: How we can make it happen in our lifetime*, London: Penguin.

Tchernina, N. (1996) *Economic transition and social exclusion in Russia*, Research Series No 108, Geneva: International Institute for Labour Studies.

Townsend, P. (1996) *A poor future: Can we counter growing poverty in Britain and across the world?*, London: Lemos and Crane.

Townsend, P. and Gordon, D. (1989) 'What is enough?', in House of Commons Social Services Committee, *Minimum Income*, House of Commons 579, London: HMSO.

Townsend et al (1997) 'An international approach to the measurement and explanation of poverty: statement by European social scientists', in P. Townsend, D. Gordon, J. Bradshaw and B. Gosschalk (1997) *Absolute and overall poverty in Britain in 1997: What the population themselves say*, Bristol: Bristol Statistical Monitoring Unit, University of Bristol.

Townsend, P. and Gordon, D. (2002) *World poverty: New policies to defeat an old enemy*, Bristol: The Policy Press.

UN (United Nations) (1995) *The Copenhagen Declaration and Programme of Action, World Summit for Social Development, 6-12 March 1995*. New York: United Nations.

UNICEF Innocenti Research Centre (2000) *A league table of child poverty in rich nations*, Innocenti Report Card No 1, Florence: UNICEF.

UNICEF Innocenti Research Centre (2005) *Child poverty in rich countries*, Innocenti Report Card No 5, Florence: UNICEF.

UNDP (United Nations Development Programme) (1997) *Human development report*, New York, NY and Oxford: UNDP.

UNDP (1998) *Human development report*, New York, NY and Oxford: UNDP.

UNDP (1999) *Human development report*, New York, NY and Oxford: UNDP.

UNDP (2000) *Human development report*, New York, NY and Oxford: UNDP.

World Bank (1996) *Poverty reduction and the World Bank: Progress and challenges in the 1990s*, Washington DC: World Bank.

Appendix 3.1: Absolute deprivation index

The 39 PSE variables, which could be used to construct an absolute poverty deprivation index, have been discussed by Gordon and his colleagues (2000). The adult and child socially perceived necessity items and activities from the PSE Survey were first allocated on the basis of normative judgements based on the UN definitions of absolute and overall poverty; then the allocation was adjusted in the light of the proportion of the population that identified each item as a socially perceived necessity (items that all adults should be able to afford and should not have to do without). Only items that more than 50% of the population thought were necessities were included as potential indicators of absolute poverty. In the case of the children's items, only the proportion of adults with children has been taken.

Also included are some indicators derived from other parts of the survey that can be used as indicators of absolute and overall poverty in addition to the socially perceived necessities – on the grounds that the socially perceived necessity items do not cover these elements of absolute and overall poverty.

Table A3.1: Potential absolute poverty indicators in the PSE Survey

Absolute poverty	% choosing item as a necessity
Adult items	
Beds and bedding for everyone	95
Heating to warm living areas	94
Damp-free home	93
Two meals a day	91
All medicines prescribed by doctor	90
Fridge	89
Fresh fruit and vegetables every day	86
A warm waterproof coat	85
Meat/fish/vegetables every other day	79
Dictionary	53
Adult activities	
Visits to friends/family	84
Visiting friends/family in hospital	84
Attending weddings, funerals and other such occasions	80
Children's items	
A warm waterproof coat	96
Bed and bedding for herself/himself	96
New properly fitting shoes	95
Fresh fruit or vegetables daily	94
Three meals a day	92
Books of her/his own	90
All the school uniform required	89
Enough bedrooms for every child over 10	77
Meat/fish twice a day	77
Children's activities	
Celebrations of special occasions	92
Other	
Five or more problems with accommodation	
In debt for rent, mortgage, gas, electricity, water	
Disconnected from water, gas, electricity	
Cutting down on water, gas electricity	
Housing in 'poor' repair	
Housing problems	
Health affected by poor housing	
Difficulty in accessing information by disabled people	
Personally gone without clothes, shoes, food, heating	
Partner and children gone without clothes, shoes, food, heating	
Non-use of doctor	
Non-use of dentist	
Non-use of optician	
Non-use of chemist	
Non-use of hospital	
Non-use of home help (by elderly)	

Table A3.2 shows the 21 variables that make up a valid and reliable final adult absolute deprivation index (after the exclusion of 18 variables that did not contribute to the reliability and/or the validity of the deprivation index or that relate to children).

The validity of each potential item in the index was tested by calculating the correlation (logistic odds) between the item and two health variables ('general health question' and 'limiting long-term illness') and a subjective poverty question ('genuinely poor now') after allowing for age and gender difference. The reliability of each potential item in the index was tested using a classical test theory model, the final adult index is very reliable and has a Chronbach's Alpha statistic of 0.79.

Table: A3.2: Final absolute deprivation index (21 variables)

Absolute poverty	% choosing item as a necessity
Adult items	
Beds and bedding for everyone	95
Heating to warm living areas	94
Damp-free home	93
Two meals a day	91
All medicines prescribed by doctor	90
Fresh fruit and vegetables everyday	86
A warm waterproof coat	85
Meat/fish/vegetables every other day	79
Dictionary	53
Adult activities	
Visits to friends/family	84
Visiting friends/family in hospital	84
Attending weddings, funerals and other such occasions	80
Other	
Five or more problems with accommodation	
In debt for rent, mortgage, gas, electricity, water	
Disconnected from water, gas, electricity	
Cutting down on water, gas electricity	
Housing in 'poor' repair	
Difficulty in accessing information by disabled people	
Personally gone without food, heating	
Partner and children gone without food, heating	
Non-use of home help (by elderly)	

Reference

Gordon, D., Adelman, L., Ashworth, K., Bradshaw, J., Levitas, R., Middleton, S., Pantazis, C., Patsios, D., Payne, S., Townsend, P. and Williams, J. (2000) *Poverty and social exclusion in Britain*, York: Joseph Rowntree Foundation.

FOUR

The necessities of life

Christina Pantazis, David Gordon and Peter Townsend

Introduction

One of the primary purposes of the Poverty and Social Exclusion (PSE) Survey was to establish what possessions and activities the public perceive as necessary – that no adult in modern society should have to go without due to a lack of money. This type of social inquiry reflects a long tradition within poverty research of attempting to establish what constitutes human needs. For example, Charles Booth (1902, p 33) argued that the "'poor' may be described as living under a struggle to obtain the necessities of life and make both ends meet". The 1983 Living in Britain Survey (published as *Poor Britain* (Mack and Lansky, 1985)), which set the precedent for the PSE Survey, was the first in Britain to capture what 'standard of living' is considered unacceptable by society as a whole. In a radical departure from previous poverty studies, which relied on the role of 'experts', the central idea of the Living in Britain Survey was:

> to try to discover whether there is a *public consensus* on what is an unacceptable standard of living for Britain in 1983 and, if there is a consensus, who, if anyone, falls below that standard. The idea underlying this is that a person is in 'poverty' when their standard of living falls below the minimum deemed necessary by current public opinion. (Mack and Lansley, 1985, p 50, emphasis added)

One of the major achievements of the Mack and Lansley study was that it established that this minimum covered not only the basic essentials for survival (such as food and shelter) but also the ability to participate in society and play a social role:

> for the first time ever, ... that a majority of people see the
> necessities of life in Britain in the 1980s as covering a
> wide range of goods and activities, and ... that people judge
> a minimum standard of living on socially established criteria
> and not just the criteria of survival or subsistence. (Mack
> and Lansley, 1985, p 55)

The validity of this consensual approach to measuring poverty rests
on the assumption that there is a universal minimum accepted by
society that also reflects actual living conditions. The implication of
this, which is central to the approach, is that differences in views
between social groups, including ranked social strata, concerning what
constitutes an acceptable living standard are relatively small. Otherwise,
the definition of an unacceptable standard of living just becomes the
opinion of one group against another. The subsequent 1990 Breadline
Britain Survey confirmed that there was "a high degree of consensus,
across all divisions in society, on the necessity of a range of common
possessions and activities. Society as a whole clearly does have a view
on what is necessary to have a decent standard of living" (Gordon and
Pantazis, 1997, p 96).

The 1999 PSE Survey developed and extended the methodologies
of the 1983 and 1990 studies dealing with indicators of a substantial
list of necessities – prompted partly by intervening research into social
conditions, consumer behaviour and household interaction. In 1999
respondents were asked substantially more questions about material
goods and social activities (84 compared with 44 in 1990 and 35 in
1983). The additional questions relate mainly to social activities (which
were selectively few in number in the first two surveys) and with
goods and activities particularly relevant to children. These 'necessities
of life' questions were asked in the June 1999 Office for National
Statistics (ONS) Omnibus Survey, and involved face-to-face interviews
with 1,900 adults aged 16 and over (ONS, 1999). The questions added
to the 1999 Omnibus Survey were designed to establish what changes
have taken place in public perceptions of what constitutes necessities.

The question asked of respondents in the Omnibus Survey was as
follows[1]:

> On these cards are a number of different items which relate
> to our standard of living. I would like you to indicate the
> living standards you feel all adults should have in Britain
> today by placing the cards in the appropriate box.

Box A is for items which you think are necessary; which all adults should be able to afford and which they should not have to do without.

Box B is for items which maybe desirable but are not necessary.

This chapter aims to examine which adult items and activities constitute the necessities of life among the adult British population at the end of the 20th century (children's items and activities are discussed in Chapter Eleven). It also compares these results with those of the 1983 and 1990 studies in order to assess whether there has been any change in public attitude concerning what is an acceptable standard of living and, if so, to explain why. In the final section, the chapter responds to some recent criticisms of the consensual method for measuring poverty (see McKay, 2004)

Standard of living or style of living: concept and methodology

There is a long history of scientific investigation into what constitutes the necessities of life. These investigations, which go back a lot further than the 1983 and 1990 forerunner studies described above, helped inform the PSE Survey about which items to include. Seebohm Rowntree's classic study of York was framed from the very beginning to throw some light upon the "conditions which govern the life of the wage-earning classes.... [It was] a detailed investigation into the social and economic conditions of the working classes in York" (Rowntree, 1901, pp v-vi). Within this framework of conditions and action, poverty was measured as insufficient income "to obtain the minimum necessaries of the maintenance of merely physical efficiency" (Rowntree, 1899, p 86). Charles Booth had also adopted a similar framework in his approach to the conditions of social and economic life, especially in his examination of 'the standard life' when investigating the construction of a poverty line in London (Booth, 1902, p 131).

For these pioneers, broad investigation of contemporary conditions of life seemed unavoidable in order to arrive at a list of needs, and then deliberately restrict and interpret those needs to produce a measure of poverty acceptable to the public and to politicians. The fact that Seebohm Rowntree tended to enlarge the meaning he gave to the 'necessities' of life in his later work, for example, in redefining a poverty line in 1936, compared with the definition he had given in 1899

(Rowntree, 1941, pp 28-31), and in describing the income to surmount poverty as enough to "secure the necessities of a healthy life" (Rowntree, 1937, p 11) only heightens the importance of decisions that have to be made about the *scope* of investigation as well as the categorisation of its components.

Needs are not self-evident. They have to be fulfilled consciously and unconsciously in accordance with purposes concerned with maintaining and improving human life. It is not just social organisation, or individual biology and physiology, or a combination of all three, that determine needs but the style of life to which, by their behaviour and feelings, individual members of society are obliged to conform.

> There is no unitary and clear-cut national 'style of living'. Rather, there are a series of overlapping and merging community, ethnic, organisational and regional styles. By style of living I do not mean *particular* things and actions in themselves, but *types* of consumption and *customs* which are expressive of social form. Thus, the influence of national government, trading systems, education, the mass media, industry and transport systems will tend towards the establishment of diffuse cultural norms.... Certain practices gradually become accepted as appropriate modes of behaviour, and even when a group performs particular rituals of religious observance or engages in particular leisure-time activity, it shares other customs with many different groups in society. What do need to be distinguished are the customs practised by a majority of the national population, and those practised by different minorities and sub-groups. (Townsend, 1979, p 249, emphasis in original)

The procedure in identifying needs becomes easier to understand:

> A national style of living has to be defined in operational terms. Many component items, including those specific to age groups, peers, and generations, and to large units, such as regional communities and ethnic groups, have to be identified and examined and the elements common to, or approved by, the majority of the population distinguished.... The degree of cultural integration of different groups and communities could then be tentatively assessed and perhaps measured. (Townsend, 1979, p 249)

Ideally, the aim would be "to cover all activities and events in order to establish standard or majority norms, conventions and customs, so that non-participation, or marginal participation, in those norms, conventions and customs could be identified" (Townsend and Gordon, 1993, pp 57-8). But this would involve a huge exercise in definition, investigation and measurement on a national scale. Resources for such extensive research have not been available in recent years (Townsend and Gordon, 1993, p 56). Instead, drawing on precedents in social surveys, investigators of poverty and deprivation have covered a wide range of individual and social conditions and activities, generally ignoring, on the basis of everyday observation and national statistics, customs in which few participate.

One practice in recent research has been to adopt one of the primary meanings of 'need', that is, 'deprivation', and to consider its sub-categories, beginning with the distinction between material and social deprivation, and then examining the sub-categories of material deprivation, related to diet, health, clothing, housing, household facilities, environment and work, and of social deprivation, related to family activities, social support and integration, recreation and education (Townsend, 1993). The consensual investigative approaches of 1983 and 1990, and the 1999 PSE Survey, have extended that categorisation. The social scientist has to "consider deprivation as the darker side of the entire lifestyle of people" (Townsend and Gordon, 1993, p 82). Like both sides of a coin, one cannot be separated from the other, and the comprehension of one side is necessary to the other.

In developing the 1999 PSE Survey, other surveys were referred to (for example, the European Community Household Panel Survey, Harmonised Question Set (consumer durables), Small Fortunes: National Survey of the Lifestyles and Living Standards of Children, the Swedish Living Standards Survey and the Lorraine Panel Survey) and focus group discussions with 13 groups of people in different circumstances were undertaken. A major object of these focus group discussions was to negotiate "agreed lists of items, activities and facilities which all adults in Britain should be able to have and should not have to go without" (Bradshaw et al, 1998, p44). This led to the removal, addition and amendment of questions asked in the 1983 and 1990 studies. Three items which had been included in 1983 and 1990 were omitted in 1999: an inside toilet not shared with another household; a bath not shared with another household; and a pack of cigarettes every other day. The first two (toilet and bath) were dropped since almost all households now possess these housing amenities, while the reference to cigarettes was omitted as these have been demonstrated to be an addictive drug and are, therefore, not a good indicator of poverty even though it is well established that cigarette consumption is higher among lower socio-economic groups (National Statistics, 2002).

Among new items of a primarily 'material' kind were fresh fruit or fresh vegetables every day, appropriate clothes to wear for job interviews and mattresses and bedding for everyone in the household. New questions of a primarily 'social' kind were also added. They include visiting friends and/or family once a week, and going to the pub once a fortnight. Furthermore, contact with friends and family was emphasised throughout all "discussions of necessities as being vital to survival" (Bradshaw et al, 1998, p 47). Many more children's items and activities were added, building upon Middleton et al's (1997) *Small fortunes* study.

Ranking material and social necessities

The PSE Survey reveals clear majorities of public support for many consumption items and activities relating to both adults (Table 4.1) and children[2]. As with the previous Breadline Britain surveys, items and activities attracting 50% or more support from the public were considered as socially perceived necessities for the purposes of further analysis. In the PSE Survey, 18 out of 84 items and activities in the adult lists failed to satisfy this criterion, leaving 35 that were considered as necessities by the majority of the public.

Over 90% of British people in each case perceive beds for everyone, heating, a damp-free home, and visits to the hospital as items or activities that all adults should have or be able to participate in. By contrast, less than 10% see a dishwasher, a mobile phone, internet access and a satellite television as necessary. Thus, the majority of the lowest ranked items relate to consumer durables and information needs, whereas, in general, items relating to clothing, heating, housing, food and social activities tend to be ranked higher. Notwithstanding that, certain consumer durables, such as refrigerators and washing machines, are clearly perceived by the overwhelming majority to be necessities of life in modern Britain, reflecting the fact that, "in a practical sense, items that become customary also become necessary because other aspects of life are planned and built on the very fact that these items are customary" (Mack and Lansley, 1985, p 56).

Two problems with the list in Table 4.1 might be anticipated. First, the distinction between 'material' and 'social' necessities is not always as clear as it may seem and begins to break down on close examination.

Table 4.1: Percentage of respondents perceiving adult item/ activity as necessary

Adult item or activity	Necessary	Desirable	Don't know
Beds and bedding for everyone	95	4	
Heating to warm living areas	94	5	
Damp-free home	93	6	1
Visiting friends or family in hospital	92	7	1
Two meals a day	91	9	1
Medicines prescribed by doctor	90	9	1
Refrigerator	89	11	1
Fresh fruit and vegetables daily	86	13	1
A warm waterproof coat	85	14	1
Replace broken electrical goods	85	14	2
Visits to friends or family	84	15	1
Celebrations on special occasions	83	16	2
Money to keep home decorated	82	17	1
Visits to school, eg sports day	81	17	2
Attending weddings, funerals	80	19	1
Meat, fish or vegetarian equivalent	79	19	1
Insurance of contents of dwelling	79	20	1
A hobby or leisure activity	78	20	1
A washing machine	76	22	1
Collect children from school	75	23	3
Telephone	71	28	1
Deep freezer/fridge freezer	68	30	2
Carpets in living rooms and bedrooms	67	31	2
Regular savings for rainy days	66	32	2
Two pairs of all-weather shoes	64	34	2
Friends or family round for a meal	64	34	2
Leisure equipment (eg for sports)	60	38	2
Money to spend on self weekly	59	39	2
A television	56	43	2
A roast joint/vegetarian equivalent weekly	56	41	3
Presents for friends/family yearly	56	42	2
A holiday away from home	55	43	3
Replace worn-out furniture	54	43	3
A dictionary	53	44	3
An outfit for social occasions	51	46	3
New, not second-hand, clothes	48	49	3
A car	38	59	3
Coach/train fares to visit friends/family	38	58	4
An evening out once a fortnight	37	56	3
A dressing gown	34	63	4
Having a daily newspaper	30	66	4
A meal in a restaurant/pub monthly	26	71	4
Microwave oven	23	73	4
Tumble dryer	20	75	4
Going to the pub once a fortnight	20	76	4
A video cassette recorder	19	78	3
Holidays abroad once a year	19	77	4
CD player	12	84	4
A home computer	11	85	4
A dishwasher	7	88	5
Mobile phone	7	88	5
Access to the internet	6	89	5
Satellite television	5	90	5

Note: The individual weight was used for this analysis; analysis excludes those who refused to answer question.

A telephone is a 'material' good, but its function as a necessary form of communication is entirely 'social'. Similarly, a television can be a satisfying form of entertainment for the individual, but at the same time is a symbol of material prosperity and social status; and it can be a valuable means of shared family custom as well of national and local information. Similar points can be made about diet and clothing. Many items on the list are in fact multi-functional, and are interpreted accordingly by the public.

Second, it is easier to ask questions about some items and verify the answers. Usually few doubts arise about material goods such as refrigerators and telephones. The goods may be broken, unworkable or unused but rarely difficult to define and locate. However, the meaning of a damp-free home or two meals a day may be less easy to agree upon. The meaning of what are usually described as 'social' necessities – like visiting friends or family in hospital and having friends and family round for a meal – can also pose problems. Questions abound. For example, should nursing and residential homes count as equivalent to hospitals?

The answers given by respondents in the PSE Survey were analysed by region in order to examine possible regional discrepancies in respondents' views. Table 4.2 ranks the percentage of the population identifying different items and activities as necessary in 1999, comparing Welsh, English and Scottish respondents. It can be seen that there is consistency in the ranking, although caution must be expressed about the small numbers in the Scottish, and especially, Welsh sub-samples. Fortunately, the results for Wales can be compared with a 1995 survey of Wales where over 1,000 respondents were interviewed.

Ninety per cent of the population in all three countries named a damp-free home as a necessity and large majorities of the population also specified things like heating to warm living areas, beds and bedding for everyone, a refrigerator, visits to friends and family, and medicines prescribed by their doctor as items and activities that adults in Britain should have. By contrast, less than 10% of the population sees a dishwasher, a mobile phone, internet access and a satellite television as necessary.

What is perhaps remarkable is that perceptions in the three countries are so similar. In England, a majority of the population picked out 35 of the 54 items as necessary. In Scotland, the total was 34 – and all of these fell within the English list. In only one case, a roast joint or the vegetarian equivalent weekly, was there a difference among the items reaching the 50% threshold, falling short in Scotland (42%) compared with England (58%). But this example of a necessity was picked out

Table 4.2: Perception of adult necessities in England, Scotland and Wales (%)

Material goods and social customs and activities said to be necessary	England 1999 (n=1,591)	Scotland 1999 (n=165)	Wales 1999 (n=99)	Wales 1995 (n=1,007)
Heating to warm living areas	95	95	89	99
Damp-free home	94	98	90	99
Visiting friends or family in hospital	94	94	83	–
Two meals a day	92	91	75	94
Medicines prescribed by doctor	92	92	79	–
Refrigerator	90	91	80	95
Fresh fruit and vegetables daily	87	85	76	90
A warm waterproof coat	86	92	81	93
Replace broken electrical goods	86	86	83	–
Visits to friends or family	86	82	84	–
Celebrations on special occasions	85	85	74	–
Money to keep home decorated	84	83	72	84
Visits to school, eg sports day	84	78	67	–
Attending weddings, funerals	82	80	79	–
Meat, fish or vegetarian equivalent at least twice a day	81	80	76	–
Insurance of contents of dwelling	80	82	75	84
A hobby or leisure activity	80	77	77	73
Collect children from school	78	71	68	–
A washing machine	77	82	80	83
Telephone	72	69	69	64
Appropriate clothes for job interviews	71	69	66	–
Carpets in living rooms and bedrooms	70	70	77	–
Deep freezer/fridge freezer	70	69	63	–
Regular savings for rainy days	68	61	65	67
Friends or family round for a meal	66	62	60	–
Two pairs of all-weather shoes	65	71	68	80
Money to spend on self weekly	62	53	49	–
Presents for friends/family yearly	59	50	46	55
A roast joint/vegetarian equivalent weekly	58	42	72	–
A holiday away from home	57	51	55	49
A television	56	59	60	68
Replace worn-out furniture	56	53	51	–
A dictionary	55	55	58	–
An outfit for social occasions	52	54	53	–
New, not second-hand, clothes	49	46	57	59
Attending place of worship	42	46	53	–
An evening out once a fortnight	41	35	43	–
Coach/train fares to visit friends/family	41	33	34	–
A car	40	27	42	43
A dressing gown	35	34	42	–
Having a daily newspaper	29	47	40	–
A meal in a restaurant/pub monthly	27	20	26	–
Microwave oven	24	23	28	–
Tumble dryer	21	20	27	–
Going to the pub once a fortnight	21	19	24	–
A video cassette recorder	20	15	23	23
Holidays abroad once a year	20	17	21	–
A home computer	12	9	15	13
CD player	12	12	18	–
A dishwasher	7	7	14	–
Mobile phone	7	7	10	–
Access to the internet	7	4	7	–
Satellite television	5	6	9	–

Note: Don't know/not sure/unanswered responses are coded as missing. Some of the question wordings in the 1995 *Poor Wales Survey* varied slightly from the wordings used in the 1999 PSE Survey.

by a much higher proportion of Welsh respondents than respondents in the other countries (72%).

In Wales, 50% or more of the respondents named 35 items as necessary – the same as in England. Among these, 33 were identical. More of the Welsh laid stress on new, not second-hand, clothes and attending a place of worship. Fewer named money to spend on self weekly and presents for friends and/or family at least yearly – although in both these cases the number approached 50%.

There are of course certain variations. In Wales there is a tendency for fewer people than in England to list certain items as necessary. The instances of two meals a day and fresh fruit and vegetables daily stand out, but the percentage rating of many items in the middle and end of the list is rather similar. And more of the Welsh than of the English and Scottish respondents name carpets, a dressing gown and a newspaper, as well as attending a place of worship, and a roast joint or the vegetarian equivalent, among the necessities of life.

Is there a consensus on the necessities of life?

The consensual approach to poverty adopted in the PSE Survey is predicated on the assumption that there exists a broad public consensus on the necessities of life – a consensus that cuts across social divisions such as those relating to class, gender, ethnicity and age. As discussed in the introduction to this chapter, the forerunner studies to the PSE Survey demonstrated a high degree of homogeneity in opinions across different social groups. This section of the chapter considers the question how far does this assumption hold true for the 1999 Survey? The question is examined carefully by assembling information about different sub-divisions of population and presenting the information in the form of a series of scatter plot graphs that are easy to assimilate. Linear regression has been used with each scatter plot graph to show the 'best fit' straight line, which minimises the total distance between the line and each individual item.

Figure 4.1 illustrates the extent of agreement between men and women on the necessities of life. It compares the percentage of men considering an item or an activity to be necessary (on the vertical axis) with the percentage of women (horizontal axis). It shows each item or activity as a shaded circle. A random scatter of points on the graph would indicate no agreement between women and men about the necessity of different goods and activities but, in fact, the figure shows that there are generally few attitudinal differences between men and women.

Figure 4.1: Perception of necessities: comparing men and women

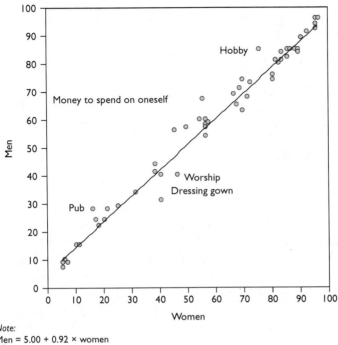

Note:
Men = 5.00 + 0.92 × women
$R^2 = 0.98$

There is one important caveat. It is that gender differences are sometimes striking. While women give priority to key aspects of an adequate family standard of living, men tend to support material goods of greatest interest or concern to them. For example, women are slightly more likely to view two meals daily, a refrigerator and a damp-free home as essential, whereas men are more likely to view a video, home computer, mobile phone, satellite television, CD player, and internet access as necessary. This gender difference is greater with respect to those items and activities that may be considered as satisfying 'personal' consumption (Goode et al, 1998). Men are more likely than women to consider as necessary those items and activities that potentially satisfy their own personal use – items such as new clothing and money to spend on oneself and activities such as a hobby and going to the pub once a fortnight. Of course, these survey results do not allow us to conclude that male respondents are thinking of an item or activity in terms of only their own individual consumption, although we can speculate that this may be the case. However, there are good grounds for believing that many women perceive needs in relation to household or familial consumption, not least because women generally have responsibility for meeting the needs of others, but also because research exists showing that women often put their own needs second to those of their children and partners, forgoing essential items for themselves in circumstances of poverty (Middleton et al, 1997; Goode et al, 1998; for further discussion of parental sacrifice, see Chapters Eleven and Thirteen in this volume).

These results also confirm earlier forerunner studies examining differences in perceptions of necessities between men and women (Payne and Pantazis, 1997), as well as other European studies (for example, Nyman, 1996). Yet, in many ways, they continue to raise more questions than they answer, particularly in terms of "what they may suggest about definitions of poverty for men and women" (Payne and Pantazis, 1997, p 104). Further research, of a qualitative nature, is required to tease out why these differences exist and what the implications might be for consensual studies of poverty. Nevertheless, the results shown in Figure 4.1 demonstrate that with regard to most items and activities the views of men and women are indistinguishable, with effectively identical percentages of men and women in agreement (or disagreement) about what constitute the necessities of life.

There is a greater diversity in opinion between different age groups (Figure 4.2). The general trend is for younger respondents (aged 16 to 24) to view fewer items and activities as essential than older respondents (aged 65 plus). Some have attracted strong disagreement, particularly clothing items. The extent of difference in relation to these is so great that Gordon et al (2000a, p 29) have argued that "the consensus between age groups on the necessities of life that all people should be able to afford and have not have to do without appears to have broken down particularly in relation to clothing items". But younger respondents have adopted a similarly stringent view in relation to a number of disparate items, including a roast joint or vegetarian equivalent, a telephone, a television, a washing machine, a car, a dictionary, money to spend on self weekly, and presents for friends and family. This is not a uniform pattern as there are some exceptions: for example, young adult respondents are more likely to consider collecting children from school and attending school events such as sports day and parents' evening as essential.

While tastes and attitudes towards fashion may explain some of the differences with regard to why there is greater support for clothing items among older people, the fact that they feel the cold more may also be important in relation to items such as a dressing gown. Similarly, cultural attitudes may explain why a greater proportion of older people view a weekly roast joint or its vegetarian equivalent as essential. The

Figure 4.2: Perception of necessities: comparing younger and older respondents

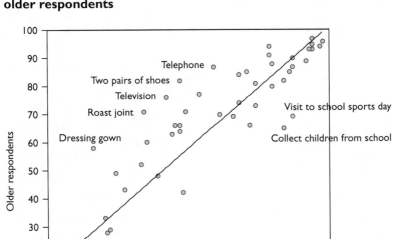

Note:
Older = 14.72 + 0.86 × younger
$R^2 = 0.81$

high support for a telephone among older people is suggestive of this form of communication being especially important to them because they are more likely to have restricted mobility that limits their ability to meet up with friends and family outside of the home (see Chapter Five in this volume), whereas their higher levels of support for a television indicates a reliance on home entertainment. In fact, many of the differences discussed may reflect the fact that older people are more home-bound and younger people are much more likely to go out and enjoy themselves (Mack and Lansley, 1985). The support among younger adults for activities relating to children, for example collecting children from school and attending school events, probably reflects long-term shifts in societal ideas concerning children's safety. There may also be strong cultural shifts between the generations to explain why younger respondents tend to take a harsher view of what items and activities constitute the necessities of life, and these are explored below when considering changes over time.

A less varied picture emerges when considering differences in perceptions among ethnic groups (Figure 4.3). All minority ethnic

Figure 4.3: Perception of necessities: comparing minority ethnic respondents and non-minority ethnic respondents

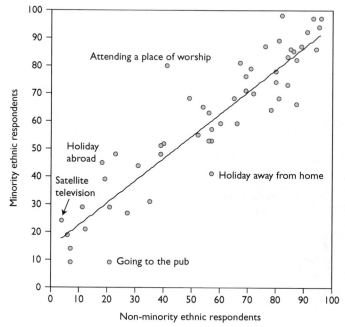

Note:
Ethnic = 14.50 + 0.80 × non-ethnic
$R^2 = 0.84$

groups are combined into one category because of the small numbers of minority ethnic respondents in the PSE sample, but we must acknowledge that this is not a satisfactory procedure because there are likely to be socio-economic and cultural differences between Black and Asian respondents, as well as differences within these groups (see Modood et al, 1997). Berthoud (1997), for example, found that while Asian people as a whole often score more highly than Caribbean people on a range of socio-economic indicators, people from the Caribbean score more highly than Bangladeshis and Pakistanis. Furthermore, as there are only 72 respondents in the combined minority ethnic group, there are still problems relating to reliability.

Nevertheless the data in Figure 4.3 are not randomly dispersed and there is some evidence of a consensus, although there are a number of items and activities attracting differences in opinion. Respondents from minority ethnic groups are more likely to view new, not second-hand clothes, a home computer, a microwave oven, a satellite TV, holidays abroad once a year, attending a place of worship and visits to school as necessary. Items such as a warm waterproof coat, a washing machine and activities including a holiday away from home are more likely to be perceived as necessities by non-minority ethnic respondents. Some of these differences may reflect actual differences in lifestyles: for example, a greater proportion of minority ethnic respondents probably travel overseas to visit family and friends, and this may account for the strong support given to this activity. However, for some items (for example, a washing machine) there are no obvious reasons to explain the differences.

Thus, strong patterns have not emerged from this analysis but it may be that combining all minority ethnic groups into one category has obscured possible distinctions in people's perceptions. This points to the need for surveys to contain larger samples of minority ethnic respondents so that potential differences in people's views on what needs are can be disentangled more sufficiently according to their ethnic background.

Despite much recent discussion about the demise of social class (for example, see Pakulski and Waters, 1999) the class system is still strongly entrenched within British society and people's attitudes, including voting behaviour (see, for example, Geoffrey, 1999; Anderson and Heath, 2002), continue to be strongly influenced by class. This leads to an expectation that there should be marked differences on the necessities of life by social class group. For purposes of broad comparison, social classes I/II (professionals and managers) and IV/V (the partly skilled and unskilled) have been compared (Figure 4.4). However, the figure reveals small differences in the perceptions of social classes – at least in comparing social class I/II heads of households with IV/V. However, the general trend is for respondents in social classes IV/V to specify more items and activities necessities.

This pattern was found in both the earlier Breadline Britain Surveys, and two explanations were offered. First, differences in opinion could be linked to possession so that people with property and material goods attach less importance to them than those who "have had to struggle and save, or even go without" (Mack and Lansley, 1983, p 62). Possession of items and participation in activities was generally higher among social classes I/II than social classes IV/V, so the argument that people's perceptions are linked to what they possess is still a very plausible one (see below for critique of this method). The second argument relates to cultural homogeneity and whether these differences are a result of differing lifestyles, tastes and aspirations.

Some strong patterns emerge that can indeed be linked to lifestyles. People in social classes IV/V are more likely to consider items that

Figure 4.4: Perception of necessities: comparing respondents in social classes I/II and IV/V

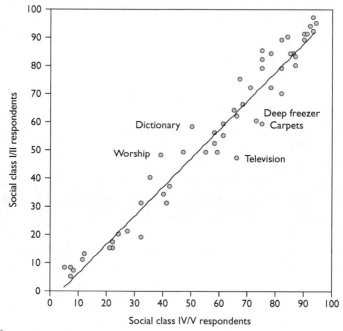

Note:
High = –3.97 + 1.02 × low
$R^2 = 0.95$

provide cheap forms of entertainment as essential (for example, a television and a video cassette recorder). Applying the 50% rule, a television is a socially perceived necessity among lower social class groups but not among higher social class groups: 66% of social class IV/V respondents perceive this item as a necessity compared with only 46% of respondents in social classes I/II. Televisions, like videos and computer games, provide cheap forms of entertainment and distractions from the pressing problems some people find themselves in (Mack and Lansley, 1985). As Pamela, a lone parent with a nine-month-old child living on Supplementary Benefit in an attic flat, who was interviewed in the 1983 study, put it succinctly:

> I watch TV from first thing in the morning till last thing at night, till the television goes off. I sit and watch it all day. I can't afford to do other things at all. The only thing I can do is sit and watch television. I can't go anywhere, I can't go out and enjoy myself or nothing. I should be able to take my daughter out somewhere. I would take her to the

zoo and things like that. Places she's never been, or seen, and half the places I haven't seen in London myself. Things that I can't afford to do. (Mack and Lansley, 1985, pp 63-4)

Differences in tastes may explain why social classes IV/V respondents give greater support to carpets in living rooms, for example. Or, it could reflect their circumstances, namely that respondents in social classes IV/V are more likely to be living in accommodation with concreted floors where alternative floorings such as pine floors are not an option. A deep freezer/fridge freezer is also more likely to be seen as essential by people in lower social class groups. We can speculate that this is due to their greater consumption of frozen foods because of their relative affordability.

Similar patterns emerge when we compare respondents in the bottom and highest household income quintile groups (Figure 4.5), such that people living in the poorest income households consider many more items and activities as necessary than those in the richest households[3].

Figure 4.5: Perception of necessities: comparing the richest and poorest respondents

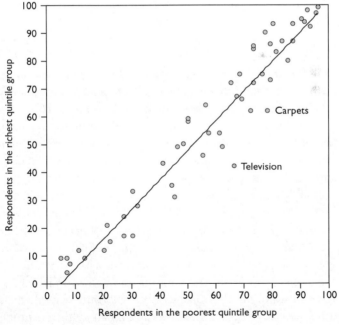

Note:
Richest = −5.27 + 1.07 × poorest
$R^2 = 0.94$

Significant differences can be found in relation to items corresponding to cheap forms of entertainment (for example, a television). Carpets in living rooms and bedrooms also attract greater support from poorer people.

Attitudinal change over time

Gordon and Pantazis (1997) have argued that the relative theory of poverty predicts that as society gets richer, so will the number of people perceiving common possessions and activities as necessary. Goods and services that are luxuries at first become generally available as a result of mass production:

> Since the real income of average households increased between 1983 and 1990, we would expect that number of respondents considering items to be necessary would also have increased between 1983 and 1990.... this is true for 30 out of 33 items. There has clearly been a large shift in public attitudes between 1983 and 1990, with greater numbers in 1990, perceiving as necessities, a whole range of common possessions and activities. (Gordon and Pantazis, 1997, p 72)

However, they have since questioned their original proposition based on the results of other consensual poverty surveys (Gordon et al, 2000b). Surveys in Finland (Kangas and Ritakallio, 1998) and Vietnam (Davies and Smith, 1998) found that over 90% of respondents consider having 'all medicines prescribed by their doctor' to be a necessity – a similar figure to the much wealthier Britain. One explanation for this apparent paradox could lie in the greater consequences, in terms of premature morbidity and mortality, of not having access to necessary medicines. For example, it is estimated that only about 50% of the Vietnamese population has 'regular access to essential drugs' compared with almost 100% of the British population (WHO, 1998). But cultural factors are also important when comparing the perception of necessities between different countries and communities; for example, France has a relatively high level of medicinal drug use compared with other European countries (Bradshaw, personal communication). Since Vietnam was a French colony until the 1950s, it could be that some of the Vietnamese population may have been influenced by French cultural attitudes to medicinal drug use.

Similarly, the PSE findings suggest that it is too simplistic to expect that on average a greater proportion of people would consider common possessions and activities to be necessities in 1999 than in 1990 or 1983 because of increases in general wealth and income. Figure 4.6 demonstrates that support for a number of goods and activities actually *fell* between 1990 and 1999, rather than increased. These results are detailed in Table 4.3. The main observation is that marginally more items and activities were considered essential in 1990 than in 1999. In 1999, a slightly smaller proportion of respondents considered the highest ranked items to be necessities than did respondents in either 1990 or 1983. This attitudinal change is most striking with respect to clothing possessions. For example, the proportion of respondents considering that there is a need to have two pairs of all-weather shoes has steadily declined from 78% in 1983, to 74% in 1990 and 67% in 1999. This may reflect cultural and commercial changes in the footwear market, particularly the growth in popularity of trainers over the past 16 years. There has also been a marked reduction in the percentage of people who think new, not second-hand clothes are a necessity (from 65% in 1990 to just 50% in 1999). This may be because there is less

Figure 4.6: Percentage of households considering items and activities as necessary, 1990-99

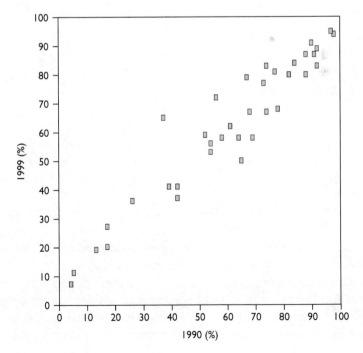

Table 4.3: Percentage of households perceiving items and activities as necessary, 1999, 1990 and 1983

Item	1999	1990	1983
A damp-free home	94	98	96
Heating to warm living areas	95	97	97
Beds for everyone	95	97	97
A decent state of decoration	83	92	–
Fridge	89	92	77
Warm waterproof coat	87	91	87
Three meals a day for children	91	90	82
Two meals a day for adults	91	90	64
Insurance	80	88	–
Fresh fruit	87	88	–
Toys for children	84	84	71
Separate bedrooms for children aged 10 plus	80	82	77
Carpets	68	78	70
Meat and fish every other day	81	77	63
Celebrations on special occasions	83	74	69
Two pairs of all-weather shoes	67	74	78
Washing machine	77	73	67
Presents for friends/family	58	69	63
Regular savings	67	68	–
Hobby or leisure activity	79	67	64
New, not second-hand clothes	50	65	64
A roast joint or equivalent	58	64	67
Leisure equipment for children	62	61	57
Television	58	58	51
Phone	72	56	43
Annual week's holiday	56	54	63
A best outfit	53	54	48
Children's friends round for tea	59	52	37
A dressing gown	37	42	38
A night out fortnightly	41	42	36
Fares to visit friends	41	39	–
Friends/family for a meal	65	37	32
Car	36	26	22
Restaurant meal	27	17	–
Holidays abroad	20	17	–
Video	19	13	–
Home computer	11	5	–
Dishwasher	7	4	–

Note: Don't know responses are coded as missing.

stigma attached to buying second-hand clothing, particularly 'vintage' clothing, which may be popular with younger respondents.

On the other hand, when it comes to the lower ranked, more luxury items, such as videos, dishwashers and cars, a greater proportion of respondents considered these to be necessities in 1999 than previously. Similarly, many social and leisure activities, such as celebrations on special occasions and being able to afford a hobby or leisure activity, were thought to be a necessity by more respondents in 1999 than in the two previous surveys. This is also true for certain consumer durables, such as telephones and washing machines.

What is the explanation for these complex patterns of change in the perception of necessities over the past 16 years? Why has the prediction of Gordon and Pantazis (1997, p 72) that as "a society gets richer, the number of people who perceive common possessions and activities as necessary will increase" proved to be over-simplistic? There are a number of possible explanations for these findings. Some of the changes may result from the differences in the sampling methods used in the surveys. The PSE Survey used highly accurate random sampling to select respondents, whereas the 1990 and 1983 surveys used less accurate (but less expensive) quota samples, with booster samples in 'poor' areas that were then weighted to match the national population profile. Another part of the explanation for some of these results may be due to continuing demographic changes that have an impact on lifestyles.

However, some more fundamental explanation is required in order to understand the surprising results. One possible explanation for these changes in public opinion on what constitute the necessities of life is that the profound socio-economic and cultural changes, that resulted from the policies of successive Conservative governments between 1979 and 1997 have changed public attitudes so radically that the results can now be detected in a relatively small sample survey.

One of the most significant social changes to have occurred under 18 years of Conservative government was the growing divide between the rich and the poor (Pantazis, 2000; see also Chapter One in this volume). For example, the poorest 10% of the population became £520 per year poorer, whereas the richest 10% saw their median incomes more than double, a gain of £12,220 per year (Gordon, 2000). The massive increase in inequality and social polarisation during this period was accompanied by continued attacks on various groups of 'poor' people as 'scroungers' by both the government and the media. Lone-parent mothers, asylum seekers, the young unemployed and the homeless were particularly targeted (Cook, 1997). The 'underclass' debate even revived the 'undeserving poor' and the 'transmitted deprivation' theses for a time in the late 1980s and early 1990s (see for example, Murray, 1990). It is possible that these profound socio-economic changes have resulted in attitudinal changes on the minimum standard of living that all adults should have in Britain today and be able to afford. If this explanation is correct, then the most profound changes in attitude would be expected among the younger age groups, the 'Thatcher' generation, whose formative years were spent under Conservative rule.

Is there a Thatcher generation effect?

Several commentators have remarked that the children who grew up knowing only Conservative 'rule' may as adults have rather more 'conservative' views than their parents who grew up during the 1960s and 1970s (see Pilcher and Wagg, 1996). This may explain why children growing up under Thatcher's governments are more stringent than previous generations in their views on what standard of living every person in Britain should be entitled to.

The 1990 Breadline Britain Survey found that there were only a few variations in the perception of necessities among different age groups, although older people were more likely than younger people to consider items such as a dressing gown, two pairs of all-weather shoes, a telephone and having a roast joint or its vegetarian equivalent once a week as necessities (Gordon and Pantazis, 1997). Conversely, younger people were more likely to consider leisure activities and items relating to going out and meeting friends as essential. These differences were as expected and are relatively unremarkable. They are repeated in the PSE Survey, with the major exception that for every item and activity, there are fewer younger people considering them as necessary (see Chapter Twelve for further discussion). Table 4.4 shows how the attitudes of younger people have changed between 1990 and 1999 compared with the adult population as a whole. The items and activities are highlighted in bold where there is a marked difference between young people's perceptions in 1999 with all adults in 1999 and younger people in 1990. The results reveal that in 1999 younger people were less likely to see a whole range of items and activities as necessary compared with other adults, as well as with younger people nine years earlier. This is especially the case in relation to all clothing items.

However, before a 'Thatcher's children' effect can be confirmed, a number of possible confounding factors need to first be examined. Young men and women suffered from profound adverse socio-economic changes during the 1990s, which resulted in fewer young people being employed in full-time jobs in 1999 than in 1990 (see, for example, MacDonald, 1997). Large numbers of young men and women now enter post-school education and training schemes than was the case in 1990. This relative impoverishment of youth may be as

Table 4.4: Thatcher's children?

Item/activity	16 to 24 (1999)	16 to 24 (1990)	All adults (1999)	All adults (1990)
A damp-free home	94	95	94	98
Heating to warm living areas	94	97	95	97
Beds for everyone	98	95	95	97
A decent state of decoration	79	91	83	92
Fridge	92	92	89	92
Warm waterproof coat	**79**	**85**	**87**	**91**
Three meals a day for kids	94	93	91	90
Two meals a day for adults	97	95	91	90
Insurance	**71**	**87**	**80**	**88**
Fresh fruit	**80**	**87**	**87**	**88**
Toys for children	83	90	84	84
Separate bedrooms for children aged 10 plus	72	77	80	82
Carpets	68	82	68	78
Meat and fish every other day	74	70	81	77
Celebrations on special occasions	86	77	83	74
Two pairs of all-weather shoes	**47**	**63**	**67**	**74**
Washing machine	68	68	77	73
Presents for friends/family	**49**	**72**	**58**	**69**
Regular savings	66	68	67	68
Hobby or leisure activity	80	67	79	67
New, not second-hand clothes	**35**	**59**	**50**	**65**
A roast joint or equivalent	**34**	**55**	**58**	**64**
Leisure equipment	56	62	62	61
TV	**42**	**53**	**58**	**58**
Phone	59	45	72	56
Annual week's holiday	47	46	56	54
A best outfit	**45**	**54**	**53**	**54**
Children's friends round	61	50	59	52
A dressing gown	**16**	**24**	**37**	**42**
A night out fortnightly	48	50	41	42
Fares to visit friends	39	31	41	39
Friends/family for a meal	61	35	65	37
Car	27	22	36	26
Restaurant meal	22	13	27	17
Holidays abroad	20	23	20	17
Video	16	17	19	13
Home computer	13	4	11	5
Dishwasher	7	4	7	4

important a factor in explaining the change in attitudes among the younger cohort than any cultural effect of 18 years of Conservative rule. In order to distinguish the relative importance of these different effects, it would be necessary to undertake a multivariate, longitudinal quasi-cohort analysis.

Recent criticisms of the consensual approach

McKay (2004) has recently analysed the PSE Survey data and made criticisms of the consensual method for measuring deprivation. He has argued that:

> First, there is only limited agreement about which items families should be able to afford. Secondly, different social groups are more (or less) likely to say the absence of a 'necessity' is due to choice. Families who cannot afford two or more 'necessities' invariably have a number of 'non-necessities', often many. Their patterns of preferences (and spending) are not typical and they are choosing to buy other goods – through preference rather than poverty. Simply checking whether people lack items for any reason provides results empirically as reliable, but subject to similar criticisms. (McKay, 2004, p 201)

These claims will be examined in turn. First, it has been repeatedly shown that there is a group of deprivation items relating to housing conditions (damp-free home, and so on), diet (three meals a day for children, two meals a day for adults, and so on), warmth (heating to warm the living areas of the home) and social activities (visiting friends or family in hospital) that almost everyone (approximately 90%) agrees are 'necessities'. There is not just a consensus that the items listed are necessities, there is virtual unanimity. This unanimity of opinion has been demonstrated to persist across social groups, time and space. For example, it exists across social groups, by gender, age, social class, ethnicity, education level, and so on. The same virtual consensual opinion on these deprivations or their equivalents is found in all countries and regions in Europe that have so far been surveyed, for example, Britain (Gordon et al, 2000b), Belgium (van den Bosch, 1998, 2001), Finland (Kangas and Ritakillio, 1998), Ireland (Callan et al, 1996), Northern Ireland (Hillyard et al, 2003) and Sweden (Halleröd, 1998). The unanimity on the necessity of these deprivation items across time holds true at both the social group level (see Mack and Lansley 1985; Gordon and Pantazis, 1997; Gordon et al, 2000b) and at individual level in countries where longitudinal data on perception of necessities are available (see van den Bosch, 1998 research on Belgium panel data).

Similarly there are a large number of items covering deprivation of social participation, clothing and consumer possessions for example, that substantial majorities of the population agree are necessities of life. These substantial levels of agreement have been repeatedly demonstrated to be consistent across social groups, space and time, although there are some specific exceptions (see Mack and Lansley, 1985; Gordon and Pantazis, 1997; van den Bosch, 2001 for a detailed discussion of some of these specific exceptions). McKay (2004, p 203) argues that the "variation in different people's ideas of what is necessary... cannot easily be understood or explained". This claim is questionable, as a significant proportion of the variance in perceptions of necessities has been explained. Research has shown that possession status, and, to a lesser extent, life stage and culture that explain the differences in perception of necessities. Van den Bosch (1988, p 149) concluded "possession status (i.e. whether or not the household possesses the given item, and if not, whether it desires it or not) has evidently a very large effect on perceptions of necessities, which generally surpasses that of all other variables combined. After the inclusion of possession status, the effect of the other variables are generally much smaller, and in many cases no longer significant"[4]. McKay did not have data that would have allowed him to repeat this kind of analysis to explain the "variation in different people's ideas of what is necessary", and unfortunately the 1999 PSE Survey asked about perceptions of necessities in the Omnibus survey, but did not include questions on possession of necessities.

Consensus means agreement in the judgment or opinion reached by a group as a whole. It does not mean that there are no individual differences of opinion. As discussed earlier, Mack and Lansley (1983) argued that if 50% of the population agree that an item is a necessity, then this represents a democratic consensus. Halleröd et al (1997, p 215) disagreed with this position by arguing that "'majority' is not the same as 'consensus'". It is, of course, possible to use higher threshold levels to define a consensus. However, if, for example, a two thirds majority (67% agree) is used to define a group consensus, the results on who is poor and how many people are poor change very little. Halleröd et al (1997) used a very detailed weighting method (proportional deprivation index) to allow for differences in the perception of necessities by gender, age and household type. The empirical result was to "confirm the robustness and reliability of the Mack and Lansley method" (p 234).

There is a considerable body of high quality scientific research that can be used to counter McKay's (2004) first criticism that "there is only limited agreement about which items families should be able to afford". In fact, the questions about necessities in the PSE Survey refer specifically and deliberately to adults or children and not to families; therefore, his specific criticism about 'families' is misplaced.

This is not to deny that there are considerable differences of opinion among individuals on what are necessities. For example, the PSE Survey shows that one in 20 people believe that satellite television is a necessity; conversely one in 20 people believe that a damp-free home is not a necessity. The overwhelming majority (95%) disagree. What is important is not that there are differences of opinion among individuals but that these differences do not vary systematically by social group – otherwise, the definition of a necessity would just become the opinion of one group against another. The evidence in this chapter shows that while there are differences of opinion among individuals within social groups, there are relatively few systematic differences of opinion between social groups. For example, Figure 4.1 shows that if 50% of men think an item is a necessity, so will 50% of women and if 80% of women think an item is a necessity, so will 80% of men, and so on. There is a consensus of opinion between social groups, although this does not mean that all individuals have the same opinion.

McKay's second criticism is that since families who cannot afford necessities often possess a number of non-necessities, then this shows that they have atypical preferences and choose to spend their money on 'luxuries' not 'necessities'. He concludes that "such families may be classified as poor using deprivation indicators, when it might be more accurate to say that their consumption preferences deviate from the average" (McKay, 2004, p 220). This argument is problematic; first, it takes no account of the fact that people may possess non-necessities, such as a video recorder, that were purchased before they became 'poor'. Poverty is dynamic and consumer durables and other non-necessities can last for many years. Only 4% of respondents in the PSE Survey who were multiply deprived (could not afford two or more necessities) had been poor 'most of the time' in the past. Over 95% of multiply deprived respondents reported that they had been poor in the past less frequently (if at all). Figure 4.7 shows that there is a clear and unsurprising relationship between the average number of non-necessities a respondent has and their deprivation index score (the number of necessities they don't have and cannot afford). Thus as deprivation increases, the average number of non-necessities a respondent possesses decreases.

There is also a similar clear and unsurprising relationship between the average number of non-necessities a respondent possesses and their self-reported history of poverty (Figure 4.8). The more frequently a respondent reports being poor in the past, the fewer non-necessities they possess.

Figure 4.7: Average number of non-necessities, by respondent's deprivation score

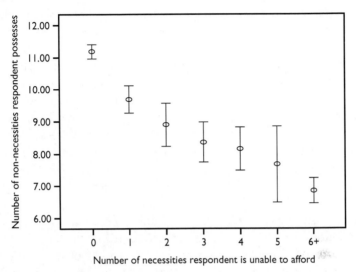

Number of necessities respondent is unable to afford

Note: Bars are 95% Confidence Intervals of the mean.

Figure 4.8: Average number of non-necessities, by respondent's history of poverty

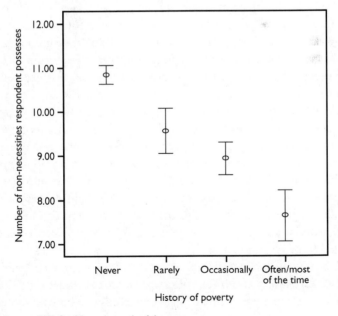

History of poverty

Note: Bars are 95% Confidence Intervals of the mean.

Muffels and his colleagues in the Netherlands developed the subjective deprivation scale (SDS) method to examine exactly the question that McKay has raised (see Muffels, 1993). In the SDS method a respondent is only considered deprived if the item they cannot afford, they or their head of household also consider to be a necessity. A weighting is also applied based on the percentage of the reference group that has the item, reflecting the assumption that not having a necessity is 'worse' if more people in your reference group have it (see Muffels and Driven, 1998, Appendix 1, for details). This kind of complex weighting scheme meets the criticism of McKay, yet the research results show that there is little obvious advantage in using such a complex weighting scheme over the much simpler Mack and Lansley method used in the PSE Survey. For example, results on the longitudinal relationship between income and deprivation showed that in both Belgium and the Netherlands "low levels of deprivation contribute to a decrease in income-to-need, while low levels of income-to-need contribute to an increased level of deprivation", irrespective of whether the SDS method or the Mack and Lansley method is used to measure deprivation (Driven and Fouarge, 1998, p 275).

McKay's final conclusion that "simply checking whether people lack items for any reason provides results empirically as reliable" as the consensual deprivation indicator method. This is an empirical claim that is incorrect. The term 'reliability' often causes confusion because the common usage of the word differs from its scientific meaning. In common usage, a reliable measurement is a correct measurement, that is, something that can be relied upon. However, in scientific terms, a reliable measurement is not necessarily correct – but it is precise. For example, if you were to repeatedly measure an object with a one foot ruler, which in reality was only 11 inches long, you would produce a series of very similar measurements. This series of measurements would be highly reliable even though they were very inaccurate. Scientific reliability is about the consistency of a measurement, not its accuracy and there are a number of statistics that can be used to measure the internal consistency (reliability) of scales such as deprivation indices. The most widely used statistical measure of reliability is Cronbach's Alpha statistic (Nunnally, 1981), which can be interpreted as the average correlation between the set of questions asked (the deprivation index) and all other possible sets of deprivation questions (deprivation indices) of equal length (equal number of questions). Cronbach's Coefficient Alpha for the 35-item deprivation index produced by McKay using the consensual method (don't have and can't afford) is 0.885, whereas for the 35-item non-possession index (can't afford and don't want combined – the original method used by Townsend, 1979) Cronbach's Alpha is smaller at 0.844. Therefore, the consensual method deprivation index used by McKay is more reliable than the non-possession index.

In conclusion, many of the claims made by McKay (2004) about the consensual deprivation method for measuring poverty are problematic. The title of McKay's paper, 'Poverty or preference: what do "consensual deprivation indicators" really measure?', seems to be based on a false premise – consensual deprivation indicators measure both poverty and preference, that is what they are designed to do.

The idea that the 'poor' live in deprived circumstances because they choose to live that way is a very old one. However, a great many scientific studies have shown that the 'rich' do not choose to live like the 'poor', and the 'poor' have no choice but to live in deprivation.

Conclusion

The general public holds ideas about what constitutes the necessities of life that are more wide-ranging, or multi-dimensional, than are ordinarily represented in expert or political assessments. As much importance is attached to some social activities as to some consumer goods. That is the first striking conclusion from the national Omnibus Survey, confirming conclusions drawn from previous but less elaborate surveys carried out in 1983 and 1990. Inevitably, this determines what balance of material goods and activities must shape the *scientific* meaning and measure of poverty.

People of all ages and walks of life do not restrict their interpretation of necessities to the basic material needs of a subsistence diet, shelter, clothing and fuel. There are social customs, obligations and activities that substantial majorities of the population also identify as among the most important necessities of life. Among the customs are celebrations on special occasions, and attendance of weddings and funerals. There are presents at least once a year for family and friends. There are regular events centred around food, like a weekly roast joint or the vegetarian equivalent, which extend our ideas of dietary needs way beyond the provision of minimal calories required of physiological efficiency. And the expression of clothing needs extends ideas about basic cover to include a warm waterproof coat, and two pairs of all-weather shoes.

Among obligations and activities described as necessary are not just those that seem on the face of it to satisfy individual physiological survival and individual occupation – like a hobby or leisure activity. They include joint activities with friends and within families, such as visits to friends or family, particularly if they are in hospital. People also recognise the need to have friends and family round for meals. What is striking is the strength of public acknowledgement that a fulfilment of a range of social activities, roles and relationships take their place among the 'necessities' of life. When establishing need, more account in research should be given to the roles – at work, in family and location – that people consider to be obligatory. The questions on social activities were designed to build on the relative few that had been asked in the pioneering surveys in 1983 and 1990. Substantial majorities of the population represented in the survey were found to believe that visiting family and friends, especially when they are in hospital, collecting children from school, paying visits to the children's schools, for example on sports days, and attending weddings and funerals, compose a necessary part of everyday life. Using a larger number of indicators, the PSE Survey showed that slightly more people specified one or more social activities among the necessities of life than those specifying one or more items concerning housing, food, clothing and consumer durables, for example.

The PSE's forerunner surveys had already confirmed that perceptions of 'necessities' were more broadly based than the corresponding assessments ordinarily made by many economists, and by governments in their policies and legislation. But because of doubts about methodology and sponsorship, the evidence unearthed in these surveys was treated with scepticism in some quarters. And perhaps because indicators of social deprivation were relatively few, compared with those of material deprivation, the implications of the conclusions may have seemed smaller than they really are.

The degree of consensus found between people of different age and gender, and among different groups, was surprisingly strong. There is little doubt that perceptions of necessities are related to individual circumstances at the time of asking, and to the changes in privation and prosperity that individuals may have experienced in the past. Nonetheless, many more people than might have been expected reflect a sensitive awareness of developments that have taken place nationally in living standards. There is greater consensus about national living standards than there is direct experience of those standards.

There are, of course, some important differences between sections of the population. More of the poor than of the rich in the survey considered certain items to be necessities: there was a marked difference, for example, in the case of carpets and a television. But such differences seem to be partly explained by circumstances – more of the rich than the poor live in accommodation with alternative floor coverings, and more of the rich similarly have alternative or multiple forms of entertainment.

The third striking conclusion is that the public's perception of necessities reflects the conditions and dependencies of contemporary life – whether these are created by market availability or by developments in social structure and interaction. They are relative to contemporary conditions. The evidence for this conclusion comes primarily from the comparative analysis of the successive surveys of 1983, 1990 and 1999. One example of the way in which perceptions become updated is easy to understand. Technology and mass production throw up examples as the years pass. Ownership of a telephone has spread, and the percentage of the population finding a telephone a necessity of life has grown rapidly. Although not a majority (in 1999), the proportions of the population finding a car, a video recorder and a home computer a necessity have also grown.

Finally, a notable difference between the 1999 PSE Survey and the previous surveys in 1983 and 1990 is that there are now greater levels of disagreement by age on the definition of necessities. On average, slightly fewer young people consider many items and activities to be necessities than people over 30 years old. This may be a result of the impoverishment of youth (see Chapter Twelve in this volume) during the 1980s and 1990s or it may represent a cultural shift between generations. However, overall there is a widespread consensus in British society on what are the necessities of life that all adults should be able to afford and should not have to do without.

Notes

[1] Survey respondents were asked the same question in relation to children's items and activities.

[2] The ranking of children's items and activities are discussed in Chapter Eleven.

[3] Household income has been equivalised according to the measure developed by Jonathan Bradshaw and Sue Middleton in conjunction with the Office for National Statistics. The scale, unlike the McClements equivalence scale, gives greater weight to children (see Appendix 4 in Gordon et al, 2000b).

[4] Other variables in this analysis included household type, education level, social class, income and region.

References

Andersen, R. and Heath, A. (2002) 'Class matters: the persisting effects of contextual social class on individual voting in Britain, 1964-97', *European Sociological Review*, vol 18, no 2, pp 125-38.

Andreß, H.J. and Lipsmeir, G. (1995) 'Was gehört zum notwendigen Lebensstandard und wer kann ihn sich leisten? Ein neues Konzept zur Armutsmessung', *Aus Politik und Zeitgeschichte, Beilage zur Wochenzeitung Das Parlament*, B, 31-32/95 (28 July).

Berthoud, R. (1997) 'Income and standard of living', in T. Modood, R. Berthoud, J. Lakey, J. Nazroo, P. Smith, S. Virdee and S. Beishon (eds) *Ethnic minorities in Britain: Diversity and disadvantage*, London: Policy Studies Institute.

Booth, C. (1902) *Life and labour of people in London*, Poverty Series, vol 1. London: Macmillan and Co. Limited.

Bradshaw, J., Gordon, D., Levitas, R., Middleton, S., Pantazis, C., Payne, S. and Townsend, P. (1998) *Report on preparatory research*, Bristol: Centre for International Poverty Research, University of Bristol.

Callan, T., Nolan, B., Whelan, B.J., Whelan, C.T. and Williams, J. (1996) *Poverty in the 1990s: Evidence from the 1994 Living in Ireland Survey*, Dublin: Oak Tree Press.

Cook, D. (1997) *Poverty, crime and punishment*, London: Child Poverty Action Group.

Davies, R. and Smith, W. (1998) *The Basic Necessities Survey: The experience of Action Aid Vietnam*, London: Action Aid.

Driven, H.-J. and Fouarge, D. (1998) 'Impoverishment and social exclusion: a dynamic perspective on income and relative deprivation in Belgium and the Netherlands', in H.J. Andreß (ed) *Empirical poverty research in a comparative perspective*, Aldershot: Ashgate. pp 257-82.

Geoffrey, E. (1999) *The end of class politics? Class voting in comparative context*, Oxford: Oxford University Press.

Goode, J., Callender, C. and Lister, R. (1998) *Purse or wallet?: Gender inequalities and income distribution within families on benefits*, London: Policy Studies Institute.

Gordon, D. (2000) 'Inequalities in income, wealth and standard of living in Britain', in C. Pantazis and D. Gordon (eds) *Tackling inequalities: Where are we now and what can be done?*, Bristol: The Policy Press.

Gordon, D. and Pantazis, C. (eds) (1997) *Breadline Britain in the 1990s*, Aldershot: Ashgate.

Gordon, D., Pantazis, C. and Townsend, P. (2000a) *Changing necessities of life*, York: Joseph Rowntree Foundation.

Gordon, D., Adelman, L., Ashworth, K., Bradshaw, J., Levitas, R., Middleton, R., Pantazis, C., Patsios, D., Payne, S., Townsend, P. and Williams, J. (2000b) *Poverty and social exclusion in Britain*, York: Joseph Rowntree Foundation.

Halleröd, B. (1998) 'Poor Swedes, poor Britons: a comparative analysis of relative deprivation', in H.J. Andreß (ed) *Empirical poverty research in a comparative perspective,* Aldershot: Ashgate, pp 283-312.

Halleröd, B., Bradshaw, J. and Holmes, H. (1997) 'Adapting the consensual definition of poverty', in D. Gordon and C. Pantazis (eds) *Breadline Britain in 1990s*, Aldershot: Ashgate, pp 213-41.

Hillyard, P., Kelly, G., McLaughlin, E., Patsios, D. and Tomlinson, M. (2003) *Bare necessities: Poverty and social exclusion in Northern Ireland: Key findings.* Belfast: Democratic Dialogue (www.democraticdialogue.org/ PSEtsvqxf.pdf.pdf).

Kangas, O. and Ritakallio, V.M. (1998) 'Different methods – different results? Approaches to multidimensional poverty', in H.J. Andreß (ed) *Empirical poverty research in a comparative perspective.* Aldershot: Ashgate.

MacDonald, M. (ed) (1997) *Youth, the 'underclass' and social exclusion,* London: Routledge.

Mack, J. and Lansley, S. (1985) *Poor Britain,* London: George Allen & Unwin.

McKay, S. (2004) 'Poverty or preference: what do 'consensual deprivation indicators' really measure?', *Fiscal Studies,* vol 25, no 2, pp. 201-23.

Middleton, S., Ashworth, K. and Braithwaite, I. (1997) *Small fortunes: Spending on children, childhood poverty and parental sacrifice*, York: Joseph Rowntree Foundation.

Modood, T., Berthoud, R., Lakey, J., Nazroo, J., Smith, P., Virdee, S. and Beishon, S. (1997) *Ethnic minorities in Britain,* London: Policy Studies Institute.

Muffels, R.J.A. (1993) *Welfare economic effects of social security. Essays on poverty, social security and labour market: Evidence from panel data,* Series on Social Security Studies, Reports No 21, Tilburg: Tilburg University.

Muffels, R.J.A. and Driven, H.-J. (1998) 'Long-term income and deprivation-based poverty among the elderly', in H.J. Andreß (ed) *Empirical poverty research in a comparative perspective,* Aldershot: Ashgate, pp 229-56.

Murray, C. (1990) *The emerging British underclass,* London: Institute for Economic Affairs.

National Statistics (2002) *Living in Britain – 2001*, London: The Stationery Office.

Nunnally, J.C. (1981) *Psychometric theory*, New Delhi: Tate McGraw-Hill Publishing Company Ltd.

Nyman, C. (1996) 'Inside the Black Box: intra-household distribution of consumption in Sweden', in E. Bihagen, C. Nyman and M. Strand (eds) *Three aspects of consensual poverty in Sweden – work, deprivation, attitudes towards the welfare state and household consumptional distribution*, Umea: Umea University.

ONS (Office for National Statistics) (1999) *ONS Omnibus*, London: ONS.

ONS (2000) *Living in Britain: Results from the 1998 General Household Survey*, London: The Stationery Office.

Pakulski, J. and Waters, M. (1999) *The death of class*, London: Sage Publications.

Pantazis, C. (2000) 'Introduction', in C. Pantazis and D. Gordon (eds) *Tackling inequalities: Where are we now and what can be done?*, Bristol: The Policy Press, pp 1-23.

Payne, S. and Pantazis, C. (1997) 'Poverty and gender', in D. Gordon and C. Pantazis (eds) *Breadline Britain in the 1990s*, Aldershot: Ashgate, pp 97-110.

Pilcher, J. and Wagg, S. (1996) (eds) *Thatcher's children? Politics, childhood and society in the 1980s and 1990s*, London: Falmer Press.

Rowntree, B. (1901) *Poverty: A study of town life*, London: Macmillan.

Rowntree, B. (1937) *The human needs of labour* (new edn), London: Longman.

Rowntree, B. (1941) *Poverty and progress: A second social survey of York*, London: Longman.

Townsend, P. (1979) *Poverty in the United Kingdom*, London: Allen Lane.

Townsend, P. and Gordon, D. (1993) 'What is enough? The definition of a poverty line', in P. Townsend (ed) *The international analysis of poverty*, Hemel Hempstead: Harvester Wheatsheaf, pp 40-78.

Townsend, P. (ed) (1993) *The international analysis of poverty*, Hemel Hempstead: Harvester Wheatsheaf.

van den Bosch, K. (1998) 'Perceptions of the minimum standard of living in Belgium: is there a consensus?', in H.J. Andreß (ed) *Empirical poverty research in a comparative perspective*, Aldershot: Ashgate, pp 135-54.

van den Bosch, K. (2001) *Identifying the poor: Using subjective and consensual measures*, Aldershot: Ashgate.

WHO (World Health Organisation) (1998) *The world health report 1998 – Life in the 21st century: A vision for all*, Geneva: WHO.

FIVE

The concept and measurement of social exclusion

Ruth Levitas[1]

Introduction

The concepts of social exclusion and inclusion are now firmly entrenched in both British and European government policy, as well as having increasingly wide currency outside the European Union (EU) in international agencies such as the International Labour Office (ILO), United Nations, UNESCO and the World Bank (Gore and Figueiredo, 1997; Estivill, 2003). This chapter focuses primarily on the deployment of 'social exclusion' in the United Kingdom, in the context of EU policy, although many of the issues have wider application. The first part of the chapter addresses the development of definitions and indicators of social exclusion at UK national and at EU levels, showing that the distinctively *social* aspects of social exclusion have not been at the centre of these debates. The second part of the chapter outlines the findings of the Poverty and Social Exclusion (PSE) Survey itself, whose unique feature is its direct attention to exclusion from social relations and patterns of sociability. Two key points emerge. First, poverty has a profound effect on some, though not all, aspects of social participation. An objective relationship can be demonstrated here, casting doubt on the significance of the distinction between chosen and enforced non-participation. Second, although paid work is correlated with increased social participation on some measures, there is tentative evidence that this is principally an indirect effect mediated by poverty, and that paid work itself may in some cases limit social inclusion. 'Economic inactivity' does not, in itself, necessarily lead to exclusion from social relations. These findings cast doubt on the emphasis on work that is central to both European and UK policy.

Defining exclusion

Since the Lisbon Summit in 2000, the promotion of social inclusion and social cohesion have been central strategic goals of the EU. Member states are now required to produce biennial National Action Plans for Social Inclusion[2], addressing four key objectives specified at the Nice summit in December 2000, although allowing considerable scope for member states to interpret these in different ways through the 'open method of coordination'. This method means that common objectives are set at European level, while member states design nationally appropriate policies and report on these and on their outcomes, thus both monitoring progress and sharing best practice. The Nice objectives are:

- facilitating participation in employment and access by all to resources, rights, goods and services;
- preventing the risks of exclusion;
- helping the most vulnerable; and
- mobilising all relevant bodies in overcoming exclusion.

Monitoring the progress of such a policy requires the development of appropriate modes of measurement. Thus under the Belgian presidency in 2001, moves were made towards establishing common indicators across the EU, while incorporating the national variation endorsed by the open method of coordination. Debates over indicators involve both issues of definition and pragmatic considerations about the availability of appropriate data. These are discussed below in relation to Britain and Europe, showing how the PSE approach to social exclusion at its inception differs both in theory and in practice from many other approaches, although aspects of it have subsequently been adopted elsewhere.

Despite its current prevalence within and beyond the EU, the terminology of social exclusion and inclusion is of relatively recent origin. In France, it originated with the publication of *Les exclus* (Lenoir, 1974), drawing attention to those excluded from social protection, and it is largely from these origins that it entered the European agenda. In Britain, 'social exclusion' has a separate origin in critical social policy in the 1980s. This draws on the work of Peter Townsend, who argued in 1979 that a proper understanding of poverty should not be limited to questions of subsistence, but should incorporate people's inability to participate in the customary life of society: "Individuals, families and groups can be said to be in poverty when ... their resources are so seriously below those commanded by the average individual or family that they are, in effect, excluded from ordinary living patterns, customs and activities" (Townsend, 1979, p 32). Social exclusion was increasingly used to capture this consequence of poverty, together with its multi-faceted and processual character. It also gained currency in a political climate where Conservative politicians from 1979-97 denied the existence of poverty. There are therefore different national traditions in thinking about exclusion. Hilary Silver (1995) explored national interpretations of social exclusion in relation to Esping-Andersen's model of welfare regimes. Analysis of British public discourse and policy in the 1990s, with some reference to Europe, identified different understandings within as well as between nation states, and offered a model for tracking alternative, shifting and contested meanings (Levitas, 1996, 1998, 2005). This model distinguishes three discourses, with different embedded meanings of social exclusion, its causes, and appropriate policy responses. In the first, RED or redistributive discourse, which is exemplified by British critical social policy, the central problem is that the poor lack resources – not just money, but also access to collectively provided services; poverty remains at the core. Dominant in European discourse in the mid-nineties was a different model, concerned with social integration (hence SID), in which social exclusion was primarily construed as labour market exclusion or lack of paid work, either at an individual or household level. Long-term unemployment and the consequences of economic restructuring were key concerns of the European Observatory on social exclusion in the 1990s (Room, 1995), and this concern with work remains central to the National Inclusion Plans across the EU. In Britain, SID became increasingly visible in New Labour's Welfare to Work programmes and their concerns about 'workless households'. But also detectable was a third discourse, MUD or moral underclass discourse, focusing on the imputed behavioural or moral deficiencies of 'problem' groups. This model was initially used to trace shifts and contradictions in public policy in the 1990s, but also constitutes an analytic device through which the significance of particular indicators can be illuminated.

Discourse and policy have to be excavated in this way to work out what is meant by social exclusion because it is so rarely clearly defined, despite the fact that such definition would seem to be a necessary precursor to effective measurement. The Social Exclusion Unit (SEU), set up in 1997 in the wake of New Labour's first electoral victory, defines it as "a shorthand label for what can happen when individuals or areas suffer from a combination of linked problems such as unemployment, poor skills, low incomes, poor housing, high crime environments, bad health and family breakdown" (SEU, 1997) – although this fails to identify what it is that happens. Walker and Walker (1997, p 8), from a British critical social policy tradition, offer "the dynamic process of being shut out ... from any of the social, economic, political and cultural systems which determine the social integration of a person in society". The Economic and Social Research Council, in making social exclusion a thematic priority for research funding in the UK, glossed it as "the processes by which individuals and their communities become polarised, socially differentiated and unequal". In a European context, Duffy (1995) suggests "inability to participate effectively in economic, social, political and cultural life, alienation and distance from the mainstream society". Estivill, exploring the transferability of the concept beyond Europe, offers a less individualised but more abstract definition: "Social exclusion may be understood as an accumulation of confluent processes with successive ruptures arising from the heart of the economy, politics and society, which gradually distances and places persons, groups, communities and territories in a position of inferiority in relation to centres of power, resources and prevailing values" (Estivill 2003, p 19).

There is, however, a difficulty in distinguishing 'social exclusion' from 'poverty' – sometimes masked by references to 'poverty and social exclusion' as an inseparable dyad. Walker and Walker (1997, p 8) regard them as analytically distinct, reserving 'poverty' for a "lack of material resources, especially income, needed to participate in British society". But some definitions of poverty incorporate aspects of social exclusion. Thus the definition of overall poverty adopted by the Copenhagen World Summit for Social Development involves:

> lack of income and productive resources to ensure sustainable livelihoods; hunger and malnutrition; ill health; limited or lack of access to education and other basic services; increased morbidity and mortality from illness; homelessness and inadequate housing; unsafe environments and social discrimination and exclusion. It is also characterised by lack of participation in decision-making and in civil, social and cultural life. (United Nations, 1995, p 57)

Elements of exclusion from social participation, were, as we have seen, part of Townsend's conceptualisation of poverty in the 1970s. The PSE Survey is a direct descendant of this tradition, with the original

Living in Britain Survey (published as *Poor Britain* (Mack and Lansley, 1985)) addressing criticisms of Townsend's approach by using a consensual definition of poverty, and asking whether lack of necessities was 'chosen' or imposed by lack of resources. Seven of the items in the original list of 35 (potential) necessities could be described as aspects of social exclusion, including a hobby or leisure activity, a holiday away from home once a year, celebrations and gifts for special occasions, and having friends and family – or children's friends – round for a meal. The subsequent Breadline Britain Surveys used the same approach. Consequently, the Breadline Britain/PSE definition of poverty and deprivation in terms of lack of necessities has always incorporated aspects of what is now termed social exclusion.

Indicators of exclusion

If disentangling poverty and social exclusion is conceptually difficult, establishing appropriate measures and indicators is even more challenging. Since both are multi-faceted, they require sets of indicators rather than single ones. Which indicators are chosen, and which are seen as the most important, depends on views of both the nature of social exclusion and its causal connection to poverty, which frequently remain implicit rather than explicit. But the necessity of multiple indicators means that it is possible to draw up a provisional set without clarifying underlying definitions and relationships, and without any statement of priorities. Pragmatic considerations also encourage the use of existing data sets; these are not only relatively cheap and convenient, but permit projection back in time. The effect of this is that rather than moving, as social research ideally should, from definition to operationalisation to data collection, the process is reversed. This has been true of most of the attempts to derive indicators of social exclusion in a British context, a problem that began to be addressed some years before it became a central question for the EU.

The problem was first posed when the SEU was set up in 1997. Its initial remit was to provide 'joined-up solutions to joined-up problems' through reports and recommendations relating to intractable problems crossing departmental boundaries; but it was also charged with the responsibility for deriving appropriate indicators for monitoring progress in reducing exclusion. The general approach of the SEU was – in keeping with its remit – to focus on specific problems. Its first five reports addressed truancy and school exclusions, rough sleeping, poor neighbourhoods, teenage pregnancy and 16- to 18-year-olds not in education, employment, or training, giving rise to the acronym NEET

(SEU, 1998a; 1998b; 1998c; 1999a; 1999b). More recently, it has looked at reducing reoffending, at young runaways, and looked-after children (SEU, 2002a, 2002b, 2003a), as well as at the role of transport in effecting access to services (SEU, 2003b)[3]. Much of the rhetoric around the SEU reports was characterised by the moral underclass discourse, and indeed the truancy and teenage pregnancy reports focused on the traditional demons of the 'dangerous classes' (Morris, 1994) – idle criminal young men and sexually/reproductively delinquent young women (Murray, 1993). There is, of course, a necessary normativity in the definition and measurement of both poverty and social exclusion, in so far as they refer to exclusion from minimally acceptable standards of living, or from common socially sanctioned forms of participation. But the normative judgements implicit in social indicators need to be explicit and interrogated, rather than taken for granted.

By February 1999, however, the responsibility for defining the indicators had been removed from the SEU as the question of social exclusion became more central to government policy and Alistair Darling (in his capacity as Secretary of State for Social Security) announced a commitment to an annual audit of poverty and social exclusion. At that point, the SEU's advice was to consult the recent independent report from the New Policy Institute (NPI), *Monitoring poverty and social exclusion: Labour's inheritance* (Howarth et al, 1998). This was intended to form the basis of an annual audit of poverty and social exclusion, and is indeed sustained as an annual series, offering a battery of 50 indicators. It was only one contribution to the debate taking place in think-tanks and among overlapping groups of academics and policy advisers, including an earlier report from the Institute for Public Policy Research (IPPR) (Robinson and Oppenheim, 1998; see also Howarth et al, 1998; Lessof and Jowell, 2000). The following month, Blair made a further commitment to the abolition of child poverty over a 20-year period (Walker, 1999), reiterated in his 1999 speech to the Labour Party Conference. In October 1999, the Department for Social Security published *Opportunity for All: Tackling poverty and social exclusion* (DSS, 1999). Among other things, this set out the 40 indicators on which the assessment of the government's progress in tackling poverty and social exclusion would be based. Some would be collected for the whole of the UK, while others covered areas of devolved responsibility and thus might differ for England, Wales, Scotland and Northern Ireland.

In none of these reports is there a clear definition of social exclusion and how it might be seen as distinct from poverty. The NPI elides them: "Poverty and social exclusion are concerned with a lack of possessions, or an inability to do things, that are in some sense considered normal by society as a whole" (Howarth et al, 1998, p 18). Indeed, they appear to be treated as synonymous, since "the notion of poverty that has guided the ... report is that where many people lack the opportunities that are available to the average citizen. ... This broad concept of poverty coincides with the emerging concept of social exclusion" (Howarth et al, 1998, p 13). The first *Opportunity for All* (OFA) report similarly fails to distinguish adequately between the two, although it manages also to redefine poverty in terms of lack of opportunity rather than lack of resources. Again, poverty is seen as multi-dimensional: "Lack of income, access to good-quality health, education and housing, and the quality of the local environment all affect people's well-being. Our view of poverty covers all these aspects" (DSS, 1999). But the emphasis shifts to opportunity: "Poverty ... [exists] when people are denied opportunities to work, to learn, to live healthy and secure lives, and to live out their retirement years in security"; "Poverty exists when those on low incomes lack opportunities to improve their position" (DSS, 1999). Low income may be "an important aspect of poverty", but the strategy is focused on those who "are, or are at risk of becoming trapped on low incomes for long periods, especially those who have limited opportunities to escape" (DSS, 1999, p 23). Although the report says that "there are some further dimensions to the concept of social exclusion" they are not clearly defined. The report reiterates the SEU definition, cited above: social exclusion is: "A shorthand label for *what can happen when* individuals or areas suffer from a combination of linked problems such as unemployment, poor skills, low incomes, poor housing, high crime environments, bad health and family breakdown" (my emphasis). It goes on to say that 'social exclusion *occurs where* different factors combine to trap individuals and areas in a spiral of disadvantage" (DSS, 1999, p 23, my emphasis). Both these formulations actually fail to specify *what* 'happens' or 'occurs', and therefore what constitutes social exclusion.

There are both general problems about the use of such large batteries of indicators, and specific difficulties about the indicators chosen. The general issues include: the distinction between measures, indicators, and risk factors; the quality of individual indicators; their individual relevance; their relative importance or priority; the danger of stigmatising certain groups in defining their behaviour or situation as socially excluded; and the implied causal processes involved in choosing indicators (Levitas and Guy, 1996; Dorling and Simpson, 2000; Levitas, 2000; Watt and Jacobs, 2000). For example, 'worklessness' may be included because where a household has no-one in paid work this typically (although not always) results in poverty, although this is an artefact of the wage and benefit system, not a 'natural' process. It reflects a moral value placed on paid work, which stigmatises those outside it and ignores the high proportion of socially necessary labour that takes place outside the labour market. The depth of this assumption is picked up by the NPI, which identifies "a lack of clarity about what social exclusion might mean" for older people, "because neither inclusion within education and training nor inclusion within paid work will be central to overcoming any problem" (Howarth et al, 1998, p 14) – embodying additional assumptions about the significance of age. Many of the indicators in both the NPI and OFA reports relate to low income and labour-market status. The OFA reports also contain indicators relating to the SEU priorities, such as rough sleeping, teenage pregnancy and truancy, as well as drug use, smoking and suicide. The NPI indicators have a broader focus on quality of life, including financial exclusion (Kempson and Whyley, 1999), fear of crime, anxiety and depression, but also include (for children) having divorced parents. There are some striking differences as a result of indicators chosen: the NPI reports show that homelessness has been rising steadily since 1997, while the OFA reports celebrate the fall in rough sleeping over the same period[4].

European indicators

The OFA reports effectively metamorphosed into the National Action Plan for Social Inclusion. Like most member states, for the 2001 'NAPincl', Britain simply reorganised its existing policy and statistics under the Nice headings, emphasising the Sure Start programme as its main example of good practice. However, in December 2001, the Social Protection Committee endorsed a first set of 18 harmonised indicators of social exclusion and poverty, organised in two tiers of 10 primary and eight secondary measures. As can be seen from Table 5.1, the understanding of exclusion implied by these indicators is very much a RED/SID model. Most of the indicators relate either to income or to labour-market position, with data to be derived from the European Community Household Panel (ECHP) Survey and the European Union Labour Force Survey (EU-LFS). The indicators were slightly revised in 2003, dividing the indicator of persons in jobless households into two to separate children and persons of working age, and adding a new secondary indicator, incidence of in-work poverty risk. The terminology used to describe what is being measured changed from 'low income' to 'at risk of poverty', and strong emphasis is placed on

Table 5.1: Harmonised indicators of social exclusion adopted by the European Union in 2001

Primary indicators
1. Low income rate after transfers with low-income threshold set at 60% median income, with breakdowns by gender, age, activity status, household type and housing tenure
2. Distribution of income, using income quintile ratio
3. Persistence of low income
4. Median low income gap
5. Regional cohesion (measured by variation of employment rates)
6. Long-term unemployment rate
7. Persons living in jobless households
8. Early school leavers not in education or training
9. Life expectancy at birth
10. Self-defined health status by income level

Secondary indicators
1. Dispersion around the low income threshold using 40%, 50% and 70% median national income
2. Low income rate anchored at a fixed time-point
3. Low income rate before transfers
4. Gini coefficient
5. Persistent low income (below 50% median income)
6. Long-term (over 12 months) unemployment share
7. Very long-term (over 24 months) unemployment share
8. Persons with low educational attainment

Source: Social Protection Committee (2001)

the need to disaggregate statistics by age and gender. Besides the primary and secondary indicators, member states are expected to use tertiary indicators that would not need to be comparable at supra–national level but would reflect the special circumstances and priorities of different countries.

The indicators eventually adopted by the Social Protection Committee charged with developing them differ from those proposed in a major report to the committee. While the principle of primary, secondary and tertiary indicators is central to the Atkinson report (Atkinson et al, 2002), the scope of the indicators proposed is wider (Table 5.2). They additionally include a number of indicators relating to education, housing and health, thus moving in the direction of a battery of indicators of multiple deprivation. The report also identifies eight areas where significant investment needs to be made in developing appropriate indicators. Most of these relate to aspects of deprivation and inequality, with particular emphasis on educational inequality, but two do reflect on more social aspects of social exclusion: access to public and private services (which is part of the first Nice criterion); and social participation. Any proposal must, of course, be constrained by pragmatic considerations of the kind of data that might practically be collected on a comparable basis. Interpretation of its significance

Table 5.2: Proposed European indicators of social exclusion

Level one
1. The risk of financial poverty as measured by 50% and 60% of national median income
2. Income inequality as measured by the quintile share ratio, ie the ratio of the share of national income received by the top 20% of households relative to the bottom 20% of households
3. The proportion of those aged 18-24 with only lower secondary education (and not in education or training)
4. Overall and long-term unemployment rates measured on ILO basis.
5. Proportion of population living in jobless households
6. Proportion of population dying before the age of 65, or the ratio of those in bottom and top income quintile groups who classify their health as bad or very bad on the WHO definition
7. Proportion of people living in households lacking specified amenities or with specified housing faults

Level two
1. Proportion of persons in households below 40% and below 70% of median income, and proportion below 60% of the median fixed in real terms at a particular date
2. Value of 60% of median threshold in purchasing power standards for one- and four-person households
3. Proportion of the population living in households permanently at risk of financial poverty
4. Mean and median equivalised poverty gap for a poverty line set at 60% median income. (This measures depth of poverty by calculating the extent to which those in poverty fall below the poverty line.)
5. Income inequality as measured by the decile ratio and the Gini coefficient
6. Proportion of the population aged 18-59 (64) with only lower secondary education or less
7. Proportion of discouraged workers, proportion non-employed and proportion in involuntary part-time work, as a percentage of total 18-64 population excluding those in full-time education
8. Proportion of people living in jobless households with current income below 60% median
9. Proportion of employees living in households at risk of poverty (60% median)
10. Proportion of employees who are low paid
11. Proportion of people unable to obtain medical treatment for financial reasons or because of waiting lists
12. Proportion of the population living in overcrowded housing
13. Proportion of people who have been in arrears on rent or mortgage payments
14. Proportion of people living in households unable in an emergency to raise a specified sum

Indicators to be developed
1. Non-monetary indicators of deprivation
2. Differential access to education
3. Housing of poor environmental quality
4. Housing cost
5. Homelessness and precarious housing
6. Literacy and numeracy
7. Access to public and essential private services
8. Social participation and access to internet

Source: Atkinson et al (2002)

must also bear in mind that these are explicitly indicators, not measures, of social exclusion. Nevertheless, while the Atkinson proposals do extend the implicit notion of 'social exclusion' somewhat beyond that of multiple deprivation, there is still a very limited focus on the social.

Alternative approaches

The difficulties of prioritising indicators from the long lists provided by the NPI and the OFA reports, and the slight attention to more social aspects of social exclusion, are partly addressed by two other models, from the IPPR (Robinson and Oppenheim, 1998) and the Centre for the Analysis of Social Exclusion (CASE) (Burchardt, 2000; Hills et al, 2002). The IPPR suggests a more compact index with one lead indicator and some supplementary ones in each of four areas – income poverty, (un)employment, education and health. These four areas are reduced from an initial seven drawn from the SEU definition: unemployment, poor skills, low incomes, poor housing, high crime environments, bad health and family breakdown. The final shortlist of indicators is seen as a first step:

> In the future, we hope further indicators will be developed to assess disadvantage from poor housing, high crime environments, family breakdown, and social and political exclusion, omitted from this report as they are difficult to extract from existing data sources. It is essential to develop indicators of social capital at a later date. Initial suggestions include the proportion of population who are members of a civic organisation and the extent of social support networks. (Robinson and Oppenheim, 1998, p ii)

They note the "genuine difficulties in quantifying ... less tangible aspects of social exclusion" (Robinson and Oppenheim, 1998, p 26), and argue that "it is as yet unclear how one would define, measure and track social and political exclusion". They suggest the possibility of using the British Household Panel Survey (BHPS) to measure 'social capital' by looking at data on social support networks and membership of civic organisations.

The definition of social exclusion later deployed by CASE is rather different, although its empirical data is drawn, as the IPPR suggests, from the BHPS. Burchardt (2002) suggests that there are two distinct ways of thinking about exclusion, one of which is to focus, as the SEU does, on relatively small groups whose problems are seen as extreme or intractable, and the other which is to think in terms of detachment from the core activities of society. The initial definition adopted by CASE is a tripartite one: "an individual is socially excluded if he or she does not participate in key activities of the society in which he or she lives; ... the individual is not participating for reasons beyond his/her control; and he or she would like to participate" (Burchardt et al, 2002, p 30, p 32). The operational model is limited to the first of these clauses – "an individual is socially excluded if he or she does not participate in key activities of the society in which he or she lives" – the issue of choice, discussed further below, being side-stepped for pragmatic reasons. The key activities are defined as: consumption, or the capacity to purchase goods and services; production, or the participation in economically or socially valuable activities; political engagement, or involvement in local or national decision making; and social interaction, or integration with family, friends and community. This model is used to explore empirical data drawn from the BHPS, and therefore has to select indicators from the data contained in that survey.

The CASE model does include some limited attention to social and political engagement, but there are both problems about the definition of 'key activities', and severe limitations deriving from the need to operationalise these dimensions in terms of the data available in the BHPS. The merit of the model is that it is conceptually clear, simple, and capable of retrospective application to the data set. The problem is that the indicators do not map very well on to the definition, or do so only by glossing over problematic hidden assumptions. The indicator for consumption is a proxy indicator of equivalised net household income of less than half mean income, which, unlike the PSE Survey, does not directly address questions of material deprivation. Moreover, access to goods and services is not only dependent on the capacity to purchase them, but on their availability (for example, a functioning public transport system). Participation in economically or socially valuable activities (production) is measured using the now prevalent 'NEET' formula (not in employment, education or training) plus 'looking after family'. The inclusion of the last clause gives a welcome recognition to some unpaid work. However, since those defined as excluded are the unemployed, long-term sick or disabled, early retired, or 'other', the indicator reflects a further embedded assumption: the situation of non-employment for women over 60 and men over 65 does not constitute social exclusion, whereas for those under 'normal' retirement age, it does. The difference, of course, is that prevailing social norms make non-employment legitimate at some ages and not at others. This indicator thus embeds age and gender assumptions (even though from 2006 age discrimination, like gender discrimination, will become illegal across the EU) and is essentially normative rather than descriptive.

Paid work is also prioritised as socially useful whatever its character. However, 'production', especially where this chiefly means participation in the formal economy, and the 'participation in economically or socially valuable activities' are not necessarily the same thing: some forms of production (including cosmetic surgery, cigarettes and arms manufacture) may be considered damaging to individuals, society or the environment, while other economically or socially valuable activities do not constitute production in any meaningful sense. Political engagement is measured simply by voting behaviour and membership of a campaigning organisation. Exclusion in terms of social interaction is assessed by whether an individual lacks support in one of five respects: someone to listen, comfort, help in a crisis, relax with, or who really appreciates them. These, of course, while giving some indication of perceived support, do not directly address the question of social interaction, or integration with friends, family and community.

Social exclusion in the Poverty and Social Exclusion Survey

The PSE Survey has considerable similarities at a conceptual level with the approach of CASE. It is concerned with several dimensions of potential exclusion, and with social, as well as economic (production and consumption), issues. As well as collecting data on impoverishment, labour market exclusion and service exclusion, it operationalises social exclusion in terms of exclusion from social relations, thus offering a much wider range of data than the CASE model draws from the BHPS. Most importantly, unlike the CASE model, it addresses the question of social exclusion directly, rather than drawing on batteries of existing indicators. The focus on social relations pioneered by the PSE Survey has been very influential, and has been subsequently incorporated into regular surveys at both national and European levels. For example, the new 'social capital' section of the General Household Survey 2000/1 now asks questions about civic engagement, social networks, social support and views of the local area, though not participation in common social activities (GHS, 2000/1; ONS, 2001). However, the conceptual background and political implications of 'exclusion from social relations' and 'social capital' are not the same. As Burchardt et al (2002) point out, social exclusion may be considered a problem either from the point of view of the individual or the state. The language of social capital is closely linked to that of social cohesion, and is often primarily concerned with social order and stability. The PSE approach is more explicitly concerned with people's quality of life and the place of social relations in this – and at the impact of poverty and (lack of) paid work on these social relationships. It distinguishes between four dimensions of social exclusion. The first of these, discussed in Chapter Two, is impoverishment, or exclusion from adequate resources or income. The other three are labour market exclusion, service exclusion and exclusion from social relations. Both labour-market participation and access to services are dealt with at greater length in Chapters Six and Eight respectively, but brief general results are set out here, together with an overview of the findings on the main indicators of exclusion from social relations.

Labour market exclusion

Chapter Six considers exclusion from the labour market for both individuals and households. Individual labour-market activity is frequently promoted for its intrinsic benefits in providing an arena of social contact and interaction and as the basis of self-esteem and social recognition, as well as the instrumental benefit of affording a (potential) route to an adequate income. It has therefore both a normative and a practical significance – even though particular jobs may afford neither social satisfaction nor an income sufficient to lift workers out of poverty, or out of dependence on benefits. Linking social inclusion to labour-market activity can imply that adults of any age not in paid work are to be considered socially excluded, whether or not they live with other adults who are in paid work, and whether or not they are poor. Both UK and European indicators of exclusion look at levels of labour-market participation, but also at 'workless' or 'jobless' households, although generally only for those below normal retirement age[5]. Jobless households are at risk of poverty, and possibly other forms of social exclusion.

What the PSE Survey data suggest is that treating either labour market exclusion, or living in a jobless household, as *in themselves* indicative of social exclusion is problematic: a very high proportion of the population constituting 'society' are in these situations. Both, of course, may still work as *indicators* of exclusion, where they correlate with exclusion from social relations. Similarly, both may constitute *risk factors* because of their impact on household incomes, but that makes poverty the real problem. Overall, in 1999 when the survey was carried out, 43% of all adults (50% of women and 36% of men) were not in paid work, and 34% (30% of men and 38% of women) lived in a jobless household. With such high levels of non-participation in paid work, treating this as *constitutive* of social exclusion becomes problematic. The figures do not simply represent those over the statutory 'retirement' or pension age. In the 55-64 age group, nearly two thirds (62%) are not in paid work. A substantial proportion of that age group describe themselves as sick or disabled (15%) or engaged in domestic and caring activities (8%) rather than as retired (33%). Overall, caring responsibilities are six times as likely to take women out of paid employment as men. Those with a long-standing illness are more than twice as likely to be labour-market inactive, and half as likely to be in paid work, compared with those who are well. Similarly, 44% of the 55-64 age group live in a household where no-one is in paid work, as do about one in eight of adults aged between 16 and 24, one in 10 of those aged between 35 and 54, and over half of those with a long-standing illness.

Service exclusion

Exclusion from a range of public and private services is discussed in Chapter Eight. Here Tania Fisher and Glen Bramley show that there are constraints on the use of services of availability, suitability and cost – described in the original PSE report (Gordon et al, 2000) as 'collective' exclusion where the service is unavailable or unsuitable, and 'individual' exclusion where it is unaffordable. The services most affected by these constraints are play facilities, school meals, youth clubs and public transport for children, but as many as one in four of all households are constrained in their use of public transport by inadequate service delivery. Overall, Fisher and Bramley find a strong relationship between service exclusion and poverty, arguing that "poor households face poorer quality services and/or that poverty reinforces constraints on service usage" (p 227). They also find a similar relationship between living in a working-age jobless household and service exclusion, which does not hold for retired households. There does not seem to be a similar correlation between service exclusion and exclusion from common social activities.

An additional aspect of the PSE's conceptualisation of service exclusion is lack of access to basic services inside the home. Utility disconnections can be seen as an exclusion from basic services (gas, electricity, water, telephone) that most people take for granted. In addition, many people who are not disconnected restrict their consumption. Six per cent of respondents have experienced disconnection of one or more services, but 11% have used less than they needed because of cost. Younger respondents are more likely to have been disconnected. One in five of those unemployed have been disconnected, and one in three have restricted consumption; the figures for those in working-age jobless households are slightly lower. One in six of those with a long-standing illness have also used less than they needed because of cost, and the same is true for a similar proportion of households with children.

Exclusion from social relations

Direct exploration of exclusion from social relations was pioneered by the PSE Survey. Five different sets of information address aspects of social participation and sociability:

- non-participation in common activities, some of which have always been included in the Breadline Britain Surveys, but are here given separate and more extended treatment;
- the extent and quality of social networks and the extent to which individuals are socially isolated;
- the support available to individuals on a routine basis and in times of crisis;
- disengagement from political and civic activity; and
- confinement, resulting from fear of crime, disability or other factors.

Confinement resulting from fear of crime is covered in Chapter Nine, although Pantazis argues that fear of crime is more likely to result in risk-avoidance strategies than lead to confinement. Thus the emphasis in this chapter is predominantly on the first four dimensions[6]. Besides a general descriptive overview of the findings, two key issues are addressed: whether work necessarily generates social inclusion in this sense; and the question of voluntary self-exclusion.

Common social activities

The method of enquiry about participation in common social activities is identical to that for the (non)possession of material necessities (Chapter Two). The initial Omnibus survey asked a cross-section of the population what activities they regarded as essential options for all (Chapter Four). The main sample was presented with a shuffle-card question asking, in relation to a range of activities, whether they participate in them; whether they don't do them because they cannot afford them; or whether they don't do them because they don't wish to do so. There is a follow-up question, in which respondents who 'don't do' each specified activity are asked which of a wider list of reasons are important in preventing them. The PSE annotated questionnaire (www.bris.ac.uk/poverty/pse/welcome.htm) lists the activities and the proportion of the population participating in each, and Table 4.1 in Chapter Four details the proportion of the Omnibus sample regarding each activity as a necessity. Some key aspects of social participation regarded by the Omnibus sample as essential were not a regular part of the lives of many of our sample:

- 33% of the population do not have a week's annual holiday away from home;
- 41% do not have an evening out once a fortnight;
- 41% do not have a meal out in a pub or restaurant once a month;
- 22% have no hobby or leisure activity; and
- 18% rarely have friends or family round for a meal, snack or drink[7].

In fact, only a small minority (5%) engages in all the listed activities; 45% are non-participants in one to three activities, and a further 30% in four to six. Nearly a fifth (19%) of the population are participants in half or less of the listed activities, with 6% showing very low participation[8].

There are demographic variations in levels of participation (see Table 5.3). Categories where the risk of non-participation is highest are young adults aged between 16 and 34, and those aged over 65, especially single pensioners; women; single people with children; those who are outside the labour market or (especially) unemployed, or in a jobless household; those with long-standing illness; and those who are poor. Participation is highest among non-pensioner couples and single people without children, and those with a worker in the household. The relationship between paid work and participation is, however, far from straightforward: non-pensioner jobless households show lower participation than those in retirement, with the participation of pensioner couples only just below that for the sample as a whole. And in some categories there is a marked polarisation: women who are labour-market-inactive and/or in jobless households are more likely than average to participate in all activities *and* more likely to be non-participant in seven or more.

Table 5.3: Percentage of respondents not participating in common social activities, by key social and economic variables

	Number of common social activities not participated in			
	1	2	3-4	5+
Age group				
16-34	16	20	23	41
35-54	14	20	30	37
55-64	14	15	32	39
65+	10	10	29	52
Sex				
Male	17	20	24	38
Female	10	14	31	45
Family type				
Pensioner couple	10	14	31	45
Single pensioner	8	8	23	60
Couple with children	10	16	28	46
Couple without children	16	24	31	28
Single adult with children	9	4	21	66
Single adult without children	19	23	27	31
Other	18	16	25	41
Economic status of respondent				
Working	18	21	29	33
Unemployed	20	5	26	50
Economically inactive	7	13	26	54
Workers in household				
No workers	7	11	28	55
Workers	17	20	28	35
Retired	9	11	28	53
Long-standing illness				
Yes	12	15	25	48
No	14	18	30	38
*Below 60% median income**				
Below	8	6	21	65
Above	16	20	30	35
PSE poor				
Yes	3	4	15	78
No	18	22	32	28
Generally poor				
Yes	8	9	21	63
No	17	20	30	34
Social class				
Higher manager and professional	26	28	25	22
Lower manager and professional	16	14	36	34
Intermediate occupations	15	22	33	30
Small employers and own workers	9	23	26	42
Lower supervisory and technical occupations	12	14	35	38
Semi-routine occupations	13	15	21	52
Routine occupations	10	9	22	59
Total	**14**	**17**	**28**	**42**

* Based on the OECD equivalisation scale.

The association between poverty and reduced social participation is clear. The PSE Survey deploys three different measures of poverty (see Chapter Two): income poverty (below 60% median income); general poverty (subjective poverty)[9]; and the PSE index (low income plus material and social deprivation)[10]. Whichever measure is chosen, those who are poor are far more likely not to engage in a wide range of social activities, and all three measures show poverty to be a severe risk factor (Tables 5.4 and 5.5). The income measure alone shows that those below the 60% threshold are three times as likely as those above it to be non-participant in seven or more activities. The pattern is

Table 5.4: Lack of participation in common social activities, by different measures of poverty[11]

	Percentage of respondents		
	Lacks participation in at least one activity	'Can't afford' participation in at least one activity	'Doesn't want' participation in at least one activity
PSE poor			
Yes	99	85	89
No	93	21	93
*Below 60% median income**			
Below 60%	97	60	90
Above 60%	95	30	93
General poverty			
Yes	98	59	93
No	96	30	95

* Based on the OECD equivalisation scale.

Table 5.5: Mean number of common social activities not participated in, by different measures of poverty

	Number of activities		
	Mean number of activities not participated in	Mean number 'can't afford'	Mean number 'don't want'
PSE poor			
Yes	6.4	3.7	2.6
No	3.2	0.4	2.8
*Below 60% median income**			
Below	5.4	2.3	3.1
Above	3.6	0.9	2.7
General poverty			
Yes	5.4	2.5	2.9
No	3.6	1	2.7

* Based on the OECD equivalisation scale.

similar for general poverty. The complex relationship between work and participation is discussed further below, but there is no doubt that it has an indirect effect, since non-participation in paid work at the level of the household often results in poverty.

Social isolation and social networks

Indicators of social isolation include both living alone and the degree of contact with friends and family outside the household. In the PSE sample, 18% live alone. In the younger age groups (16-34, 35-54) men are more likely to live alone than women. The probability of men living alone rises slightly with age, while for women it increases sharply, so that overall women are more likely than men to live alone. One in four of the population over 65 are women living alone, as are one in 10 of the 55-64 age group.

Respondents were asked about the numbers of relatives and friends outside their immediate household whom they saw or spoke to on a daily, weekly or annual basis, including both face-to-face and telephone contact. The key findings here are:

- Only 59% of the sample has at least one relative outside the household whom they see or speak to on a daily basis but 91% have at least one family member they see at least weekly;
- Nine per cent of the population have no family member outside the household whom they see or speak to at least weekly; and
- One per cent has no effective family contact outside the household (that is, no family member they see or speak to at least once a year).

Most respondents have active friendships. However:

- 7% have no friend they see or speak to at least weekly;
- 3% have no friend they see or speak to at least yearly; and
- Just over 1% of respondents have neither a family member nor a friend with whom they are in contact at least weekly. All of these are men. Although this is a tiny percentage, 1% of the population is in excess of half a million people, equivalent to a city the size of Bristol.

In contrast with the pattern of participation in common social activities, there are not large differences between the poor and non-poor using any of the three measures of poverty. There is some evidence of minor differences in network mix. Contacts are biased towards family for the poor and friends for the non-poor. 'Economic inactivity', both for individuals and households, is associated with networks more focused on family than friends, but unemployed individuals are more likely to have regular contact only with friends rather than family. Whereas much policy has focused on the alleged social exclusion of lone parents, the PSE Survey suggests that adults living alone with children are among the least likely to be socially isolated, and the most likely to have both family members and friends with whom they are in regular contact[12]. Poverty also affects the extent of social networks, and here the PSE measure is the best discriminator, with the PSE poor being more likely to have smaller combined networks.

Social support

One of the important aspects of social networks is the support they offer in times of need. Respondents were asked how much support would be available to them in a range of situations:

- needing help around the home if in bed with flu/illness;
- needing help with heavy household or gardening jobs;
- needing someone to look after their home or possessions while away;
- needing someone to look after children or an adult dependant;
- needing advice about an important life change;
- being upset because of problems with spouse/partner; and
- feeling depressed and wanting someone to talk to.

The first four items relate to practical support, the following three to emotional support. Such questions are, of course, partly speculative, and reflect a mixture of people's expectations and experience. They therefore generate data that say as much about the sense of social integration people have as about the practical realities of their lives – and both of these are vital to a proper understanding of inclusion and belonging. The results (Table 5.6) show unequivocally that those who are PSE poor have weaker support than the non-poor, on both practical and emotional indicators[13]. Those in working-age jobless households have support profiles very similar to those in pensioner households, and both groups have much poorer support than those in households with at least one person in paid work. Although the pattern of anticipated support varies slightly, both the 'economically inactive' and the unemployed have relatively poor support. But those most vulnerable to social exclusion on the social support indicators are

Table 5.6: Levels of practical and emotional support, by key social and economic variables

	Practical support			Emotional support			Practical/ emotional support		
	Good	Reasonable	Poor	Good	Reasonable	Poor	Good	Reasonable	Poor
Age group									
16-34	69	27	4	78	20	2	61	31	8
35-54	65	31	4	71	24	5	54	39	8
55-64	60	37	3	64	32	4	46	49	5
65+	54	37	9	35	26	9	48	37	16
Sex									
Male	64	32	4	66	30	4	51	40	9
Female	61	33	6	76	19	6	56	35	9
Family type									
Pensioner couple	64	32	5	74	20	5	57	32	11
Single pensioner	47	39	14	54	34	12	40	41	19
Couple with children	74	23	3	77	20	3	60	36	4
Couple without children	60	35	5	71	24	5	51	41	8
Single adult with children	67	26	7	80	15	5	60	33	7
Single adult without children	46	44	10	65	29	7	43	42	15
Other	67	32	1	71	27	3	57	36	8
Economic status of respondent									
Working	68	29	3	75	21	3	58	36	6
Unemployed	51	38	11	58	36	5	45	43	11
Economically inactive	56	36	8	65	27	7	48	39	13
Workers in the household									
No workers	55	35	10	64	28	8	47	41	12
Workers	67	31	3	74	23	3	56	37	6
Retired	55	36	9	64	27	9	49	36	15

(continued)

Table 5.6: Levels of practical and emotional support, by key social and economic variables (continued)

	Practical support			Emotional support			Practical/ emotional support		
	Good	Reasonable	Poor	Good	Reasonable	Poor	Good	Reasonable	Poor
Long-standing illness									
Yes	62	31	7	67	27	6	52	37	10
No	63	33	4	73	23	5	54	38	8
*Below 60% median income**									
Below 60%	60	31	9	65	28	7	50	39	11
Above 60%	35	32	3	74	22	4	56	38	6
PSE poor									
Poor	52	37	11	59	32	10	41	41	18
Not poor	66	31	3	75	22	3	58	37	6
General poverty									
In general poverty	60	30	10	66	29	6	50	41	9
Not in general poverty	67	30	3	74	23	3	56	37	6
Social class									
Higher manager and professional	71	24	4	74	25	1	57	39	4
Lower manager and professional	57	39	4	70	25	5	52	41	8
Intermediate occupations	65	30	5	79	12	9	60	30	10
Small employers and own workers	58	39	3	62	34	4	46	40	15
Lower supervisory and technical occupations	67	30	3	71	26	3	53	42	5
Semi-routine occupations	64	29	7	75	20	6	58	33	9
Routine occupations	61	34	5	66	30	4	48	42	11
Total	**63**	**32**	**5**	**71**	**24**	**5**	**54**	**38**	**9**

* Based on the OECD equivalisation scale.

those living alone, whether pensioners or working-age adults. Less than half the solo non-pensioners have good expectations of practical support, and 10% have poor support; just over half have good emotional support. In contrast, lone parents have relatively good support, only marginally less than the most-supported groups, couples with children, and slightly better than the sample as a whole. Indeed, although they have slightly lower levels of practical support than couples with children, lone parents are the most likely of any group in the sample to report good emotional support (80%). Generally, lone parents are more like other families with children in terms of anticipated support than like other households with only one adult (see also Chapter Fourteen). Living alone leaves people uncertain of access to social support at times of need. Those living with others (even if those others are children) anticipate better support. Among those who live alone, women in fact fare rather worse than men on both practical and emotional support as well as on the combined indicators.

Civic participation

The PSE Survey collected two sets of information on civic engagement, sometimes referred to as active citizenship. Respondents were asked about a list of activities in which they might have participated in the past three years, ranging from voting to taking part in a political campaign or standing for civic office. Some 73% claimed to have voted in the last general election (1997). While this is not inconsistent with the turn-out, 65% claimed to have voted in the last local election, which by far exceeds the level of voting in these. About 17% had taken none of the listed actions. Respondents were also asked about current active involvement in civic organisations such as sports clubs, parents associations, trade unions and community groups. Here, 44% have no active involvement, with sports clubs claiming the highest number of participants at 18%. Combining the activities and organisations from both questions, 88% of respondents are engaged in some way, leaving only 12% disengaged. However, if voting is excluded, some 30% of the population are disengaged. Analyses of the data, both for the separate and combined variables, show that young people, those not in paid work, and those who are poor have lower levels of participation (Gordon et al, 2000; Bradshaw and Williams, 2000).

Lack of work or lack of money?

For both participation in common social activities and the availability of social support, it is worth exploring a little further whether work in itself has a protective effect in relation to inclusion in social relations, or whether any such effect is indirect, through the relief of poverty. This is an important question in policy terms, for the current dominant assumption is that paid work always promotes inclusion. The PSE Survey suggests that greater scepticism is needed about this, as well as more targeted, probably qualitative, research. There are difficulties in extrapolating from the PSE sample because the numbers in some sub-groups are very small, so the discussion below must be treated as tentative and exploratory. But in looking at the reasons people give for reduced participation, there is some cause to think that paid work can have an inhibiting impact on inclusion in social relations.

One of the limitations of the main shuffle-card question about necessities in the PSE Survey is that it forces a choice between 'don't want' and 'can't afford' as the two alternative reasons for non-participation in common social activities. The forced choice, however, excludes other possible constraints on participation. A secondary question, however, invites respondents to specify a range of reasons that are important in preventing participation, including lack of interest, lack of money, pressure on time from paid and unpaid work, illness and confinement. The 'don't want' category turns out to mask a range of reasons, including lack of interest, but also including sickness and disability, and lack of time. For no activity do these factors compete in importance with lack of money, but significant minorities are affected. For example, for 15% of the whole sample, lack of money is an important factor in not having an evening out once a fortnight, while lack of time resulting from childcare commitments is important for 5% of the whole sample, lack of time due to paid work for 4%, and illness or disability for 3%. For 6% of the whole sample lack of money is important in preventing a hobby or leisure activity, but 3% of the whole sample cite lack of time because of childcare, 3% lack of time because of paid work, and 1% lack of time because of other caring responsibilities. Although these numbers and percentages are small, they indicate substantial numbers in the population whose social participation is squeezed by the time constraints of paid and unpaid work. Pressures on time as a result of paid work ranked in the top five reasons for non-participation for all but two of the listed activities, as did confinement through age, illness or disability. Both men and women, principally in the 16-54 age groups, report time pressures, and those in paid work are most likely to cite both the paid work itself and childcare as important constraints on the time available for social participation.

In relation to social networks, respondents were also asked if they had as much contact with family and friends as they would like, and if not, for the reasons for this. These responses also suggest that paid work is not an unequivocally positive factor in promoting social inclusion. Only 7% of respondents directly cite money as an inhibiting factor, although distance (27%), lack of a car (6%) and poor public transport (4%) might also involve questions of cost. Much more prevalent are claims of pressure of time: 27% cite lack of time due to paid work, 9% lack of time due to childcare responsibilities, and 4% lack of time due to caring responsibilities. For more than one in four of the adult population as a whole (and thus for a significantly higher proportion of those in paid work), employment is a brake on social contact and integration. Indeed, 42% of respondents in paid work, and 38% of all those in households with paid workers, said that work prevents them from seeing friends and family. The time pressures of work get in the way of building and sustaining relationships with families and friends – and 'economic inactivity' does not necessarily result in social exclusion in this regard.

Where social support is concerned, the relationship with work and poverty is again complex. We divided the working-age population into four groups – those not in paid work and in poor households; those in work and in poor households; those in work and not poor; and those not in paid work and not poor (Table 5.7). Those not in

Table 5.7: Levels of practical and emotional support among working and poor households (%)

	In paid work and in poor households (n=70)	Not in work and in poor households (n=36)	In work and not in poor households (n=707)	Not in work and not in poor households (n=11)
Practical support				
Good	70	50	70	73
Reasonable	23	47	29	27
Poor	7	3	2	0
Emotional support				
Good	73	53	78	91
Reasonable	25	42	20	9
Poor	3	6	3	0
Total support				
Good	54	42	60	73
Reasonable	41	56	36	27
Poor	4	3	4	0

work and in poor households have weaker practical and emotional support than the working poor, and the working poor are less likely to have good support than workers in non-poor households. But the very small group not in paid work but not living in a poor household has both the best practical support and by far the best emotional support in the sample. The small size of this group means that it is essential to be cautious about the result. But its implication, if confirmed by further research, would be that non-participation in paid work, when not accompanied by poverty, does not produce social exclusion. It may indeed provide the basis for greater social participation and integration, because of the freeing up of time to invest in social relationships.

Poverty, non-participation and choice

The question of choice has been the topic of debate in social policy for over 20 years. Townsend's (1979) original deprivation index was criticised for not distinguishing between those who chose not to have certain items, and those whose deprivation was enforced. This is why the question of choice is embedded in the CASE definition, discussed above. It is also one reason why the original Breadline Britain methodology was initially devised (Mack and Lansley, 1985) and continued in the PSE Survey itself. On the initial shuffle-card question, for all items except having a week's holiday and having holidays abroad, the proportion saying the activity is unwanted exceeds the proportion saying they cannot afford it. While the poor are three to four times as likely as the non-poor to claim exclusion from at least one activity on the grounds of cost, there is very little difference between poor and non-poor in the extent to which they claim non-participation in at least one activity out of lack of interest. These might be taken as the self-aware responses of rational actors, indicating that a great deal of non-participation even by the poor is chosen. And if we are talking about voluntary self-exclusion, then perhaps this is not a matter for tremendous concern.

However, the shuffle-card and the follow-up questions on individual activities produce different results. The forced choice between 'don't want' and 'can't afford' in the shuffle-card question privileges 'don't want'. The follow-up question, in contrast, allows a wider range of responses. Although lack of interest remains an important expressed reason for non-participation, on this question lack of money rather than lack of interest emerges as the most important inhibiting factor for most of the listed activities. Forcing a choice between 'don't want' and 'can't afford' not only excludes alternative constraints, but conflates the three quite different phenomena of objective, experienced and expressed financial constraint, and suggests that the reasons people give for their (in)actions cannot straightforwardly be treated as causes. Shame is also a likely factor in responses to this question. In a society where identity is increasingly defined in terms of consumption and choice (Bauman 2004), (admission to) the lack of either carries an increased burden of shame. The response 'don't want' preserves individual dignity above 'can't afford'.

The demographic pattern of expressed financial constraint embodied in the 'don't do/can't afford' responses differs from the general pattern of non-participation (Table 5.8, and compare Table 5.3). Generally, the presence of children in the household is associated with a strong sense of financial constraint, with lone parents reporting the greatest financial restriction to social participation. Only 26% of lone parents report no exclusion on grounds of cost, compared with 63% overall; and 31% are excluded by cost from five or more activities, compared with 10% overall and 5% of over those aged over 65. The PSE poor experience levels of exclusion higher than any other group in the sample: 37% are excluded by cost from five or more activities, and 62% from three or more. They are more than three times as likely as the population as a whole to experience exclusion from common social activities because they cannot afford them[14]. But if the impact of poverty is clear, the PSE Survey provides additional evidence for the now established point that people learn to be poor, that is, that the habit of limited consumption and/or participation results in people learning not to want what they cannot afford. Younger people are far more likely than older age groups to attribute their lack of participation to lack of money, bearing out the hypothesis that older people have brought their expectations and aspirations in line with their resources.

These factors led us to expect that the reported pattern of financial constraint understated its objective impact. We therefore looked directly at the relationship between income and non-participation, irrespective of the professed reasons. We plotted the number of activities not participated in against mean equivalised household income (Figure 5.1), which shows declining participation with declining income. Below about £260 equivalised OECD income, social participation is increasingly severely curtailed.

What this suggests is that whatever people say about not wanting to participate in, or not being interested in, particular activities, low income restricts participation, and does so progressively. Of course, no correlation can in itself establish a causal link, but in the absence of any other plausible account of causation at work here, it seems

Table 5.8: Percentage of respondents not participating in common social activities because unable to afford them, by key social and economic variables

	Number of common social activities				
	Can afford all	Can't afford 1	Can't afford 2	Can't afford 3-4	Can't afford 5+
Age group					
16-34	51	13	9	11	16
35-54	65	10	4	11	10
55-64	72	9	4	9	7
65+	70	10	7	8	5
Sex					
Male	65	11	6	9	9
Female	61	10	6	11	12
Family type					
Pensioner couple	72	7	9	8	4
Single pensioner	64	12	6	11	8
Couple with children	47	14	10	13	17
Couple without children	74	10	4	6	7
Single adult with children	26	8	12	24	31
Single person	68	8	4	8	12
Other family type	66	10	4	11	9
Economic status of respondent					
Working	67	12	6	8	8
Unemployed	36	6	5	21	32
Economically inactive	60	9	7	12	12
Workers in the household					
No workers	40	10	9	15	27
Workers	66	11	5	9	8
Retired	69	9	7	9	6
Long-standing illness					
Yes	62	8	7	11	13
No	64	12	6	9	9
*Below 60% median**					
Below 60%	40	12	10	17	21
Above 60%	70	10	5	8	6
PSE index					
Poor	15	11	11	25	37
Not poor	79	10	4	5	1
General poverty					
In general poverty	41	9	8	17	25
Not in general poverty	70	10	6	9	6
Total	**63**	**11**	**6**	**10**	**10**

* Based on the OECD equivalisation scale.

reasonable to conclude that poverty has a direct impact on levels of social participation. This is a somewhat different conclusion from that drawn by Mack and Lansley, who argue that "overall the relationship

Figure 5.1: Household income, by participation (smoothed results)

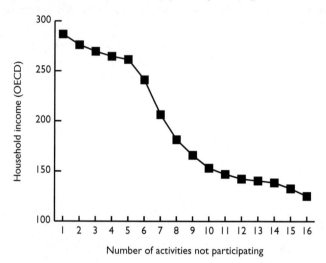

between income and lack of necessities because of lack of desire suggests that … people are, indeed, choosing to go without rather than being forced into this situation" (1985, p 94). Mack and Lansley, however, also acknowledge that there is a serious problem about expressed 'choice' reflecting low expectations, and that "deprivation among those on low incomes may be more extensive than that suggested by people's own judgements of what they can afford and what they want" (1985, p 117).

The implications of this analysis of the PSE results also run directly counter to McKay's (2004) arguments, discussed in Chapter Four. McKay's position is essentially a recapitulation of traditional claims about 'secondary poverty': people are unable to afford 'necessities' because they (mis)spend their money on non-essentials[15]. While he argues that many of the PSE poor are really not poor, since they could afford items they say they cannot afford, this analysis shows, at least in relation to social necessities, that the reverse is the case. Low income restricts participation, even for those who do not give this as a reason.

How much social exclusion?

The multi-dimensional character of social exclusion makes it difficult to give a headline figure for its overall extent as can, with qualifications, be done for poverty. This would be somewhat easier if the different dimensions of social exclusion were more closely associated. Not only

Table 5.9: Percentage of poor people experiencing social exclusion

	PSE poor (26%)	Income poor[6] (24%)	Generally poor (24%)	Total (%)
Not in paid work	57	79	67	44
In jobless household	47	69	61	34
Service exclusion[1]	22	22	20	13
Non-participation in social activities[2]	77	63	62	10
Socially isolated[3]	14	12	11	15
Poor social support[4]	18	11	9	9
Disengaged[5]	20	9	16	12

Notes: 1= excluded from 3 plus services because unaffordable or unavailable/unsuitable; 2 = does not participate in 5 plus social activities for any reason; 3 = no daily contact with either friends or family; 4 = poor support on 4 plus indicators; 5 = not currently involved or involved in the past three years (includes voting); 6 = 60% median income (OECD).

do the proportions of the population excluded on different dimension vary, as Table 5.9 shows, but the relationships between the dimensions are complex, and different indicators of poverty give startlingly different results.

All measures of poverty are associated with an increased risk of detachment from the labour market at both individual and household level. Yet although similar proportions of the population are poor on each poverty measure, it is income poverty rather than deprivation as measured by the PSE Survey that shows the closest association. Poverty is also associated with service exclusion, but has the strongest association with exclusion from common social activities. As we have already seen, poverty does have a strong causal effect on participation in common social activities, and intensity of poverty is associated with intensity of social exclusion on the PSE measures (Bradshaw et al, 2000). Those who are poor have between six and eight times the risk of non-participation in five or more social activities. However, the social isolation dimension, if the cut-off is taken as having no daily contact with either friends or family, is if anything negatively associated with poverty. Contradictory results are obtained for social support and disengagement depending on the poverty measure selected. Among the implications of this finding is that using social support (as the GHS does) or social networks/social capital will produce a rosier picture of inclusion in social relations than the 'common social activities' element of the PSE.

Figure 5.2 looks at social exclusion across eight dimensions, including a single dimension of poverty made up of those defined as poor on any one of the three measures, plus the remaining seven dimensions from Table 5.9: not in paid work; in jobless household; service exclusion;

Figure 5.2: Number of indicators of social exclusion and poverty reported by respondents, out of a possible eight

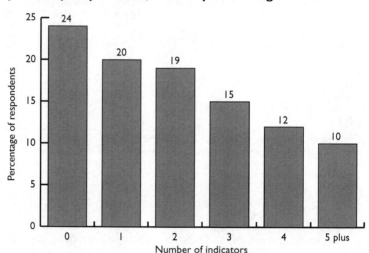

Note: Respondent is poor if counted as poor on any one poverty measure (that is PSE poor, below 60% median income, in general poverty).

non-participation in social activities; socially isolated; poor social support; disengaged. Roughly three quarters (76%) of the population is socially excluded on one or more indicators, but less than a quarter (22%) on four or more out of a possible eight. Even the indicators of exclusion from social relations turn out not to cohere into a single dimension.

The question might therefore be posed as to whether social exclusion is a coherent or useful concept. Given that much of what social exclusion covers, even in the extended form operationalised in the PSE Survey, is either integral to or consequent on the concept of overall poverty (see Chapter Three), it might be seen as dispensable. On the other hand, social exclusion does draw attention to the social aspects and consequences of poverty, which, despite being incorporated into the definition of overall poverty, are not necessarily at the forefront of people's minds.

Conclusion

The key issues that emerge from the PSE's data on exclusion from social relations are these:

- Levels of social participation are affected by age, gender, household type and employment status as well as poverty.
- Poverty has the strongest (negative) effect on social relationships and participation of any of these variables.
- About 9% of the population have low levels of expectation around the amount of social support that might be available to them in times of need or personal crisis.
- Although those in paid work are less likely to be poor, employment does not necessarily promote social inclusion. Pressures on time, both from paid work and informal caring, inhibit social participation for significant numbers of the population.
- People of working age not in paid work and not poor do not appear to suffer exclusion from social relations. This suggests that it is poverty rather than joblessness that is the key problem in terms of the social element of social exclusion.
- Older people in particular may report less exclusion on the grounds of cost because they 'learn to be poor' (see Chapter Fifteen).
- The objective effect of poverty is stronger than would appear from asking people whether they can afford particular activities, suggesting that the long-running question of 'choice' is methodologically problematic.

In some cases, these results are tentative. Three broad conclusions can, however, be drawn. The first is that indicators of social inclusion need routinely to include some that directly address the fabric of social life. The agreed indicators at both UK and European level are overly concentrated on employment and poverty. Without appropriate indicators, the complex relationships between different dimensions of social exclusion cannot be explored. Second, there is a need for more research, probably of a qualitative kind, to explore the impact of poverty and worklessness on social relations. This would facilitate the refinement and development of the indicators used in the PSE Survey. Third, the policy emphasis on paid work as a mechanism for delivering social inclusion is a double-edged sword. Paid work may reduce poverty (although that depends on the level of income it generates) but it simultaneously can create acute problems of work–life balance, reducing the time necessary for social participation and social support.

Notes
[1] The latter part of this chapter draws substantially on Levitas et al (2004). Thanks also to Christina Pantazis for additional analysis for this chapter.

[2] The National Action Plans for the UK can be found at the websites of the Department for Work and Pensions (www.dwp.gov.uk/publications/dwp/2003/nap/index.asp) and the Department of Social Security (www.dss.gov.uk/publications/dss/2001/uknapsi/uknap2001_03.pdf).

[3] For a full discussion of the work of the SEU up to the end of 2004, see Levitas (2005).

[4] For a detailed examination of the IPPR, NPI and OFA indicators, see Levitas (2000).

[5] 'Jobless' is to be preferred to 'workless', since the latter neglects the unpaid work that takes place in all households, especially those with children, as well as any unpaid work outside the home.

[6] A more detailed description of the results may be found in Levitas et al (2004).

[7] These figures include the very small percentages, shown separately in Table 4.1, for whom the recorded reply was 'not applicable'.

[8] In making this calculation, the items relating to schools are included for relevant households, that is, those with school-aged children, only. The total number of relevant items for this group is 15, for the rest of the sample 13.

[9] Respondents in general poverty have been defined as having a net weekly household income that is less than the income estimated by respondents as necessary to need to keep their household out of general poverty.

[10] The closer association between PSE poverty and participation in common social activities is partly generated by an overlap between these two variables.

[11] See note 10.

[12] Throughout this section, since the numbers in each group without significant contact are small, the results must be treated with caution.

[13] We defined 'good', 'reasonable' and 'poor' levels of support on practical and emotional sets of indicators, and for both combined. In all cases, 'good' support means lacking support on *none* of the listed items. 'Reasonable' support means lacking support on one or two items, and 'poor' support means lacking support on three or more items. On the practical items, 63%

of the sample had good support, 32% reasonable and 5% poor support. On the emotional items, 71% had good support, 24% reasonable and 5% poor support. On the combined measure, 54% had good support, 38% reasonable and 9% poor support.

[14] See note 10.

[15] Rowntree defined two types of poverty: primary and secondary poverty. Those in primary poverty were those "whose earnings were insufficient to obtain the minimum necessities for the maintenance of merely physical efficiency" and those in secondary poverty were those 'whose total earnings would have been sufficient for the maintenance of merely physical efficiency were it not that some portion of them was absorbed by other expenditure". Rowntree rejected the argument of his critics that those in secondary poverty were not 'really' poor. In December 1901 he wrote to the *Times:*

> With regard to what I have called 'secondary poverty', I include in this class all those families which proved upon observation and enquiry to be living in obvious want and squalor, but whose poverty was not due solely to insufficiency of income. Your reviewer suggests that these families should not have been returned as living 'in poverty', because their condition was in part due to wasteful and ignorant expenditure. But from the statistical standpoint I was concerned with conditions as they were, and families which were living in 'obvious want and squalor' − i.e. under conditions which rendered them economically inefficient − could surely not be counted as being above the poverty line, whatever the cause of their condition. (Rowntree 1902, quoted in Harris, 2000)

References

Atkinson, T., Cantillon, B., Marlier, E. and Nolan, B. (2002) *Social indicators: The EU and social inclusion*, Oxford: Oxford University Press.

Bauman, Z. (2004) *Work, consumerism and the new poor*, Milton Keynes: Open University Press.

Bradshaw, J. and Williams, J. (2000) 'Active citizenship, social exclusion and social norms', PSE Working Paper No 17 (www.bris.ac.uk/poverty/pse).

Bradshaw, J., Williams, J., Levitas, R., Pantazis, C., Patsios, D., Townsend, P., Gordon, D. and Middleton, S. (2000) *The relationship between poverty and social exclusion in Britain*, Paper presented at the 26th General Conference of the International Association for Research in Income and Wealth, Kracow, Poland, 27 August-3 September (www.bris.ac.uk/poverty/pse).

Burchardt, T. (2000) 'Social exclusion: concepts and evidence', in D. Gordon and P. Townsend (eds) *Breadline Europe: The measurement of poverty*, Bristol: The Policy Press, pp 385-406.

Burchardt, T., Le Grand, J. and Piachaud, D. (2002) 'Degrees of exclusion: developing a dynamic, multidimensional measure', in J. Hills, J. Le Grand and D. Piachaud (eds) *Understanding social exclusion*, Oxford: Oxford University Press, pp 30-43.

Dorling, D. and Simpson, S. (1999) (eds) *Statistics in society*, London: Arnold.

DSS (Department of Social Security)(1999) *Opportunity for All: Tackling poverty and social exclusion*, Cm 4445, London: The Stationery Office.

Duffy, K. (1995) *Social exclusion and human dignity in Europe*, Council of Europe.

Estivill, J. (2003) *Concepts and strategies for combating social exclusion*, Geneva: International Labour Office.

General Household Survey (2000/1) (www.statistics.gov.uk/ssd/surveys/general_household_survey.asp).

Gordon, D., Adelman, L., Ashworth, K., Bradshaw, J., Levitas, R., Middleton, S., Pantazis, C., Patsios, D., Payne, S., Townsend, P. and Williams, J. (2000) *Poverty and social exclusion in Britain*, York: Joseph Rowntree Foundation.

Gore, C. and Figueiredo, J. (eds) (1997) *Social exclusion and anti-poverty policy: A debate*, Geneva: International Labour Organization.

Harris, B. (2000) 'Seebohm Rowntree and the measurement of poverty, 1899-1951', in J. Bradshaw and R. Sainsbury (eds) *Getting the measure of poverty: The early legacy of Seebohm Rowntree*, Aldershot: Ashgate. pp 60-84.

Hills, J., Le Grand, J. and Piachaud, D. (2002) *Understanding social exclusion*, Oxford: Oxford University Press.

Howarth, C., Kenway, P., Palmer, G. and Street, C. (1998) *Monitoring poverty and social exclusion: Labour's inheritance*, London: New Policy Institute/Joseph Rowntree Foundation.

Kempson, E. and Whyley, C. (1999) *Kept out or opted out? Understanding and combating financial exclusion*, Bristol: The Policy Press.

Lenoir, R. (1974) *Les exclus*, Paris: Seuil.

Lessof, C. and Jowell, R. (2000) *Measuring social exclusion*, CREST Working Paper 84, Oxford: Centre for Research into Elections and Social Trends.

Levitas, R. (1996) 'The concept of social exclusion and the new "Durkheimian" hegemony', *Critical Social Policy*, no 46, pp 5-20.

Levitas, R. (1998) *The inclusive society: Social exclusion and New Labour*, Basingstoke: Macmillan.

Levitas, R. (2000) 'What is social exclusion?', in D. Gordon and P. Townsend (eds) *Breadline Europe: The measurement of poverty*, Bristol: The Policy Press.

Levitas, R. (2005) *The inclusive society: Social exclusion and New Labour* (2nd edn), Basingstoke: Palgrave Macmillan.

Levitas, R. and Guy, W. (eds) (1996) *Interpreting official statistics*, London: Routledge.

Levitas, R. with Pantazis, C. and Patsios, D. (2004) 'Social exclusion as lack of social relations: a working paper on the PSE Survey' (www.bristol.ac.uk/poverty/pse).

Mack, J. and Lansley, S. (1985) *Poor Britain*, London: Allen and Unwin.

McKay, S. (2004) 'Poverty or preference: what do "consensual deprivation indicators" really measure?', *Fiscal Studies*, vol 25, no 2, pp 201-23.

Morris, L. (1994) *Dangerous classes: The underclass and social citizenship*, London: Routledge.

Murray, C. (1993) *The emerging British underclass*, London: Institute of Economic Affairs.

ONS (Office for National Statistics) (2001) *Social capital matrix of surveys*, London: ONS Social Analysis and Reporting Division.

Robinson, P. and Oppenheim, C. (1998) *Social exclusion indicators: A submission to the Social Exclusion Unit*, London: Institute of Public Policy Research.

Room, G. (ed) (1995) *Beyond the threshold: The measurement and analysis of social exclusion*, Bristol: The Policy Press.

Rowntree, S. (1902) 'Poverty: the York Enquiry', *The Times*, 1 January, p 13.

SEU (Social Exclusion Unit) (1997) *Social Exclusion Unit: Purpose, work priorities and working methods*.

SEU (1998a) *Truancy and school exclusion*, Cm 3957, London: The Stationery Office.

SEU (1998b) *Rough sleeping*, Cm 4008, London: The Stationery Office.

SEU (1998c) *Bringing Britain together: A national strategy for neighbourhood renewal*, Cm 4045, London: The Stationery Office.

SEU (1999a) *Teenage pregnancy*, Cm 4342, London: The Stationery Office.

SEU (1999b) *Bridging the gap: New opportunities for 16-18 year-olds not in education, employment or training*, Cm 4405, London: The Stationery Office.

SEU (2002a) *Reducing re-offending by ex-prisoners*, London: The Stationery Office.

SEU (2002b) *Young runaways*, London: The Stationery Office.

SEU (2003a) *Making the connections: Transport and social exclusion*, London: The Stationery Office.

SEU (2003b) *A better education for children in care*, London: The Stationery Office.

Silver, H. (1995) 'Reconceptualising social disadvantage: three paradigms of social exclusion', in G. Rodgers, C. Gore, and J.B. Figueiredo (eds) *Social exclusion: Rhetoric, reality, responses*, Geneva: International Labour Organization.

Social Protection Committee (2001) 'Social Protection Committee: Report on indicators in the field of poverty and social exclusion', European Commission (http://europa.eu.int/comm/employment_social/social_protection_commitee/spc_indic_en.htm).

Townsend, P. (1979) *Poverty in the United Kingdom,* Harmondsworth: Penguin.

UK National Plan on Social Inclusion 2001-3 (www.dss.gov.uk/publications/dss/2001/uknapsi/uknap2001_03.pdf).

UK National Plan on Social Inclusion 2003-5 (www.dwp.gov.uk/publications/dwp/2003/nap/index.asp).

United Nations (1995) *The Copenhagen Declaration and Programme of Action: World Summit for Social Development 6-12 March 1995,* United Nations Department of Publications.

Walker, A. and Walker, C. (eds) (1997) *Britain divided: The growth of social exclusion in the 1980s and 1990s,* London: Child Poverty Action Group.

Walker, R. (ed.) (1999) *Ending child poverty: Popular welfare for the 21st century*, Bristol: The Policy Press.

Watt, P. and Jacobs, K. (2000) 'Discourses of social exclusion: an analysis of *Bringing Britain together: A national strategy for neighbourhood renewal*', *Housing, Theory and Society*, vol 17, no 1, pp 14-26.

Part Two:
Processes

SIX

Does work pay? Employment, poverty and exclusion from social relations

Nick Bailey

Introduction

There have been radical changes in welfare and labour market policies across developed countries over the past decade or so, and Britain has been at the forefront of many of these. At a time of major economic restructuring and change in the nature of employment opportunities available, traditional welfare policies have been criticised for failing to facilitate adaptation by individuals to the new 'realities'. They are seen as doing little to encourage retraining or upgrading of skills and, in the opinion of some, they may even prove a barrier to work through financial disincentives. This has led to an emphasis on 'activation' or the use of welfare benefit and labour market policies to promote individual re-entry to work. This is apparent in European Union (EU) and Organization for Economic Cooperation and Development (OECD) policy statements as well as those of many individual countries (OECD, 1994; European Council, 1997; Lødemol and Trickey, 2001).

One aspect of these policies is an increased emphasis on ensuring that individuals have positive financial incentives to move from welfare to work, and that they are supported in this process. In the UK, changes include the introduction of the National Minimum Wage in April 1999 combined with progressive extension of financial support for those in employment through tax credits, starting in October of that year. There has also been the introduction of personal advisers for the unemployed, first for particular groups through the various New Deal schemes, and then for all those on out-of-work benefits through the JobCentre Plus arrangements being rolled out nationally between 2001 and 2006 (DWP, 2004). Such individual support has also been a feature of the area-based Employment Zones (Hales et al, 2003). The other, more controversial, aspect is the growing use of sanctions and compulsion to pressure 'those who can work' to do so. In the UK, there has been a progressive increase in the conditions attached to the receipt of some forms of unemployment benefit over the past 20 years, but the current government has extended this in two key respects: by introducing compulsory activities as a condition of benefit receipt for those under 25 through the New Deal for Young People; and by extending other activation efforts to groups previously seen as being outside the labour market through, for example, compulsory work-focused interviews for lone parents or those on long-term sickness benefits (Trickey, 2001; DWP, 2004).

Two main arguments are used to justify this approach by government. First, there is a concern about the impacts on society as a whole of high levels of unemployment. This leads to high levels of welfare expenditure but also a reduced supply of labour and hence higher labour costs. These have a negative impact on national economic competitiveness. Second, there is a concern with individual welfare. Unemployment and economic inactivity are seen as having negative impacts on individuals, through reduced income and hence higher risks of impoverishment but also through processes of exclusion. Government can argue, therefore, that it is protecting individuals by taking more active steps to encourage them to take paid work (DWP, 2004, for example). This attitude to the promotion of work has been further bolstered by a discourse about social exclusion that defines employment as necessary for inclusion (Levitas, 1998).

A number of criticisms can be made of activation approaches, not least that they place too great an emphasis on the supply side and on the obligation for labour to adjust to the new economic conditions, rather than focusing on the demand side and the obligation on government to ensure that there genuinely is work available for those who want it. This chapter takes a different focus, addressing the question of whether those in work are actually better off than those unemployed or economically inactive. With the rise in insecure or marginal forms of employment, and with growing income inequality, it is clear that not everyone in work escapes poverty or social exclusion. The question here, however, is whether those in work tend to be better off than those not in work – does work pay? This is not just a question about financial rewards, although these are clearly important. If society is going to compel individuals to work partly on the grounds of promoting social inclusion, then the government ought to be clear that work does in general offer these other benefits as well. The concern is that the government's policies are motivated more by national economic considerations than by evidence that work benefits individuals in these different ways.

Within this general focus, two more specific themes are examined. First, there is a question about whether the benefits of work are continuous; in other words, is more work always better in the sense that it leads to greater reductions in the risk of individual poverty or exclusion? Certainly, this appears to be the government's assumption (Hirsh, 2002). The Working Families Tax Credit, for example, encouraged full-time rather than part-time working by providing benefit only if individuals worked at least 16 hours per week and higher levels of benefit for those working more than 30 hours per week. In the analysis presented here, the category of the 'employed' is therefore broken down to distinguish between those working part-time and those full-time. Previous studies have tended to make distinctions between those employed in permanent or secure employment and those in more marginal forms of employment, described as 'insecure' or 'flexible'. This leads to a clear hierarchy, with more secure forms of employment seen as bringing greater benefits (Burchall, 1994; Paugam, 1995). The categorisation into part- and full-time cuts across that hierarchy to some extent. Unfortunately, there are no data in the Poverty and Social Exclusion (PSE) Survey that would permit the construction of categories based on job security as well.

Second, there is a particular focus on whether the benefits of work are equally great for men and women. Previous research suggests that women gain less from employment than men. On the one hand, women tend to be less skilled than men, less well-paid and have fewer opportunities for career progression, so the positive impacts of work on income and status may be less. On the other hand, women tend to have greater domestic responsibilities that are not only an additional burden for those in paid employment but may also be an alternative source of identity and sociability, reducing the social benefits of working (Gallie and Marsh, 1994). On average, women may not need paid work to provide a sense of identity or self-worth to the same extent.

For those not in employment, there have been debates about the boundary between unemployment and inactivity, with much criticism of official approaches to measuring unemployment and research into the scale of the 'hidden unemployed' (Beatty et al, 1997). The government has added to the problems by starting to extend the definition of those who might reasonably be expected to look for work. The approach in this chapter is to treat those not in paid employment as a single group. This is, in part, a pragmatic decision driven by the relatively small number of cases in the various sub-groups of the non-employed. Looking at the indicators of poverty and exclusion, it also appears reasonable to take this approach as differences between the non-working groups are relatively minor.

Throughout this chapter, the focus is on people of working age. The data in this analysis are drawn from two sources – the PSE Survey itself and the original General Household Survey (GHS) from which the PSE sample was drawn. One issue is the difference in timing between the two surveys, as reinterviews for the PSE Survey occurred six to 18 months after the initial survey. Some cases are omitted where data on employment status may be incomplete; details are provided in Appendix 6.1. It should also be noted that the timing of the PSE Survey is significant. It occurred relatively early in New Labour's period of office. Some of the key changes in relation to welfare benefits and the labour market had barely been introduced or were not in effect. The introduction of the National Minimum Wage occurred shortly before the survey while the first in-work tax credits were introduced shortly after it (October 1999) and have since been extended. The effects of the latter are not captured in this work.

The structure of the remainder of the chapter is as follows. The second section looks at the distribution of work and the characteristics associated with higher or lower probabilities of being in work. The third section looks at the relationship between employment status and poverty, while the fourth explores relationships between employment and one dimension of social exclusion – exclusion from social relations. The fifth section provides a summary and concluding comments.

Exclusion from employment

Within the PSE framework, lack of employment is seen as a form of social exclusion in itself. This view, which has been influential with both the UK government and the European Commission, sees paid work for those who want it as a necessary condition for inclusion – the 'social inclusion discourse' in Levitas' (1998) framework. There is thus an implied obligation on the state to ensure that there is work available for those who want it, although governments have been keener to stress the reciprocal obligation that those able to work should do so. There are clear links between this discourse and moves by government to promote more active labour market policies, as the introduction noted. Identifying who is not in paid work is fairly straightforward as this is based on a relatively objective measure, but identifying who wants work but is denied it (or, from the government's point of view, who ought to be working) involves more complex and subjective judgements. Cultural norms are used to define exemptions from the obligation to work based on age, health or other responsibilities such as childcare. This section therefore focuses on the simpler task of describing the characteristics of those in or out of work, as background for the sections on poverty and social exclusion below.

The results from the PSE Survey reinforce what is already known about the distribution of work (Table 6.1). First, they show the important influences of individual characteristics such as gender or age. Overall, the proportion of women working is 8% lower than for men but the gap is greater for middle-age cohorts where the impacts of child bearing and child rearing are most concentrated. For older men and women, the difference in employment rates narrows considerably, although, for those not working, the reasons given are quite different. Older men are more likely to cite early retirement or

Table 6.1: Employment rates, by gender and individual characteristics (%)

	All	Male	Female
All	74	78	70
Age group			
16-24	55	60	48
25-34	85	92	78
35-44	81	95	69
45-54	81	86	78
55-64	52	52	51
Household type			
Single	67	70	59
Couple	73	71	75
3+ adults	72	76	66
Adults with children (youngest under 5)	79	87	75
Adults with children (youngest 5-10)	81	97	68
Adults with children (youngest 11+)	70	75	66
Lone parent			
Not lone parent	75	78	72
Lone parent	50	57	48
Educational attainment			
Degree/other higher qualification	84	89	79
1+ A-level or equivalent	82	82	82
1+ O-level or equivalent	76	83	69
1+ CSE or equivalent	80	86	74
Other or no qualifications	52	58	43
Health/disability			
No limiting long-term illness or disability	81	86	75
Limiting long-term illness or disability	40	42	38

inability to work on health grounds, while women are more likely to be recorded as economically inactive with domestic responsibilities.

Second, the results show how household situation impacts on employment levels. In particular, the presence of younger children in the household is a major influence on employment rates but has very different impacts on men and women (see also Chapter Thirteen in this volume). For households with no children, the proportion of women in paid work is just two percentage points lower than for men but, in households with children, this gap rises to 19 percentage points. This difference is the result not of women with dependent children being less likely to work than those without (69% compared with 70%) but, rather, of men with dependent children being *more* likely to be in employment (88% compared with 72%). This might be seen as evidence that having children encourages men to make greater efforts to seek or remain in employment. Alternatively, it has been suggested that men with poor employment prospects find it more difficult to form or to remain in relationships and hence are less likely to live in households with children (Wilson, 1987). In a longitudinal study, Lampard (1994) showed that a move from employment to unemployment for men is associated with a 70% increase in the probability of a relationship breaking down in the next year. Assuming children are more likely to remain with the mother, this could equally explain the difference between male and female employment rates in households with children.

Other factors are also confirmed as influencing employment rates, including educational attainment and health or disability. With education, the results suggest that any qualification is better than none. The employment rates for those with degrees, A-levels, O-levels or CSEs (or their equivalents) are very similar (between 76% and 84%) but those with none of these qualifications have an employment rate of just 52%. Poor health or disability appears to be the strongest influence on employment of the factors covered here. For those reporting a limiting long-term illness (LLTI) or disability, the employment rate is just 40%, compared with 81% for others. People with an LLTI or disability are much more likely to be recorded as economically inactive for health reasons but it should be noted that there are more people with an LLTI or disability in work than in that category. The effects of health on employment also vary by age, with the gap in employment rates greatest for older people (over 55).

Women are much more likely than men to work part-time (25% compared with 5%) and much less likely to work full-time (45% compared with 73%). Having children in the household also impacts on the likelihood that women will work part-time. In households with no children, the gap between men and women is just 10 percentage points, but this rises to 29 percentage points in households with children. Looking at those not working, the proportion counted as unemployed (on the International Labour Organization definition) is the same for men and for women. Of the economically inactive, men are more likely to be recorded as permanently unable to work or as retired. Women are much more likely to be recorded as looking after the house, but also as students or others.

Logistic regression models are used to confirm that the effects of gender and household type are maintained even when the impact of other factors is controlled for (see Table 6.2.1 in Appendix 6.2). Two models are compared. The first is based on individual and household characteristics with no differences between men and women, while the second allows for the interaction between gender and household type. The models confirm that young people (16-24), those with few qualifications and those with an LLTI/disability are significantly less likely to be in employment. The first model shows that people living alone have a slightly lower employment rate than people in any other household type (with the exception of lone parents), although differences are not very significant. The second model reinforces the point that the presence of dependent children in the household has very different impacts on men and women. Men living in households with children under 10 have significantly higher employment rates than other men, while women in such households have employment rates only marginally lower than other women.

Employment and poverty

For poverty, the impacts of employment are generally expected to be positive. Earnings from paid work are the biggest single source of income and lack of earnings is the major cause of poverty (Sutherland et al, 2003). Changes in employment status or earnings are the main cause of movements into or out of poverty (Jenkins and Rigg, 2001). Employment levels within the household are a major determinant of poverty levels for all members including children, while lifetime employment influences levels of poverty in retirement. Nevertheless, there are important questions over the nature of the relationship between work and poverty. For this chapter, a key question is whether men and women derive the same benefit from working, following the discussion outlined in the introduction. The PSE Survey is particularly useful in this respect as it includes both objective and subjective measures of poverty. The former have the advantage of applying the same objective standard in all cases but the weakness is that they are based on the assumption that resources are equally shared by all household members. The latter apply a much simpler methodology but do allow individual perceptions to be captured and hence, to some extent, permit intra-household inequalities to emerge.

Overall, objective and subjective measures provide similar pictures of the incidence of poverty for men and women. On the PSE's objective measure, some 27% of the working age population are regarded as being in poverty. This is higher for women than men (30% compared with 24%), reflecting the fact that more women are in households with children and that women in work tend to have lower earnings, partly because more work part-time. Looking at the three subjective poverty measures, the patterns are very similar, with working-age women reporting higher poverty levels than men in each case, although the absolute percentages in poverty vary. The general poverty measure falls between overall and absolute measures (19% of the working age population in poverty on this measure, compared with 25% and 15%, respectively). This is the one used for the remainder of this chapter.

Looking at the impacts of individual employment status on poverty levels, objective and subjective measures both show that the benefits of work are positive and continuous (Figure 6.1). Individuals in work

Figure 6.1: Poverty rates, by individual employment status and gender

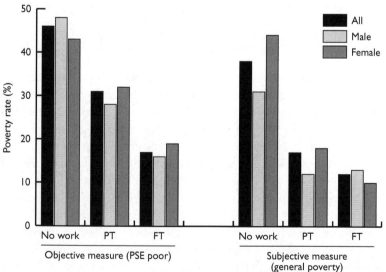

Note: 'PT' – part-time (up to 24 hours per week); 'FT' – full-time (more than 24 hours per week).

have lower poverty rates than those not in work, and full-time workers have lower poverty rates than part-time workers on both measures. While the objective measure suggests that men derive greater benefits from working, however, the subjective measure suggests that it is women who gain more. On the objective measure, non-working women have a lower poverty rate than non-working men, but working women have a higher poverty rate than working men, suggesting that men gain more from a move into employment. On the subjective measure, non-working women have much higher poverty rates than non-working men even though objective measures suggest they are better off on average. As working women have the same poverty rate as working men, it is women who see the biggest gains from work on this measure. Indeed, women working full-time have a slightly lower subjective poverty rate than men in the same situation.

Again, these findings can be formalised through logistic regression models, with the objective and subjective poverty measures as the dependent variables (Table A6.2.2 in Appendix 6.2). The same set of independent variables is used as previously with the addition of a measure of employment status (not working, part-time and full-time). Gender and employment status are combined to allow for differing impacts of employment for men and women (interaction effects). Individual characteristics (age, household type, educational attainment, health) have very similar impacts on objective and subjective poverty rates, suggesting consistency between the two measures, at least for working-age people. By controlling for the effects of these characteristics, the models confirm that the benefits of work are positive and continuous for men and women, with a slightly stronger relationship between employment status and objective poverty than between it and subjective poverty.

The models also show that, while objective measures suggest that men derive much greater benefits from working than women, subjective measures suggest that women derive slightly greater benefits than men (Figure 6.2). Further confirmation can be obtained by looking at men and women separately – in effect, allowing for interactions between gender and all the individual characteristics. Again, using the objective measure, this shows that employment has a much stronger impact on the probability that men will be in poverty than for women. With the subjective measure, however, the benefits of work remain greater for women. Further extensions of the model are possible by restricting cases only to those households with two or more adults and by including an indicator that picks up whether other members

Figure 6.2: Objective and subjective poverty, by employment status and gender

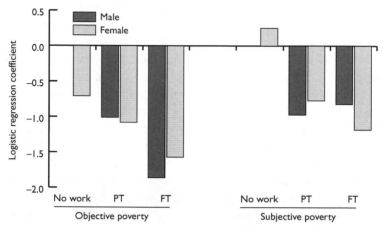

Notes:
'PT' – part-time (up to 24 hours per week);'FT' – full-time (more than 24 hours per week).
Default case for both models is men, not working. Scale shows coefficients for employment status and gender only.
Other characteristics (age, household type, education and health) are controlled for. See Table A6.2.1.

of the household are working or not. In all cases, the picture that emerges is the same.

These findings have a number of implications. First, they support evidence produced elsewhere on the uneven distribution of resources within some households that contributes to the higher levels of poverty experienced by women (Adelman et al, 2000, see also Chapter Thirteen in this volume). The explanation is as follows. Work on the intra-household distribution of resources has shown that, in low-income households in particular, women are more likely to receive less than an equal share of resources, and that they are more likely to forgo items for personal consumption in order to purchase items for children or the household as a whole. Given this, it follows that women are more likely to perceive that a given level of income is insufficient to prevent their household falling into poverty, particularly when on a low income. It has also been shown that the sources of income matter, with problems for women greater when income comes through male earnings (Adelman et al, 2000). Hence, women are likely to see a greater benefit if they themselves are working and gaining direct control over a larger part of the household income. The PSE Survey's objective measure obscures this difference and, as a result, underrepresents the degree of poverty experienced by women. As a consequence, objective measures, including measures based on household income, understate the financial value of work for women. Using subjective measures, work appears more beneficial for women than for men.

Employment and exclusion from social relations

One of the most significant implications of the move from talking about poverty to a focus on social exclusion is that this signals a shift away from a concern with material resources or distributional issues to a concern with social or relational issues (Room, 1995). Critics of this view rightly point out that Townsend's (1979) definitions of poverty and deprivation are framed directly in social or relational terms. These concepts are about the inability of some people to fulfil the *social roles* expected of them by virtue of their membership in society as a result of a lack of material resources. Nevertheless, attempts to operationalise poverty and deprivation measures have tended to focus on the more easily measurable material dimensions. The shift to a social exclusion perspective makes the relational aspects central rather than secondary.

If exclusion from social relationships is seen as important in itself, then labour-market marginalisation may matter if there is a relationship between this and the extent of social interaction. There has been a long-standing interest in the impact of unemployment on *sociability* or the number and frequency of social contacts. The original work in this area comes from a study in Marienthal, Austria in the inter-war period where it was argued that unemployment led to a collapse in sociability as the unemployed isolated themselves from social contact outside the home (Lazarsfeld et al, 1933). Evidence from the UK in the 1980s was more mixed. One qualitative study argued that (male) unemployment was associated with a reduction in sociability (McKee and Bell, 1986, on Britain). Other quantitative studies argued that average levels of contact were little changed by unemployment and that there was wide variation with individuals seeing both increases and decreases (Gallie et al, 1994; Russell, 1999). Gender differences have also been noted with Russell (1999) finding that unemployment led to increased sociability for women but decreased sociability for men, suggesting that work has more benefits for men than women. Further analysis showed that the positive impact of unemployment for women applied much more strongly to those with a history of part-time work, where strong networks existed based around domestic or childcare roles. Women who had always worked full-time were in a similar situation to men, with a loss of employment associated with a reduction in social contact.

The work in Marienthal also examined participation in *social activities*, arguing that (male) unemployment was associated with a withdrawal from public activities into passivity or inactivity. Here, feminist critics have highlighted the way in which this early research equated social activities with those non-domestic, more expensive activities more typically enjoyed by men (Russell, 1999). Looking at a wider range of activities, the change appears rather as the replacement of non-domestic activities with cheaper, home-centred ones (Gallie et al, 1994; Russell, 1999). Seen in these terms, men may experience a greater change on becoming unemployed but this reflects rather different starting points or expectations, and possibly unequal access to resources to pursue social activities in the first place.

As well as being an end in themselves, social relationships may also be important because they are a means to something else. They can act as a resource, providing material or non-material benefits. From a labour-market perspective, there has been a concern with the impacts of employment status on *social segregation* precisely because this is seen as reinforcing exclusion. This has been a feature of the 'underclass' debate, in both conservative and liberal writings (Gallie et al, 2003). Explanations for this effect vary, with conservatives more likely to stress the loss of positive (employment-oriented) role models or attitudes to work, while liberals stress the inability of the unemployed to access information on job vacancies that circulates by word of mouth among the employed. Here there is strong agreement that unemployed people are much less likely to have regular contact with people in employment and this affects both men and women (Gallie et al, 1994; Russell, 1999).

Employment status has also been studied for the impacts it has on *social support* or the practical, emotional and informational resources individuals are able to draw on through their social networks. Research suggests that unemployment has a negative impact on support and that this results from their social segregation (Gallie et al, 1994). Russell (1999) showed that unemployed women did not suffer a loss of support compared with employed women and that they had greater levels of support than unemployed men.

The PSE data are used to examine two of these issues – sociability and social support. On sociability, the PSE Survey includes questions on the total number of friends each person has and on the frequency of contact with friends and family. This permits the construction of two dichotomous variables – 'low number of friends' and 'low levels of contact with friends/relatives' – which can be used as indicators of exclusion from social relationships. For the purposes of this chapter, people were regarded as having a 'low number of friends' if they said they had five or fewer people whom they spoke to or saw every day or nearly every day. They were regarded as having low levels of contact with close friends or family if they saw or spoke to fewer than two a day (or nine a week if none on a daily basis). The thresholds were chosen so that a similar proportion was regarded as excluded on each measure. For both variables, people the respondent lived with were excluded.

On support, there is a series of seven questions on how much support an individual felt they would get with a range of domestic or personal matters, with answers on a five-point scale (Table 6.2). Again this can be used to construct a dichotomous variable indicating which individuals can be considered excluded by having 'low levels of support', defined as those answering not much/none at all to three or more of the support questions. This overall measure of support can be further broken down into measures of practical and emotional support. Individuals were recorded as having 'low levels of practical support' if they answered not much/none at all to two or more of the relevant questions, and as having 'low levels of emotional support' if they answered not much/none at all to one or more of the relevant questions.

Before discussing the findings, there is an important limitation of the PSE Survey to note. The PSE data result from a single cross-sectional survey and the analyses presented here merely contrast the situation of people in different employment situations in terms of levels of social exclusion at one point in time. As a result, it is not

Table 6.2: Support questions in the PSE Survey

Situations	Type
• Help around the home if you are in bed with flu or other illness	Practical
• Help with heavy household or gardening jobs that you cannot manage alone (eg moving furniture)	Practical
• Needing advice about an important change in your life (eg changing jobs, moving to another area)	Emotional
• Being upset because of problems with your spouse or partner	Emotional
• Feeling a bit depressed and wanting someone to talk to	Emotional
• Needing someone to look after your children, an elderly or a disabled adult you care for	Practical
• Needing someone to look after your home or possessions when away	Practical

Note: The statements are prefaced by the question: 'How much support would you get in the following situations?'. Answers are recorded on a four-point scale: a lot; some; not much; none at all.

possible to draw any firm conclusions about the direction of causality. It may be, for example, that differences in social networks, patterns of sociability or levels of support explain differences in employment status, rather than the other way around. Indeed, this is explicit in some of the theories discussed. This is not a problem when looking at the relationship between employment status and poverty because the direction of causality is clear – obtaining work increases income and reduces the risk of poverty. Even here, it could be argued that access to resources (for job search, for example) may mean that the situation is not entirely one-way. For now, all the results presented above are interpreted as if the direction of causality were solely or at least predominantly from employment status to these social outcomes. In the end, only longitudinal data will resolve these questions.

Sociability

Before examining the relationships between employment status and sociability, it is useful to summarise the impacts of personal characteristics on the latter. Overall, 18% of the working-age population are regarded as having few friends and the same proportion have low levels of contact with friends or family. Men are slightly less likely to have a low number of friends but differences are small (17% compared with 18%). Men are slightly more likely to have low levels of contact (19% compared with 16%). Young people tend to have more friends and to be in more frequent contact with family and friends. People with higher educational qualifications tend to have more friends but have lower levels of contact. People with young children (under 11) and those with an LLTI/disability are much more likely to have few friends and low levels of contact. Controlling for all these other factors using logistic regression, there is still no difference between men and women in terms of the probability of having a low number of friends but women are slightly less likely to have low levels of contact with family or friends (that is, women had more contact on average).

Employment status has rather different impacts on the number of friends and on the frequency of contact with family and friends (Figure 6.3). Being in work has a positive and continuous but weak impact on number of friends. It is associated with a modest reduction in the proportion of individuals with a low number of friends from 24% to 15%, with a greater reduction for full-time workers than part-time (14% compared with 19%). Differences between men and women are very small, with both registering gains from employment. Logistic

Figure 6.3: Social relationships, by employment status and gender

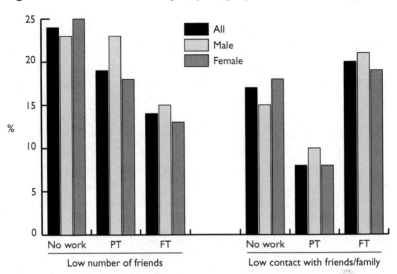

Note: 'PT' – part-time (up to 24 hours per week); 'FT' – full-time (more than 24 hours per week).

regression models confirm this pattern but show that none of the differences is statistically significant (Table A6.2.3 in Appendix 6.2).

By contrast, the relationship between employment status and frequency of contact is discontinuous as well as being slightly stronger. Those in part-time employment are less likely to have low levels of contact than either those with no employment or those working full-time (8%, compared with 17% and 20%, respectively). The effect is stronger for women and logistic regression shows that it is significant for this group once other factors have been controlled for (see Table A6.2.3 in Appendix 6.2). Indeed, full-time work is associated with lower levels of contact than non-employment for both men and women, although differences are not significant when compared with those not in employment.

Social support

Overall, 14% of the working-age population fall into the low support group, with the same proportion identified as having low levels of practical support but a rather higher proportion with low levels of emotional support (29%), reflecting the choice of cut-off points for these indicators. In general, groups with higher levels of sociability, particularly social contact, have higher levels of support, particularly emotional support, as might be expected. Women report slightly higher levels of support with just 12% in the low support group, compared with 17% for men, and this mirrors their higher levels of social contact noted above. The difference is driven by the much higher levels of emotional support reported by women (22% in the low emotional support group, compared with 36% of men). For practical support, there is no difference between men and women. For young people (under 25), high levels of sociability (numbers of friends and contact with family or friends) are accompanied by low levels of support overall, but this is the result of high levels of emotional support offset by low levels of practical support. For people with an LLTI/disability, low scores on both measures of sociability are accompanied by low levels of support overall, driven largely by very low levels of emotional support. People with children have fewer friends but relatively high levels of contact, and this is mirrored in high levels of support, particularly for those with very young children (under five).

Employment status has a much greater impact on levels of support than it does on sociability (Figure 6.4). The relationship is positive but discontinuous, with the highest levels of support experienced by those working part-time rather than full-time. In addition, the benefits of work appear to be greater for men than women. Men not working have the lowest levels of overall support, significantly lower than either women not working or men or women in work (part-time or full-time). For men and women, levels of support are highest for those working part-time. Breaking overall support down into the two components, both relationships remain positive and discontinuous but it is clear that there is a much stronger relationship with emotional than with practical support (Figures 6.5 and 6.6). Men appear to derive

Figure 6.4: Social support, by employment status and gender

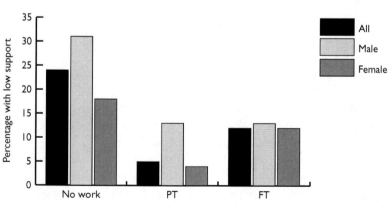

Note: 'PT' – part-time (up to 24 hours per week); 'FT' – full-time (more than 24 hours per week).

Figure 6.5: Practical support, by employment status and gender

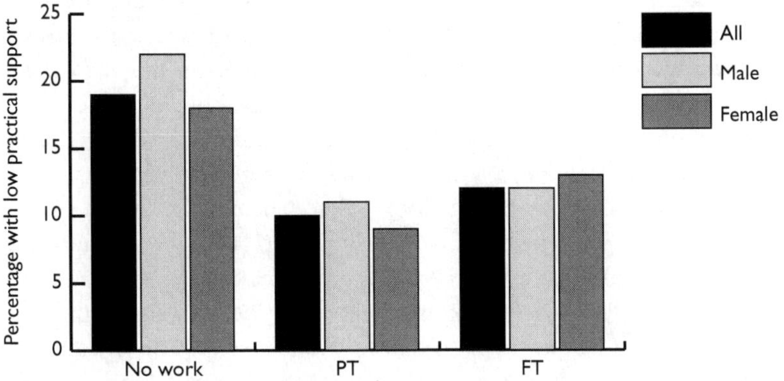

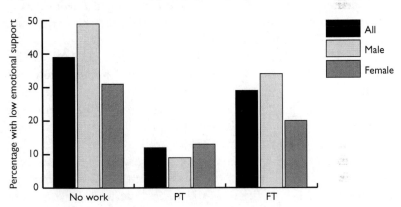

Note: 'PT' – part-time (up to 24 hours per week); 'FT' – full-time (more than 24 hours per week).

Figure 6.6: Emotional support, by employment status and gender

Note: 'PT' – part-time (up to 24 hours per week); 'FT' – full-time (more than 24 hours per week).

slightly greater benefits from work than women, at least in respect of overall support and practical support. For emotional support, there is no difference between men and women in this respect. Logistic regression models confirm these details (see Table A6.2.4 in Appendix 6.2).

Summary and conclusions

This chapter explores the relationships between employment status, poverty and exclusion from social relationships, paying particular attention to differences between men and women and to the situation of part-time and full-time workers. The PSE Survey has made possible a particularly detailed analysis, due to the fact it includes a range of measures covering objective and subjective definitions of poverty, as well as sociability and social support. With this framework, the answer to the question 'Does work pay?' is a complex one. Overall, the picture is positive, with work associated with significantly lower levels of poverty on both objective and subjective measures, and higher levels of support, particularly emotional support. In general, the impacts of employment on poverty are far greater than on exclusion, casting some doubt on the view that work is 'necessary' for inclusion in social relationships. Indeed, it may be as much the case that inclusion raises the chance of being in work as much as the other way around; this analysis cannot lead to firm conclusions on the direction of causality, as noted above. It is also clear that more work is not always better, particularly in relation to social inclusion. In terms of support and in terms of contact with family and friends, part-time employment was associated with significantly lower levels of exclusion than either no work or full-time work. The analysis also stresses that women may gain more from employment in financial terms than objective measures of poverty or income statistics would suggest.

One implication must be the need to pay more attention to the positive value of part-time working and to challenge the view that sees this as second-best. In some respects, the analysis presented here suggests that working longer hours brings not just diminishing but negative returns. Part-time working for many people should be seen as preferable and should be rewarded accordingly – and the incentives or pressures to work full-time should be reduced. This issue may become more important as the government seeks to extend its definition of who 'ought to work' to include a range of groups previously considered out of the labour market – the long-term sick or lone parents, for example. If these groups are to be 'reconnected' to the labour market, it is most likely to be on a part-time basis.

Government has made some attempt to recognise this, for instance in its extension of the right of those on Incapacity Benefits to undertake modest amounts of work under 'therapeutic earnings' rules. Overall, the benefit system remains geared towards full-time employment. From an international perspective, the benefits system in Britain appears unusual in the barriers or disincentives for part-time working (Hirsh, 2002). This analysis also supports work by the Department of Trade and Industry on promoting a better 'work–life balance', and highlights the tensions between that perspective and the drive to reduce welfare bills.

Second, the analysis reinforces findings from other research on the unequal distribution of resources within households. These problems are obscured by the PSE Survey's objective poverty measure, which is based on the assumption that each individual enjoys the same share of household income. Subjective poverty measures do not suffer from the same limitation and, as a result, these suggest that women gain more from employment in material terms. As well as providing a different perspective on the relative value of paid work for men and women, this finding also emphasises the need to continue to pay attention to how resources are channelled into low-income households. With the move from Family Credit to tax credits, a greater proportion of household income may be directed through male partners (Adelman et al, 2000), and that seems to be a step backwards from this perspective.

While the value of the PSE Survey is clear from this analysis, a number of directions for further work are also suggested. The findings reported here are the result of a survey carried out in one country at one point in time. Comparative studies have shown how both material and social benefits of work are shaped by national and temporal contexts, including aspects of welfare policy as well as social structures (Gallie and Paugam, 2000). Since 1999, a number of changes to welfare policy have been implemented in Britain, not least in an effort to increase the financial benefits of work for those on low incomes. It would therefore be extremely interesting to see the exercise repeated to update the picture. Refinements to the data on employment status could enable quality of work to be taken into account as well as quantity. It would also be valuable to extend the work through longitudinal analysis, so that the direction of causality between employment and social relationships could be clearly identified.

Finally, although this chapter has focused on the relative situations of the employed and the non-employed, a large differential between these two groups is not necessarily a positive feature of the welfare regime. The employed may be better off either because of the high level of wages or because the level of welfare support is very low. In terms of poverty rates, for example, the relative gap between employed and unemployed is greater in the UK than in any of the other European countries studied by Gallie et al (2003). This reflects the fact that the UK unemployed are more likely to be in poverty than the unemployed of any of the other countries. Absolute levels of poverty and exclusion in both groups need to be addressed. Work brings some benefits in financial and social terms, but there remain very large numbers of in-work poor and excluded.

References

Adelman, L., Ashworth, K. and Middleton, S. (2000) *Intra-household distribution of poverty and social exclusion*, Loughborough: Centre for Research in Social Policy.

Beatty, C., Fothergill, S., Gore, T. and Herrington, A. (1997) *The real level of unemployment*, Sheffield: Centre for Regional Economic and Social Research, Sheffield Hallam University.

Burchall, B. (1994) 'The effects of labour market position, job insecurity and unemployment on psychological health', in D. Gallie, C. Marsh and C. Vogler (eds) *Social change and the experience of unemployment*, Oxford: Oxford University Press, pp 188-212.

DWP (Department for Work and Pensions) (2004) *Building on New Deal: Local solutions meeting individual needs. Preliminary paper*, London: DWP.

European Council (1997) *The 1998 employment guidelines. Council Resolution of 15 December*, Brussels: DGV.

Gallie, D., Gershuny, J. and Vogler, C. (1994) 'Unemployment, the household and social networks', in D. Gallie, C. Marsh and C. Vogler (eds) *Social change and the experience of unemployment*, Oxford: Oxford University Press, pp 231-63.

Gallie, D. and Marsh, C. (1994) 'The experience of unemployment', in D. Gallie, C. Marsh and C. Vogler (eds) *Social change and the experience of unemployment*, Oxford: Oxford University Press, pp 1-30.

Gallie, D. and Paugam, S. (2000) *Welfare regimes and the experience of unemployment in Europe*, Oxford: Oxford University Press.

Gallie, D., Paugam, S. and Jacobs, S. (2003) 'Unemployment, poverty and social isolation', *European Societies*, vol 5, no 1, pp 1-32.

Hales, J., Taylor, R., Mandy, W. and Miller, M. (2003) *Evaluation of Employment Zones: Report on a cohort survey of long-term unemployed people in the Zones and a matched set of comparison areas*, London: Department for Work and Pensions.

Hirsch, D. (2002) *How much work for those who can?* Presentation to IFS conference 'Social security policy under New Labour: a critical analysis', May 2002, York: Joseph Rowntree Foundation.

Jenkins, S.P. and Rigg, J.A. (2001) *The dynamics of poverty in Britain. Research Report 157*, Leeds: Department for Work and Pensions.

Lampard, R. (1994) 'An examination of the relationship between marital dissolution and unemployment', in D. Gallie, C. Marsh and C. Vogler (eds) *Social change and the experience of unemployment*, Oxford: Oxford University Press, pp 264-98.

Lazarsfeld, P., Jahoda, M. and Zeisel, H. (1933) *Marienthal: The sociology of an unemployed community*, London: Tavistock.

Levitas, R. (1998) *The inclusive society? Social exclusion and New Labour*, Basingstoke: Macmillan.

Lødemel, I. and Trickey, H. (2001) 'A new contract for social assistance', in I. Lødemel and H. Trickey (eds) *'An offer you can't refuse': Workfare in international perspective*, Bristol: The Policy Press, pp 1-40.

McKee, L. and Bell, C. (1986) 'His unemployment, her problem: the domestic and marital consequences of male unemployment', in S. Allen, A. Watson, K. Purcell and S. Woods (eds) *The experience of unemployment*, Basingstoke: Macmillan, pp 134-49.

OECD (Organisation for Economic Cooperation and Development) (1994) *New orientations for social policy. Social Policy Studies No 12*, Paris: OECD.

Paugam, S. (1995) 'The spiral of precariousness: a multidimensional approach to the process of social disqualification in France', in G. Room (ed) *Beyond the threshold: The measurement and analysis of social exclusion*, Bristol: The Policy Press, pp 49-79.

Room, G. (1995) 'Poverty and social exclusion: the new European agenda for policy and research', in G. Room (ed) *Beyond the threshold: The measurement and analysis of social exclusion*, Bristol: The Policy Press, pp 1-9.

Russell, H. (1999) 'Friends in low places: gender, unemployment and sociability', *Work, Employment and Society*, vol 13, no 2, pp 205-24.

Sutherland, H., Sefton, T. and Piachaud, D. (2003) *Poverty in Britain: The impact of government policy since 1997*, York: Joseph Rowntree Foundation.

Townsend, P. (1979) *Poverty in the UK*, Harmondsworth: Allen Lane.

Trickey, H. (2001) 'Comparing workfare programmes: features and implications', in I. Lødemel and H. Trickey (eds) *'An offer you can't refuse': Workfare in international perspective*, Bristol: The Policy Press, pp 249-94.

Wilson, W.J. (1987) *The truly disadvantaged: The inner city, the underclass and public policy*, Chicago, IL: University of Chicago Press.

Appendix 6.1: Note on methodology

Data for the PSE Survey were collected six to 18 months after the General Household Survey (GHS) from which the sample was drawn. While the PSE Survey supplied information on poverty and social exclusion, much of the data on individual and household characteristics comes from the GHS. This includes data on incomes, household composition and employment status. While the PSE Survey rechecked the data on incomes and household composition, it did not check for changes in employment status directly. For the analyses conducted for this chapter, two sets of problems may arise, resulting from changes in household composition and from changes in employment status for existing members.

Changes in household composition may impact on employment status for the household as a whole. There were no changes in 1,420 households, while 43 saw individuals leave and 78 saw individuals arrive (with seven seeing both leavers and arrivals). In cases where all new arrivals are children (36 individuals, 34 households), there is no problem with employment figures and these are included. In cases where some or all new arrivals are adults (52 individuals, 44 households), the employment status of the new arrivals is unknown and these households are therefore excluded from analyses in this chapter. Where individuals left between the GHS and the PSE Survey (58 individuals in 43 households), the individuals can be excluded when estimating employment levels for the household at the time of the PSE Survey so these households can be included in employment analyses.

The employment status of existing residents was not rechecked at the time of the PSE Survey but there is some indirect information on this through questions on changes in household income. Where there has been a significant change in income for the respondent or the household as a whole, supplementary questions ask the main reasons for this, and some of the responses are employment-related. Households can be included where it is reasonable to assume that there has also been no change in employment status for any household member. That includes households where:

- there has been no change in household income (905 households out of 1,534);
- there has been a change in income *and* this is due to employment reasons not related to starting or finishing work (for example, changing job, promotion or pay rise – 207 households);

- there has been change in income *and* this is due to non-employment-related reasons (increase in occupational pension, in interest rates or 'other' – 323 households).

Households are excluded from the analyses where:

- there has been change in income *and* this is due to change in the amount of employment (job loss, (re-)entering employment or retirement – 77 households);
- there are no data on changes in household income (22 households).

Thus a relatively cautious approach has been adopted that excludes cases where information on employment status is not known and cannot be reasonably inferred.

Appendix 6.2: Logistic regression tables

Table A6.2.1: Logistic regression models – employment rates

	B	Sig	Exp(B)	B	Sig	Exp(B)
Female	−0.98	***	0.38	−0.42		0.66
Age (16-24)						
25-34	1.75	***	5.76	1.76	***	5.81
35-44	1.42	***	4.13	1.39	***	4.03
45-54	1.83	***	6.25	1.78	***	5.91
55-retirement age	0.25		1.28	0.31		1.36
Education (Degree)						
A-level/equivalent	0.05		1.05	0.10		1.10
O-level/equivalent	−0.48	*	0.62	−0.46	*	0.63
CSE/equivalent	0.06		1.06	0.04		1.04
Other/none	−1.34	***	0.26	−1.37	***	0.25
LLTI/disability	−1.61	***	0.20	−1.59	***	0.20
Household type (Single)						
Couple	0.69	*	1.99	0.66	*	1.94
Adults (3+)	0.47		1.60	0.61		1.84
Adults + child(ren) under 5	0.72	*	2.06	1.70	*	5.46
Adults + child(ren) aged 5-10	0.51		1.66	1.95	**	7.05
Adults + child(ren) aged 11+	0.22		1.24	0.35		1.42
Lone parent	−1.04	**	0.36	−0.89	*	0.41
Female and household type						
Female and couple				−0.12		0.89
Female and adults (3+)				−0.40		0.67
Female and adults + child(ren) under 5				−1.57		0.21
Female and adults + child(ren) aged 5–10				−2.13	**	0.12
Female and adults + child(ren) aged 11+				−0.48		0.62
Constant	0.84	*	2.31	0.62		1.87

Model summaries		
	Model 1	Model 2
Cox and Snell R Square	0.23	0.24
Nagelkerke R Square	0.33	0.35

Notes:

1. Dependent – working (not working). Independent variables show default category in brackets unless dichotomous variables. 'LLTI' – limiting long-term illness.

2. Significance levels: * <0.1; ** <0.01; *** <0.001.

3. Second model includes interaction term for gender and household type. Hence 'household type' coefficients for that model refer to men only so the default category is single men. The 'female' coefficient shows the position of single women (relative to single men). The position of women in couple households (relative to single men) is given by adding the coefficients for 'couple' to the coefficient for 'female' and the coefficient for 'female and couple' (0.66 + −0.42 + −0.12 = 0.12).

Table A6.2.2: Logistic regression models – objective and subjective poverty

	PSE poverty (objective)			General poverty (subjective)		
	B	Sig	Exp(B)	B	Sig	Exp(B)
Age (16-24)						
25-34	0.32		1.37	0.31		1.36
35-44	−0.80	*	0.45	−0.13		0.88
45-54	−0.19		0.82	0.21		1.23
55-retirement age	−1.68	***	0.19	−0.80	*	0.45
Household type (Single)						
Couple	−0.93	**	0.39	−0.63	*	0.53
Adults (3+)	−0.95	**	0.39	−0.77	*	0.46
Adults + child(ren) under 5	0.76	*	2.13	0.82	*	2.28
Adults + child(ren) aged 5-10	0.36		1.43	−0.05		0.95
Adults + child(ren) aged 11+	−0.56		0.57	0.19		1.21
Lone parent	1.10	**	2.99	1.39	***	4.01
Education (Degree)						
A-level/equivalent	0.16		1.17	0.45		1.57
O-level/equivalent	0.73	**	2.07	1.18	***	3.26
CSE/equivalent	1.61	***	4.98	1.48	***	4.38
Other/none	1.68	***	5.38	1.64	***	5.15
LLTI/disability	1.07	***	2.91	1.22	***	3.37
*Gender **and** employment status (Male – no work)*						
Male – PT	−1.01	*	0.37	−0.97		0.38
Male – FT	−1.86	***	0.16	−0.82	*	0.44
Female – no work	−0.71	*	0.49	0.25		1.28
Female – PT	−1.08	**	0.34	−0.77	*	0.46
Female – FT	−1.57	***	0.21	−1.18	**	0.31
Constant	−0.20		0.82	−2.08	***	0.13

Model summaries	PSE poverty (objective)	General poverty (subjective)
Cox and Snell R Square	0.24	0.19
Nagelkerke R Square	0.35	0.30

Notes:

1. Dependent – in poverty on objective or subjective measure (not in poverty). Independent variables show default category in brackets unless dichotomous variables. 'LLTI' – limiting long-term illness.

2. Significance levels: * <0.1; ** <0.01; *** <0.001.

3. The combined effects of gender and employment status are shown as a single variable, with the default category being men not in employment.

'PT' – part-time (up to 24 hours per week); 'FT' – full-time (more than 24 hours per week).

Table A6.2.3: Logistic regression models – social relationships

	Low number of friends			Low levels of contact with friends/family		
	B	Sig	Exp(B)	B	Sig	Exp(B)
Age (16-24)						
25-34	1.27	**	3.56	0.88		2.40
35-44	0.53		1.69	2.05	**	7.76
45-54	1.54	**	4.67	2.57	***	13.02
55-retirement age	1.20	*	3.34	2.01	**	7.45
Household type (Single)						
Couple	−0.15		0.86	−0.30		0.74
Adults (3+)	0.00		1.00	−0.49		0.61
Adults + child(ren) under 5	0.58		1.79	0.85	*	2.34
Adults + child(ren) aged 5–10	1.07	**	2.92	0.58	*	1.78
Adults + child(ren) aged 11+	−0.18		0.83	−0.30		0.74
Lone parent	−0.10		0.91	−0.14		0.87
Education (Degree)						
A-level/equivalent	0.48		1.61	−0.09		0.91
O-level/equivalent	0.54	*	1.72	0.04		1.04
CSE/equivalent	1.53	***	4.62	−0.76	*	0.47
Other/none	1.37	***	3.93	−0.29		0.75
LLTI/disability	0.91	***	2.47	0.83	***	2.29
*Gender **and** employment. status (Male – no work)*						
Male – PT	0.32		1.38	−0.22		0.80
Male – FT	−0.26		0.77	0.46		1.58
Female – no work	0.09		1.09	0.09		1.09
Female – PT	−0.06		0.94	−0.92	*	0.40
Female – FT	−0.26		0.77	0.41		1.50
Constant	−3.72	***	0.02	−3.64	***	0.03

Model summaries		
	Low number of friends	Low levels of contact with friends/family
Cox and Snell R Square	0.11	0.10
Nagelkerke R Square	0.19	0.16

Notes:

1. Dependent – low number of friends or low levels of contact with friends or family (not low). Independent variables show default category in brackets unless dichotomous variables. 'LLTI' – limiting long-term illness.

2. Significance levels: * <0.1; ** <0.01; *** <0.001.

3. The combined effects of gender and employment status are shown as a single variable, with the default category being men not in employment.

'PT' – part-time (up to 24 hours per week); 'FT' – full-time (more than 24 hours per week).

Table A6.2.4: Logistic regression models – social support

	Low levels of support – overall			Low levels of support – practical			Low levels of support – emotional		
	B	Sig	Exp(B)	B	Sig	Exp(B)	B	Sig	Exp(B)
Age (16-24)									
25-34	−0.96	*	0.38	−0.59		0.55	0.38		1.46
35-44	−1.24	**	0.29	−0.46		0.63	0.35		1.41
45-54	−0.72	*	0.48	−0.94	*	0.39	0.84	**	2.33
55-retirement age	−1.27	**	0.28	−1.41	**	0.24	0.43		1.54
Household type (Single)									
Couple	−0.58	*	0.56	−0.48		0.62	−0.16		0.85
Adults (3+)	−1.52	***	0.22	−1.45	**	0.24	−0.21		0.81
Adults + child(ren) under 5	−2.60	**	0.07	−0.61		0.54	−0.17		0.84
Adults + child(ren) aged 5-10	0.12		1.12	−0.28		0.76	0.10		1.11
Adults + child(ren) aged 11+	−0.66		0.52	−0.86	*	0.42	0.22		1.25
Lone parent	−0.03		0.98	−0.10		0.90	−0.56		0.57
Education (Degree)									
A-level/equivalent	−0.26		0.77	−0.50		0.60	−0.14		0.87
O-level/equivalent	0.35		1.42	−0.16		0.85	0.26		1.29
CSE/equivalent	1.22	***	3.40	0.54		1.72	0.56	*	1.75
Other/none	0.28		1.33	0.24		1.27	0.40	*	1.50
LLTI/disability	0.58	*	1.78	0.24		1.27	0.35	*	1.42
*Gender **and** employment status (Male – no work)*									
Male – PT	−1.57	*	0.21	−0.98		0.38	−2.28	**	0.10
Male – FT	−1.19	***	0.30	−1.01	**	0.36	−0.57	*	0.56
Female – no work	−0.84	*	0.43	−0.53		0.59	−0.73	*	0.48
Female – PT	−2.28	***	0.10	−1.23	**	0.29	−1.77	***	0.17
Female – FT	−1.15	**	0.32	−0.78	*	0.46	−1.25	***	0.29
Constant	0.25		1.28	0.11		1.11	−0.74	*	0.47

Model summaries

	Low support – overall	Low support – practical	Low support – emotional
Cox and Snell R Square	0.10	0.05	0.08
Nagelkerke R Square	0.18	0.09	0.12

Notes:

1. Dependent – low levels of support overall, instrumental and emotional (not low). Independent variables show default category in brackets unless dichotomous variables. 'LLTI' – limiting long-term illness.

2. Significance levels: * <0.1; ** <0.01; *** <0.001.

3. The combined effects of gender and employment status are shown as a single variable, with the default category being men not in employment.

'PT' – part-time (up to 24 hours per week); 'FT' – full-time (more than 24 hours per week).

SEVEN

Debt and financial exclusion

Stephen McKay and Sharon Collard

Introduction

This chapter discusses the concepts of debt and financial exclusion, and shows what light may be shed on these issues by the Poverty and Social Exclusion (PSE) Survey. As well as being one of the first major surveys to investigate these issues, the PSE Survey is in a unique position to consider how far both debt and financial exclusion are related to poverty, low income and social exclusion.

The issues of debt and financial exclusion are often studied in parallel in academic, government and other commentaries (for example, Drakeford and Sachdev, 2001; Church Action on Poverty, 2002; DWP, 2003). But these two topics are conceptually distinct and should not be conflated. In particular, people who make little or no use of financial services are not necessarily in arrears with their credit or other household commitments. Indeed, they may have eschewed financial products, in favour of cash, as one means of minimising their risk of arrears. The risks of being financially excluded or having arrears are both, however, increased among people who live on low incomes (Kempson and Whyley 1999a; Kempson, 2002).

There are also a number of important causal links between debt and financial exclusion. Certainly, being financially excluded can lead a person into debt, for example by having to use more expensive forms of credit (such as moneylenders) to deal with an emergency. However, some forms of debt, such as on credit cards or bank loans, presuppose a degree of financial inclusion within the mainstream of financial products. It is also possible that indebtedness later leads to exclusion. A record of default may, through credit scoring in the industry, prevent a person gaining further access to products. Conversely, some people use a range of financial products without getting into financial difficulties. We might therefore construct the following table indicating the four main possibilities (Table 7.1).

Table 7.1: Typologies of debt and financial exclusion

		Financial exclusion	
		Excluded	**Not excluded**
Debt status	**In debt**	Use of non-standard lenders with high interest rates. Past history of debt.	Using loans, credit cards, etc. perhaps over-committed or affected by change in circumstances.
	Not in debt	Low-income cash economy, some careful managers, often older group.	Managing financial products with no problems, and/or on a high income.

Many financial products have long been restricted to richer groups. In recent times, access to financial services has become much more widespread. In 1975, for example, just 45% of adults had a current account; that figure is now 87% (DWP, 2005). It is this growth that has perhaps focused attention on those excluded from or not participating in mainstream financial services. Now those lacking such access are more clearly isolated from the mainstream. Within an increasingly cashless or electronic economy (Pahl, 1999), the consequences of remaining outside the mainstream financial services market have become more serious. In particular, it is far more costly to operate a household budget without basic financial services – conservative estimates put the cost at over £200 a year.

In addition, the likelihood of having limited access to financial products and services is concentrated both geographically and among certain groups of people (Kempson and Whyley, 1999a). As a result, it forms an important component of a much wider social exclusion and has become a prominent aspect of social exclusion debates in the UK (Kempson et al, 2000). For example Ruth Kelly, while a minister at the Treasury, said that: "The Government attach great importance to tackling financial exclusion – it is a key part of our strategy for ending social exclusion" (*Hansard*, 15 Oct 2001, column 862W).

Defining financial exclusion

Although the term 'financial exclusion' has gained common currency in recent years, its definition remains rather ambiguous. In some of the earliest academic work on financial exclusion, it was used to refer to "those processes that prevent poor and disadvantaged social groups from gaining access to the financial system" (Leyshon and Thrift, 1995, p 312). This focused largely on *geographical* access to financial services, particularly in relation to bank and building society branch closures in both urban and rural areas.

More recent studies have centred on the types of people who make little or no use of financial services, and the complex processes by which they are excluded (Ford and Rowlingson, 1996; Kempson and Whyley, 1998; Kempson and Whyley, 1999a; OFT, 1999). In particular, several specific dimensions of financial exclusion have been identified, including:

- *access exclusion*: the restriction of access through the processes of risk assessment by financial institutions;
- *condition exclusion*: where the conditions attached to financial products make them inappropriate for the needs of some people;
- *price exclusion*: where some people can only gain access to financial products at prices they cannot afford; and
- *self-exclusion*: people may decide that there is little point applying for a financial product because they believe they would be refused. In some cases, this is a result of having been refused personally in the past, in others because they know someone else who has been refused, or because of a belief that 'they don't accept people who live round here' (Kempson and Whyley, 1999a).

Kempson et al (2000) list a number of different examples in their review of financial exclusion. They range from lacking a bank account (of any kind), to lacking a non-state pension, to having no life insurance. However, they do not offer a succinct definition of financial exclusion. In another review, Sinclair (2001, p 6) suggests that "financial exclusion means the inability to access necessary financial services in an appropriate form". In the National Action Plan on Social Inclusion 2003-05 (DWP, 2003, p 10), financial exclusion is defined as "the lack of access to, and inability to take advantage of, basic financial services and products".

Defining debt

The rather emotive term 'debt' is used to describe two quite different situations. First, it is frequently used to refer to use of credit, and having outstanding money to repay. So someone is said to be 'in debt' if they, say, have a personal loan from a bank, owe money on a credit card, or have bought goods on hire purchase or through a mail order catalogue. At any one time, half the population owes money on consumer credit but 94% of credit borrowers are up to date with the repayments (Kempson, 2002).

At the same time, debt is also used to refer to financial difficulties, and people are said to be 'in debt' if they have fallen behind with the payments on any of their household bills or other commitments. Sometimes the term 'problem debt' is used for this.

The recent survey *Over-indebtedness in Britain* (Kempson, 2002), commissioned by the Department of Trade and Industry (DTI), showed that 20% of households were in financial difficulty. A minority (7%) were struggling financially but not actually in arrears, while 13% had fallen behind with payments on either household bills or other regular commitments (Kempson, 2002). Households at greatest risk of being in arrears included families with children, and especially lone parents. The risk of arrears was highest among young people and fell with increasing age. There was also a strong link with income, but only among non-pensioners. These findings are very much in line with earlier studies (Berthoud and Kempson, 1992).

The Poverty and Social Exclusion Survey

The PSE Survey makes a number of contributions towards studying financial exclusion and debt. The questionnaire probed a number of relevant areas, as follows:

- whether the respondent or their partner/spouse has a bank or building society current account;
- whether they can afford home contents insurance;
- whether they can afford to make regular savings (at least £10 a month) for rainy days or retirement;
- whether there have been times during the past year when they have been seriously behind in paying within the time allowed for any of a long list of items (for example, credit cards, loans, utility bills); and
- if there have been times in the past year when they have borrowed from pawnbrokers or moneylenders (excluding banks or building societies), or from friends or family, in order to make ends meet.

Dimensions of financial exclusion and debt

A range of different dimensions that may be taken to characterise financial exclusion and indebtedness is shown below (Table 7.2). The financial problem areas listed range from one in 20 lacking a current account, to one in four who cannot afford regular savings or who worry about the prospect of debt. Close to one in three (32%) do not have any regular savings, mostly through being unable to afford to

Table 7.2: Dimensions of financial exclusion

Dimension of financial exclusion	% of respondents excluded on each measure
Has no bank or building society current account	5
Cannot afford home contents insurance	8
[cannot afford or doesn't want]	[13]
Has used informal kinds of borrowing, such as moneylenders or family	11
Doesn't use banks, or thinks the local service is inadequate	13
Has been seriously behind with repaying bills or credit in last year	14
Cannot afford regular savings	24
[cannot afford or doesn't want]	[32]
Is 'worried' about having financial debts	26
Any of the above	48
Unweighted base	1,534

save. Some 14% have been in arrears with household bills or credit commitments within the last year, while 11% have borrowed in a range of fairly non-standard ways simply to make ends meet. Taking all these different features together, almost half (48%) report one or more of these dimensions of financial exclusion or debt, while 23% report two or more such problems.

Overlaps with poverty

Each of these dimensions of financial exclusion or debt is more common among those in poverty, often by a very large margin (Table 7.3). Only 1% of the non-poor lack a current account, compared with 16% of those in poverty. Similarly, some 42% of the poor have current or previous problems repaying credit or bills, compared with just 4% of the non-poor. There are also strong links between this measure of poverty and respondents being unable to afford either savings or contents insurance – but since these two questions are constituent parts of the poverty definition the link is at least partly circular.

The association between debt and financial exclusion, and a more subjective personal impression of poverty over time, is also very strong (Table 7.4). This measure removes the problem of circularity of using the earlier poverty definition to explore links between financial exclusion and poverty. Among those saying they are poor now 'all the time', half cannot afford home contents insurance, and three-quarters cannot afford regular savings. Similarly, one in five of those poor 'all the time' do not have a current account. The link to debt is also very

Table 7.3: Poverty, financial exclusion and debt (%)

Dimension of financial exclusion	Poor	Not poor	All
Has no bank or building society current account	16	1	5
Cannot afford home contents insurance	30	1	8
Has used informal kinds of borrowing, such as moneylenders or family	34	3	11
Doesn't use banks, or thinks the service is inadequate	19	10	13
Has been seriously behind with repaying bills or credit in past year	42	4	14
Cannot afford regular savings	75	7	24
Is 'worried' about having financial debts	53	16	26
Unweighted base	572	962	1,534

Table 7.4: Poverty over time, financial exclusion and debt (%)

	Do you think you could genuinely say you are poor now?		
Dimension of financial exclusion	All the time	Sometimes	Never
Has no bank or building society current account	20	10	2
Cannot afford home contents insurance	50	17	2
Has used informal kinds of borrowing, such as moneylenders or family	50	28	3
Doesn't use banks, or thinks the service is inadequate	28	16	10
Has been seriously behind with repaying bills or credit in past year	61	34	4
Cannot afford regular savings	78	49	12
Is 'worried' about having financial debts	72	53	14
Unweighted base	151	398	972

strong. Among those poor all the time, some 61% are behind with bills or credit, as are 34% of those saying they are sometimes poor. These figures compare with 14% overall, and just 4% of the never poor.

The following sections look separately at financial exclusion, and then debt, before examining policy reactions to them. But next we analyse the links between financial exclusion and debt.

Linking financial exclusion and debt

Although it has been stated that financial exclusion and debt are distinct, they often affect the same people. Something of the overlap between them may be gauged from Table 7.5. Among those lacking a bank account, and aged 16-59, over half have borrowed to make ends meet,

Table 7.5: Extent of debt, by bank account ownership

| | % of each group with arrears or borrowing | | |
	Has account	No account	Total
Among those aged 16-59			
Has arrears	16	56	18
Borrowed	13	50	15
Among those aged 60+			
Has arrears	3	26	4
Borrowed	3	4	3
Unweighted base: aged 16-59	740	118	858
Unweighted base: aged 60+	614	62	676

and slightly more are in arrears. The incidence of debt and arrears is much lower among those aged 60 or more, as we show above and as is clear from the final column, but among this group having arrears is strongly associated with not having a bank account.

Financial exclusion

Analysis of the PSE Survey clearly indicates that certain types of people are much more likely to be financially excluded than others. Those who run the highest risk of financial exclusion: tend to live on low incomes; are members of minority ethnic groups; rent their home from a local council or housing association; are lone parents; live in households where no one works; have no or low educational qualifications; and live in large urban areas. Age also has an impact and there is some evidence of regional effects. To a large extent, these findings confirm the results of earlier work, which show that the chances of being financially excluded depend not only on who you are but also where you live (Kempson and Whyley, 1999a).

The following sections examine in more detail each of these measures of financial exclusion, looking at those most likely to be excluded and the consequences of that exclusion.

Access to current accounts

A current account from a bank or building society is perhaps the most basic financial product. Without one, money management – and bill payment in particular – can be complex, time-consuming and considerably more expensive. During the past decade, direct debits have become the most common way of paying regular household bills such as electricity, gas, water and telephone. In 2002, over half of regular bills were paid by direct debit compared with around one in three in 1995. Moreover, 60% of gas and electricity bills are now settled in this way (APACS, 2003).

People who are unable to use direct debits because they do not have a current account instead employ a range of bill-payment methods, including paying in cash at a post office or a bank branch, using pay-as-you-go methods such as prepayment meters or buying savings stamps (Kempson and Whyley, 1998). The most important drawback of settling bills in these ways is that it is much more expensive, particularly for people who make small, frequent payments or use a prepayment meter (Kempson and Whyley, 1999a). In addition, cash payment of bills excludes people from the discounted energy tariffs available to direct debit users (Kempson and Whyley, 1998; Speak and Graham, 2000). Indeed, consumers typically pay more than £70 extra a year if they cannot pay their utility bills by direct debit (Klein et al, 2004).

As well as providing a cost-effective means of bill payment, a current account can also provide access to other financial products and services, including short-term credit facilities such as an overdraft (Kempson and Whyley, 1998; Kempson and Whyley, 1999a). In addition, some financial products and services require customers to have access to a current account. In particular, many insurance policies can only be paid for by cheque or direct debit (Whyley et al, 1998).

Who does not have a current account?

Overall, 5% of respondents in the PSE Survey do not have access to a current account, that is, neither they nor their partner have an account. Current account holding is lowest among the under-25s (Table 7.6). Many of these young people would, however, be likely to open an account in the future, when they move into paid employment.

Income, ethnicity, and educational qualifications all have a significant impact on current account holding. Where people live is also important, with those in the North West of England and Scotland being less likely to have an account than people living in other areas of Britain. Other research has found higher proportions lacking accounts in Northern Ireland (DWP, 2003).

The most pronounced effects, however, are in relation to household type, tenure and economic status. A third of lone parent families manage their money without a current account, compared with just 3% of two-parent families (Figure 7.1).

In addition, people living in jobless households and those who rent

Table 7.6: Access to current accounts, by age group

Age group	Unweighted base	% with no current account
16-24	97	11
25-29	77	2
30-39	266	5
40-49	199	5
50-59	219	4
60-69	267	5
70 or over	409	5
All	1,534	5

their home from a social landlord are four times more likely not to have an account than the average.

The PSE Survey also provides some insight into why people do not have a current account. Overall, half of those who do not have access to an account state that it is a matter of choice – they either do not want to use banks or building societies or feel they are irrelevant to their lives. Earlier research has also shown that many people value the financial control that operating a cash budget provides, particularly in relation to bill payment (Collard, 2001a; Kempson and Whyley, 2001; MORI, January 2001; University of Warwick and University of East Anglia, 2001).

Despite these views, 60% of the people excluded from banking consider it essential to have access to banks and building societies (Table 7.7). So not having a current account does not appear to be the result of downplaying the significance of their role in society. Overall, three quarters of people think that having access to banks is essential.

Figure 7.1: Percentage of respondents lacking a current account

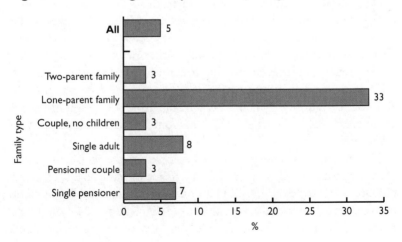

Table 7.7: Importance of access to banks, among those with and without accounts (%)

Do you think having access to banks is:	Has current account	No current account	All
Essential	77	60	76
Desirable, but not essential	22	38	23
[Don't know, spontaneous]	1	4	1
Unweighted base	1,348	178	1,526

Home contents insurance

Previous research has indicated that the people most likely to be excluded from insurance products tend to have low incomes, little if any money saved, and no access to a current account that might offer them short-term credit facilities. As a result, their ability to cope financially with unforeseen events is extremely limited (Kempson et al, 2000).

People with few resources of their own may have family or friends they can turn to for help. More often than not, however, their friends and relatives are in a similar financial position and so can only offer limited assistance, if any (Whyley et al, 1998). State support for people who have suffered a fire, flood or burglary is similarly limited. They could, in some circumstances, apply to the Social Fund for help. There are, however, strict eligibility criteria for all the discretionary elements of the Social Fund. It also has a limited budget and, as a result, a high proportion of applications are turned down (see, for example, Collard and Kempson, 2005).

The PSE Survey indicates that 13% of people do not have a home contents insurance policy. In 8% of cases, this is because they cannot afford the premiums. Those least able to afford insurance cover in the event of a fire, flood or burglary mirror the overall patterns of financial exclusion. It is worth noting, however, that nearly four in 10 lone parents (39%) said they are unable to afford this type of insurance. A third (32%) of non-white respondents are in the same position. In addition, people living in the West Midlands and London are more likely to say they cannot afford home contents insurance than those living in other parts of Britain.

Previous studies have shown that people unable to obtain home contents insurance are deprived of the peace of mind that such cover provides (Whyley et al, 1998). The PSE Survey suggests a high degree of correlation between not having insurance and concerns about being burgled. Nearly four in 10 people (39%) with no home contents insurance are very worried about being burgled, compared with just under two in 10 (17%) of those with cover. To some extent, these concerns are well-founded, as people without insurance are nearly four times as likely to have been burgled in the past year than those who have insurance (15% compared with 4%, respectively). Moreover, poor people living in areas with high levels of crime are unlikely to be able to afford home contents insurance simply because they *are* very likely to be burgled and consequently face high insurance premiums (Pantazis and Gordon, 1997; Whyley et al, 1998).

Regular savings

Like insurance cover, savings give people the peace of mind of knowing they have a financial safety-net they can draw on to cope with emergencies or to cover unexpected or 'lumpy expenditure'. Financial security is a particular concern among parents, and lone mothers especially, who aspire to put money aside to pay for their children's weddings, help them through higher education and, ultimately, leave as an inheritance (Rowlingson et al, 1999). But while many people living on low incomes save informally to help make ends meet or for discretionary spending, few are able to put money aside regularly for the longer term.

The threat of a 'pensions crisis' in Britain has fuelled concerns among government, the financial services industry and consumer groups that people are generally not saving anywhere near enough money for their retirement (see, for example, Pensions Commission, 2004). Yet, among those surveyed, about a quarter (24%) said they cannot afford to save regularly for a rainy day or retirement.

The ability to save regularly was, as we would expect, closely correlated with income. So while around four in 10 people in the two lowest income groups cannot afford to put money aside, this is true of less than one in 10 people on the highest incomes (Table 7.8). Once again, lone parents, people from minority ethnic groups and those living in socially rented accommodation are among those least able to save.

There are also some regional variations – people living in the North East, West Midlands and London are most likely to say they cannot afford to save regularly, in contrast to those living in the eastern part of England and the South West.

Table 7.8: Income groups unable to afford to save regularly, by income (PSE-equivalised) (%)

All	24
Lowest quintile	36
Second	40
Third	27
Fourth	13
Highest quintile	7

Debt

As mentioned earlier, households at greatest risk of being in arrears tend to include families with children, and lone parents in particular. The risk of arrears is highest among young people. There is also a strong link with income among non-pensioners (Berthoud and Kempson, 1992; Kempson, 2002). Various changes in circumstance have also been identified as being strongly correlated with arrears, including having a new baby, separation/divorce and a fall in income.

People living on low incomes usually have limited access to many forms of high street credit. Their financial situation means they are unlikely to pass the credit checks carried out by mainstream consumer credit companies (Kempson et al, 2000). Instead, they often turn to their family and friends for small amounts of money to tie them over from one week to the next. This is particularly common among women, with mothers and daughters frequently lending to one another in this way (Kempson et al, 1994). However, for larger sums of money, family and friends are often unable to help out. As a result, people may then use moneylenders or pawnbrokers, each of which is a high-cost source of credit. Licensed moneylenders, for example, may charge an annual percentage rate (APR) of between 100% and 500%, depending on the size and length of the loan (Rowlingson, 1994; Kempson and Whyley, 1999a). The APRs charged by pawnbrokers typically range between 70% and 200% (Collard and Kempson, 2003). As a last resort, people may even borrow from unlicensed moneylenders, who charge even higher rates of interest and may use intimidating and sometimes aggressive behaviour to recover the money they are owed (Burrows, 1999; Kempson and Whyley, 1999a; Whyley et al, 2000).

The main empirical analyses of debt to date have been the Office of Fair Trading's 1979 report (OFT, 1979), the Policy Studies Institute report in 1992 on credit and debt (Berthoud and Kempson, 1992), and the DTI-sponsored report on debt in 2002 (Kempson, 2002). The DTI survey provides the most recent data, but contains very little on patterns of poverty or social exclusion, certainly compared with the PSE Survey. Otherwise, there has been relatively little research on the extent and nature of debt in Britain. This lack of evidence, and the lack of debt questions in most large surveys, is increasingly remarked upon, Bridges and Disney (2002, p 3) calling it "an extraordinary collective omission". The PSE Survey provides new evidence.

A total of 14% of respondents have arrears on one of their household bills or credit commitments (Table 7.9). The most common arrears relate to council tax, and bills for the use of water and telephone. Among those with any arrears, some 61% have two or more arrears and the average is to have nearly three different types.

In addition, PSE respondents were asked whether there had been times in past year when they had had to borrow from sources other than mainstream lenders, 'in order to pay for your day-to-day needs'. Across the PSE Survey, 11% have used one of these sources, with most turning to family or friends in priority to commercial lenders (Table 7.10). Most (71%) have used just one such source (an average of 1.3 credit providers for this group – although this counts sources rather than occasions of borrowing). Like the patterns of exclusion already described, people from minority ethnic groups, lone parents and social tenants are all heavy users of these types of borrowing, along with those on the very lowest incomes.

Previous research has found marked differences in attitudes to borrowing by age group (Rowlingson and McKay, 2002). In an analysis of the British Social Attitudes Survey, the youngest group (aged between 18 and 24) are no less than six times more likely than those aged 65 or more to advocate borrowing money to replace an old sofa (one of the

Table 7.9: Arrears in the past year

Type of debt	% of respondents with each type of debt
Council tax	6
Water	5
Telephone	5
Credit card payments	3
Gas	3
Mail order catalogues	2
Electricity	2
Rent	2
Television licence	2
Mortgage	2
Goods on hire purchase	1
Other	2
Any of these	14
Average number, among those with any	2.8
Unweighted base	1,534

Table 7.10: Types of borrowing

Type of debt	% of respondents with each type of loan
Family	8
Friends	5
Moneylender	2
Pawnbroker	1
Any of these	11
Average number, among those with any	1.3
Unweighted base	1,534

items asked about). Empirical research (Berthoud and Kempson, 1992; Kempson, 2002) has confirmed that older people are the least likely to be facing financial problems, including debt, often despite having a low income. This is largely due to their more negative attitudes towards credit use. In addition, the greatest need to borrow is when people are setting up home and bringing up a family.

Older groups in the PSE Survey are much less likely to be in debt, or having to borrow to make ends meet, than younger people. This is very clear from Figure 7.2. The incidence of arrears goes from highs of 28%, among those aged 25-29, to barely 1% among those aged 70 or more. Having to borrow follows a similar pattern by age, with very low rates for all those aged 50 or more.

The determinants of debt for those aged 60 or more are likely to be elusive in this analysis. Relatively few of this group have debts or have

Figure 7.2: Extent of arrears and borrowing, by age group

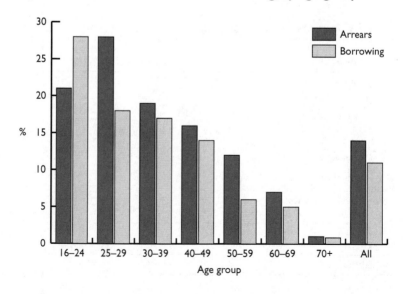

to borrow. Conversely, any links we find between socio-demographic characteristics and debt need to control for or at least take account of this very strong age-based link. As shown in Figure 7.3, even those on the lowest incomes, and aged 60 or more, tend to avoid getting into debt. Conversely, there is a very strong link between having a low level of income and getting into debt among those aged 16-59. In much of what follows we restrict attention to those of working age, to avoid conflating results that are due to age with other characteristics.

There is a particularly strong relationship between housing tenure and having debts (Table 7.11). Among those aged under 60, half of social tenants have debts, and a similar proportion have had to borrow to make ends meet from family, friends, moneylenders or a pawnbroker. Owner-occupiers, particularly those with no outstanding mortgage, are the least likely to have debts.

Looking at the location of respondents more broadly, being in debt is most common in the larger cities and towns, but also in the rural areas. In the former case, this may be related to low incomes, and in the latter case to networks of contacts and low rural wages.

Having arrears is more common in Wales (27%) than in either Scotland (20%) or England (20%). Sub-prime and informal varieties of borrowing follow a similar pattern: Wales (19%), Scotland (18%) and England (14%). Among respondents from a minority ethnic background, 43% are in arrears, and a similar proportion have borrowed to make ends meet.

Figure 7.3: Links between income and debt, by age group

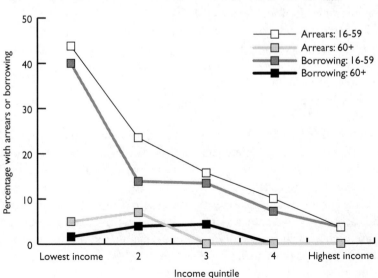

Table 7.11: Extent of debt among respondents aged under 60, by residence (%)

	Unweighted base (*n*)	Has arrears (%)	Has borrowed to make ends meet (%)
Housing tenure			
Owner-occupied, owned outright	105	6	6
Owner-occupied, with mortgage	402	12	9
Rented from council/			
housing association	267	50	47
Rented privately	83	26	15
Location			
1 million or more residents	210	23	24
100,000 to 999,999 residents	241	21	13
10,000 to 99,999 residents	206	16	16
1,000 to 9,999 residents	101	9	6
Less than 1,000 residents	100	17	11

Debt and psychiatric health

One of the benefits of a major study, such as the PSE Survey, is that questions may be 'adopted' by other surveys. This enables analysts to track trends over time, and look at results within different samples with alternative kinds of information.

The questions on debt and borrowing provide a good example of this kind of process. In 2000, the Office for National Statistics conducted a study of psychiatric morbidity among adults living in private households (ONS, 2000)[1]. In an attempt to capture a few simple measures of social exclusion, it included the same questions as the PSE Survey on debt and borrowing. There were few other questions in this health survey relating to social exclusion – unsurprisingly, the focus of the study was psychiatric problems, alcohol/drug use and behaviour. The inclusion of the PSE-style questions now mean it is possible to explore some of the links between debt and psychiatric health.

It is unusual to be able to combine data from a more medical perspective with those measuring social exclusion, especially with a fairly generous sample size (over 8,500 individuals). The direction of causation may not always, of course, be clear. Being in debt could generate problems as well as result from them. But in general, poverty and debt tend to cause mental health problems rather than be a consequence of them (see discussion in Chapter Ten in this volume). The strength of the association between debt and mental health may be judged from the following results.

Overall, 13% of those aged 16-59 have been in arrears in the past year, while 16% have borrowed (from family, friends, moneylenders or pawnbrokers) to make ends meet (Table 7.12). These figures are generally at least twice as high among those with different psychiatric conditions. Among those exhibiting moderate depression, 38% are in arrears, while 45% have borrowed in one of the four ways described. For those with one of a list of phobias, 31% are in arrears, while 39% have borrowed in one of the four ways described. These are extraordinarily powerful figures, which are likely to have wider significance (for further discussion on the links between debt and poor mental health, see Chapter Ten in this volume).

Table 7.12: Extent of debt among respondents aged under 60, by psychiatric health

	Unweighted base (*n*)	Has arrears (%)	Has borrowed to make ends meet (%)
Any neurotic disorder	1,264	26	30
Depressive episode	221	34	39
Moderate depression	137	38	45
Any phobia	157	31	39
Agoraphobia	89	35	38
Had suicidal thoughts in past year	319	27	34
Suicide attempt in lifetime	377	34	37
Severity of alcohol dependence			
None	6,014	12	15
Mild	497	24	32
Moderate or severe	40	49	62
Has spent time in an institution up to the age of 16	176	32	31
Total	**6,573**	**13**	**16**

Policy initiatives to tackle financial exclusion and debt

Financial exclusion

Following the Social Exclusion Unit's report on neighbourhood renewal in 1998 (SEU, 1998), 18 Policy Action Teams were established to look at a wide range of issues around social exclusion. One of these, Policy Action Team 14, examined the scope for widening access to financial services. Its report was published in 1999 (HM Treasury, 1999) and, since then, financial exclusion has become the focus of increasingly widespread interest – among government, the financial services industry, community-based organisations, consumer groups and the academic community.

In its report, Policy Action Team 14 made a number of recommendations about how access to financial services could be improved. These included the development of credit unions, to provide affordable credit and promote small-scale saving; the promotion and extension of local authority Insure with Rent schemes, which provide low-cost home contents insurance for tenants; and the development and promotion of basic account services by banks, building societies and other providers.

There have been varying degrees of progress in each of these areas. The government has provided financial support to expand and consolidate the existing credit union network and, between 1995 and 2000, the number of credit unions in Great Britain grew by around 30% (DWP, 2003). More recently, the government announced plans to establish a growth fund for not-for-profit lenders like credit unions to increase their coverage, capacity and sustainability (HM Treasury, 2004).

In relation to home contents insurance, research indicates that the number of local authorities and housing associations offering Insure with Rent schemes had increased steadily from 1997 to 1999 and was almost certain to continue (Kempson, 1999). In addition, the Association of British Insurers has developed a best practice guide for social landlords about running such schemes (DWP, 2003).

But progress has arguably been greatest in relation to banking. As a result of government pressure following Policy Action Team 14's report, most high street banks and building societies now offer a no-frills basic current account that provides transactional services such as access to cash through automated teller machines, but generally does not come with a cheque book, debit card or overdraft facility. The main benefit of this type of account for people living on low incomes is that it allows closer financial control over all monies. Most basic accounts also have direct debit facilities for bill payment. Since April 2003, all basic bank account holders have been able to make cash withdrawals from branches of the Post Office free of charge.

Progress towards improving access to transactional banking services was driven by the government's policy to pay welfare benefits and state pensions by automated credit transfer into a bank or building society account from spring 2003, rather than through girocheques and payment books. Its aim in doing so has been not only to promote financial inclusion but also to cut the considerable costs (including those of certain types of fraud) associated with paying state pensions and welfare benefits in cash.

By the end of 2004, over two million basic bank accounts had been opened that could be used through the Post Office (www.bba.org.uk).

Despite this progress, banks and building societies have been criticised for not promoting basic bank accounts sufficiently in their branches (Financial Services Consumer Panel, 2002; Citizens Advice, 2003; Knight, 2003).

Moreover, the government remains concerned that around 1.9 million households (2.8 million adults) still do not have a bank account of any kind. Consequently, as part of the 2004 Pre-Budget Report, it announced its intention to "work in partnership with the banking industry and others to achieve real progress in reducing the number of unbanked" (HM Treasury, 2004, p 17).

Alongside basic bank accounts has been the development of the Post Office Card Account, which was launched in March 2003. Partly funded by the banking sector, this account is an electronic version of the girocheque or payment book that people traditionally used to collect their welfare benefits or state pension. Benefit and pension payments are credited to the account, and the claimant can withdraw all or some of the money at a Post Office counter via a keypad, using a plastic card. The government expects that over three million Post Office Card Accounts will be opened (Trade and Industry Committee, 2003). Given its limited functionality, it seems likely that the account will have a minimal impact in tackling financial exclusion. It will, however, ensure that the Post Office network recoups some of the business lost through the introduction of direct payment of benefits and state pensions.

Policy Action Team 14 also recommended that the Department for Work and Pensions (then the Department for Social Security) explore the scope for reforming the Social Fund, a cash-limited scheme that provides grants and loans on a discretionary basis to eligible benefit recipients[2]. Despite extra funding and some welcome changes to the rules, however, the Budgeting Loan scheme still fails to meet the needs of many eligible applicants.

Credit use and debt

The DTI is responsible for consumer credit policy. Under New Labour, it has been active in looking at issues such as debt. In October 2000, it established a Task Force on Over-indebtedness, to explore the causes of over-indebtedness and look at ways of achieving more responsible lending and borrowing. This led directly to data collection on the extent of debt in Britain, covering amounts outstanding as well as arrears more specifically (Kempson, 2002).

In addition, in 2001, the government launched a wide-ranging review of the 1974 Consumer Credit Act. Among other things, the review aimed to tackle the issue of extortionate lending (DTI, 2003).

The extortionate credit provisions of the 1974 Consumer Credit Act have been widely criticised for their ineffectiveness. Few extortionate credit cases have been brought before the courts, and even fewer were proven (Kempson and Whyley, 1999b; DTI, 2003). In the light of this, there has been a concerted campaign for the introduction of an interest rate ceiling, such as exists in several European countries and some states of the USA. This has been led by Church Action on Poverty through its Debt On Our Doorstep campaign.

In August 2004, the government announced that an interest rate ceiling would not be introduced as part of the shake-up of consumer credit law. Instead, it proposed to tackle the issue of high-cost credit in other ways. These included legislative changes to broaden the existing 'extortionate credit' provisions to encompass unfair terms and practices as well as the cost of credit and to bring consumer credit within the remit of the Financial Ombudsman Service, to make it easier for individual consumers to seek redress. These proposals were included in the Consumer Credit Bill, which was introduced in the House of Commons in 2005.

A European Directive Proposal on consumer credit from the European Commission was made on 11 September 2002, and might have made considerable changes to the credit market (especially moneylending). Its underlying aim was to harmonise the laws, regulations and administrative procedures of the European Union member states – however, it now looks very unlikely to be fully passed into law by the European Parliament.

Government policy remains mostly focused on ensuring competition. The use of credit does not create problems for most borrowers. In a free market, so long as firms are free to enter the market and consumers are well-informed, economists (influential in policy formulation) may see little reason for further regulation. In line with this approach, in 2004 the Competition Commission launched an investigation into the home credit industry. This was based on research carried out by the National Consumer Council, which identified a number of practices in the industry that were considered to be against the consumer interest (Whyley and Brooker, 2004).

Promoting saving and asset building

As well as trying to increase access to financial services, the government is very keen to promote saving and asset accumulation, particularly in relation to lower-income households. This has led to a range of policy initiatives, including the introduction of Individual Savings Accounts and Stakeholder Pensions. Neither of these products, however, has had the desired impact among lower-income consumers (Collard, 2001b; Association of British Insurers, 2002; Institute for Public Policy Research, 2003).

Consequently, government attention has recently turned to the concept of matched funding as a means of encouraging a 'strong saving habit' (HM Treasury, 2001), with the announcement of proposals for the Saving Gateway (www.hm-treasury.gov.uk). This would be a national savings scheme for people of working age who are in receipt of state benefits or in-work tax credits that offers matched funding of one pound for every pound saved, up to a certain limit. Five Saving Gateway pilots were launched around England during 2002 and were the subject of an extensive evaluation that found that the scheme not only encouraged saving among people on low incomes but also had a positive impact on their attitudes to saving (Kempson et al, 2005). A second, larger pilot scheme was launched in 2005 that aimed to examine, among other things, the impact of different match rates for savings. It is intended that this second pilot "will inform the development of matching as a central pillar in the Government's strategy for prompting saving and asset ownership" (HM Treasury, 2005, p 112).

Conclusions

The PSE Survey has provided a unique opportunity to research debt and financial exclusion, particularly in relation to wider questions of poverty and social exclusion. It has also been possible to consider debt and financial exclusion separately, and to look at the overlaps and interactions between them. It is clear that both financial exclusion and getting into debt are associated with being on a low income, subjective conceptions of poverty, and the main PSE poverty measure. Debt is much less common among older groups, while financial exclusion is concentrated on young and old alike.

Since 1997, the government has taken a close interest in financial exclusion. This is linked both to its wider objective of tackling social exclusion, and to a cost-reduction agenda in paying benefits into bank accounts rather than in cashable girocheques. The introduction of basic bank accounts is one outcome from policy but they have not been a priority for most providers.

We have also looked at the strong links between a range of psychiatric health problems and debt. This analysis uses the PSE questions, which were used in a later Office for National Statistics survey. They show such strong associations that one must suspect either that poverty and debt are creating or exacerbating such problems, or that a particular group of people does not receive adequate support in making financial decisions.

Financial exclusion and, increasingly, debt are high on the policy agenda. To date, the main emphasis has been on tackling financial exclusion. Government action on debt has been to begin closer monitoring of the situation, at a time when good data on individuals (rather than on products) are lacking. One of the main messages from this chapter is the strong extent to which the problems of debt and financial exclusion are so closely related to poverty and to low incomes.

Notes

[1] Data were collected by the Office for National Statistics, sponsored by Department of Health, Scottish Executive Health Department and the National Assembly for Wales. Data were supplied by the Data Archive at Essex University. None of these groups is responsible for any of the analysis or interpretations in this chapter.

[2] Limited financial assistance is also available to people who are not in receipt of benefits.

References

APACS (Association for Payment Clearing Services) (2003) *UK payment markets trends and forecasts in brief 2003*, London: APACS.

Association of British Insurers (2002) *Stakeholder pensions – closing the savings gap?*, London: Association of British Insurers.

Berthoud, R. and Kempson, E. (1992) *Credit and debt: The PSI report*. London: Policy Studies Institute.

Bridges, S. and Disney, R. (2002) *Access to credit, and debt, among low income families in the United Kingdom: An empirical analysis*, Nottingham: Nottingham University Experian Centre for Economic Modelling.

Bridges, S. and Disney, R. (2003) *Use of credit and arrears on debt among low income families in the United Kingdom*, Nottingham: Nottingham University Experian Centre for Economic Modelling.

Burrows, B. (1999) *Living in a homeless hostel: You wouldn't credit it!*, Glasgow: Money Advice Scotland.

Church Action on Poverty (2002) *Forgive us our debts*, London: Church Action on Poverty.

Citizens Advice (2002) 'The CAB Service's submission to the Treasury Committee Inquiry into Banking' (www.publications.parliament.uk/pa/cm200102/cmselect/cmtreasy/818/818ap17.htm).

Collard, S. (2001a) *Ending fuel poverty and financial exclusion: A market feasibility report*, London: Office of Gas and Electricity Markets.

Collard, S. (2001b) *Consumers in the financial market: Financial Services Consumer Panel annual survey of consumers 2000*, London: Financial Services Authority.

Collard, S. and Kempson, E. (2003) *Pawnbrokers and their customers*, London: National Pawnbrokers Association.

Collard, S. and Kempson, E. (2005) *Affordable credit: The way forward*. Bristol: The Policy Press.

Drakeford, M. and Sachdev, D. (2001) 'Financial exclusion and debt redemption', *Critical Social Policy*, vol 21, no 2, pp 209-30.

DTI (Department of Trade and Industry) (2003) *Fair, clear and competitive: The consumer credit market in the 21st century*, Cm 6040, London: The Stationery Office.

DWP (Department for Work and Pensions) (2003) *UK National Action Plan on Social Inclusion 2003-2005*, London: DWP.

DWP (2005) *Family Resources Survey, United Kingdom 2003-04*, London: DWP.

Financial Services Consumer Panel (2002) *Basic banking research*, London: Financial Services Consumer Panel.

Ford, J. and Rowlingson, K. (1996) 'Low-income households and credit: exclusion, preference and inclusion', *Environment and Planning A*, vol 28, pp 1345-60.

Gibbons, D. (2003) *Reducing the cost of credit to low income households*, London: Debt on our Doorstep.

HM Treasury (1999) *Access to financial services*, London: HM Treasury.

HM Treasury (2001) *Savings and assets for all: The modernisation of Britain's tax and benefit system, Number eight*, London: HM Treasury.

HM Treasury (2004) *Promoting financial inclusion*, London: HM Treasury.

HM Treasury (2005) *Budget report 2005*, London: HM Treasury.

Hillyard, P., Kelly, G., McLaughlin, E., Patsios, D. and Tomlinson, M. (2003) *Bare necessities: Poverty and social exclusion in Northern Ireland: Key findings*, Belfast: Democratic Dialogue.

Institute for Public Policy Research (2003) *Tax efficient saving: The effectiveness of ISAs*, London: Institute for Public Policy Research.

Kempson, E. (1999) 'Insured with rent schemes', in *Insurance Trends*, vol 23, pp 1-13.

Kempson, E. (2002) *Over-indebtedness in Britain*, London: Department of Trade and Industry.

Kempson, E. and Whyley, C. (1998) *Access to current accounts*, London: British Bankers' Association.

Kempson, E. and Whyley, C. (1999a) *Kept out or opted out? Understanding and combating financial exclusion*, Bristol: The Policy Press.

Kempson, E. and Whyley, C. (1999b) *Extortionate credit in the UK – A report to the Department of Trade and Industry*, London: Department of Trade and Industry.

Kempson, E. and Whyley, C. (2001) *Payment of pensions and benefit: A survey of social security recipients paid by order book and girocheque*, Department for Work and Pensions Research Report 146, Leeds: Corporate Document Services.

Kempson, E., Bryson, A. and Rowlingson, K. (1994) *Hard Times? How poor families make ends meet*, London: Policy Studies Institute.

Kempson, E., McKay, S. and Collard, S. (2005) *Incentives to save: Encouraging saving among low-income households*, London: HM Treasury, (www.hm-treasury.gov.uk/media/A64/28/incentivestosave_150305.pdf).

Kempson, E., Whyley, C., Caskey, J. and Collard, S. (2000) *In or out? Financial exclusion: A literature and research review*, London: Financial Services Authority.

Klein, G., Whyley, C., O'Reilly, N. and Lowe, J. (2004) *Mind the financial gap: Access to financial services*, London: National Consumer Council.

Knight, R. (2003) *Survey of subscriber institutions on basic bank accounts*, London: Banking Code Standards Board.

Leyshon, A. and Thrift, N. (1995) 'Geographies of financial exclusion: financial abandonment in Britain and the United States', *Transactions of the Institute of British Geographers*, New Series, vol 20, no 3, pp 312-41.

MORI (Market and Opinion Research Institute) (January 2001) *Experience of the competitive market: The domestic electricity and gas markets*, London: Office of Gas and Electricity Markets.

OFT (Office of Fair Trading) (1979) *Over-indebtedness: A report by the Director General of Fair Trading*, London: OFT.

OFT (1999) *Vulnerable consumers and financial services*, Report No OFT 255, London: OFT.

Office for National Statistics Social Survey Division, 'Psychiatric Morbidity Among Adults Living in Private Households, 2000' [computer file]. Colchester, Essex: UK Data Archive [distributor], 7 May 2003. SN: 4653.

Pahl, J. (1999) *Invisible money: Family finances in the electronic economy*, York: Joseph Rowntree Foundation.

Pantazis, C. and Gordon, D. (1997) 'Poverty and crime', in D. Gordon and C. Pantazis (eds) *Breadline Britain in the 1990s*, Aldershot: Ashgate, pp 115-34.

Pensions Commission (2004) *Pensions: Challenges and choices*, London: Pensions Commission.

Rowlingson, K. (1994) *Moneylenders and their customers*, London: Policy Studies Institute.

Rowlingson, K. and McKay, S. (2002) 'Buy now, pay later?', in A. Park, J. Curtice, K. Thomson, L. Jarvis and C. Bromley (eds) *British social attitudes: The 19th Report*, London: Sage Publications and National Centre for Social Research, pp 27-41.

Rowlingson, K., Whyley, C. and Warren, T. (1999) *Wealth in Britain – a lifecycle perspective*, London: Policy Studies Institute.

SEU (Social Exclusion Unit) (1998) *Bringing Britain together: A national strategy for neighbourhood renewal*, London: Cabinet Office.

Sinclair, S. (2001) *Financial exclusion: An introductory survey*, Edinburgh: Centre for Research into Socially Inclusive Services, Edinburgh College of Art/Heriot Watt University.

Speak, S. and Graham, S. (2000) *Service not included: Social implications of private sector service restructuring in marginalised neighbourhoods*, Bristol: The Policy Press.

Trade and Industry Committee (2003) *People, pensions and post offices: The impact of 'direct payment' on post offices and their customers*, London: The Stationery Office.

University of Warwick (Centre for Management under Regulation) and University of East Anglia (Centre for Competition and Regulation) (2001) *Affording gas and electricity: Self-disconnection and rationing by prepayment and low income credit customers and company attitudes to social action*, London: Electricity Association.

Whyley, C. and Brooker, S. (2004) *Home credit: An investigation into the UK home credit market*, London: National Consumer Council.

Whyley, C., McCormick, J. and Kempson, E. (1998) *Paying for peace of mind*, London: Policy Studies Institute.

Whyley, C., Collard, S. and Kempson, E. (2001) *Saving and borrowing*, Department of Social Security Research Report 125, Leeds: Corporate Document Services.

EIGHT

Social exclusion and local services

Tania Fisher and Glen Bramley

Introduction

This chapter considers the use and adequacy of local services. It is largely based on data from the 1999 Poverty and Social Exclusion (PSE) Survey and draws on previous analysis of the 1990 Breadline Britain Survey undertaken by Bramley (1997) in order to assess trends over time. This is set in the context of wider research on the distributional impact of local services (Bramley and Le Grand, 1992; Bramley and Smart, 1993; Hills, 1996; Bramley, 1996; Sefton, 1997; Bramley et al, 1998) and on how adequate and accessible people regard these services as being (Duffy, 2000; Bailey and Hastings, 2002). The main aim of the chapter is to investigate whether local services are an effective mechanism of redistribution in favour of the 'poor', or whether these services are used more by the better off. In doing so, the chapter examines both use of and attitudes towards local services. It addresses the following specific questions:

- What is the *distributional profile* of local public services in terms of individual households, class, income and poverty in 1999? Are certain services used more by the poor or by the better off?
- Which local services are regarded as *essential* by most households? Are the 'poor' more or less likely to regard particular services as essential?
- Has the distributional profile of service usage *changed* since 1990? What factors might account for these changes? Is this service exclusion for the 'poor' becoming greater or diminishing?
- How does the distributional profile of usage for local *private services* compare with that for local public services?
- For which services are *constraints* of access, inadequacy or affordability most significant? Which types of household are more affected by these constraints?

- How important are *class, income and poverty*[1] in explaining service usage alongside other demographic and socio-economic factors?
- How far does the *geographical area* affect use of local services? Are there distinguishable differences between urban and rural areas, regions, or high- and low-spending local authorities?
- To what extent is the 'service excluded' population also excluded from other aspects of life, such as work and social activities?

The PSE Survey asks well-structured questions on service usage that can (for some services) be compared with the 1990 Breadline Britain Survey. These include:

- Whether the respondent rates a service as essential and should be available or whether the service is desirable but not essential.
- Whether the respondent uses any of the listed services and, for those services they do use, whether they are adequate or inadequate. For the services that are not used, the respondent is asked to give reasons for not using, including 'don't want/not relevant', 'unavailable or unsuitable' and 'can't afford'.

The range of services included in the 1999 PSE Survey has been extended from the original 11 services included in the 1990 Breadline Britain Survey and now includes a number of private local services. The provision of public services is subject to significant local authority discretion, while the private services will be subject to market forces and a variety of external demand factors. Some of these services are available to the population as a whole, while others are targeted at particular groups and rationed on the basis of some method of needs assessment.

Distributional profile of local service usage

Access to local services may affect and be affected by people's standard of living. While good local services can improve people's standard of living, the importance of different services varies according to people's level of income. Some services are used in conjunction with high levels of expenditure in other areas. For example, people may take advantage of subsidised public sports facilities while spending more of their income on cars, sportswear and sports equipment. Other services may be substituted by private expenditure as incomes rise, for example, library usage may decrease as people become better off and are more likely to buy books. The relationship between usage and income affects not just the distributional profile but also the trend over time in average levels of usage.

Figure 8.1 shows the average usage rate for the 11 services that were also included in the 1990 Breadline Britain Survey[2]. The first group of services is open to all households. In all cases the usage rate has declined in 1999, compared with 1990. Declining usage is particularly apparent for bus services and public sports facilities. This may be a function of increases in charges or reduced access, but in the case of buses this is part of a longer-term trend associated with rising car ownership and use. Usage rates have remained fairly consistent over time for the services targeted at both households with children and households with elderly/disabled members.

Declining overall usage rates for 'universal' local public services pose several potential challenges. First, some such services may become less economically viable, leading to a downward spiral of cutbacks and declining quality. Second, they may attract less attention from local politicians, reinforcing this process. Third, they may become perceived less as 'mainstream' activities and more as provision for the less well-off, a process referred to as 'residualisation' in some contexts.

Figure 8.2 shows a similar display of usage rates for a wider group of 17 public and private services, although these were only included in

Figure 8.1: Percentage of households using service, 1990 and 1999

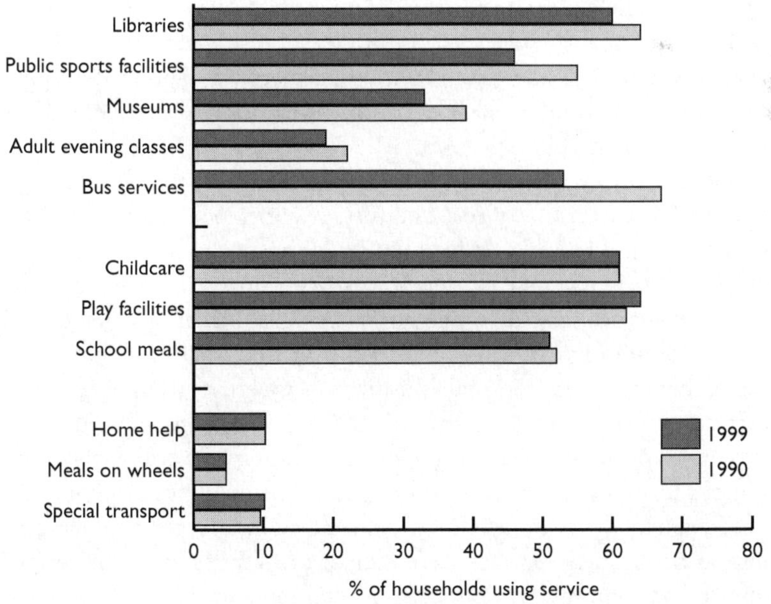

Source: Calculated from 1990 Breadline Britain Survey and 1999 PSE Survey.

Figure 8.2: Percentage of households using service, 1999

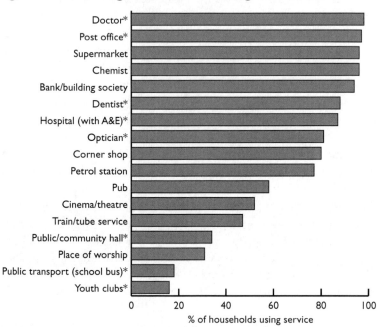

Note: * Public services usually provided by local councils or other public bodies.
Source: Calculated from 1999 PSE Survey

the 1999 PSE Survey and hence comparisons over time cannot be made. Many of these services are provided by private businesses and most are open to all households, with the exception of public transport for children (school bus) and youth clubs, which are targeted at households with children.

The services in Figure 8.2 are ranked by overall usage. The top five services (doctor, post office, chemist, supermarket, bank/building society) are used almost universally by all households. The next five services (dentist, hospital, optician, corner shop, petrol station) are also used by most households, while services such as places of worship and public/community halls are only used by a third of households.

The central distributional question is whether service usage is distributed evenly, or more towards the poor or more affluent. Here usage rates of the range of public and private services are tabulated by household types against a number of measures of socio-economic (dis)advantage. It is important to take household type into account here, as many local services are either of greater relevance to certain types of households or are specifically targeted at particular groups, such as the elderly or households with school aged children. Important redistributions effected by local services may be 'horizontal', between different age groups and household types, rather than between different income or class groups ('vertical'). For example, the confounding effects of demography may mean that simple comparisons of usage rates by income are misleading. Cross-tabulating by household type enables us to observe different socio-economic profiles within different demographic groups and also to perform a general standardisation procedure[3].

Table 8.1 summarises the results of this procedure for the 11 local public services identified in both the 1990 Breadline Britain Survey and the 1999 PSE Survey. Three socio-economic measures are used: social (occupational) class; equivalent income (adjusted for household structure); and poverty[4]. In each case, Table 8.1 shows the ratio of usage by the top (most advantaged) group to usage by the bottom (least advantaged) group, after standardisation for household type.

Apart from bus services, a pro-rich bias has remained consistent for all of this group of services over the two surveys, and in many cases this bias has increased somewhat in 1999. These services (apart from buses) are essentially demand-led leisure and information services and represent economic goods that 'better-off' people are more likely to use. The pro-middle-class pattern exists across the three measures of (dis)advantage used. Social class is particularly important in the case of museums and galleries and adult evening classes, with an increase in the pro-rich bias in 1999. In the case of museums and galleries, the importance of income has increased in 1999; this may reflect the introduction of charges in the mid-1990s. Poorer households make

Table 8.1: Standardised usage ratios, by class, equivalent income and poverty, for public local services, 1990 and 1999

Service	Usage ratio by class		Usage ratio by equivalent income[4]		Usage ratio by poverty[5]	
	1990	1999	1990	1999	1990	1999
Libraries	1.40	1.42	0.95	1.11	1.36	1.26
Public sports facilities	1.34	1.33	1.39	1.41	1.19	1.44
Museums and galleries	2.03	2.09	1.60	2.22	1.56	1.98
Adult evening classes	1.88	2.80	1.29	1.11	1.52	1.76
Bus service	0.77	0.77	0.77	0.75	0.85	0.84
Childcare[6]	0.92	1.18	0.75	1.94	1.26	1.12
Play facilities	0.93	1.46	0.80	0.47	1.31	1.56
School meals	0.70	1.24	0.71	0.81	0.79	0.86
Home help	0.62	0.61	0.93	1.37	0.84	1.15
Meals on wheels	0.32	0.61			0.57	0.73
Special transport	0.29	0.23	0.06	0.44	0.94	0.33

Source: Calculated from 1990 Breadline Britain Survey and 1999 PSE Survey[7].

significantly less use of these 'leisure' services, with an increase in this disparity in 1999, except in the case of libraries.

In both 1990 and 1999, bus services remain consistently pro-poor across all three measures. More detailed analysis of the data reveals that bus usage peaks among poor lone-parent households and low-income couple households with children. Furthermore, only 60% of those using bus services in 1999 were employed, and 10% were unemployed/ unable to work.

Services used primarily by households with children show a more mixed picture (again, Table 8.1). While usage rates for the three services have remained consistent over time, there has been a shift towards a pro-rich bias in relation to class. For childcare services (nurseries, playgroups, mother and toddler groups and after-school clubs), the distribution has shifted towards higher-income households in 1999. In contrast, there has been a shift towards lower incomes, but also higher-class and poor households in the usage of children's play facilities. School meals display a more consistent pro-poor bias, although there was a shift towards higher class in 1999.

The final group of services is targeted mainly at the elderly and disabled. Meals on wheels and special transport consistently show a pro-poor bias across all three measures in both 1990 and 1999, although special transport was even more likely to be used by the poor in 1999. In the case of home help, the bias has shifted towards higher income and non-poor households in 1999.

Table 8.2 analyses distributional patterns for the wider group of services identified in Figure 8.2. Again, these have been ranked by usage rate and, as the top five services are used by virtually all households, these therefore inevitably show a fairly neutral ratio across all three measures. Banks/building societies are something of an exception, which as expected shows a slight bias in favour of higher-income households. A pro-rich bias, particularly in terms of income, is more apparent in services such as petrol stations, cinema/theatres, pubs, train/tube services and places of worship. This reflects the importance of the ability to pay for the use of most of these services. Although only a third of households report using a public/community hall or place of worship, these services display a pro-rich bias on all measures, particularly in relation to class. There is evidence here that some aspects of 'social capital' are positively associated with economic status. Only corner shops and post offices show a slight bias in favour of the poor, suggesting that these more 'local' services are important for this group.

The final two services in Table 8.2 are used mainly by households

Table 8.2: Standardised usage ratios, by class, equivalent income and poverty, for selected public and private local services, 1999 (ranked by usage rate)

Service	Usage ratio by class	Usage ratio by equivalent income[4]	Usage ratio by poverty[5]
Doctor*	1.00	0.98	1.00
Post office*	1.02	1.00	0.99
Chemist	1.01	1.03	1.02
Supermarket	1.06	1.06	1.02
Bank/building society	1.10	1.17	1.10
Dentist*	1.03	1.10	1.04
Hospital (with A&E)*	1.06	0.94	1.02
Optician*	1.05	1.07	1.05
Corner shop	1.11	0.98	0.95
Petrol station	1.46	1.76	1.34
Pub	1.07	1.38	1.31
Cinema/theatre	1.69	2.16	1.61
Train/tube service	1.56	1.38	1.10
Public/community hall*	1.56	1.38	1.46
Place of worship	1.86	1.32	1.27
Public transport (school bus)*	1.35	0.35	1.10
Youth clubs*	1.50	0.45	1.24

Note: * Public services.
Source: Calculated from 1999 PSE Survey

with children. Both public transport (school bus) and youth clubs seem to be used more by higher-class and non-poor households. However, they seem to be used less by higher-income households. The reason for this apparent inconsistency is not clear, although it may relate to factors like urban–rural differences and/or car ownership (for example, higher-income households have more cars and are less likely to use these services).

How essential are local services?

Both the 1990 Breadline Britain Survey and the 1999 PSE Survey asked respondents to indicate which of the selected services they believed to be essential, and should be generally available, as opposed to being desirable, but not essential. Figure 8.3 shows the proportion of respondents rating the services as essential in both the 1990 and 1999 surveys. While the proportion of respondents rating the services as essential is very high, this proportion has declined in all cases in 1999, and this reflects the decline in usage of mainstream services shown in Figure 8.1. This decline is particularly evident for adult evening classes, museums and galleries, and services targeted at households with children and elderly/disabled members (Figure 8.3).

Figure 8.3: Percentage of respondents regarding selected local services as essential, 1990 and 1999 (ranked according to 1999 %)

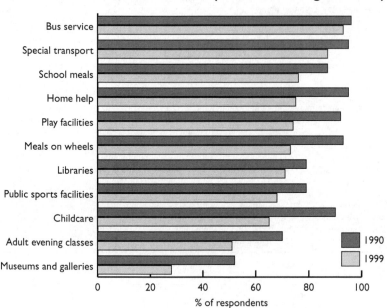

Source: Calculated from 1990 Breadline Britain Survey and 1999 PSE Survey

This suggests that declining usage of these services is not necessarily due to their reduced availability or affordability, but because fewer people see them as relevant to their needs. However, in the case of elderly/disabled services, this has also been a period when community care policies have led to a narrower targeting of more intensive services on fewer clients. It is unlikely that needs have declined, with an ageing population and more disabled people living in the community. Although there has been an expansion of private home care services, supply/rationing factors are probably involved as well. In contrast, the proportion regarding bus services as essential has remained high in both surveys (more than 90%). This is in spite of the declining usage of buses mentioned earlier.

Figure 8.4 shows that many of the additional services that were included in the PSE Survey are regarded as essential by the majority of households. It may be that many people regard these services as being 'essential' even if they do not actually use them, as they signify a potential 'backup' service if required. Exceptions include places of worship, pubs and cinema/theatres, which are more likely to be regarded as 'desirable, but not essential'. In the case of services such as pubs, supermarkets, corner shops and even banks/building societies,

Figure 8.4: Percentage of respondents regarding selected local services as essential and desirable, 1999 (ranked)

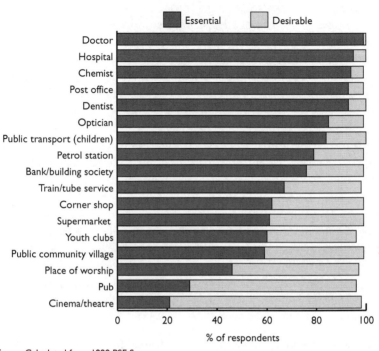

Source: Calculated from 1999 PSE Survey

there is now a wider variety of alternative outlets that perform the same or similar service, and hence they may not be seen as individually essential to a household's needs. The rise in the use of the internet for banking, shopping, payment of bills and email may have an impact on the degree to which households see associated local services such as banks, post offices and supermarkets as being essential.

Supply constraints and inadequacies

Further insights into the patterns of local service usage can be gained by considering the incidence of problems associated with the availability, quality and cost of services, problems that are referred to collectively in this chapter as 'constraints'. In both the 1990 Breadline Britain Survey and the 1999 PSE Survey, possible responses to the question on service usage include ways in which supply constraints or inadequacies can affect usage. These include: using the service, despite perceiving it as inadequate; not using the service because it is unavailable or inadequate; and not using the service because the respondent cannot afford to. Here these three responses are used together to provide a broad index of constraint.

Figure 8.5 shows the top 15 services ranked according to the proportion of households reporting some form of constraint or inadequacy[8]. Constraint appears to be greatest for a number of public children's services (play facilities, school meals and youth clubs), with around a third of households with children reporting some degree of constraint, particularly in relation to availability. This may reflect increasing privatisation of these services and households opting for the private services. Indeed, this may be the case for many other services, as 10 out of the top 15 services in Figure 8.5 are publicly provided services. Approximately one in four households are constrained in their use of transport services (buses, trains, school buses) and this is largely due to inadequate service delivery, while only a small proportion of households do not use services because they cannot afford to. This supports the findings of Duffy (2000) and reinforces the need to target particular services for improvement.

Lack of availability or perceived inadequacy appear to be the main barriers to use of both public and private services, rather than affordability. Less than 5% of households are unable to use public and

Figure 8.5: Service constraint or inadequacies for top 14 public and private local services, 1999 (ranked by % constrained)

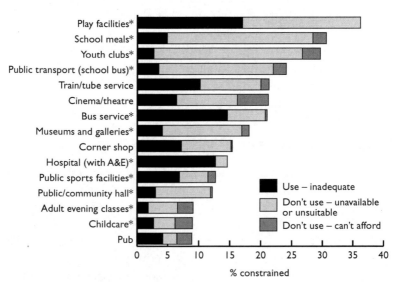

Note: * Public services.
Source: Calculated from 1999 PSE Survey

private services because of cost, compared with around 25% of households that are unable to use these services due to lack of availability. Further analysis of the data shows that households with children are more likely to be constrained in their use of all services because of cost, but are particularly constrained in their use of public services because of their unavailability. For school meals, youth clubs and school transport, unavailability deters usage substantially; while people are more likely to use play facilities, buses and hospitals despite seeing them as inadequate.

Table 8.3 summarises the constraint responses for high and low equivalent income groups and households below or above the poverty threshold in both 1990 and 1999. For most services in 1990, the lowest-income group reports either a similar level of constraint or a lower level than the top group, with the exception of adult evening classes and children's play facilities. A similar pattern is evident in 1999, except that the difference between the top and bottom groups has increased in the case of public sports facilities and bus services and the lowest-income group is more constrained in its usage of childcare services. Poor households tend to be more constrained in their use of all services, except public sports facilities and school meals, a pattern that has persisted across both surveys. Hence, it may be concluded that poor households face poorer-quality services and/or that poverty reinforces constraints on service usage. This is more clear-cut than the relationship with income or class.

Table 8.3: Supply, quality or cost: constraints on usage, by equivalent income and poverty, for local services, 1990 and 1999

	Proportion of households constrained (%)							
	Equivalent income				Poor			
	1990		1999		1990		1999	
Service	Top	Bottom	Top	Bottom	No	Yes	No	Yes
Libraries	12	12	9	11	9	14	7	12
Public sports facilities	20	18	20	11	20	15	13	11
Museums and galleries	25	19	22	18	17	21	17	21
Adult evening classes	9	16	9	11	9	20	7	15
Bus service	35	24	22	24	25	29	19	27
Childcare	38	30	12	39	29	28	24	50
Play facilities	26	55	32	57	39	57	29	60
School meals	35	33	13	15	19	33	11	14

Source: Calculated from 1990 Breadline Britain Survey and 1999 PSE Survey.

Table 8.4 shows the results of a similar exercise for the wider set of 17 services included in 1999. The main conclusion here is that, when comparing both the top and bottom equivalent income groups and households below or above the poverty threshold, the level of reported constraint is very similar for the majority of services. Exceptions include public/community halls, pubs, cinema/theatre and youth clubs, where both the poor and lowest-income groups are more constrained. The lowest-income group is more constrained in its usage of the corner shop, while poor households are more constrained in their use of pubs. Public transport for children (school bus) is the only service that is significantly pro-poor, that is, the poor are less constrained. In many cases, income is a key factor in the use of private services, as the ability to pay will determine usage.

Some additional services, including some important local public goods, are considered in Table 8.5. These services deal with local environmental quality, open space, school resources (teacher availability, books and so on), housing disrepair and crime (being a victim or feeling unsafe). Care needs to be taken here in the interpretation of results shown, as some of the questions asked in the 1999 PSE Survey were not directly comparable with those asked in the 1990 Breadline

Table 8.4: Supply, quality or cost: constraints on usage, by equivalent income and poverty, for public and private local services, 1999

	Proportion of households constrained			
	Equivalent income		Poor	
	Top	Bottom	No	Yes
Doctor*	6	5	5	7
Post office*	8	6	4	5
Chemist	4	3	3	5
Supermarket	11	9	5	9
Bank/building society	12	10	8	10
Dentist*	8	8	6	8
Hospital (with A&E)*	16	15	14	15
Optician*	3	5	4	5
Corner shop	12	17	16	14
Petrol station	3	6	4	6
Pub	7	12	7	16
Cinema/theatre	15	27	18	32
Train/tube service	24	23	21	23
Public/community hall*	10	19	10	19
Place of worship	4	5	3	5
Public transport (school bus)*	19	13	15	8
Youth clubs*	6	29	15	31

Note: * Public services.

Source: Calculated from 1999 PSE Survey

Table 8.5: Supply, quality or cost: constraints on selected additional services, by equivalent income and poverty, for local services, 1990 and 1999 (% of all households reporting problems)

Service	Equivalent income		Poor	
	Top	Bottom	No	Yes
1990				
Local area dirty[9]	20	39	22	42
Lack open space	13	37	19	43
School resources	5	10	n/a	n/a
Home disrepair	2	16	3	19
Crime victim/unsafe[10]	29	30	22	39
1999				
Local area dirty	80	87	85	84
Lack open space	9	10	7	14
School resources	10	15	22	20
Home disrepair	3	11	2	16
Crime victim/unsafe	29	49	35	44

Note: Analysis of school resources by poverty not available for 1990.
Source: Calculated from 1990 Breadline Britain Survey and 1999 PSE Survey

Britain Survey (particularly questions on local area, and also to some extent the crime question) (see also Chapter Nine for further discussion on crime).

In 1990, there was a very strong tendency for the lowest-income and poor groups to experience supply constraints or quality problems. In 1999, this tendency exists, although not to quite the same extent. The proportions of households reporting problems with the local area (dirty, lacking in open space) differ significantly from those reported in 1990 and this is due to issues of comparability. Nevertheless, almost equal proportions of both the highest- and lowest-income and poor/not-poor groups report problems associated with a dirty local area. The poor are more likely to report lack of public open spaces. They are also more likely to experience various aspects of crime and home disrepair, which may reflect the association between the 'poor' and bad housing and neighbourhoods. The previous study concludes that the poor appear to be particularly disadvantaged by their local environment. This situation still appears to stand, with some qualifications, and may be consistent with the finding of Burrows and Rhodes (1998) and Bramley et al (2000) that the poor live in 'unpopular places'.

Use of local services and area characteristics

This section addresses the question of how far people's location affects their access to adequate local services. The question of how far location affects outcomes in general has attracted much recent debate, generally associated with the term 'area effects'.

If poor people use poorer-quality or fewer services, this may be because they live in 'poor areas' and these areas tend to be less well served. The SEU (1998, 2001) reports launching the national strategy for neighbourhood renewal included local services as one of the ways in which poor neighbourhoods often lost out. Such work as has been published provides mixed evidence on this assumption. For example, Duffy (2000) found that for a number of services satisfaction was not markedly less in deprived neighbourhoods. Bailey and Hastings (2002) found in Scotland that satisfaction is significantly lower in deprived neighbourhoods for local authority services overall and for schools, general practitioners and parks/open space. Past studies (Bramley and Le Grand, 1992; Bramley and Smart, 1993) have shown, like this one, certain systematic associations of service usage with socio-economic status, and one would expect these to map onto the socio-economic geography of Britain. Other evidence on area distributions of public spending confirms that this is indeed the case (Bramley et al, 1998; Bramley and Evans, 2000).

In this context, the question of area effects is about whether area-level processes influence and modify this general socio-economic mapping, either reinforcing it or alleviating it. To echo a recurrent question of the past 30 years, is disadvantage a matter of 'who you are or where you live?'. The research question then becomes one of separating the independent influence of location from the influences of individual/household attributes, typically using some kind of multivariate statistical modelling technique. There has been a growth of such research in recent years, using large-scale household surveys, in the investigation of a range of outcomes relating to deprivation and social exclusion. A recent example of such research is that by McCulloch (2000), which spawned a clutch of responses debating and disputing the central argument of the paper, that area effects were relatively marginal (Dorling, 2001). Most of the other contributors to this symposium accepted the general statistical finding that area attributes did not add much to the explanation contained in individual attributes, but they disagreed widely about the interpretation and policy implications (see Glennerster et al, 1999, Burrows and Bradshaw, 2001; Joshi, 2001; Pattie, 2001; Smith et al, 2001; Hills et al, 2002; Lupton and Power, 2002).

A general framework to explain and account for usage of local services needs to encompass the following types of explanatory factors:

- the demographic characteristics of individuals and households that affect relevance, need and demand;
- socio-economic characteristics of individuals and households relating to occupation, economic activity, income and wealth that affect the demand for services and for complementary or substitute goods and services;
- cultural factors, which may be proxied by variables like ethnicity as well as social class, length of residence and so on, that affect preferences;
- the supply of services in the locality, including the budgets of local authorities and other agencies;
- physical accessibility of those services to residents, affected by facilities, settlement pattern and transport;
- rationing/eligibility rules where applicable;
- time to use services, related to economic activity and to domestic responsibilities; and
- social, cultural and environmental aspects of the neighbourhood that may affect people's willingness to use services.

While many of these factors are essentially attributes of the individual or household in question, some are attributes of the service and some are attributes of the area and/or of the collectivity of people living in it. It is these latter factors, and the way that they interact with individual factors, that raises the possibility of 'area effects' on service usage.

The ability to investigate area effects in the PSE Survey is severely limited by the area type variables contained in the dataset. The analysis presented here concentrates on two area characteristics: urban/rural location (settlement size) and broad regional (north/south) location. The impact of local authority expenditure variations is also tested (although rather unsuccessfully). More neighbourhood-level effects are explored further in separate work, drawing mainly on a different survey but cross-referring to the PSE Survey (Bramley and Fisher, 2002).

Turning first to the urban/rural indicator, the usage rates are tabulated using a four-way, settlement-size classification, which ranges from large cities (more than one million residents) to rural areas (less than 9,999 residents) (see Figure 8.6). For most services, usage rates are fairly uniform across the four settlement types. This is surprising given that many services are provided centrally and, as a result of geography, one would assume that access would be reduced in rural areas. Bramley and Fisher (2002) suggest that this may be because of offsetting effects of poverty and accessibility. Nevertheless, there are some services where usage is lower in more rural areas, such as museums/galleries, bus

Figure 8.6: Usage rates for selected services, by urban/rural indicator, 1999

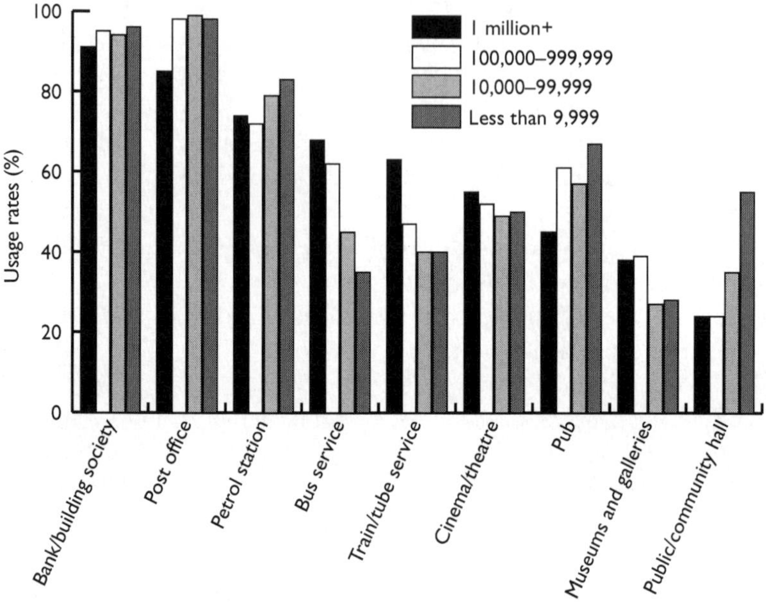

Source: Calculated from 1999 PSE Survey

services, train/tube services and cinema/theatres, and this is likely to reflect the greater access and convenience to these types of service in urban areas. In contrast, services such as petrol stations, bank/building societies, pubs and post offices have higher usage rates in smaller settlement areas (Figure 8.6).

Services used primarily by households with children or disabled/ elderly members display a more mixed picture with regard to usage by urban/rural area. Figure 8.7 shows that the general pattern is one of greater usage by households living in medium-sized urban centres and also the smallest, rural settlements. The exception is children's play facilities, which displays a consistent upward slope from more urban to more rural, and school meals, which displays a U-shaped pattern.

Rates of service usage have also been tabulated for households living in the North (North West, North East, Yorkshire and Humberside and Midlands regions), those living in Greater London and those living in the Rest of the South (South West, South East, East regions) of England. Figure 8.8 shows that services such as opticians, libraries, cinema/ theatres and children's play facilities are utilised more by households living in the South and London. Use of buses and trains/tubes is

Figure 8.7: Usage rates for services targeted at children, the elderly and disabled, by urban/rural indicator, 1999

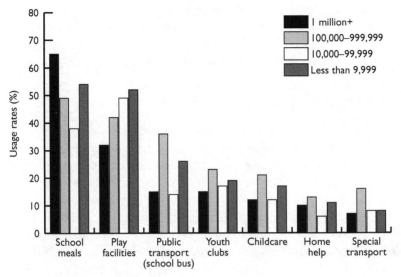

Source: Calculated from 1999 PSE Survey

Figure 8.8: Usage rates for selected services, by North/South indicator, 1999

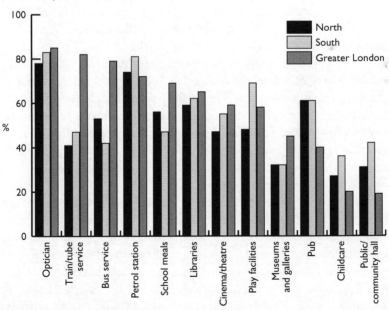

Note: Excludes Wales and Scotland.
Source: Calculated from 1999 PSE Survey

greater in London, which is what would be expected given the much more extensive services available within the capital. A number of other services, such as petrol stations and pubs, are utilised more by households outside of London, perhaps because they are more associated with car-based access. Childcare and public/community halls are also used more outside London, which may reflect provision levels.

Multivariate models

While the previous section addressed the patterns of service usage, the underlying reasons for the differences in usage are still not clear. Although higher-income households may use a particular service more than lower-income households, this might not be a direct result of income alone, but may have more to do with indirect factors such as higher car ownership, more direct access or size and type of household. The next section reports on a multivariate statistical analysis, which tries to separate out the simultaneous influence of a large number of factors that may influence the outcome. The relative influence of particular explanatory variables within a plausible set of relevant characteristics can be assessed empirically. The analysis builds on previous work by Bramley (1996, 1997).

In the previous section, a general explanatory framework was set out for local service usage using the PSE data, subject to the limitations of available indicators (particularly area-level measures). The list of household and area attributes used in the analysis is shown in Appendix 8.1. The analysis first only includes variables that represent the attributes of households and excludes, at this stage, measures of the characteristics of areas. Up to 20 household characteristics are included in the analysis, and include class, income, poverty, age, sex, household types, economic activity factors, housing tenure, health and disability, ethnicity, car ownership and receipt of benefits. In some cases, the number of variables included in the analysis is reduced for certain services as appropriate.

The following tables concentrate on class, income and poverty, and indicate whether the three variables are working in the same 'pro-rich' way, a negative relationship with poverty and a corresponding positive relationship with income and class would be expected, or vice versa for pro-poor. However, some of the other variables included (see Appendix 8.1) may also capture some of the effects of poverty and deprivation (for example, car ownership). Table 8.6 summarises the key findings for the three socio-economic measures, using t-statistics from a logistic regression model to indicate the direction and statistical significance of the effects.

For the first four services, the pattern is fairly consistent with the results from Table 8.1 discussed earlier. Higher social class exerts a positive influence on usage in both 1990 and 1999 cases, except public sports facilities. As was shown in Table 8.1, the extent of this influence increased in 1999 for museums and galleries and adult evening classes. Income has a largely negative influence on the use of these services, but particularly in the case of bus services, which underlines the issue of affordability of bus fares for lower-income households. It may also reflect use of private substitutes. Although the strong negative effect of income has declined slightly in 1999, this is continuing even after allowing for the strong negative effect of car ownership, which has increased in 1999. Most of the other significant influences are demographic, particularly age and household type. Being of Asian or Black ethnic background has a strong negative influence on the use of public sports facilities, but a positive influence on the use of bus services.

Poverty has a consistently negative effect on use of all services, except school meals and special transport, a pattern that confirms earlier results. Nevertheless, the negative effect of poverty is considerably stronger on public sports facilities and museums and galleries in 1999. Being

Table 8.6: Influence of class, equivalent income and poverty on usage of local services in multivariate models, 1990 and 1999 (t-statistics* in logistic regression model including up to 20 individual household attributes)

Service	Class AB		Class C1		Equivalent income		Poverty	
	1990	1999	1990	1999	1990	1999	1990	1999
Libraries	**3.54**	**3.92**	**3.06**	0.65	**-2.00**	**-2.12**	-1.23	-1.82
Public sports facilities	1.26	1.27	1.50	1.17	2.11	0.90	-1.49	**-3.22**
Museums and galleries	**2.82**	**4.50**	**2.14**	1.15	0.71	-0.42	-1.76	**-4.61**
Adult evening classes	1.36	**5.59**	**2.93**	1.22	1.25	-1.27	-1.54	-0.66
Bus service	-0.42	-1.71	-0.05	-1.87	**-3.12**	**-2.92**	-1.54	-0.16
Childcare	**-3.20**	0.12	-1.67	-1.76	0.92	**2.10**	**-2.50**	-0.40
Play facilities	-1.72	1.28	-1.02	-0.80	-0.19	1.24	**-2.20**	**-3.08**
School meals	1.49	0.61	0.11	0.21	-1.15	**2.35**	0.64	0.00
Home help	1.77	1.28	1.13	1.74	-0.09	-0.25	-1.13	**-2.31**
Meals on wheels	0.26	0.47	0.22	0.03	0.59	0.09	0.01	0.22
Special transport	0.58	-0.60	1.10	1.00	-0.92	0.06	-0.73	**2.49**

Note:* t-statistics indicate the direction and significance of the effect of the particular variable on the probability of usage of each service, allowing for the simultaneous influence of all of the other variables included in the analysis; values greater than 2.0 (shown in bold) indicate significance at the 5% level.

Source: Calculated from 1990 Breadline Britain Survey and 1999 PSE Survey. Other variables included in models listed in Appendix 8.1.

in full-time employment has a positive influence on the use of museums and galleries and reinforces the conclusion that, generally, these services are used more by higher socio-economic groups and less by the poorest groups, and this effect was stronger in 1999.

In the case of childcare, the pattern has changed to one more related to income and less to class and poverty. This may reflect increasing costs involved with good-quality childcare, higher demand from working households for the service or increased privatisation. The poor are less likely to use children's play facilities in the local area and this may reflect issues of access to safe and good-quality play facilities. In contrast, the relationship between income and school meals has shifted from being pro-poor in 1990 to pro-rich in 1999 and this may be due to an increase in two-parent working families requiring schools to provide meals for their children.

The influence of the three variables is generally minimal in relation to the services targeted at the elderly and the disabled. While neither income nor class has a strong or significant influence on any of the three services, poverty has an increasingly strong influence on home help and special transport; the poor are less likely to use home help, but more likely to use special transport.

In relation to the additional services included in the 1999 PSE Survey, Table 8.7 shows that higher-class households are more likely to use private local services such as cinemas/theatres, train/tube services and places of worship. Access to transport, particularly car ownership, is likely to influence the usage of many services listed in Table 8.7. Although this effect is not as strong as expected, car ownership does exert a strong influence on the use of petrol stations, but a negative influence on the use of train/tube services, as would be expected.

Income has a significant relationship with many of the services listed in Table 8.7 and exerts a positive influence on the use of dentists, hospitals, petrol stations and places of worship, but a negative influence on the use of opticians, train/tube services and public/community halls. Other income-related factors, such as receiving benefits, being a council tenant, and being in full-time employment, are significant influences on the use of opticians, corner shops, pubs, places of worship and cinema/theatres. Generally, poverty has a negative influence on the use of all the services listed in Table 8.7, but particularly doctors, chemists, opticians, cinema/theatres, public/community halls and places of worship. The only exception is, again, corner shops.

As with the previous set of services, other demographic factors, such as age and household type, exert a strong influence on the services in Table 8.7. Interestingly, ethnicity has a strong influence on the use

Table 8.7: Influence of class, car ownership, equivalent income and poverty on usage of local services in multivariate models, 1999 (t-statistics* in logistic regression model including up to 20 individual household attributes)

Service	Class AB	Car ownership	Equivalent income	Poverty
Doctor**	−0.04	0.02	1.28	**−2.17**
Post office**	0.23	1.34	0.10	0.28
Chemist	0.74	−1.42	1.63	**−2.08**
Supermarket	−0.05	0.67	1.28	0.36
Bank/building society	−0.13	1.82	1.91	−1.51
Dentist**	0.05	1.19	**3.09**	−0.38
Hospital**	0.65	0.88	**3.23**	−1.05
Optician**	−0.06	0.52	**−3.13**	−1.98
Corner shop	−0.97	−0.30	0.33	1.65
Petrol station	−0.24	**15.27**	**3.94**	−0.86
Pub	−1.17	0.02	0.10	**−2.00**
Cinema/theatre	**5.46**	0.13	0.67	**−3.34**
Train/tube service	**3.50**	**−3.33**	**−2.94**	−0.40
Public/community hall**	1.37	0.60	**−3.38**	**−2.76**
Place of worship	**3.32**	1.13	**3.74**	**−2.85**
Public transport (school bus)**	−0.95	0.82	−0.41	−0.51
Youth clubs**	−1.47	−0.52	−0.76	−0.63

Notes: * t-statistics indicate the direction and significance of the effect of the particular variable on the probability of usage of each service, allowing for the simultaneous influence of all of the other variables included in the analysis; values greater than 2.0 (shown in bold) indicate significance at the 5% level.

** Public services.

Source: Calculated from 1999 PSE Survey

of services, a reflection of wider cultural and lifestyle issues. Specifically, coming from a Black or Asian background has a strong negative influence on the use of banks/building societies, chemists, dentists and pubs, but a positive influence on the use of places of worship, supermarkets and public/community halls.

This multivariate modelling exercise can be extended to include the influence of factors associated with the area in which households live. Accessibility to services may be affected by the geographical characteristics of local areas and here two area indicators are included in the logit model to test this: north/south and urban/rural. Table 8.8 summarises the influence of these area characteristics on service usage, once allowance has been made for the household/individual variables.

Although households living in the South are more likely to use trains/tubes, largely a result of greater access to this service, the influence of living in the South of England (including Greater London) on other services is minimal and implies that the regional differences identified in Figure 8.8 are mainly due to socio-economic factors. Households living in large cities are more likely to use bus and train/

Table 8.8: Influence of area characteristics on usage, 1999
(t-statistics* in logistic regression models including up to 20 individual household attributes)

Service	South	City	Rural
Libraries**	0.90	0.28	**−2.70**
Public sports facilities**	1.92	−0.91	1.13
Museums and galleries**	0.58	−0.05	**−4.20**
Adult evening classes**	−0.31	−0.16	−1.34
Bus service**	−0.33	**2.18**	**−6.69**
Doctor**	−0.78	0.25	−0.55
Post office**	−0.20	**−2.57**	0.31
Chemist	−1.20	−1.24	**−2.58**
Supermarket	0.99	−0.80	−0.85
Bank/building society	1.03	−1.91	−0.40
Dentist**	−0.05	1.41	0.56
Hospital**	−1.47	−1.42	−2.21
Optician**	**2.59**	0.27	−0.25
Corner shop	1.42	0.56	0.79
Petrol station	0.10	0.64	0.64
Pub	−1.14	**−3.72**	1.18
Cinema/theatre	**2.45**	0.90	**−2.89**
Train/tube service	**4.80**	**4.37**	**−2.83**
Public/community hall**	0.41	−0.44	8.62
Place of worship	**−2.44**	−0.46	1.11
Childcare**	−0.56	−1.54	0.17
Play facilities**	0.93	−1.51	0.35
School meals**	−1.77	1.50	1.41
Public transport (school bus)**	−1.87	**−3.48**	−1.16
Youth clubs**	**−2.32**	−1.54	−0.91
Home help**	**2.09**	−0.68	0.20
Meals on wheels**	−0.34	1.33	1.28
Special transport**	−1.30	**−2.64**	−1.21

Notes: 'South' includes the South West, South East, East and London regions; 'city' is defined as having 1 million or more residents; 'rural' is defined as having less than 9,999 residents.

* t-statistics indicate the direction and significance of the effect of the particular variable on the probability of usage of each service, allowing for the simultaneous influence of all of the other variables included in the analysis; values greater than 2.0 (shown in bold) indicate significance at the 5% level.

** Public services usually provided by local councils or other public bodies.

Source: Calculated from 1999 PSE Survey.

tube services, which reflects the greater access to these services in cities. On the other hand, households living in large cities are less likely to use post offices and pubs and this may reflect access to alternatives in large cities. Many of the services provided by post offices can now be found in a wide variety of alternative outlets, while wine bars, cafes and restaurants offer alternatives to the pub.

Public transport for children and special transport for the elderly is also less likely to be utilised by city dwellers and this reflects the concentration of these services in smaller and more rural areas.

Households living in a rural location are far more likely to utilise public/community halls and this is a direct result of greater accessibility to this service in these areas. As expected, many of the services often associated with large cities, such as museums and galleries, cinema/theatres, bus services and train/tube services, are negatively associated with a rural location.

Table 8.9 shows the influence of high relative local authority expenditure per head on frequency of usage. The variable used is a crude categorical measure relating to expenditure on all local authority services, relative to the need for spending assessed in the government's grant system. Generally, this variable is not significant, after allowing for individual and household characteristics. High relative expenditure has a positive influence on the use of bus services and children's school buses and (marginally) on public sports facilities and special transport for the elderly and disabled, but a negative influence on the use of public/community halls. These rather weak results are disappointing but reflect the crudity of the expenditure measure, and the fact that in 1999 local authority expenditure did not vary all that widely after allowing for assessed needs.

Table 8.9: Influence of local authority expenditure* on usage, 1999 (t-statistics** in logistic regression model including up to 20 individual household attributes)

Service	High relative expenditure
Libraries	−0.70
Public sports facilities	1.45
Museums and galleries	0.08
Adult evening classes	0.18
Bus services	**2.97**
Public/community hall	−1.62
Place of worship	0.33
Childcare	−0.16
Play facilities	−0.81
School meals	−1.35
Public transport (school bus)	1.85
Youth clubs	−0.69
Home help	1.44
Meals on wheels	1.13
Special transport	1.72

Notes: * Local authority expenditure is per head (bands).

** t-statistics indicate the direction and significance of the effect of the particular variable on the probability of usage of each service, allowing for the simultaneous influence of all of the other variables included in the analysis; values greater than 2.0 (shown in bold) indicate significance at the 5% level.

Source: Calculated from 1999 PSE Survey

The findings presented in this section have been exploratory in nature, but do provide confirmation for some of the key findings on local service usage and constraints experienced by different socio-economic groups. In addition, more detailed insights into some of the factors that affect use of services have been gained.

Relationship between service exclusion and other excluded groups

The final question addressed in this chapter is whether there is a relationship between people who are excluded from local services and those who suffer from other forms of exclusion. Gordon et al (2000, p 6) identify four dimensions of exclusion: impoverishment (or exclusion from adequate income or resources); labour market exclusion; service exclusion; and exclusion from social relations. Clearly, each aspect of exclusion can be assessed independently, just as this chapter has focused on service usage and exclusion. However, one aspect of exclusion may correlate with or be caused by another and a significant relationship may exist between the various forms of social exclusion. Are those people who are excluded from social relations or the labour market also excluded from local services? Someone lacking in social networks may rely more on local services for support and a means of participating in the community.

Table 8.10 looks at the patterns of association between service exclusion and the other dimensions of exclusion. Service exclusion is defined here as households not using three or more of the public and private services identified earlier because the service is unavailable or unaffordable. Lack of social participation is defined as not undertaking four or more out of seven activities selected to represent participation in family or social interactions (see note to table). Exclusion from work is defined as being in a jobless household, with retired households shown separately. Impoverishment is defined in two ways – being poor (lacking two or more necessities) or being in the lowest equivalent income quintile.

Table 8.10 suggests that there is only a very weak relationship between service exclusion and social participation. It suggests that there is a stronger relationship between service exclusion and joblessness. It further confirms that there is a slightly stronger relationship again between service exclusion and poverty or low income. Cross-tabulating combinations of these factors suggests that the number of households excluded on three or more dimensions simultaneously is very low indeed.

Table 8.10: Association between service exclusion and other dimensions of exclusion

Exclusion category	Excluded from 3+ services (%)*
Poor household (lacking 2+ necessities)	25
Lowest quintile equivalent income	23
Jobless household (working age)	22
Lack of social participation (4+ activities**)	16
Retired household	16
Not lacking social participation	15
With workers in household	12
Not lowest quintile	12
Not poor	11
All households	**15**

Notes: * Exclusion from three or more services because not available or unaffordable.

** From seven activities: evening out each fortnight; meal out each month; family meal each fortnight; visits to family each fortnight; go to pub each fortnight; attend church; guest at wedding, funeral, etc.

These findings are encouraging in one sense. They suggest that it is not automatically the case that poverty or joblessness leads to exclusion on the other dimensions of local services or social isolation. Lack of social participation in particular seems to be a separate dimension with its own causes and dynamic. However, this does imply that, if lack of social participation is a problem to be addressed by policy, the nature of these policies is likely to be different from those designed to address poverty or service access.

The relationship between service exclusion and impoverishment has already been addressed to some extent in this chapter. Much of the earlier analysis concluded that poverty does seem to reinforce constraints on service usage. Table 8.10 confirms this relationship by showing the extent to which the poor are more likely to be excluded from significant numbers of services – roughly speaking, the chance of such exclusion from services is doubled. More detailed analysis confirms that the impact of poverty is greater in relation to those private services where ability to pay is more of a factor.

Conclusions

General public services open to all have tended to display a decline in usage over the 1990s, and this is associated with a decline in the proportion of people regarding these services as essential. This retreat from universalism, which partly reflects the wider range of alternatives, may pose problems for maintaining political and financial support for such provision. The services that remain most universal (and essential) in 1999 are doctors, post offices, supermarkets and chemists.

A pro-rich bias has remained consistent for usage of demand-led leisure and information services over the 1990s, and in many cases this bias has increased somewhat. Bus services remain pro-poor in their distribution of usage. Children's services display a mixed picture, with some shift in favour of higher incomes in the case of childcare. Services for elderly people show a generally pro-poor pattern, although this lessened somewhat for home care over the 1990s. For the wider group of private and public services considered in 1999, most are either neutral or pro-rich in their distribution. Only corner shops and post offices show a slight bias in favour of the poor, suggesting that these more 'local' services are important for this group.

The services for which constraints of inadequacy, unavailability or unaffordability are most widely cited are play facilities, school meals, youth clubs, and public transport for children. Unavailability/ unsuitability is the dominant type of constraint, rather than affordability. These services are clearly priority targets for improvements in supply and quality, and families with children are the key group affected. It appears that poor households face poorer-quality services and that poverty reinforces constraints on service usage; this is more clear-cut than the general relationship with income or class, although income/ affordability is more important for private services. Poor households are also much more likely to report problems of local environmental quality, lack of open space, housing disrepair and crime, patterns that have broadly persisted throughout the 1990s.

Local service usage, quality and satisfaction are more driven by household than by area characteristics, although neighbourhood location is more important for some outcomes such as those just mentioned. Regional differences are not very apparent, apart from London. For many services there is surprisingly little difference between urban and rural areas, partly because of the offsetting effects of poverty and accessibility. Nevertheless, services like public transport, cinemas/ theatres and museums/galleries are used more by city dwellers, while pubs, petrol stations and community halls are used more by rural dwellers. For quite a few services, larger towns score better than either cities or smaller settlements. Overall, local authority spending levels do not seem to impact much on service usage.

While there is some association between exclusion in the job market and poverty on the one hand and service exclusion on the other, there is very little association with a lack of social participation, which seems to be a separate dimension of exclusion.

Notes

[1] Poverty has been defined as households lacking two or more socially perceived necessities. See note 5.

[2] Calculation of the usage rate in Figure 8.1 is based on all relevant households and includes those who used the service but classified it as inadequate, with the denominator being all relevant households including those answering 'don't know'.

[3] Usage rates are calculated for each household type by socio-economic category. We then calculate a weighted average usage rate for each socio-economic group, assuming it had the same household type composition as the population as a whole.

[4] Equivalised weekly household income, which is total net income divided by scales that vary according to the number of adults and the number and age of dependants in the household.

[5] The PSE measure of poverty is defined as lacking two or more socially perceived necessities, whereas the same measure in the 1990 Breadline Britain Survey was defined as lacking three or more socially perceived necessities.

[6] Childcare includes nurseries, playgroups, mother and toddler groups and after-school clubs.

[7] Usage ratios are the ratio between the usage rate for the least disadvantaged group and that for the most disadvantaged group, with four class groups, five income groups and two deprivation groups. For the first of these services, the relevant population is all households; for the second group, households with children under five or school age; for the third group, all elderly, plus households with one or more disabled member.

[8] 'Constraint' refers to the percentage of relevant households using a service but finding it inadequate, not using it because it is inadequate/unavailable, or who can't afford it, excluding don't knows.

[9] In 1990, a single question was asked (with only three possible responses): "Thinking about the area where you live, please tell me whether each of the following applies: 'the local area is dirty and unpleasant', 'there is a lack of pleasant, open spaces within easy reach' and 'there are houses boarded up/ with broken windows nearby'". In 1999, two questions were asked: the first asked the respondent to choose up to 10 problems that might be common

to the area, and the second question asked the respondent to choose up to six problems that may occur in their area. In an attempt to make these comparable with the 1990 survey, the following has been analysed: 'the local area is dirty and unpleasant' (1990 Breadline Britain Survey) and 'graffiti on walls and buildings', 'rubbish or litter lying around', 'dogs and dog mess in this area' and 'pollution, grime or other environmental problems caused by traffic and industry' (1999 PSE Survey); 'there is a lack of pleasant, open spaces within easy reach (1990 Breadline Britain Survey) and 'lack of open public spaces' (1999 PSE Survey).

[10] In 1990, a single question was asked: 'Which, if any, of the following applies to you or other members of your household?'. Responses included 'burgled in the last year', 'mugged/robbed in the last year', 'assaulted in the last year' and 'feel unsafe in local neighbourhood'. In 1999, a series of questions were asked relating to different aspects of crime that may have happened to the respondent only (that is, not including other members of the household as in 1990). In order to gain a fairly comparable measure, responses to the following questions were included: 'Has anyone broken or tried to break into your home to steal something?', '... stolen anything you were carrying?', '... deliberately hit or assaulted you?'; 'Has any adult member of your household hit or kicked you, or used force or violence in any other way?'; and 'How safe do you feel walking alone in this area after dark?'.

References

Bailey, N. and Hastings, A. (2002) 'Public services in deprived neighbourhoods: "spatial injustices" from mainstream services', Paper presented at Scottish Centre for Research on Social Justice launch conference, Aberdeen, September 2002.

Bramley, G. (1996) 'Who uses local services: need, demand and rationing in action', in D. King (ed) *Local government economics in theory and practice*, Cheltenham: Edward Elgar.

Bramley, G. (1997) 'Poverty and local public services', in D. Gordon and C. Pantazis (eds) *Breadline Britain in the 1990s*, Aldershot: Ashgate.

Bramley, G. and Evans, M. (2000) 'Getting the smaller picture: small-area analysis of public expenditure incidence and deprivation in three English cities', *Fiscal Studies*, vol 21, no 2, pp 231-67.

Bramley, G. and Fisher, T. (2002) 'Services, social exclusion and the neighbourhood', Paper presented at 'Cities and Regions in the 21st Century' conference, Newcastle, 17-18 September.

Bramley, G. and Le Grand, J. (1992) *Who uses local services? Striving for equity*, The Belgrave Papers, No 4, Luton: Local Government Management Board.

Bramley, G. and Smart, G. (1993) *Who benefits from local services? Comparative evidence from different local authorities*, Welfare State Programme Paper WSP/91, London: London School of Economics.

Bramley, G., Evans, M. and Atkins, J. (1998) *Where does public spending go? Pilot study to analyse the flows of public expenditure into local areas*, London: Department of the Environment, Transport and the Regions.

Bramley, G., Pawson, H. and Third, H. (2000) *Low demand housing and unpopular neighbourhoods*, London: Department of the Environment, Transport and the Regions.

Burrows, R. and Bradshaw, J. (2001) 'Evidence-based policy and practice', *Environment and Planning A*, 33, pp 1345-48.

Burrows, R. and Rhodes, D. (1998) *Unpopular places? Area disadvantage and the geography of misery in England*, Bristol: The Policy Press.

Dorling, D. (2001) '"Anecdote is the singular of place", Overview and introduction to forum on "How much does place matter?"', *Environment and Planning A*, 33, pp 1335-40.

Duffy, B. (2000) *Satisfaction and expectations: Attitudes to public services in deprived areas*, CASE Paper 45, London: Centre for Analysis of Social Exclusion, London School of Economics.

Glennerster, H., Lupton, R., Noden, P. and Power, A. (1999) *Poverty, social exclusion and neighbourhood: Studying the area bases of social exclusion*, CASE Paper 22, London: London School of Economics.

Gordon, D., Adelman, L., Ashworth, K., Bradshaw, J., Levitas, R., Middleton, S., Pantazis, C., Patsios, D., Payne, S., Townsend, P. and Williams, J. (2000) *Poverty and social exclusion in Britain: Report of the poverty and social exclusion survey of Britain*, York: Joseph Rowntree Foundation.

Hills, J. (ed) (1996) *New inequalities: Changes in the distribution of income and wealth in the United Kingdom*, Cambridge: Cambridge University Press.

Hills, J., Le Grand, J. and Piachaud, D. (2002) *Understanding social exclusion*, Oxford: Oxford University Press.

Joshi, H. (2001) 'Is there a place for area-based initiatives', *Environment and Planning A*, 33, pp 1349-52.

Lupton, R. and Power, A. (2002) 'Social exclusion and neighbourhoods', in J. Hills, J. Le Grand and D. Piachaud (eds) *Understanding social exclusion*, Oxford: Oxford University Press.

McCulloch, A. (2000) 'Ward level deprivation and individual social and economic outcomes in the British Household Panel Study', *Environment and Planning A*, 33, pp 667-84.

Pattie, C. (2001) 'On reinventing wheels', *Environment and Planning A*, 33, pp 1353-6.

Sefton, T. (1997) *The changing distribution of the social wage*, STICERD Occasional Paper 21, London: London School of Economics.

Smith, G., Noble, M. and Wright, G. (2001) 'Do we care about area effects?', *Environment and Planning A*, 33, pp 1341-4.

SEU (Social Exclusion Unit) (1998) *Bringing Britain together: A national strategy for neighbourhood renewal*, London: Cabinet Office.

SEU (2001) *A new commitment to neighbourhood renewal, National strategy action plan*, London: Cabinet Office.

Appendix 8.1: Variable definitions (survey based, household level)

a. Demographic

FMALE	Male respondent
YOUNG	Respondent aged under 25 years
OLD	Respondent aged 75+
SINGRET	Single adult of retirement age
SINGLE	Single-person household
LPAR	Lone-parent household
CPLCHILD	Household with children
MULTI	Household with three or more adults
NKIDS	Number of children
NDISAB	Household with disabled or ill member
ASIAN	Black or Asian respondent

b. Socio-economic

PSEEQUIV	Equivalised household income £ per week
BENEFIT	Household receives state benefits
POOR	Household lacks and cannot afford two or more 'essentials'
OWNER	Outright home owner
COUNCIL	Council tenant
CLASSAB	Social class of HOH professional/managerial
CLASSDE	Social class of HOH other non-manual
CLASSC1	Social class of HOH semi/unskilled manual
FULLTIME	Respondent works full-time
CARS	Household has one or more cars

c. Area characteristics

EXPBAN2	Local authority expenditure per head (bands) – high relative expenditure
EXPBAN3	Local authority expenditure per head (bands) – high absolute expenditure
CITY	Household lives in large city (1 million+ residents)
SMALL	Household lives in a small town (10,000 to 99,999 residents)
RURAL	Household lives in a rural area (less than 9,999 residents)
SOUTH	Household lives in the South of England (Eastern, London, South East, South West regions)

NINE

Crime, 'disorder', insecurity and social exclusion

Christina Pantazis

Introduction

Crime is an inescapable feature of everyday modern life. According to the government's own sources, crime has grown considerably in post-war Britain. Whereas 500,000 crimes were recorded in 1955, the extent of police recorded crime had reached 4.5 million crimes by the time New Labour took office in 1997 (Barclay and Tavares, 1999)[1]. Yet there is widespread acknowledgement that these crimes are just the tip of the iceberg, with a vast amount of crime being unreported, unrecorded and undetected (Coleman and Moynihan, 1996). According to the more reliable British Crime Survey (BCS), crime rose steadily in the decade from 1981, and continued to rise during the early 1990s, peaking in 1995 to over 16.5 million crimes. The most recent sweep, however, shows that since 1995, the risk of becoming a victim of crime has fallen from 40% to 26% (representing a drop in BCS crime by 40%), the lowest level recorded since the survey began in 1981 (Dodd et al, 2004).

Despite being a vastly improved measurement method, the BCS is still likely to considerably underestimate the amount of crime. One study (Green, 2004) found that at least 10.9 million offences are missed from the most recent survey but even this estimate fails to include a whole raft of other crimes such as white-collar, corporate crime and environmental crime (Garside, 2004), which would indicate that the problem of crime is a much bigger one than evidenced by either police-recorded crime or victimisation surveys like the BCS (Box, 1983).

In addition to these high levels of crime, the government argues that acts of 'disorder', which often make people's lives intolerable, have now reached unacceptable levels. For example, on a one-day count, 1,500 organisations reported more than 66,000 incidents of 'anti-social behaviour' (encompassing behaviours such as litter, vandalism, street drinking, intimidation and prostitution among others), estimated to be costing agencies £3.4 billion per year (Home Office, 2005a).

The high crime rates in countries such as the UK and the US have stirred important debates about the changing nature of societies (Carrabine et al, 2002). The criminologist David Garland (2000, p 348), for example, describes the high crime rates affecting such societies from the 1960s onwards as becoming a "normal social fact" notwithstanding the problems inherent with the crime statistics. In later work (2001, p 90) he discusses this trend in terms of the "causal link between the coming of late modernity and society's susceptibility to crime". Garland argues that this susceptibility can be accounted for in terms of a number of factors, including: the growing consumer boom which has increased the number of goods available to steal; the reduction of situational controls (for example, caused by lifestyle changes relating to the shift to dual-earner households, which mean that more houses are being left unattended for longer periods in the day); demographic changes that have led to a larger pool of potential offenders; and finally, a relaxation of informal social controls in families, as well as in neighbourhoods and schools. As a result of these changes, crime is a problem that affects the whole of society and not just the poor (Garland, 2000, p 359). It now increasingly transforms the middle-class experience of crime, as it becomes a consideration for anyone owning a car, using public transport, leaving his or her house unattended during the day, or walking the city at night.

Beyond criminology, Ulrich Beck (1992) has identified "the emergence of 'risk society' where individuals have to negotiate a quantitatively higher level and range of 'risks' and contingencies unknown to previous generations as they go about their daily routines" (Carrabine et al, 2002, p 56). While some risks are global in their origins (for example, the risk of flooding from climatic change), crime risks are localised, for example associated with living in high crime areas (Kempshall, 2003). Responsibility for managing these crime risks in late modernity is shared and individuals have a key role to play in risk management: including avoiding risky behaviours, places and times, and purchasing risk protection such as home insurance, alarms and other security. In this context, individuals are characterised as processing and adapting to risk information, and thus being in a constant state of reflexivity and anxiety about their choice of actions (Giddens, 1991). However, risk (including the risk of being victimised) is indiscriminate. "*Poverty is hierarchic, smog is democratic*" argues Beck (1992, p 36; emphasis in original), so that class divisions become less relevant in the 'risk' society[2].

The purpose of the chapter is not to evaluate these theoretical propositions; it has the more modest aim of assessing the extent to which crime risks (as well as other risks) are distributed evenly throughout society. Can the common assumption that social groups experience crime as equal risks in high crime societies be supported, or are particular social groups more susceptible to becoming victims and, if so, how? The overall objective of the chapter, therefore, is to provide empirical evidence, from the Poverty and Social Exclusion (PSE) Survey, on people's experiences of crime, 'disorder' and concerns about victimisation at the end of the 20th century. It seeks to do this by, first, examining the impact of poverty and aspects of social exclusion on the risks of victimisation and insecurity in order to explore the extent to which social groups experience these differentially. Second, it utilises a social harm approach to add depth to the understanding of these experiences (see Hillyard et al, 2004)[3] by placing crime, 'disorder' and insecurity in the context of a whole range of other harmful life events, situations and concerns.

If our aim is to gauge the breadth and depth of harm experienced by individuals in late 20th-century Britain, then our focus needs to be greater than a narrow interpretation offered by conventional victimisation surveys such as the BCS. For example, loss of employment, illness and accidents are all significant conditions or events which create trauma and may have long-lasting consequences. By contrast many events defined as crime do not constitute particularly important events in most people's lives. Although some crimes, particularly those of a violent or sexual nature, often have serious and long-standing impacts on the lives of victims (and non-victims), many criminal events are minor and do not score particularly highly on a scale of personal hardship (Hulsman, 1986).

Hillyard et al (2004) have argued that a social harm approach may be more useful than crime in both capturing the range of harms people experience from the cradle to the grave, as well as offering more imaginative policies in responding to them. By examining crime as well as other aspects of social harm, this chapter therefore aims to provide a more balanced understanding of the harmful conditions, events and insecurities that people may experience during their lives.

The chapter is divided into four discrete, but ultimately related, parts. With poverty and aspects of social exclusion as the central themes of the chapter, the first part examines people's experiences of crime and non-criminal harm. The second part looks at the issue of 'disorder' and considers this alongside other aspects of area deprivation. The third part examines the extent of 'fear' of crime, as well as other insecurities among the population. The final part considers the Labour government's response to crime, 'disorder' and insecurity, and suggests that recent policy responses may be directly and indirectly leading to the escalation of exclusion from society for certain already vulnerable groups.

Social harm and unequal risks

Criminal harm

Although crime is a routine feature of modern societies, Garland argues, "the collective experience of crime will tend to be highly differentiated and stratified. Social groups are differently placed in respect to crime – differentially vulnerable to victimization, [and] differentially fearful about its risks..." (2000, p 355). The experience of crime is certainly contingent upon a number of factors, including gender, ethnicity, class, and sexual preference, as well as geographical location. This important insight was first brought to our attention by feminist researchers demonstrating the extent of hidden crimes against women and children (Russell, 1982; Hanmer and Saunders, 1984), as well as by left realist criminologists who argue that the extent and impact of crime is greater for working-class communities (Lea and Young, 1984; Kinsey and Young, 1985).

Through the development and implementation of local victimisation surveys in the 1980s (Kinsey, 1985; Jones et al, 1986), left realist criminologists have sought to expose the extent to which crime was socially and geographically concentrated. The first Islington Crime Survey, for example, confirmed that women had much higher victimisation rates than men, suffering to a greater extent from particular crimes, such as street robbery, as well as sexual crimes, and experiencing a much greater risk of sub-criminal harassment (Jones et al, 1986). Consequently, the authors argued, women were living under a virtual curfew. However, the survey also revealed a more complicated relationship between crime and other aspects of socio-economic status: namely, that the highest risks of burglary, vandalism, theft from the person, and sexual assault were reported by higher income groups. Their results were similar to those found in the Canadian Urban Victimization Study, which reported that changes in urban development, resulting in the closer proximity of people with lower and higher incomes, had contributed to the wider distribution of victimisation risks (Provisional Task Force on Justice for Victims of Crime, 1983, cited by Jones et al, 1986, p 50).

While the first BCS paid only scant attention to the social distribution of crime risks (see Hough and Mayhew, 1983), preferring instead to talk of risks for the 'statistically average person', one of the impacts of left realist and feminist criminologies was to encourage the Home Office to produce much more detailed analyses of who is most at risk of becoming a victim. Thus, the most recent national survey identifies the unemployed, social renters and low-income households as being most at risk of burglary, but it also reports that the highest income individuals are at most risk from vehicle-related theft, while the poorest and richest are shown to be equally at risk of total violence (Dodd et al, 2004)[4].

If the relationship between poverty and individual crime risks seems somewhat contradictory, there is more conclusive evidence on the association between higher crime rates and poor areas, stretching as far back as the 19th century with Henry Mayhew's (1851-62) comprehensive survey which detailed the 'rookeries' (that is, slum criminal quarters) of London. This geographical theme has continued to be researched throughout the 20th century (see, for example, Morris, 1957; Baldwin et al, 1976; Hirshfield and Bowers, 1996). In recent years there has been increasing interest in the association between crime and council housing (see, for example, Barke and Turnball, 1992; Foster and Hope, 1993; SEU, 1998). Sometimes this interest has got caught up in debates about the underclass and morality. Watt and Jacobs (1999), for example, argue that the Social Exclusion Unit's (SEU's) report, *Bringing Britain together: A national strategy for neighbourhood renewal*, identifies the problems of social housing mainly in terms of crime and anti-social behaviour (rather than, for example, underfunding, unemployment or poverty). However, there are exceptions to this moralistic interpretation of the problems associated with social housing. Murie (1997), for example, discusses the dynamics between individual housing tenure and area tenure and argues that high crime rates are not simply related to individual council housing tenure but also whether council housing and, in particular, poor council housing, dominates the tenure of an area. Indeed, the elevated rates of victimisation found among social renters is confirmed by the most recent BCS which shows them having higher than average risks of vehicle-related thefts, burglary, and violence (Dodd et al, 2004). Hard-pressed areas, which include council areas, also have higher than average crime risks (Dodd et al, 2004).

However, the BCS reveals that of all areas, urban prosperous areas have the highest risks; while national rates of burglary affected 3% of households, rates are almost double that for households in affluent urban areas. Households in these areas also experience the highest levels of vehicle-related theft, and theft from the person (Dodd et al, 2004). Furthermore, any discussion of area victimisation rates should also consider the issue of the ecological fallacy[5]. For instance, Pantazis (2000a) considered whether the predominant victims in deprived areas are people who are also living in circumstances of poverty, and found that the richest income individuals experienced significantly higher victimisation risks than the poorest in 'striving' areas[6], and this was the case even after vehicle-related crimes were excluded from the total victimisation rate.

What the evidence suggests, therefore, is that the simple assumption that poor areas have the worst crime levels is misconceived. In a high-crime rate society, both poor and wealthy urban areas will be blighted by crime, but it also appears that better-off individuals in close proximity to poor people may be particularly attractive targets for offenders. However, the better-off are in a more advantageous position to withstand the impact of victimisation, most obviously with regards to acquisitive crimes. Furthermore, no analysis has been done addressing the issue of multiple victimisation and its relationship to poverty. Thus, it may be the case that multiple victimisation rates are higher for those living in poverty.

Non-criminal harm

According to the approach put forward by Hillyard and Tombs (2004), social harm has many facets, only a few of which are covered by the criminal law but most are not. Their approach identifies three main categories of harm, including emotional or psychological, physical harm and financial or economic harm. The latter category incorporates:

> ... both poverty and various forms of property and cash loss ... which includes pension and mortgage 'mis-selling', mis-appropriation of funds by government, private corporations and private individuals, increased prices for goods and services through cartelisation and price-fixing, and the redistribution of wealth and income from the poorer to the richer through regressive taxation and welfare policies. (Hillyard and Tombs, 2004, p 19)

Although the definition of social harm is still in its infancy, what is interesting for this chapter's purpose is that poverty itself is considered a social harm, if not the most serious of all harms, which can lead to ill health, disability and even death (Gordon, 2004). Furthermore, there is an explicit recognition that much harm is "the wreckage of neo-liberal globalisation" (Hillyard et al, 2004, p 3). If this is the case, then we can expect to find people who are at the sharp end of market forces or government policies to suffer a greater share of harm. For instance, UK government tax and welfare policies throughout the 1980s had major impacts on poverty and inequality. In short, in order to make the rich richer, government policies were pursued which made the poor poorer, often with other serious related repercussions (see Chapter Two in this volume).

Poverty is harmful in its own right because it denies people the possibility of meeting their basic needs in relation to, for example, food, clothing, and housing, and restricts their capabilities to act as social beings. However, the very conditions of living in poverty also expose people to other forms of harm, sometimes with fatal consequences. Although the precise mechanisms by which people in impoverished circumstances experience elevated risks of other harms are not always clear, there is a large evidence base demonstrating the links between socio-economic inequality and harm. For instance, adults of low social and economic status face higher risks of fire accidents (OPDM, 2003); ill health, both physical and mental (Pantazis and Gordon, 1997b; Payne, 1997; Shaw et al, 1999; Payne, Chapter Ten in this volume); suicide (Drever and Bunting, 1997; Lewis and Sloggett, 1998); injury or death while on the road (Roberts and Power, 1996); as well as injury within the home. Doyal and Nandy (2000), in their review of intentional and unintended harm within the domestic setting, argue that the relationship between injury and socio-economic status is strongest among children and young people:

> The gap between social classes in deaths from all unintended injuries has widened over the past decade (Roberts and Power 1996; Roberts 1997a). A child in social class V is now twice as likely to be fatally injured before the age of 15 as a child in social class I (Roberts and Power 1996). These inequalities are even more marked in the context of household injuries. Children from social class V are 10 times more likely than those in I to die as a result of a fall at home (Roberts and Pless 1995). They are also significantly more likely to be injured or to die in a fire (Warda et al 1999). (Doyal and Nandy, 2000, p 11)

Having reviewed some of the existing evidence on the distribution of criminal and non-criminal harm, the next part of this chapter examines the findings from the PSE Survey.

Findings from the PSE Survey

The PSE Survey utilises a selection of the validated questions from the BCS and supplements them with others relating to white-collar crime. Consequently it goes some way towards meeting the criticisms made of the BCS for focusing on a restricted range of crimes (for example, Pantazis and Gordon, 1997a; Garside, 2004). Respondents were asked about their experiences in relation to a number of different crimes over the previous 12 months. Some of these related to individual experiences[7] (for example, assaults, mis-selling of financial services), whereas others related to victimisation affecting the whole household (for example, burglary). Respondents were also asked about a range of other harmful events which may have affected them in the previous year in order to provide empirical evidence for the approach proposed by Hillyard et al (2004).

Because the risk of becoming a victim can be low for some types of crime (at least at the national level), the analysis for this chapter looks at harm using four broad categories (that is, financial; physical; sexual; and psychological[8]). The effect of this is to boost the sample size, with the intention of making the interpretation of results more reliable. One anticipated problem, however, is that some crimes could be said to fall into more than one category. A judgement was made concerning which harms fell into the most appropriate category, with this being dependent on what the immediate impact was considered to be, although it has to be recognised that this process is far from ideal. Burglary, for example, is categorised as a financial criminal harm because its most direct impact on the victim is financial, although psychological harm may well result. A second potential problem is that individual differences in victimisation rates are obscured, so where possible, therefore, the chapter comments on some of these results.

Table 9.1 demonstrates the proportion of the population experiencing criminal harm in the previous 12 months. Overall, 39% of the population experienced crime in the previous year but risks are higher for people living in circumstances of poverty, with rates ranging from 37% to 55%, depending on the poverty measure. Using the subjective measure of poverty yields the greatest inequalities: more than half (55%) of those respondents who are poor 'all the time' report being victimised compared to just 38% who are 'never' or 'only

Table 9.1: Percentage of respondents experiencing criminal harm in the previous year, by a selection of poverty and social exclusion variables

Poverty and social exclusion variables	Financial	Physical	Sexual[a]	Psychological	Total crime[b]
PSE poor					
Yes	34	7	6	13	45
No	31	6	4	9	37
Income poor					
Below 50% average	30	7	4	12	37
Above 50% average	32	6	5	8	39
Subjectively poor					
All the time	46	9	**7**	**17**	**55**
Only sometimes/never	31	6	5	9	38
Social class					
Routine occupation	29	7	2	9	37
Management/professional	**35**	4	**7**	11	41
Economic status					
Working	**37**	7	4	10	**44**
Unemployed	32	**14**	6	**25**	**44**
Economically inactive	25	4	5	8	30
Jobless household					
No workers	25	7	**9**	**14**	37
Workers	**38**	7	5	11	**45**
Retired	17	2	2	3	20
Housing tenure					
Owner	32	6	4	8	37
Social renter	31	7	8	11	40
Private renter	**38**	6	3	**22**	**45**
Total % in the population	**32**	**6**	**5**	**10**	**39**

Notes: [a] Relates to any time in the past; [b] excludes the experience of sexual criminal harm.

sometimes' poor. The elevated risks of crime for this group is reported consistently across all four categories of crime, although the greatest differentials relate to psychological criminal harm where their risk almost doubles.

There are more complicated patterns in the distribution of victimisation risks when different aspects of social exclusion are considered (Table 9.1). Total risks of crime are greatest among the unemployed and private renters, as well as respondents in paid work, and those living in in-work households. They are lowest among owner-occupiers, the economically inactive, and especially low among the retired. While the risk of becoming a victim of financial crime is highest among respondents in paid work, those living in in-work households, and private renters, the risk of physical crime is especially high among the unemployed (14% compared to the sample average of 6%). Psychological crimes are also high for this group, as well as for those living in jobless households, and social renters. Although the results concerning sexual criminal harm should be treated cautiously because of the small numbers, those respondents describing their situation as poor 'all the time', the unemployed, and those living among other jobless people have the highest risks. Interestingly, the results by social class show that managers and professionals have increased risks over those in routine occupations, especially concerning financial and sexual crimes.

Yet, categorising crimes in this way disguises individual differences in risk, which, when disaggregated, reveals some interesting findings. For instance, poor respondents reported higher risks of fraud and the mis-selling of financial services – crimes normally considered as white-collar crimes and, potentially, with middle-class victims. Using the PSE measure (socially perceived necessities deprivation), people in poverty were more than twice as likely as others to report being mis-sold a financial service (9% compared to 4%). It may be that white-collar offenders deliberately seek out victims who may be less well-informed about financial services and/or that better-off respondents (who perhaps also have a higher level of education) are better able to protect themselves from being a victim of this kind of crime. However, interpretation of these results can be only speculative at this stage.

The risk of criminal harm is further examined by gender and age and Table 9.2 shows that the risks are slightly higher for men. However, Chan and Rigakos (2002) argue that risk is highly gendered in the sense that women and men have to confront and negotiate different

Table 9.2: Percentage of men and women and younger and older respondents experiencing criminal harm in the previous year, by poverty status

Poverty variables	Financial	Physical	Sexual[a]	Psychological	Total crime[b]
PSE poor					
Male	36	4	–	9	44
Female	33	9	11	16	42
Younger (16-24)	43	15	13	30	62
Older (65+)	20	1	1	4	22
Not PSE poor					
Male	32	6	–	10	39
Female	31	5	8	7	36
Younger (16-24)	29	16	9	16	52
Older (65+)	17	2	2	4	20
Total % in the population	**32**	**6**	**5**	**10**	**40**

Notes: [a] Relates to any time in the past; [b] excludes the experience of sexual criminal harm.

types of risk, although it has not always been recognised as such because what is defined as 'risky' tends to be filtered through a masculine lens. Nearly one in nine women in the PSE sample report being sexually interfered with at some point in their lives by either someone they know or a stranger, while there is a slighter greater risk among women in poverty. This latter group of women also face particularly high risks of psychological criminal harm (their risk is double that of better-off women, and also almost twice that of poor men), as well as physical harm (almost double the risk experienced by other females). These results highlight the extent to which crime risks can be highly gendered, and illustrate the interplay between gender and poverty in accounting for differentials in risk.

However, the results are even more pronounced when the effects of age are considered. Overall, younger people (16-24) are three times more likely to be victims than older respondents (55% compared to only 20%), but the risk of being victimised increases considerably if the respondent is also poor. Almost two thirds (62%) of young poor respondents report being victimised in the previous year (Table 9.2). The greatest inequalities exist in relation to psychological crime, where risks are twice as high for poor young respondents compared to their better-off counterparts (30% compared to 16%). Thus, although politicians and the media seem only too ready to demonise the young (Cohen, 1972; Levitas, 2005, chapter 5) for wreaking havoc in the lives of law-abiding citizens, the PSE Survey shows that it is young people, and especially young poor people, who are the main victims of crime. This is all the more pertinent as the Survey excludes respondents below the age of 16. Yet, when studies do consider the experiences of children, there has been found to be a link between, for example, low economic status and physical and emotional abuse, although not sexual abuse, which is considered to cut across class boundaries (Bradshaw, 2001; see also Harrington and Mayhew, 2001).

As was discussed earlier, adopting a social harm framework requires considering the experience of criminal harm alongside a whole range of other harmful events and incidents in order to provide a more balanced understanding of people's experiences. Respondents were asked about a range of conditions and events that may have affected them in the previous year. For consistency, these have been grouped into three categories (financial, physical and psychological)[9]. The data in Table 9.3 reveal that people living in poverty experience much greater risks of non-criminal harm. In this sense, risk is not indiscriminate; while just more than half of the sample (55%) reports

Table 9.3: Percentage of respondents experiencing non-criminal harm in the previous year, by a selection of poverty and social exclusion variables

Poverty and social exclusion variables	Financial	Physical	Psychological	Total non-criminal harm
PSE poor				
Yes	31	17	56	71
No	8	11	39	50
Income poor				
Below 50% average	15	18	48	62
Above 50% average	12	12	41	53
Subjectively poor				
All the time	**53**	13	**70**	**83**
Only sometimes/ never	11	13	41	53
Social class				
Routine occupation	15	13	43	56
Management/professional	12	10	41	50
Economic status				
Working	16	9	41	53
Unemployed	**25**	11	**56**	**64**
Economically inactive	10	**18**	46	58
Jobless household				
No workers	**18**	15	**57**	**66**
Workers	16	11	42	55
Retired	3	**17**	39	49
Housing tenure				
Owner	12	11	42	52
Social renter	20	15	**48**	**65**
Private renter	**24**	**28**	40	63
Total % in the population	**14**	**13**	**43**	**55**

a non-criminal harm, this rises to four fifths (83%) among those people living in a permanent state of poverty.

Their exceptionally high risks of harm are evident with respect to financial and psychological aspects, although not the physical dimension. Unsurprisingly, it is in relation to financial harm that the worst inequalities exist: among those poor 'all the time', the risk of financial harm is nearly five times as high compared to others (53% compared to 11%). At this point it is relevant to recognise that categorising financial harm separately from psychological harm has its limitations; we know from numerous studies that being in poverty and having financial difficulties can have significant repercussions on people's mental well being (Oppenheim, 1990, chapter 3; see Chapters Seven and Ten in this volume).

The unemployed, respondents in jobless households, and those in rented accommodation, also report high rates of non-criminal harm. These groups have the greatest risks of financial and psychological harm, and above-average risks of physical harm are reported by private renters, the economically inactive and those in retired households. Age is obviously an important intervening variable here; elderly people are often particularly at risk from injury due to their fragility (Doyal and Nandy, 2000). Conversely, the risk of total non-criminal harm is lowest for: managers and professionals; those in paid work; those living in retired households; and homeowners. What is interesting is that, unlike the relationship between poverty, social exclusion and crime, which has a complex pattern, the association between other forms of social harm and poverty and social exclusion is much clearer; social harm (excluding criminal harm) increases disproportionately for people in poverty and experiencing different aspects of social exclusion.

Figure 9.1 provides further detail of individual risks of social harm by poverty status using the PSE Survey socially perceived necessities measure. People in poverty report consistently higher risks of harm with the exception of work injuries where they are equally likely to experience an injury. Inequalities between the two groups are greatest

Figure 9.1: Percentage of respondents experiencing harmful events and conditions in the previous year, by poverty status (PSE measure)

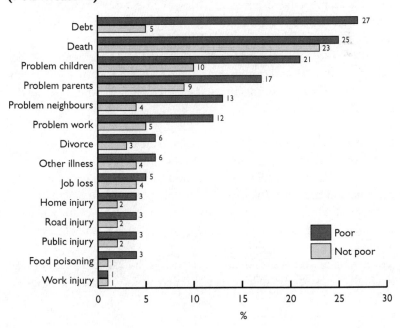

inevitably with respect to debts such as hire purchase (HP) or falling behind with mortgage payments (27% compared to 5%), but large differences also emerge with respect to problems with parents or close relatives, children, neighbours, or problems at work. The data do not allow us to properly understand the dynamics between poverty and relationship problems, but being able to get on well with family members, friends, colleagues and neighbours appears conditional on the level of material comfort such that social relationships may become highly strained by living in circumstances of poverty.

'Disorder' and area deprivation

The notion of 'disorder' has become an increasingly important focus of debates on crime and fear of crime in recent years. The issue first rose to the attention of academics and policy makers through the 'broken windows' thesis developed by Wilson and Kelling in the 1980s. This sought to explain the impact disorder on crime rates: "if a window in a building is broken and *is left unrepaired*, all the rest of the windows will soon be broken.... One unrepaired window is a signal that no one cares and so breaking more windows costs nothing" (Wilson, 1985, p 78, emphasis in original). In other words, a broken window, a littered street or unkempt garden does not harm that neighbourhood but if left unchecked it sends a signal that the residents do not care, and as a result it becomes easier to vandalise property and commit robbery, particularly as more and more people remove themselves from the streets.

Wilson and Kelling's approach has been highly influential in the Labour government's thinking on crime. In an exclusive interview with the *Daily Express*, the Prime Minister repeated the logic of the broken windows thesis:

> If you are tolerant of small crimes, and I mean vandalism and the graffiti at the end of the street, you create an environment in which pretty soon the drug dealers move in, and then after that the violent people with their knives and their guns and all the rest of it, and the community is wrecked. (quoted in Young and Mathews, 2003, p 41)

The government has successfully promoted a discussion about disorder through the language of 'anti-social behaviour':

I wholly disagree with those who argue that if we tackle relatively minor disorder that behaviour will be displaced into more serious offending. Indeed the reverse is true. Stopping people from being involved in anti-social behaviour can prevent that behaviour from escalating into more serious forms of crime. (Straw, 1995, p 18)

Although there is no single definition of 'anti-social behaviour', the 1998 Crime and Disorder Act defines it as acting "in a manner that caused or was likely to cause harassment, alarm or distress to one or more persons not of the same household as [the defendant]" (SEU, 2000). Some behaviours that are commonly included are: noise, conflicts (including harassment, domestic violence and racist incidents); litter and rubbish dumping; graffiti and vandalism; uncontrolled pets; using and selling drugs; nuisance from vehicles; unkempt gardens; and young people hanging around street corners (SEU, 2000). Consequently, the definition of 'anti-social behaviour' is wide-ranging, conflating serious criminal incidents (such as domestic violence and racial harassment) with seemingly innocuous non-criminal activities such as young people hanging around.

Some of these behaviours are concerned with the breaching of set standards or informal rules concerning the governance of neighbourhoods and the relationships between individuals and families within them. The introduction of recent policies to control these behaviours could be seen as an attempt to produce social conformity in an effort to shore up 'community cohesion'. Acts of vandalism or unkempt gardens could, therefore, be conceptualised as indicators of 'social non-conformity'[10], although academics have used alternative language to describe the same activities. For example, Burrows and Rhodes (1998) use the term 'neighbourhood dissatisfaction', while Hough (1995) describes these activities as 'cues about disorder'.

No matter which term is used, the emerging evidence points to the existence of inequalities in the experience and impact of such activities both between areas and different social groups. The SEU (2000), for example, reports that a greater proportion of people living in deprived neighbourhoods perceive 'anti-social behaviour' as a problem in their area (see Figure 9.2), while Burrows' and Rhodes' (1998) research shows that social renters express the highest rates of neighbourhood dissatisfaction. However, homeowners and private renters also report problems.

The PSE Survey does not contain data at the area level so it is not possible to confirm whether these issues affect poor neighbourhoods

Figure 9.2: Perception of a serious problem in the respondent's local area, 1997-98

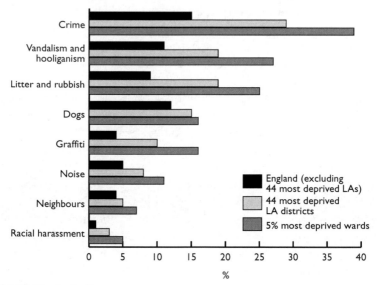

Note: LA = local authority.
Source: SEU (2000, Figure 6, p 22)

disproportionately. However, it is able to assess differential rates of reporting of these local issues by social groups (Table 9.4). PSE Survey respondents were additionally asked a set of questions relating to area disadvantage in order to provide a more comprehensive assessment of the kinds of issues that affect people in their localities. The questions were intended to capture aspects of quality of life that get overlooked in discussions about 'disorder', and these findings are also reported in Table 9.4. Sixty per cent of the PSE sample report local issues such as vandalism and noise as common in their area and a further 45% report area disadvantage such as pollution and traffic. Rates vary by population group, and people living in a permanent state of poverty report higher levels of both area disadvantage and other local issues. This is also the case for unemployed respondents, those living in jobless households, and social renters. Conversely, those least affected are managers and professionals, those in paid work, those living in in-work households, the retired and homeowners.

The results are explored in further detail in Figures 9.3 and 9.4. Figure 9.3 demonstrates that, with the exception of the presence of 'homeless people or people begging', poor people are more likely to report these activities occurring in their local area. The most common

Table 9.4: Percentage of respondents reporting issue as common in their area and other area disadvantage, by a selection of poverty and social exclusion variables

Poverty and social exclusion variables	Local issue	Local area disadvantage
PSE poor		
Yes	71	59
No	53	41
Income poor		
Below 50% average	65	51
Above 50% average	55	42
Subjectively poor		
All the time	**80**	**66**
Only sometimes/never	56	44
Social class		
Routine occupation	60	47
Management/professional	54	41
Economic status		
Working	56	42
Unemployed	**69**	**67**
Economically inactive	59	47
Jobless household		
No workers	**70**	51
Workers	58	45
Retired	48	42
Housing tenure		
Owner	54	42
Social renter	71	55
Private renter	59	55
Total % in the population	**57**	**45**

behaviour mentioned by poor respondents is 'teenagers hanging around on the streets' (50% compared to only 30% among other respondents). However, it cannot be inferred from this that half of poor respondents considers teenagers to be a problem in their area. It may be that in areas where poor people live, teenagers simply do not have access to indoor leisure activities which would make them less visible on the streets. Fisher and Bramley, for example, in this volume (Chapter Eight) found that people living in poverty were more likely to report constraints (in terms of supply, quality and cost) on the usage of youth facilities[11], although it cannot be ruled out that 'teenagers hanging around on the streets' is not seen as more problematic by poor respondents.

People living in poverty also report higher levels of disadvantage associated with their local area (Figure 9.4). Street noise from traffic,

Figure 9.3: Percentage of respondents perceiving issue as common in their local area, by poverty status (PSE measure)

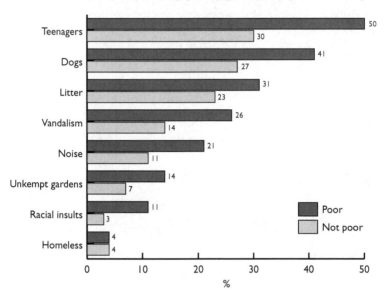

Figure 9.4: Percentage of respondents reporting disadvantages in their area, by poverty status (PSE measure)

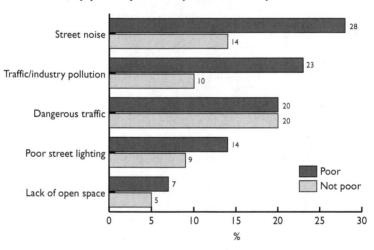

businesses and factories represents the greatest problem, affecting 28% of poor people – twice the rate for the remaining population. Similarly, the poor are more than twice as likely to report problems relating to pollution from traffic or industry as others. Poor street lighting and the lack of open spaces are also problematic issues.

Insecurity

In this section, we examine the relationship between social exclusion and insecurity, as well as fear of crime more specifically. The concept of 'fear of crime' is now well established in the criminological vocabulary, where fear of crime has traditionally been a term used to describe the concerns and anxieties that people have about crime which is seen as separate from the actual risk of experiencing crime (Hough, 1995). More recently, however, the term has been questioned in terms of both methodological and conceptual adequateness (Innes and Fielding, 2002). Some work has shown that people may not be feeling afraid but do express an awareness about crime (see, for example, Ditton et al, 1999; Farell and Ditton, 1999). On the other hand, others have argued that when people talk about crime they may be also inadvertently articulating a number of other and diffuse sets of anxieties (see, for example, Girling et al, 2000).

Putting aside these arguments about the adequacy of the term, a significant focus of fear of crime research has been to look into the social distribution of risks. Issues of gender and age, and their interplay, have dominated these discussions (see, for example, Clarke and Lewis, 1982; Pain, 1997), although far less attention has been paid to the effects of poverty and social exclusion. What evidence does exist shows that the poor have significantly higher rates of fear of crime. For instance, Pantazis and Gordon (1997a) found that multiply deprived individuals in the 1990 Breadline Britain Survey had substantially higher rates of fear of crime than others in the population, but lower risks of victimisation. Pantazis (2000b) explained the higher rates of 'fear' among people living in poverty in terms of aspects of their financial vulnerability, which means that they are less able to afford the protective measures available to others (for example, their own private transport, home security and insurance). However, this lack of control over security feeds into, and is interrelated to, other forms of insecurity such as job loss and debts (Pantazis, 2000b). Furthermore, perceptions of insecurity are strengthened when poverty interacts with other dimensions of vulnerability (for example, such as those associated with gender and age). For example, Pantazis (2000b) found that the highest risks of anxiety were among elderly women, without private transport, and struggling on a low income. Considering the interplay between gender, age and poverty is therefore crucial in understanding people's sense of insecurity.

One of the most common approaches to measuring fear of crime in victimisation surveys is to ask respondents how safe they feel when walking alone in their local area after dark. This 'global' question attempts to encompass "'any threat perceived by the respondent' and respondents who say that they feel 'very unsafe' can rightly be said to be fearful" (Hough, 1995, p 2). But because the question is framed broadly, it also allows respondents to register other concerns such as being in the dark or being alone, which do not necessarily relate to crime. For this reason, victimisation surveys often supplement this question with others including those asking respondents how safe they feel when alone in their home at night, as well as further questions about specific worries. The PSE Survey utilises all three approaches but, additionally, asks respondents about other non-criminal worries so that people's perceptions about crime can be further contextualised.

In common with the BCS, the PSE Survey reveals that respondents are much more fearful about being out on the streets than being at home alone (Table 9.5), with three times as many people reporting feeling unsafe on the streets than in their home (29% compared to 10%). The survey therefore provides evidence that the notion of 'stranger-danger' is still prevalent in attitudes. The table also shows that fear of crime is higher among all poor groups, with 25% and 42% of people living in poverty 'all the time' reporting that they feel unsafe at home and on the streets, respectively. Those in routine occupations, the economically inactive, the retired and social renters express the highest concerns about being out alone in the street after dark. Conversely, managers and professionals, workers, those living in in-work households, and homeowners are more likely to feel safe. Different patterns emerge with feeling unsafe at home, with rates being higher among the unemployed, those living in jobless households, and all renters.

Although the PSE Survey findings demonstrate that almost a third of the population is fearful, 'fear' does not appear to restrict their participation in social activities. Very few respondents cite fear of crime as a reason preventing their participation in common social activities, the most common factor being lack of money (see Chapter Five in this volume). Thus, while fear of crime is unquestionably an unpleasant feeling, the PSE Survey does not provide evidence that it leads to outright exclusion from social participation. However, other research has found that some social groups live under a de facto night-time curfew. For example, Hough (1995) reports that more than one in 10 women aged 60 and living in cities never went out after dark. Furthermore, feeling unsafe encourages the development of risk-avoidance strategies (for example, walking on some streets but not others) as people, especially women, go about the normal day-to-day

Table 9.5: Percentage of respondents feeling unsafe alone on the streets after dark or at home at night, by a selection of poverty and social exclusion variables

Poverty and social exclusion variables	Unsafe alone on the streets after dark	Unsafe alone at home at night
PSE poor		
Yes	37	17
No	27	8
Income poor		
Below 50% average	41	15
Above 50% average	25	7
Subjectively poor		
All the time	**42**	**25**
Only sometimes/never	29	9
Social class		
Routine occupation	**33**	11
Management/professional	27	10
Economic status		
Working	25	9
Unemployed	29	**16**
Economically inactive	**37**	11
Jobless household		
No workers	36	**14**
Workers	26	9
Retired	**39**	11
Housing tenure		
Owner	26	8
Social renter	**42**	**16**
Private renter	**37**	**16**
Total % in the population	**29**	**10**

business (see, for example, Chan and Rigakos, 2002). One limitation therefore of the PSE Survey is that it is only concerned with exclusion from outright participation, which affects a minority of the population, and not with restricted participation which, it can be assumed, impacts on a larger group of people.

Perceptions of safety among men and women and younger and older groups according to poverty status are shown in Table 9.6. Gender is more significant than poverty in explaining fear; women express the highest levels of concern, with 42% reporting feeling unsafe on the streets and 16% feeling unsafe at home. However, there is a clear hierarchy of insecurity evident, with poor women reporting the highest levels of fear and better-off men showing the least concern (Table 9.6). Nearly half of the poor female sample report feeling unsafe about walking alone in their local area after dark, but one in five also report feeling unsafe within their own home.

Table 9.6 also reveals the disaggregated results by age and demonstrates a more complicated pattern. Among people in poverty, younger and older respondents are equally likely to feel unsafe on the streets after dark (49%), although younger people feel less safe within their home. In contrast, better-off younger people are the least 'fearful'.

Moving beyond these general indicators to consider more specific concerns, Table 9.7 reveals the extent to which poverty and aspects of social exclusion impact on people's worries about being victimised. More than two thirds of the sample say that they are 'fairly' or 'very' worried about being a victim of crime. High rates of concern exist with respect to all dimensions of crime, including more than one quarter of women reporting that they are worried about being raped (27%). Again poor people express the highest concerns, with rates ranging from 74% to 77% with regards to any crime. This pattern is repeated across all three dimensions of crime; more than half of those living in poverty 'all the time' say they are worried about financial crime and physical crime, and nearly one third of women in this group express worry about being raped. Those in jobless households and social renters report significantly higher rates of concern over financial crimes, while those in routine jobs, the economically inactive, respondents in jobless households and social renters had the greatest rates of worry over physical crime. Worry about rape is highest among women who are unemployed or in routine jobs, in jobless households, and living in rented accommodation.

Table 9.6: Percentage of men and women and younger and older respondents feeling unsafe on the streets or at home, by poverty status (PSE measure)

Poverty and social exclusion variables	Unsafe alone on the streets after dark	Unsafe alone at home at night
PSE poor		
Male	22	13
Female	48	20
Younger (16-24)	49	28
Older (65+)	49	18
Not PSE poor		
Male	15	2
Female	39	14
Younger (16-24)	21	7
Older (65+)	35	8
Total % in the population	**29**	**10**

Table 9.7: Percentage of respondents concerned about crime, by a selection of poverty and social exclusion variables

Poverty and social exclusion variables	Financial crime	Physical crime	Sexual crime[a]	Any crime[b]
PSE poor				
Yes	69	52	33	74
No	60	39	25	65
Income poor				
Below 50% average	67	57	34	74
Above 50% average	60	36	23	64
Subjectively poor				
All the time	71	59	30	**77**
Only sometimes/never	62	42	27	67
Social class				
Routine occupation	61	**49**	**31**	68
Management/professional	62	33	19	65
Economic status				
Working	63	38	30	69
Unemployed	52	46	**36**	60
Economically inactive	63	**52**	24	69
Jobless household				
No workers	**68**	**56**	**42**	75
Workers	63	38	28	67
Retired	58	48	16	65
Housing tenure				
Owner	61	39	23	66
Social renter	**70**	**57**	**37**	77
Private renter	60	45	**49**	64
Total % in the population	**62**	**42**	**27**	**68**

Notes: [a] Relates to women only; [b] excludes the experience of sexual criminal harm.

Figure 9.5 presents more detailed findings about concerns over specific crimes by poverty status. The patterns are familiar, with people in poverty being more likely to worry about each type of crime. Burglary attracts the biggest concern among the poor, a finding confirmed in previous studies (for example, Hough, 1995). However, the results show a strong pattern of inequality with people living in poor circumstances being significantly more likely to worry about being attacked in their own home by a stranger (30% compared to 17%) or a known person (19% compared to 7%). While less than one in 10 of the 'not poor' group worries about being attacked in their own home by someone they know, this increases to one in five among poor respondents. There are no clear gender patterns here, with poor men and women being equally likely to express worry about experiencing this kind of attack, although younger respondents report much higher

Figure 9.5: Percentage of respondents worrying about being a victim of crime, by poverty status (PSE measure)

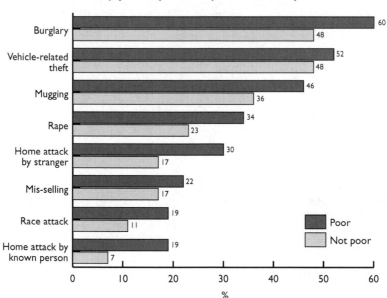

rates than older respondents. It is clear that for some social groups the home is far from being seen as a safe haven.

Indeed, the PSE Survey reveals that concerns about crime among poor respondents are not isolated experiences; people in poverty live in a perpetual state of concern about a whole range of issues (Table 9.8). The worst affected are those people who live in poverty 'all the time', with nine out of every 10 reporting at least one worry. More than 80% stated having worries about events which are psychologically harmful, and three in four worry about financial issues.

Concern over financially and physically harmful events is greatest among those in routine jobs, the unemployed, respondents in jobless households, and social renters. These groups also report a greater concern with physically harmful events, as do those in retired households. People in routine occupations, in work, or in jobless households, and social renters express the most worry about psychologically harmful events.

Figure 9.6 presents more detailed analysis on the extent to which people in poverty experience disproportionate levels of concern over harmful events and conditions. Poor people report higher levels of concern in each case. Highest among these concerns is the death of a close relative or friends (63%). Following closely behind is the issue of debt and it is that insecurity which reveals the greatest divisions within

Table 9.8: Percentage of respondents concerned about experiencing non-criminal harmful events and conditions, by a selection of poverty and social exclusion variables

Poverty and social exclusion variables	Financial harm	Physical harm	Psychological harm	Any harm
PSE poor				
Yes	58	50	77	**86**
No	28	40	66	74
Income poor				
Below 50% average	42	52	71	81
Above 50% average	33	39	68	76
Subjectively poor				
All the time	**75**	44	**82**	**91**
Only sometimes/never	33	43	68	76
Social class				
Routine occupation	**40**	**47**	71	**79**
Management/professional	25	36	66	73
Economic status				
Working	42	38	**71**	**78**
Unemployed	**54**	44	60	71
Economically inactive	24	**49**	66	76
Jobless household				
No workers	44	**52**	**75**	82
Workers	42	38	71	77
Retired	9	49	58	71
Housing tenure				
Owner	32	40	67	75
Social renter	**48**	**53**	**76**	**86**
Private renter	35	39	68	74
Total % in the population	**36**	**43**	**68**	**77**

the population. Living in poverty often involves making ends meet by getting into debt (see McKay and Collard, Chapter Seven in this volume). The PSE data show that while one in four poor people fell into debt in the previous year, more than half worry about getting into debt. Thus, even if people have been able to avoid falling into debt, living in poverty is a constant reminder of the possibility, particularly for those individuals and family who face limited chances of escaping from their impoverishment.

Labour's response to crime, 'disorder' and insecurity

Labour has made tackling crime and disorder and maintaining security central planks of government policy. In a period of just eight years, Labour has created over 1,000 new criminal offences (Liberal

Figure 9.6: Percentage of the population worrying about different harmful events and conditions, by poverty status (PSE measure)

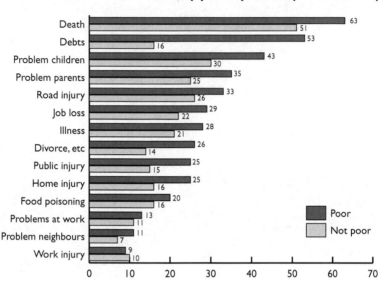

Democrats, 2005), leading Pemberton (2005) to accuse the government of 'hyper-activity' in this area while ignoring other more serious forms of harm. Indeed this hyper-activity has gathered pace since the 2001 Election, with a total of 34 anti-crime Bills being introduced by the government (*The Guardian*, 2004). In the Queen's Speech in November 2004 Labour signalled its greatest determination to date to demonstrate how far it considers crime and security as priority issues. It committed itself to eight anti-crime Bills covering a myriad of issues including the introduction of identity cards, a serious crime investigations bureau, increased police powers to deal with terrorism and anti-social behaviour – leading some political commentators to criticise the government for contributing to the politics of fear in which "the most pressing issues facing Britain are two threats now oddly twinned: terrorism and yobs" (*The Guardian*, 2004).

The government's latest stance represents a significant change in the way crime and security issues are now dealt with, a process of politicisation stemming back to the 1979 Election and Margaret Thatcher's victory. Through a series of criminal justice policies imbued with authoritarian populism (Hall, 1980), Thatcher positioned the Conservatives successfully as the Party of 'law and order', while attacking the Labour Party opposition for being soft on crime. Tony Blair managed to undermine the image of the Labour Party as soft and ineffectual in 1992, when, as the Shadow Home Secretary, he famously proclaimed that Labour would be 'tough on crime, tough on the causes of crime' – a twin-track approach that Labour argues is at the very heart of its crime reduction strategy. Being 'tough on crime' recognises that individuals have a moral choice about whether or not to commit crime and, therefore, punishment has a role in both deterring would-be offenders and making offenders pay for their crimes. Being 'tough on the causes of crime' recognises the social conditions which breed crime (Labour Party, 1996). Whereas for 'Old' Labour, issues of poverty and inequality were seen as key causes of crime, for 'New' Labour it is factors primarily related to the family (for example, poor parenting and poor parental supervision) that are prioritised (see, for example, Labour Party, 1996). The social positivism which was imbedded in 'Old' Labour's policies has been replaced by a social/ psychological positivism in which criminality can be predicted, from an early age, based on known risk factors (see, for example, Farrington, 2002).

At the area level, the twin problems of crime and 'disorder' are considered to affect the most impoverished of neighbourhoods in which high crime rates are seen as a root cause of decline rather than a symptom (Roche, undated). Crime is seen both as a product of social exclusion and a cause of it, where social exclusion is seen as a series of linked problems such as unemployment, poor skills, low incomes, poor housing, high crime environments, bad health and family breakdown (SEU, 1998). For Young and Mathews (2003, p 9) "all these interlinking factors are seen to lead to crime just as crime creates disorder and fear, thus promoting social exclusion in its own right".

Since for the government crime is a product of social exclusion, it can be tackled through policies of inclusion. Thus, measures such as the New Deal for Young People, the Minimum Wage, Sure Start, New Deal for Communities, and Connexions, among others, can be seen as part of the government's broader inclusionary strategy which also aims to contribute to reducing crime and 'disorder'. While the government promotes inclusionary policies, it simultaneously employs social exclusionary strategies which are counterproductive.

Leaving aside the exclusionary impacts of some of their so-called inclusionary policies[12], Labour's contradictory position is perhaps most clearly marked in their current strategies to deal with anti-social behaviour. Its concern for the rights of ordinary people to lead normal lives free from harassment has led to a draconian set of policies that has had the effect of criminalising and, thereby, excluding significant sections of society which also happen to be society's most vulnerable.

The government through the 1998 Crime and Disorder Act and 2003 Anti-Social Behaviour Act, in particular, now has a litany of powers to tackle crime and disorder including: on the spot fines; curfew orders against young people out at night unsupervised in designated areas; and anti-social behaviour orders (ASBOs), which prohibit the offender from specific anti-social acts or entering defined areas for a minimum of two years. Although ASBOs are made by magistrates' courts after civil proceedings, breach of an ASBO is a criminal offence and can result in up to five years in prison. Since they were introduced five years ago a total of 3,826 ASBOs have been handed out by the courts (Home Office, 2005b), but the majority of these were given in the last year alone with many orders granted against the young, homeless people, people begging, people with mental ill health and women involved in prostitution (*The Guardian*, 2005).

Beyond the impact of specific legislation, Labour has presided over unprecedented levels of imprisonment. The most recent figures show that the prison population in England and Wales stands at more than 78,000 (Home Office, 2005c), representing an increase of 28,000 since Labour came to power in the 1997. The result of these shifts towards a much more punitive and exclusionary society is that England and Wales now has the second highest imprisonment rate in Western Europe (at 142 per 100,000 of the population) (Prison Reform Trust, 2005). Yet, the government's own Social Exclusion Unit (2002) acknowledges that many prisoners have experienced a lifetime of social exclusion: prisoners are 13 times as likely to have been in care as a child; 13 times as likely to have been unemployed; and 10 times as likely to have been a regular truant. There are also high levels of mental health problems suffered by prisoners, much higher than those found in the general population (ONS, 1998).

Conclusion

This chapter began by showing how crime is a routine feature of everyday life and is sometimes perceived as such a common phenomenon that it cuts across social divisions: since crime is everywhere it affects everyone. In recent years, concern about crime has been supplemented by an emerging discourse about 'disorder' and how small acts of 'disorder' can result in more serious forms of crime from being committed, as well as with how both crime and 'disorder' can lead to increasing levels of fear of crime among individuals and communities.

The chapter analysed the PSE Survey to assess the extent to which social and economic inequality affected people's vulnerability to crime and 'disorder', and insecurity. It found a consistent relationship between poverty and social exclusion and risks of victimisation and 'disorder', as well as fear of crime. These risks were greatest for people living in poverty, especially those who live permanently in poverty.

The PSE Survey findings also illustrate the need to go beyond a narrow understanding of criminal harm to embrace a wider definition of social harm. By adopting a social harm perspective, the chapter illuminated the extent to which living in poverty is both hazardous and stressful. Poverty exposes people to other forms of harm including illness, unemployment and debt and places enormous stress on people's social relationships especially with loved ones – whether they be children, parents or partners – as well as others such as neighbours and work colleagues. Thus, government policies that seek to protect people from the impact of crime and disorder will constantly fall short if they fail to tackle the underlying cause of people's insecurity, that is, poverty.

Notes

[1] The increase in recorded crime is likely to represent a real rise in crime because there are simply more possessions to steal (for example, mobile phones, cars, etc). However, the rise may also reflect changes in recording practices and increases in the reporting of some crimes (for example, domestic violence and sexual assault).

[2] However, research by Friends of the Earth demonstrates that polluting factories are concentrated mainly in the poorest parts of the country. For example, 66% of all cancer-causing chemicals emitted into the air come from factories in the most deprived 10% of communities in England (see www.foe.c.o.uk/resource/reports/pollution_poverty_ report.pdf).

[3] The authors define social harm as any event or behaviour which has physical, psychological or financial consequences for an individual, family or community.

[4] It has been argued by some that the higher rates of crime found among better-off individuals can be explained by response bias and reflects what has become known as the 'education effect', first identified by Sparks et al (1977).

[5] The ecological fallacy refers to inappropriate inferences being made about individuals on the basis of aggregate data obtained at the area level (see Robinson, 1950).

[6] Striving areas are defined by the ACORN classification as including (i) older people, less prosperous areas; (ii) council estate residents, better-off homes; (iii) council estate residents, high unemployment; (iv) council estate residents, greatest hardship; and (v) people in multi-ethnic, low-income areas.

[7] Where the research team considered the questions sensitive (for example, in relation to threats, assaults, rape, domestic violence, racial attacks and personal safety), the survey was completed via computer-assisted interviewing techniques that allow respondents to enter their responses onto the computer directly. This method of interviewing has been used in Home Office surveys of domestic violence and rape and has been found to yield higher prevalence estimates compared to conventional methods (see, for example, Mirrlees-Black, 1999).

[8] Financial crime includes: vehicle theft or theft from or off vehicles or vehicle vandalism (those with a vehicle only), burglary, criminal damage of home, financial mis-selling, defrauded or cheated out of money, and robbery. Physical crime includes assaults, domestic violence, and racist attacks. Sexual crime includes sexual assault (females only). Psychological crime includes threats.

[9] Financial harm includes: debts and job loss. Physical harm includes: death, other illness, injury in the home, at work, on the road or somewhere else in public, as well as food poisoning. Psychological harm includes: parents having problem with their children, respondents reporting problems with their parents, neighbours, at work, and experiencing divorce or separation.

[10] I would like to thank Ruth Levitas for suggesting this term.

[11] However, this appears to have escaped the recent attention of the managers of Bluewater Shopping Centre in Kent. In early 2005, managers at Bluewater excluded young people from wearing 'hoodies' from the shopping centre and their actions received support from the government who argued that young people with 'hoodies' were intimidating to others (*The Observer*, 2005). Arguably, expectations about behavioural conduct have now spilled over to include expectations about dress, and clothing items that are perceived as threatening will not be tolerated.

[12] For example, the New Deal, with its element of compulsion, may deny recipients benefits.

References

Baldwin, J., Bottoms, A. and Walker, M. (1976) *The urban criminal: A study in Sheffield*, London: Tavistock.

Barclay, G. and Tavares, C. (1999) *Information on the criminal justice system in England and Wales*, London: Home Office Research, Development and Statistics Directorate.

Barke, M. and Turnball, G. (1992) *Meadowell: The biography of an estate with problems*, Aldershot: Avebury.

Beck, U. (1992) *Risk society: Towards a new modernity*, London: Sage Publications.

Box, S. (1983) *Power, crime, and mystification*, London: Routledge.

Bradshaw, J. (2001) (ed) *Poverty: The outcomes for children*, London: Family Policy Studies Centre.

Burrows, R. and Rhodes, D. (1998) *Patterns of neighbourhood dissatisfaction in England, findings*, York: Joseph Rowntree Foundation.

Carrabine, E., Cox, P., Lee, M. and South, N. (2002) *Crime in modern Britain*, Oxford: Oxford University Press.

Chan, W. and Rigakos, G. (2002) 'Risk, crime and gender', *British Journal of Criminology*, vol 42, pp 743-61.

Clarke, A. and Lewis, M. (1982) 'Fear of crime among the elderly', in *The British Journal of Criminology*, vol 22, no 1, pp 49-62.

Cohen, S. (1972) *Folk devils and moral panics* (2nd edn), London: Paladin.

Coleman, C. and Moynihan, J. (1996) *Understanding crime data: Haunted by the crime data*, Buckingham: Open University Press.

Ditton, J., Bannister, E., Gilchrist, E. and Farell, S. (1999) 'Afraid or angry? Recalibrating the "fear of crime"', *International Review of Victimology*, vol 6, pp 83-99.

Dodd, T., Nicholas, S., Povey, D. and Walker, A. (2004) *Crime in England and Wales 2003/2004*, Home Office Statistical Bulletin, 10/04, July, London: Home Office Research, Development and Statistics Directorate.

Doyal, L. and Nandy, S. (2000) *An integrated approach to injuries in the household: Literature review and conceptual development paper*, NHS Regional Programme C/INJ/05/05.99/Doyal, Final Report.

Drever, F. and Bunting, J. (1997) 'Patterns and trends in male mortality', in F. Drever and M. Whitehead (eds) *Health inequalities*, London: The Stationery Office.

Farell, S. and Ditton, J. (1999) 'Improving the measurement of attitudinal responses: an example from a fear of crime survey', *International Journal of Social Research Methodology*, vol 2, no 1, pp 55-68.

Farrington, D. (2002) 'Developmental criminology and risk-focused prevention', in M. Maguire, R. Morgan and R. Reiner (eds) *The Oxford handbook of criminology*, Oxford: Oxford University Press.

Foster, J. and Hope, T. (1993) *Housing, community and crime: The impact of the Priority Estates Project*, London: HMSO.

Garland, D. (2000) 'The culture of high crime societies: some preconditions of recent "law and order" policies', *British Journal of Criminology*, vol 40, no 3, pp 347-75.

Garland, D. (2001) *The culture of control: Crime and social order in contemporary society*, Oxford: Oxford University Press.

Garside, R. (2004) *Crime, persistent offenders and the justice gap*, London: Crime and Society Foundation.

Giddens, A. (1991) *Modernity and self-identity*, Oxford: Polity Press with Blackwell.

Girling, E., Loader, I. and Sparks, R. (2000) *Crime and social change in Middle England*, London: Routledge.

Gordon, D. (2000) 'Inequalities in income, wealth and standard of living', in C. Pantazis and D. Gordon (eds) *Tackling inequalities: Where are we now and what can be done?*, Bristol: The Policy Press.

Gordon, D. (2004) 'Poverty, disease and death', in P. Hillyard, C. Pantazis, S. Tombs and D. Gordon (eds) *Beyond criminology: Taking harm seriously*, London: Pluto Press.

Gordon, D. and Pantazis, C. (1997) *Breadline Britain in the 1990s*, Aldershot: Ashgate.

Green, D. (2004) *Do the official crime figures tell the whole story? 2003/ 04: Crimes omitted from the British Crime Survey*, Background Briefing, Civitas (www.civitas.org.uk.data/crimeFigures2003-04.php), accessed 4 April 2005.

Guardian, The (2004) 'Queen's Speech homes in on security', *The Guardian*, 24 November.

Guardian, The (2005) 'A triumph of hearsay and hysteria', *The Guardian*, 5 April.

Hall, S. (1980) *Drifting into a law and order society*, London: The Cobden Trust.

Hanmer, J. and Saunders, S. (1984) *Well-founded fears*, London: Hutchinson.

Harrington, V. and Mayhew, P. (2001) *Mobile phone theft*, Home Office Research Study No 235, Research Development and Statistics Directorate, London: Home Office.

Hillyard, P. and Tombs, S. (2004) 'Beyond criminology?' in P. Hillyard, C. Pantazis, S. Tombs and D. Gordon (eds) *Beyond criminology: Taking harm seriously*, London: Pluto Press.

Hillyard, P., Pantazis, C., Tombs, S. and Gordon, D. (2004) *Beyond criminology: Taking harm seriously*, London: Pluto Press.

Hirshfield, A. and Bowers, K. (1996) 'The geography of crime and disadvantage: an English case study', 5th International Seminar on Environmental Criminology and Crime Analysis, Tokyo, Japan, 1-3 July.

Home Office (2005a) 'Anti-social behaviour day count' (www.homeoffice.gov.uk/crime/antisocialbehaviour/daycount/index.html), accessed 23 January 2005.

Home Office (2005b) 'Anti-social behaviour orders' (www.crimereduction.gov.uk/asbos2.htm), accessed 5 April 2005.

Home Office (2005c) 'Population in custody', February, England and Wales, Monthly Tables (www.homeoffice.gov.uk/rds/pdfs05/prisfeb05.pdf), accessed 5 April 2005.

Hough, M. (1995) *Anxiety about crime: Findings from the 1994 British Crime Survey*, Home Office Research Study No 147, Home Office Research and Planning Unit, London: Home Office.

Hough, M. and Mayhew, P. (1983) *The British Crime Survey: First report*, A Home Office Research and Planning Unit Report, London: Home Office.

Hulsman, L. (1986) 'Critical criminology and the concept of crime', in H. Bianchi and R. van Swanningen (eds) *Abolitionism: Towards a non-repressive approach to crime*, Amsterdam: Free University Press.

Innes, M. and Fielding, N. (2002) 'From community to communicative policing: signal crimes and the problem of public reassurance', *Sociological Research Online*, vol 7, no 2 (www.socresonline.org.uk/7/2/innes.html).

Jones, T., MacLean, B. and Young, J. (1986) *The Islington Crime Survey*, Aldershot: Gower.

Kempshall, H. (2003) *Understanding risk in criminal justice*, Buckingham: Open University Press.

Kinsey, R. (1985) *Final Report of the Merseyside Crime and Police Surveys*, Liverpool: Merseyside County Council.

Kinsey, R. and Young, J. (1985) 'Crime is a class issue', *New Statesman*, 11 January, pp 16-17.

Labour Party (1996) *Tackling the causes of crime*, London: Labour Party.

Lea, J. and Young, J. (1984) *What is to be done about law and order?*, London: Pluto Press.

Levitas, R. (2005) *The inclusive society: Social exclusion and new labour* (2nd edn), London: Palgrave.

Lewis, G. and Sloggett, A. (1998) 'Suicide, deprivation, and unemployment: record linkage study', *British Medical Journal*, 7 November, vol 317, p 7168.

Liberal Democrats (2005) 'News: government creates 1,000 new criminal offences since 1997' (www.libdems.org.uk/story.html?id=8180), accessed 22 April 2005.

Mayhew, H. (1851-62) (reprinted 1967) *London labour and the London poor* (four volumes), London: Frank Cass.

Mayhew, P. and Maung, N. (1992) *Surveying crime: Findings from the 1992 British Crime Survey*, London: Home Office Research, Development and Statistics Directorate.

Mirrlees-Black, C. (1999) *Domestic violence: Findings from a new British Crime Survey self-completion questionnaire*, Home Office Research Study No 191, Home Office Research and Planning Unit, London: Home Office.

Morris, J. (1957) *The criminal area*, London: Routledge Kegan Paul.

Murie, A. (1997) 'Linking housing changes to crime', *Social Policy and Administration*, vol 31, no 5, pp 22-36.

Observer, The (2005) 'Fashion item or symbol of fear?', *Sunday Observer*, 1 May.

ODPM (Office of the Deputy Prime Minister) (2003) *Fires in the home: Findings from the 2001/2 British Crime Survey*, London: National Statistics.

ONS (Office for National Statistics) (1998) *Psychiatric morbidity among prisoners in England and Wales*, London: The Stationery Office.

Oppenheim, C. (1990) *Poverty: The facts*, London: Child Poverty Action Group.

Pain, R. (1997) 'Whither women's fear? Perceptions of sexual violence in public and private space', *International Review of Victimology*, vol 4, no 4, pp 297-312.

Pantazis, C. (2000a) 'Tackling inequalities and social harm', in C. Pantazis and D. Gordon (eds) *Tackling inequalities: Where are we now and what can be done?* Bristol: The Policy Press.

Pantazis, C. (2000b) '"Fear of crime", vulnerability, and poverty', *British Journal of Criminology*, vol 40, no 3, pp 414-35.

Pantazis, C. and Gordon, G. (1997a) 'Poverty and crime', in D. Gordon and C. Pantazis (eds) *Breadline Britain in the 1990s*, Aldershot: Ashgate.

Pantazis, C. and Gordon, G. (1997b) 'Poverty and health', in D. Gordon and C. Pantazis (eds) *Breadline Britain in the 1990s*, Aldershot: Ashgate.

Payne, S. (1997) 'Poverty and mental health', in D. Gordon and C. Pantazis (eds) *Breadline Britain in the 1990s*, Aldershot: Ashgate.

Pemberton, S. (2005) 'Moral indifference and corporate manslaughter: compromising safety in the name of profit?', in S. Tully (ed) *Research handbook on corporate legal responsibility*, London: Edward Elgar.

Prison Reform Trust (2005) *Prison fact file*, London: Prison Reform Trust.

Roberts, I. and Power, C. (1996) 'Does the decline in child injury vary by social class? A comparison of class specific mortality in 1981 and 1991', *British Medical Journal*, September, vol 313, pp 784-6.

Robinson, W. (1950) 'Ecological correlations and the behaviour of individuals', *American Sociological Review*, no 15, pp 351-7.

Roche, B. (undated) 'Crime and social exclusion', Smith Institute Seminar (www.barbararoche.labour.co.uk/ViewPage.cfm?Page=10627), accessed 6 April 2005.

Russell, D. (1982) *Rape in marriage*, New York, NY: Macmillan.

SEU (Social Exclusion Unit) (1998) *Bringing Britain together: A national strategy for neighbourhood renewal*, London: The Stationery Office.

SEU (2000) *National strategy for neighbourhood renewal, Report of Policy Action Team: Anti-Social Behaviour*, London: The Stationery Office.

SEU (2002) *Reducing re-offending by ex-prisoners*, London: The Stationery Office.

Shaw, M., Dorling, D., Gordon, D. and Davey-Smith, G. (1999) *The widening gap: Health inequalities and policy in Britain*, Bristol: The Policy Press.

Sparks, R., Genn, H. and Dodd, D. (1977) *Surveying victims: A study of the measurement of criminal victimization, perceptions of crime, and attitudes to criminal justice*, Chichester: John Wiley & Sons.

Straw, J. (1995) 'Straw and order', *New Statesman*, 15 September, p 18.

Watt, P. and Jacobs, K. (1999) 'Discourses of social exclusion: an analysis of "Bringing Britain together: a national strategy for neighbourhood renewal"', Discourse and Policy Change Conference, University of Glasgow, 3-4 February.

Wilson, J. (1985) *Thinking about crime*, New York, NY: Random House.

Young, J. and Mathews, R. (2003) 'New Labour, crime control and social exclusion', in R. Mathews and J. Young (eds) *The new politics of crime and punishment*, Cullompton: Willan.

TEN

Mental health, poverty and social exclusion

Sarah Payne

Introduction

New Labour's social exclusion strategy has in recent years extended to policy for people with mental health problems. A series of documents published by the Department of Health since 1997 has acknowledged the relationship between social exclusion and poor mental health: "mental health problems can result from a range of adverse factors associated with social exclusion and can also be a cause of social exclusion" (DH, 1999a, p 7).

However, the various strategy and policy documents published since 1997 have largely focused on mental ill health as a cause of social exclusion, and policy has concentrated on the ways in which people with mental health problems might be better included, rather than how the social exclusion and poverty which may increase mental ill health could be prevented. In May 2003, for example, the Social Exclusion Unit (SEU) published a consultation document on mental health and social exclusion, focusing on "what more can be done to reduce social exclusion among adults with mental health problems" (SEU, 2003a, p 1). The later SEU (2004) report from the consultation reiterates this focus on the exclusion of people with mental health problems, while the strategy paper *Action on mental health – A guide to promoting social inclusion* (SEU, 2003b) offers practical guidance regarding the inclusion of people with mental health problems into work, better housing and the reduction of stigma, but does not reflect on the ways in which social exclusion and poverty might increase the risks of mental distress. This failure to identify and explore in more detail the ways in which social exclusion might impair mental well being means that policy aimed at preventing or reducing mental health problems among the population as a whole is less likely to succeed, while population level health improvement targets, such as those relating to suicide in *Our healthier nation* (DH, 1999b), may also be affected[1].

However, there are significant reasons to believe that social exclusion and poverty are indeed factors which affect mental health and increase the risk of difficulties. It is becoming increasingly clear that the relationship between health and poverty is complex. The weight of evidence demonstrating an association between poverty and mortality and morbidity has grown over time (for example, Townsend et al, 1982; Drever and Whitehead, 1997; Davey Smith et al, 2001). However, it is also evident that this association is not simple and while in some respects causal pathways have been established (between damp spores in housing and respiratory illness, for example), one of the most important intervening factors appears to be that of mental health (Hunt, 1997). Wilkinson (2001) points to the importance of understanding 'psychosocial' pathways in health inequality – the part played by psychosocial factors such as sense of control over one's life, relationships with others, and life events, and this relationship has been picked up by the government in recent health policy initiatives (DH, 2001). The relationship between mental health and poverty, then, is important not simply because of the high social and public health costs of mental disorders but also because of the potential impact on health in a wider sense.

Mental illness is also a global health problem, with a growing proportion of the world's population – in both the developed and developing world – suffering from some form of mental health problem. Depression, in particular, is a major difficulty and a significant cause of disability around the world (Eisenberg, 1997; WHO, 1999). Given the impact of mental health problems as a disabling condition and significant contributor to Disability-Adjusted Life Years (DALYs), there is an urgent need to understand the distribution of such difficulties and ways in which national and global health policies might reduce this burden.

This chapter explores data from the 1999 Poverty and Social Exclusion (PSE) Survey, focusing on the relationship between experiences of poverty and social exclusion and mental health status. A range of studies, both in Britain and elsewhere, has suggested an association between poor mental health and poverty or deprivation (for example, Boardman et al, 1997; Lewis et al, 1998; Croudace et al, 2000). Intuitively, one might expect a deterioration in mental well being to result from the experience of going without the goods and services that are seen as necessary or desirable in society, particularly in the long term. It would not be surprising if individuals struggling to make ends meet, living in poor-quality housing or in high-stress environments, suffered from depression.

There is less research exploring the impact of social exclusion on mental health and well being. However, again it might be expected that being excluded from mainstream society, for whatever reason, might impact negatively on mental health just as one might hypothesise that being part of a community of friends, neighbours or family might have positive effects on mental well being. Labour government policy on social exclusion emphasises paid work as the major cause of both exclusion and poverty, and research on the association between paid employment and mental health supports the idea that people in paid work have better levels of well being than those without paid work (see Wilkinson, 1996; Payne, 1999). However, the picture is complex – mental health varies among those in paid work. One factor affecting mental health is the level and status of employment (Marmot et al, 2001); another is the 'double burden' of paid work and work outside the home, experienced most acutely by women with caring responsibilities in part-time employment (Graham and Blackburn, 1998). Thus paid work itself is not a simple protection against poor mental health – nor against social exclusion (Adelman et al, 2000; see also Chapter Five in this volume).

In addition to the policies relating to labour market exclusion, since 1997 the Labour government has also sought to tackle social exclusion through strategies for neighbourhood renewal (SEU, 2001). The aim is to reduce the problems associated with poor areas, so that "within 10 to twenty years, no-one should be seriously disadvantaged by where they live" (SEU, 2001). Within the neighbourhood renewal plans, however, references to mental illness as an outcome of social exclusion are few and far between. Mental health policies are mostly aimed at making mental health services more accessible and non-discriminatory, combined with a desire to increase safety and control. Where social exclusion is discussed alongside mental health difficulties it is as an outcome of illness rather than as a cause.

The problem of causality

A number of studies have found an association between mental health, using a variety of measurements, and socio-economic status. Much of this research has been at area level rather than at the level of the individual – for example, studies have shown higher rates of psychiatric admissions and suicidal behaviour in areas with higher levels of area-based deprivation and higher unemployment rates (Kammerling and

O'Connor, 1993; Gunnell et al, 1995; Boardman et al, 1997; Croudace et al, 2000). Some of this research – finding strong associations between the more severe psychotic illnesses, including schizophrenia, and poorer residential areas – might be explained by 'drift' factors where severely mentally ill people become poor as a result of their illness. However, Boardman et al's study (1997) found a strong correlation between social indicators of deprivation at area level and psychiatric admissions not only for psychotic conditions but also for those defined as neurotic illnesses, where such drift may occur less often. Harrison et al (1998), in a population-based study of over 38,000 respondents, compared individual mental health status with area-based deprivation scores and found highly significant correlations between psychiatric symptoms and more deprived locations.

Evidence from ecological studies relating to an association between social exclusion and poor mental health largely stems from studies showing increased psychiatric admission rates in areas with high unemployment (Kammerling and O'Connor, 1993) or during periods when national unemployment rates are elevated (for example, Brenner, 1973). However, research has also found higher levels of both suicide and parasuicide in areas with high levels of 'social fragmentation' or anomie, where there might be expected to be higher levels of social exclusion at the individual level (Congdon, 1996; Whitley et al, 1999).

Ecological surveys – focusing on indicators at area level – cannot show if there is an association between social indicators and the mental health of one individual. However, studies at the level of the individual using clinical data on diagnosis, self-reported mental health status or a psychiatric symptom screening instrument, also show an association between deprivation and mental health status. Lynch et al (1997), for example, found that people living in 'economic hardship' on a long-term basis were much more likely to be suffering from clinical depression than those not living in economic hardship, and found "little evidence of reverse causation" (p 1889) – that is, drift – over the 20 years of the study. The British OPCS (Office of Population Censuses and Surveys) Psychiatric Morbidity Survey (Meltzer et al, 1995) found higher rates of neurotic psychopathology – including depression, anxiety and phobias – among men and women with lower educational qualifications and in lower occupational groups. In the Bristol-based longitudinal ALSPAC study (Avon Longitudinal Study of Pregnancy and Childhood) of over 9,000 mothers, those reporting material deprivation and less social support also reported more ill health than those with adequate financial and social resources, with a particular connection between self-reported depression and availability of social support (Baker and Taylor, 1997).

Measuring mental health in the PSE Survey

The PSE Survey uses the short version of the General Health Questionnaire (GHQ-12), a screening instrument designed for use in general populations to detect the presence of symptoms of mental ill-health and in particular depression (Goldberg, 1972; see www.bristol.ac.uk/poverty/pse/welcome.htm). The 12 elements in the GHQ-12 focus on symptoms of depression, with four potential responses for each one ranging around either side of a 'usual' answer. For example, the first item asks, 'Have you recently been able to concentrate on whatever you're doing?' with the four possible responses being 'Better than usual', 'Same as usual', 'Less than usual' and 'Much less than usual'. Answers are treated in a bi-polar way, with 'better' and 'the same' receiving a zero score and 'less than' and 'much less than' receiving a score of one. Thus a respondent may score anywhere between zero and 12 for this screening instrument.

The GHQ-12 was developed from the longer versions of the GHQ, which have up to 60 questions in them. Both the original 60-item list and the smaller versions, including the GHQ-12, use items which have been statistically evaluated for their validity, reliability and sensitivity (Goldberg, 1972). The shorter version, the GHQ-12, was developed for use in situations such as the 1999 PSE Survey where an extended number of such questions would be inappropriate or might reduce response rates and the value of findings. A number of studies have evaluated the validity of different versions of the GHQ against other screening, including the GHQ-12 which is now one of the most used versions, and have demonstrated that the instrument does successfully identify individuals whose depression would also be diagnosed by clinicians (Papassotiropoulos and Heun, 1999). It is important to recognise that the GHQ does not give an indication of psychiatric 'caseness' in all instances (see, for example, Kessler et al, 1999; Middleton and Shaw, 2000). However, although there is some controversy over the use of the GHQ-12 as a simple indicator of clinically treatable psychiatric disorder (Heath, 1999), there is reasonable agreement that the device can indicate undue levels of distress, anxiety and depression. It is used here as an indicator of poor well being which can then be explored alongside indicators of deprivation and exclusion.

The optimum cut-off score in studies of validity, testing the GHQ-

12 against other screening devices and blind-rating of symptoms by clinically trained personnel, is between three and four, where a GHQ-12 score of four to 12 indicates the presence of mental disorder, and a score of zero to three indicates no such ill health (Papassotiropoulos and Heun, 1999).

Overall, 3% of the PSE Survey respondents have a GHQ score of between 10 and 12, that is, at the very highest end of the potential range, compared with just over half of the respondents who have a score of zero. Using a cut-off point of three and four, where scores of four and over are seen as indicative of the presence of poor mental health, 18% of respondents can be viewed as suffering from what Weich and Lewis (1998a) describe as some form of common mental disorder. This level of ill health in the sample is close to that found in other surveys. For example, the OPCS Psychiatric Morbidity Survey used a longer interview schedule designed to detect minor psychiatric disorders (CIS-R; Clinical Interview Schedule (Revised)) and found 14% of the survey population suffering from a number of psychiatric symptoms (Meltzer et al, 1995). A study of mental health and poverty in Finland using the GHQ-12 detected mental ill health in 18% of the population (Viinamäki et al, 1995).

There is a small difference between men and women in the PSE Survey, with 16% of the male respondents defined as depressed compared with 20% of female respondents. This is similar to other studies – in the OPCS Psychiatric Morbidity Survey, for example, 18% of women and 12% of men suffered from psychiatric symptoms (Meltzer et al, 1995). There are also some differences across age groups in terms of GHQ score but these are minor. Breaking responses down by ethnic group reveals some variation although the number of minority respondents is small and results must be treated with some caution. Of respondents who can be described as non-white, over a third (36%) have a GHQ score of four or more.

Adults living in family units with children have a slightly higher risk of depression than those without children, and lone parents are more likely than any other group to suffer from depression with over a quarter suffering from mental ill health. Some of this is associated with poverty and exclusion as lone parents are more likely than parents in couple households to be both poor and suffer exclusion (Baker and Taylor, 1997; Brown and Moran, 1997; see also Chapter Fourteen in this volume). However, the burden of parenting is also greater in lone-parent households and research has found higher levels of mental ill health even after controlling for poverty (Hope et al, 1999).

Poverty and mental health

A number of studies have found an association between poor mental health and the experience of poverty (Weich and Lewis, 1998a, 1998b; Whitley et al, 1999). Poverty has been seen as both a trigger and as a key part of the persistence of poor mental health (Weich and Lewis, 1998a).

Just as mental ill health is difficult to define and measure, poverty is a term open to a number of different definitions (see Chapter Two in this volume). Table 10.1 shows the distributions of poverty based on the definition of socially perceived necessities and of mental health based on the GHQ score. As the second column indicates, around a quarter of the sample population are poor with a further 10% vulnerable to poverty. However, the third column shows the risk of common mental disorders is much higher among the poor – over a half of those with mental ill health are in this group.

There are few differences between men and women in terms of the impact of poverty on mental health, with poverty presenting an increased risk of poor mental health for both. Although, perhaps unsurprisingly, poverty appears to have an effect on the mental well being of both men and women, it is likely that there are some differences in how this effect operates – associated with, for men, stresses related to self-esteem in the role of breadwinner or primary earner, providing for a family, and for women, stress revolving around caring responsibilities and managing a family budget on a low income. There is an increased risk of mental ill health for the poor compared with the non-poor for every age group. However, this risk is greatest among those under retirement age – around two fifths of the poor who are under 65 have a GHQ score of four or more. There are a range of reasons why this might be the case, partly associated with cohort effects – for example, more older people come from a generation who have lived through earlier periods of poverty and might have a different

Table 10.1: The distribution of poverty and poor mental health

	PSE Survey poverty classifications	% with GHQ score of 4+
Poor	26	50
Vulnerable to poverty	10	8
Rising out of poverty	2	1
Not poor	62	41
Sample = 1,534	100	100

reaction; those under retirement age might feel the effects of poverty more in association with self-esteem and expectations of providing a reasonable standard of living for themselves and their family.

A similar association is found between subjective accounts of poverty and poor mental health. Asking respondents if they feel poor without defining what this means is revealing – for example, a tenth of those who reply that they 'never felt poor' are revealed by the objective measures in the survey to be poor (Gordon et al, 2000; see also Chapter Two in this volume) – possibly because these respondents have developed relatively low expectations of life. However, feeling poor is associated with a higher risk of common mental disorders, as Figure 10.1 shows.

In the 1990 Breadline Britain Survey three fifths of those feeling poor 'all the time' reported isolation, and over half reported feeling depressed. In 1999, using a different measure of mental health, a similar finding emerges, with three fifths of those saying they 'feel poor all the time' also suffering from poor mental health. The association between poor mental health and poverty at the subjective level is particularly interesting.

In the PSE Survey respondents who replied that they 'never feel poor', but who are found in the objective measure to be poor, might be expected to have better mental health than those who are poor and who also feel poor, as a result of lower expectations and greater satisfaction with their lives. This appears to be the case: more than two thirds of those in the poor group who also report that they feel poor are suffering from common mental disorders compared with a quarter of those in the poor group who report not feeling poor. However, it is

Figure 10.1: Self-reported poverty and mental health

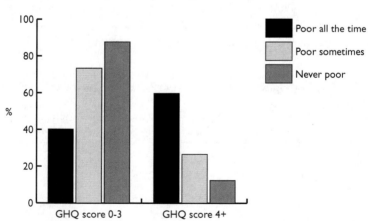

worth noting that the objective measure seems more closely connected with common mental disorders than the subjective one – that is, rates of mental ill health are higher than average among all of the poor, no matter whether they felt poor or not.

The third measure used to explore poverty and mental health is that of income. A range of measures are employed to explore equivalised incomes for households of different sizes, and each of the different measures reveals higher rates of common mental disorders among people in low-income households, particularly among the lowest incomes. For example, 25% of those living in a household with an equivalised weekly gross income of under £100 suffer from mental health symptoms compared with 12% of those in households with over £700 a week. Research suggests that income inequality is a powerful predictor of mental health. In Weich et al's study (2001) the well-off were more likely to suffer common mental disorders when living in areas with high income inequality. People on lower incomes, however, had higher rates of mental ill health in areas of greater income equality. This suggests that to some extent mental health is not only associated with the experience of being poor – but also with the subjective experience of inequality in a complex way. For example, those on high incomes in unequal areas may suffer more stress and consequent ill health than their well-off counterparts in more equal areas, perhaps as a result of their increased fear of crime (Weich et al, 2001).

Some studies have used housing tenure as an indicator of poverty and tenure has a close with association with income (Meltzer et al, 1995; Tulle-Winton; 1997). Changes in the housing market in recent years – the growth of the owner-occupied sector and the decline of social housing – have strengthened the association between social housing and being on a low income. In 1999 the odds of being poor for those who are local authority or housing association tenants are greater than for any other housing tenure, and a quarter of social housing tenants suffer common mental disorders. Similarly, being in private rented housing increases the risk of poverty, and a fifth of those in this sector in the PSE Survey have some kind of mental health problem.

Deprivation and mental health

This section explores in more detail the specific aspects of deprivation. Research has suggested that various aspects of deprivation impact in a negative way on mental well being through engendering feelings of powerlessness, lack of control, low self-esteem and distress, and increasing the psychosocial factors which increase the risk of common mental disorders (Tulle-Winton, 1997; Croudace et al, 2000; Wilkinson, 2001).

Necessities and mental health

In the PSE 'list of necessities' some items are more closely associated with poor mental health than others. In particular there are much higher rates of mental ill health among those who lack necessities such as two pairs of all-weather shoes, and insurance on the contents of their homes. Table 10.2 includes those items classified as necessities in the Omnibus Survey by more than half the population.

More than a third of those who need but are unable to afford these necessities suffer from poor mental health. There are different ways in which such necessities might impact on mental health, of course: being unable to afford insurance and savings increases financial worries and the fear of burglary or unanticipated needs – needing to replace a major item, needing to travel unexpectedly to see relatives, for example. Being unable to afford basic repairs around the home and unable to create a pleasant home affects day-to-day experiences, creating a more depressing environment. Lacking clothes for job interviews decreases self-esteem and self-belief. Wilkinson (2001) suggests that a 'sense of control' is an important aspect of the psychosocial pathways between poverty and ill health, and in lacking these necessities the respondents' sense of control over their lives is greatly reduced.

Table 10.2: Lack of necessities and mental health

Necessity	% with GHQ score of 4+[a]
Fresh fruit and vegetables	71
Warm waterproof coat	65
Two pairs of all weather shoes	54
Special outfit	49
Money to spend on self weekly	46
Money to keep home decorated	45
Roast joint	45
Replace broken electrical goods	42
Home insurance	40
Damp-free home	37
Appropriate clothes for job interviews	37
Replace worn-out furniture	35
Regular savings	34

Note: [a] Items shown where n>20.

Housing, neighbourhood and mental health

A number of studies have explored the association between poor housing and mental health problems. As we saw earlier people in social housing are more likely to suffer from poor mental health than those in owner-occupied accommodation (Meltzer et al, 1995; Lewis et al, 1998). Poor-quality housing – housing which is damp, or where there is a lack of security, or high levels of noise – has also been associated with higher levels of mental ill health, in particular depression (Hyndman, 1990; Hopton and Hunt, 1996). Such housing difficulties may affect physical health as well, of course, and mental health difficulties are often found together with poor physical health (Meltzer et al, 1995; Gomm, 1996). Housing problems may exist alongside poverty, or in isolation from it – and may also exist singly or in combination with each other.

The PSE Survey asked respondents how satisfied they were with their current accommodation. As Figure 10.2 shows, a higher proportion of respondents who are dissatisfied with their accommodation have poor mental health, compared with those who are 'fairly' or 'very satisfied' with their housing.

One of the mechanisms which might account for this connection between satisfaction with housing and mental health is again this idea of control over one's life – this applies especially to those in social tenancies who have little control over the location and style of their home and basic repairs.

However, it is not only satisfaction with accommodation that shows a relationship with poor mental health. The Survey also asked about specific problems with accommodation. Respondents with a number of accommodation problems are more likely to suffer mental health

Figure 10.2: Satisfaction with housing and mental health

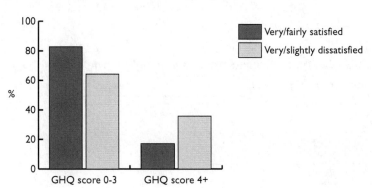

difficulties, with over a third of those with four or more accommodation problems having poor mental health, compared with 12% of those with no accommodation problems. Mental health varies slightly by the nature of the housing deprivation, as Table 10.3 shows. The most commonly reported problem is 'shortage of space'. This is mentioned by more than a fifth of respondents, and over a quarter of these have poor mental health.

Although the impact of housing deprivation on mental health is similar in every age group, the impact of poor housing appears to be greater for women than for men – particularly among those reporting very high levels of housing problem. This most probably relates to the fact that women are still largely responsible for domestic work and for maintaining a clean and comfortable home, and are more likely to suffer stress and a low sense of satisfaction if this is difficult to achieve.

Poor housing often exists in a poor environment, and research suggests that area can also exert an effect on mental health (Tulle-Winton, 1997; Yen and Kaplan, 1999). Studies have found higher rates of psychiatric admission in poor areas (Gunnell et al, 1995) and more suicidal behaviour in socially fragmented areas (Congdon, 1996; Whitley et al, 1999).

The PSE Survey asked about a range of problems – including noise, rubbish, vandalism and the state of building in the area. There is a clear relationship between poor areas and individual poverty, in that those who are poor are more likely to live in neighbourhoods with problems. Again, higher than average rates of poor mental health are found among those respondents who live in a poor environment. Thus while only a tenth of those who report no problems with their area suffer poor mental health, a third of those reporting problems with noisy neighbours suffer from common mental disorders. People who answered that they are slightly or very dissatisfied with the area where they live are more likely to suffer from poor mental health, with 38% of the men and 35% of the women who are dissatisfied having a GHQ score of four or more. Mental health is worse where there are several problems reported by respondents. Over a third of those who

Table 10.3: Type of accommodation problem and mental health

Most common problem	% with GHQ score of 4+
Damp walls, floors etc	33
Rot in window frames	32
Shortage of space	27
No place to sit outside	27
Lack of adequate heating	26
No problems	12

report four or more problems in their area had a GHQ score indicative of mental disorder.

Debt and mental health

Being in debt and the consequences of debt, such as utility disconnection and having to cut back on other expenses, might also be expected to be associated with poor mental health (Gordon and Pantazis, 1997; see also Chapter Seven in this volume for further discussion on the association between mental health and debt).

The PSE Survey asked about debt to utility companies and others in the past year, whether the respondent had ever used less than they needed of certain basic services, and also whether the respondent had ever been disconnected from a basic service such as gas or electricity.

Poor mental health is more likely among those in debt to one or more companies in the past year. The three most common services on which respondents owe money are water, council tax and telephone, all of which increase the risk of mental ill health. Over half of those who have owed money on their telephone bill in the past year are suffering from a common mental disorder. Only a small number are in mortgage arrears but of those who are, nearly 80% are suffering from mental disorder. This is likely to relate both to the very serious implications of mortgage arrears, in terms of eviction and possible homelessness, and to the fact that this kind of debt is likely to be highly indicative of poverty at all levels.

Respondents were also asked if they had to borrow at times in the past year from agencies or people other than banks and building societies, 'in order to pay for your day-to-day needs'. While most of the sample (89%) has not had to do this, those who have borrowed in this way have poorer mental health. Around 8% have borrowed from family just to meet their daily needs – and of these two fifths are suffering from poor mental health. Similarly, nearly half of those people who have borrowed from friends have poor mental health.

Social exclusion and mental health

At this point we turn to consider a relatively unexplored issue, the association between social exclusion and mental health. Social exclusion might be expected to increase risk of mental health difficulties and indeed research has suggested that good social relationships and community involvement can act to protect people in poor material circumstances from adverse effects to their mental health. Social exclusion is a concept with a range of meanings, both in research and in government policy (Levitas, 1998; SEU, 2000). The Labour government has focused on social exclusion as an explanatory tool for various social 'problems', and has focused on paid employment as the major solution to both exclusion and poverty. This section explores the relationship between mental health and three dimensions of social exclusion – exclusion from the labour market, exclusion from public services and exclusion from social relations. The fourth dimension of exclusion – impoverishment – has already been explored above.

Labour market exclusion and mental health

One of the major causes of poverty and deprivation is the experience of unemployment, and in particular long-term unemployment. A number of studies have found an association between unemployment and poor mental health. In the OPCS Psychiatric Morbidity Survey, for example, respondents defined as unemployed were the most likely group to suffer high levels of all psychiatric disorders (Meltzer et al, 1995).

Unemployment is of course notoriously difficult to define and different definitions are used in different circumstances. In particular, there are difficulties in assessing the relationship between mental health and employment status for two reasons. One problem is the direction of causality. People with pre-existing mental health problems may be less likely to be in paid work or more likely to lose their paid work as a result of their poor mental health. Alternatively, unemployment may lead to a deterioration in mental health – and of course, both of these may apply. Studies using longitudinal data, however, have suggested that unemployment is more likely to predate the onset of depression than depression causing unemployment (Wilson and Walker, 1993; Dooley et al, 1994; Montgomery et al, 1999).

The second difficulty in assessing the link between unemployment and mental health is that distinctions between two categories – unemployed and 'permanently unable to work' – are blurred; at times it may be better for an individual, either economically or emotionally, to be in one of these categories rather than another (Whiteside, 1988). Similarly, women with poor mental health who are not in paid work may take on the status of housewife, unemployed or permanently sick – depending on their eligibility for benefits and their own feelings about these different categories.

As Figure 10.3 shows, the greatest risk of poor mental health is found among respondents defined as unemployed. However, those who are permanently unable to work also have higher risks of mental

Figure 10.3: Percentage of respondents with GHQ score of 4+, by employment status

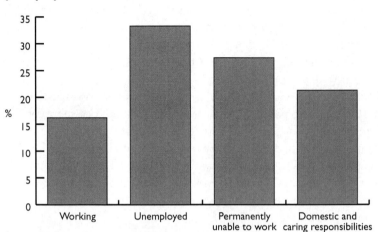

ill health compared with those in paid work. There are a number of reasons why being without paid work might have an adverse effect on mental health – over and above the poverty effect. Some research has shown that paid work can have a protective effect on mental health – providing opportunities for enhanced self-esteem or social relationships, for example (see Payne, 1999). Thus being without paid work decreases opportunities for good mental health. Conversely, the unstructured time, low status and stigma attached to being without paid work can increase negative effects on well being, which may also explain the high rates of common mental disorders among the permanently sick (although some in this category will also be people with chronic mental illness).

There is some evidence of a difference in mental health status among the employed, according to full-time or part-time status, but this is associated with the greater proportion of women in part-time work, and the generally poorer mental health of women in the Survey. Overall figures for mental health problems are similar for those in full-time and part-time work (18% and 19% respectively have poor mental health). However, among men working part time only 12% had a GHQ score of four or more, compared with 17% of the men working full time. In contrast, 20% of women working full time and 20% of those working part time suffer from common mental disorders. While these data cannot tell us whether part-time employment status is associated with a prior mental health problem for women but not for men, clearly the double burden of paid and unpaid work is likely to be of significance in explaining these figures for women (Arber, 1990; Popay, 1992; Bensing et al, 1999).

Another way of exploring the question of employment is to use the respondent's own definition of their employment status and the length of time their unemployment has lasted. The PSE Survey asked, 'Looking back over the last 10 years, for how long in total have you been unemployed?'.

Among those who have been unemployed for at least six months or more during the past decade, over a quarter have poor mental health compared with 15% of those who have not experienced unemployment in the past 10 years. Both men and women are more at risk of depression when they have experienced more than 12 months' unemployment in the last 10 years – 28% of men and 31% of women with over 12 months' unemployment have a GHQ score indicative of depression.

This finding that labour market exclusion is associated not only with poverty but also with poor mental health lends support to the idea – reflected in current Labour government policy – that finding ways of returning people to the labour market will have positive public health effects. The New Deals for different groups of unemployed people, including people with a disability such as severe mental illness, might be expected to improve this situation. The major question will be whether such policies can effectively find paid employment which reduces isolation, low status and poverty, particularly for those people suffering from poor mental health. A recent study of workers in Sweden found increased risks of mental ill health over time among those with occupational risk factors such as poor social support, shift work and job strain (Bildt and Michelsen, 2002).

One of the major causes of social exclusion is the lack of time free from responsibility to engage in activities that increase social participation. Paid work may increase inclusion by increasing financial security and reducing poverty, or by increasing the individual's feelings of self-worth, belonging, and also increasing the numbers of social contacts. For some, however, paid work reduces inclusion because it reduces opportunities for social activities – due to long hours or anti-social hours, for example, or because paid work leaves the individual too tired to participate in community or family life (see Chapter Five in this volume for further discussion). Paid work for some can also can be carried out in 'exclusionary' locations – office cleaning work, for example, often leaves the cleaner without contact with others due to the time of day it is usually performed.

Service exclusion and mental health

One of the ways in which exclusion can operate is exclusion from financial services. People who are poor more often are excluded from basic financial services such as having a bank account – a form of exclusion which increases the costs of paying bills for the poor, who are then unable to take advantage of cheaper means of paying for utilities such as direct debit payments. Very few people in the PSE Survey said that they cannot use a bank because they cannot afford it. However, among those who do not have a bank account rates of mental ill health are higher. In total 76 people say that neither they nor their partner has a bank account, and a quarter of these are suffering from depression.

The PSE Survey also looks at public and private services used by respondents, on the basis that social exclusion also extends to exclusion from such services. In these questions respondents were asked if the service was inadequate or unavailable (seen together as collective exclusion in that it is limitation at the level of provision leading to the exclusion), or if they did not use a service because they could not afford it (individual exclusion). For example, over half of those not using a service or facility because they cannot afford it have poor mental health, suggesting a powerful association between this form of social exclusion and well being. Some amenities and services are more likely to fit this 'individual' exclusion than others and show high levels of ill health among those who cannot afford them – over half of those who cannot afford to use evening classes, buses and trains, for example, have poor mental health; as do two fifths of those unable to afford the cinema and pub.

However, levels of mental ill health are also higher among those who do use many of the services or amenities listed but who find them inadequate, and also among those who do not use these because they are unavailable or unsuitable due to location or opening times, for example, suggesting that collective social exclusion is also important as a factor in well being.

Social exclusion and social relations

Social relations relates to the individual's participation in social activities, isolation, support and engagement in community life. These factors tend to interconnect in their impact on mental well being. Isolation from others, whether friends, neighbours or family, and the reasons for it, constitutes a major risk for mental health, and might be the result of a range of factors – including both absence from paid labour and participation in paid labour that restricts opportunities for being with others.

Social relationships are important. Brown and Harris (1978) found that women who had a 'close confiding relationship' with their partner were less at risk of depression, even in the face of adverse life events, than women without such a relationship. Other more recent studies have found that good social relationships or having social support can protect individuals from mental health difficulties (West, 1995; Gomm, 1996; Baker and Taylor, 1997; Schoevers et al, 2000). Seguin et al (1995), for example, found greater levels of depression among mothers who had poor material circumstances and no source of social support during pregnancy. Brown and Moran (1997) found single mothers had a greater risk of experiencing severe life events which were linked with the onset of depression but that women with low self-esteem and less support were the most at risk. Similarly, Smith et al (1993) found that the presence of social support could offset the mental health effects of such disadvantage as poor housing.

The PSE Survey asked respondents 'Have there been times in the past year when you have felt isolated and cut off from society for any of the [following] reasons?'. Over three quarters of respondents have not felt isolated in the past year, and a lower than average proportion of these (13%) is suffering from depression. Of those who have felt such a sense of isolation, however, a greater proportion also score a GHQ score indicative of depression. Higher rates of depression are found among those who report feeling isolated at times in the past year due to a range of reasons (see Figure 10.4).

Figure 10.4: Reasons for isolation from others and mental health

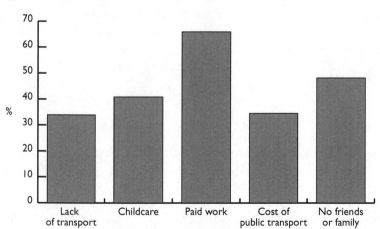

Those who report feeling isolated as a result of paid work are particularly likely to have poor mental health, again suggesting that policies to reduce social exclusion by increasing participation in paid work may be ineffective for some groups. In addition, those feeling isolated due to the lack of personal transport are more than three times as likely as the sample as a whole to have poor mental health. Those reporting isolation as a result of childcare responsibilities are more than twice as likely to be depressed, as are those feeling isolated due to a lack of family and friends. Similarly, although numbers are small, some people with poor mental health report isolation as a result of discrimination – including racism, sexism, disability-related discrimination and homophobia.

Participation in the community and mental health

Exclusion from social relations also includes participation in civic activities. Although just over a tenth of the sample is 'disengaged' in that they are not involved in any civic activities, just under a third of the sample population is disengaged in civic activities apart from voting in the General Election. National voting figures for recent elections showing the decrease in that activity suggest that a higher proportion of the population are likely to be disengaged now (Walker, 2001). However, there is very little association with mental health. Respondents who are engaged in civic activities do not differ greatly in terms of mental ill health except in one respect – those who have taken an active part in a political campaign or who have stood for civic office are much less likely to have poor mental health.

For many individuals chronic illness or disability affects all forms of participation. As Oliver (1996) and others have observed, this is the result of a society which is disabling or exclusionary – for example, the inadequacy of transport systems, pavements and public buildings for people with mobility difficulties. The disabling nature of public spaces can also arise due to stigma and discrimination, which affects the ability of people suffering some conditions to enter these spaces, or to feel relaxed when outside the home. Thus while the 'stereotype' of people with a disability encourages a focus on people in wheelchairs and access to public buildings such as cinemas or football grounds – important issues in themselves – it is important to remember also that for many with chronic health conditions the disability arises for other, more varied reasons.

Being unable to take part in activities such as going to the cinema, the library, shops, a restaurant, or a football match as a result of limiting health conditions is also associated with a higher level of common mental disorders in the PSE Survey. Over a third of those with limiting health conditions who report that they have difficulty in doing such activities also have poor mental health. For example, two fifths of those reporting difficulty in going shopping suffer from mental ill health as do over a third of those unable to go to a cinema. While to some extent this measures the impact of not being able to participate in specific activities, these are also indicators of a wider isolation – poor mental health is associated not only with being unable to go shopping but also what that represents to the individual and as an indicator of wider exclusion. Respondents who report being unable to participate in these activities mention on average just over two activities each and respondents tend to be limited in more than one way with cumulative effect on mental health.

Social relationships and mental health

Respondents were also asked about their ability to see friends and families as much as they would like to. Nearly two fifths of the sample (39%) say that they are able to see friends and family as often as they like, and among this group there is a lower rate of depression than in the sample as a whole. However, as Figure 10.5 shows, among those who feel unable to see friends and family as much as they want, the risks of poor mental health could be greater. The most common reason restricting social relationships is 'lack of time due to paid work', cited by a quarter of respondents, but this is not related to higher levels of

Figure 10.5: Mental health and factors restricting social relationships

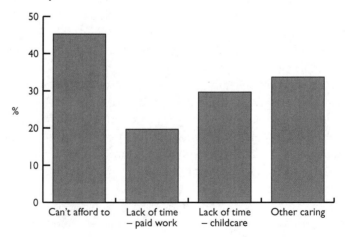

mental ill health. Similarly, those who say that distance prevents them from seeing friends and family as much as they like are not more likely than the population overall to suffer from poor mental health.

However, among respondents citing lack of money as the factor restricting social relationships, a very high proportion has poor mental health. Those saying that they lack time due to childcare or other caring responsibilities are also more likely to have poor mental health. Again the explanation for these associations might include both the impact of isolation on well being and also that a sense of control over one's life evades people who are poor, even in the area of social relationships. Thus lack of money – for travel or entertaining costs – or lack of suitable clothes, or other factors, has an effect on ordinary social participation and is also associated with increased risk of poor mental health.

Social activities and mental health

The Survey also asked about activities such as an evening out or a hobby or leisure activity, and this clearly connects with both isolation and exclusion. While a majority of respondents – 63% – are able to afford all of the activities suggested in the Survey, over a third are unable to afford one or more of these. Again, the mental health of those able to afford activities is better than the health of those respondents who cannot. Figure 10.6 shows the activities most

Figure 10.6: Social activities and mental health: percentage unable to afford activity with GHQ score of 4+

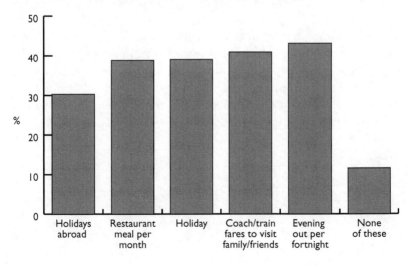

commonly given by respondents as things they cannot afford to do. More of the sample respondents who cannot afford activities such as a meal in a restaurant, for example, or a holiday away from home, or fares to enable them to visit friends or family, are suffering from poor mental health.

Conclusion

The relationship between poor mental health and various aspects of poverty, deprivation and exclusion is clearly complex. However, the 1999 PSE Survey provides evidence that, using a range of measures, people who are poor are also likely to be suffering from poor mental health. In addition, the increased risk of poor mental health is found among those reporting social exclusion, not only those who are socially excluded from labour market activity but also those excluded from other activities. Particular aspects of deprivation are also associated with higher risks of common mental disorders – poor housing conditions and area deprivation, for example. The risks appear to differ for men and women, and for those who are parents. Nonetheless, the PSE data suggest that all who experience poverty and exclusion are at an increased risk of suffering from poor mental health.

While this data cannot resolve the issue of the direction of causality, the very fact that poverty and exclusion are associated with mental well being in this way should be enough to raise concern and more specifically to raise questions about appropriate policy responses to address this health inequality. In particular, the analysis of data on social exclusion and the relationship with mental health suggests that policies aiming to reduce exclusion by labour market inclusion will fail to address the difficulties experienced by many. Running throughout this discussion is the notion of a sense of control over one's life, both material and social, as a mediating factor between the experience of poverty or exclusion and the experience of mental ill health. Policy needs most of all to address ways of returning that sense of control to these individuals if we want to address the mental health costs of poverty and social exclusion.

Note

[1] The target for improvements in mental health identified in *Saving lives: Our healthier nation* (DH, 1999b) was to reduce the death rate from suicide and undetermined injury by at least a fifth by 2010.

References

Adelman, L., Ashworth, K. and Middleton, S. (2000) 'Poverty, social exclusion and employment', Working Paper No 6, PSE study (www.bris.ac.uk/poverty/pse/99PSE-WP6.pdf).

Arber, S. (1990) 'Revealing women's health: reanalysing the general household survey', in H. Roberts (ed) *Women's health counts*, London: Routledge.

Baker, D. and Taylor, H. (1997) 'The relation between condition-specific morbidity, social support and material deprivation in pregnancy and early motherhood. ALSPAC survey team – Avon Longitudinal Study of Pregnancy and Childhood', *Social Science and Medicine*, vol 45, no 9, pp 1325-36.

Bensing, J.M., Hulsman, R.L. and Schreurs, K.M. (1999) 'Gender differences in fatigue: biopsychosocial factors relating to fatigue in men and women', *Medical Care*, vol 37, no 10, pp 1078-83.

Bildt, C. and Michelsen, H. (2002) 'Gender differences in the effects from working conditions of mental health: a four year follow up', *International Archives of Occupational and Environmental Health*, vol 75, no 4, pp 252-8.

Boardman, A.P., Hodgson, R.E., Lewis, M. and Allen, K. (1997) 'Social indicators and the prediction of psychiatric admission in different diagnostic groups', *British Journal of Psychiatry*, vol 171, pp 457-62.

Brenner, M.H. (1973) *Mental illness and the economy*, Cambridge, MA: Harvard University Press.

Brown, G.W. and Harris, T. (1978) *Social origins of depression: A study of psychiatric disorder in women*, London: Tavistock.

Brown, G.W. and Moran, P.M. (1997) 'Single mothers, poverty and depression', *Psychological Medicine*, vol 21, pp 21-33.

Congdon, P. (1996) 'Suicide and parasuicide in London: a small area study', *Urban Studies*, vol 33, no 1, pp 137-58.

Croudace, T.J., Kayne, R., Jones, P.B. and Harrison, G.L. (2000) 'Non-linear relationship between an index of social deprivation, psychiatric admission prevalence and the incidence of psychosis', *Psychological Medicine*, vol 30, pp 177-85.

Davey Smith, G., Dorling, D. and Shaw, M. (eds) (2001) *Poverty, inequality and health in Britain, 1800-2000: A reader*, Bristol: The Policy Press.

DH (Department of Health) (1999a) *National Service Framework for Mental Health*, London: Department of Health.

DH (1999b) *Saving lives: Our healthier nation*, London: The Stationery Office.

DH (2001) *Making it happen: A guide to delivering mental health promotion – written by 'mentality'*, London: Department of Health.

Dooley, D., Catalano, R. and Wilson, G. (1994) 'Depression and unemployment: panel findings from the Epidemiologic Catchment Area study', *American Journal of Community Psychology*, vol 22, pp 745-65.

Drever, F. and Whitehead, M. (eds) (1997) *Health inequalities: Decennial supplement Series DS*, no 15, London: The Stationery Office.

Eisenberg, L. (1997) 'Psychiatry and health in low-income populations', *Comprehensive Psychiatry*, vol 38, no 2, pp 69-73.

Goldberg, D.P. (1972) *The detection of psychiatric illness by questionnaire*, London: Oxford University Press.

Gomm, R. (1996) 'Mental health and inequality' in T. Heller, J. Reynolds, R. Gomm, R. Muston and S. Pattison (eds) *Mental health matters – A reader*, Basingstoke: Open University in conjunction with Macmillan Press.

Gordon, D. and Pantazis, C. (1997) *Breadline Britain in the 1990s*, Aldershot: Ashgate.

Gordon, D., Adelman, L., Ashworth, K., Bradshaw, J., Levitas, R., Middleton, S., Pantazis, C., Patsios, D., Payne, S., Townsend, P. and Williams, J. (2000) *Poverty and social exclusion in Britain*, York: Joseph Rowntree Foundation.

Graham, H. and Blackburn, C. (1998) 'The socio-economic patterning of health and smoking behaviour among mothers with young children on income support', *Sociology of Health and Illness*, vol 20, no 2, pp 215-40.

Gunnell, D., Peters, T., Kammerling, M. and Brooks, J. (1995) 'The relationship between parasuicide, suicide, psychiatric admissions and socioeconomic deprivation', *British Medical Journal*, vol 311, pp 226-30.

Harrison, J., Barrow, S. and Creed, F. (1998) 'Mental health in the north west region of England: association with deprivation', *Social Psychiatry and Psychiatric Epidemiology*, vol 33, pp 124-8.

Heath, I. (1999) 'There must be limits to the medicalisation of human distress', *British Medical Journal*, vol 318, pp 439-40.

Hope, S., Power, C. and Rodgers, B. (1999) 'Does financial hardship account for elevated psychological distress in lone mothers?', *Social Science and Medicine*, vol 49, pp 1637-49.

Hopton, J.L. and Hunt, S.M. (1996) 'Housing conditions and mental health in a disadvantaged area in Scotland', *Journal of Epidemiology and Community Health*, vol 50, pp 56-61.

Hunt, S. (1997) *Housing related disorders. Decennial supplement 11: The health of adult Britain 1841-1994*, London: Office for National Statistics.

Hyndman, S.J. (1990) 'Housing dampness and health amongst British Bengalis in East London', *Social Science and Medicine*, vol 30, no 1, pp 131-41.

Kammerling, M. and O'Connor, S. (1993) 'Unemployment rate as predictor of rate of psychiatric admission', *British Medical Journal*, vol 307, pp 1536-9.

Kessler, D., Lloyd, K., Lewis, G. and Gray, D.P. (1999) 'Cross sectional study of symptom attribution and recognition of depression and anxiety in primary care', *British Medical Journal*, vol 3180, pp 436-40.

Levitas, R. (1998) *The inclusive society? Social exclusion and New Labour*, Basingstoke: Macmillan.

Lewis, G., Bebbington, P., Brugha, T., Farrell, M., Gill, B., Jenkins, R. and Meltzer, H. (1998) 'Socioeconomic status, standard of living, and neurotic disorder', *The Lancet*, vol 352, pp 605-9.

Lynch, J.W., Kaplan, G.A. and Shema, S.J. (1997) 'Cumulative impact of sustained economic hardship on physical, cognitive, psychological and social functioning', *New England Journal of Medicine*, vol 337, pp 1889-95.

Marmot, M., Shipley, M., Brunner, E. and Hemingway, H. (2001) 'Relative contribution of early life and adult socioeconomic factors to adult morbidity in the Whitehall II study', *Journal of Epidemiology and Community Health*, vol 55, no 5, pp 301-7.

Meltzer, H., Gill, B., Petticrew, M. and Hinds, K. (1995) *The prevalence of psychiatric morbidity among adults living in private households*, OPCC Surveys of Psychiatric Morbidity Among Adults Living in Private Households, London: OPCS.

Middleton, H. and Shaw, I. (2000) 'Distinguishing mental illness in primary care', *British Medical Journal*, vol 320, pp 1420-1.

Montgomery, S.M., Cook, D.G., Bartley, M.J. and Wadsworth, M.E. (1999) 'Unemployment predates symptoms of depression and anxiety resulting in medical consultation in young men', *International Journal of Epidemiology*, vol 28, pp 95-100.

Oliver, M. (1996) *Understanding disability from theory to practice*, Basingstoke: Macmillan.

Papassotiropoulos, A. and Heun, R. (1999) 'Screening for depression in the elderly: a study on misclassification by screening instruments and improvement of scale performance', *Progress in Neuro-Psychopharmacology and Biological Psychiatry*, vol 23, pp 431-46.

Payne, S. (1999) 'Paid and unpaid work in mental health: towards a new perspective', in N. Daykin and L. Doyal (eds) *Health and work: Critical perspectives*, Basingstoke: Macmillan Press.

Popay, J. (1992) 'My health is all right, I'm just tired all the time: women's experiences of ill health', in H. Roberts (ed) *Women's health matters*, London: Routledge.

Schoevers, R.A., Beekman, A.T.F., Deeg, D.J.H., Geerlings, M.I., Jonker, C. and Van Tilburg, W.V. (2000) 'Risk factors for depression in later life: results of a prospective community based study (AMSTEL)', *Journal of Affective Disorders*, vol 59, pp 127-37.

Seguin, L., Potvin, L., St-Denis, M. and Loiselle, J. (1995) 'Chronic stressors, social support, and depression during pregnancy', *Obstetrics and Gynecology*, vol 85, pp 583-9.

SEU (Social Exclusion Unit) (2000) *National Strategy for Neighbourhood Renewal: A framework for consultation*, London: Cabinet Office.

SEU (2001) *A new commitment to Neighbourhood Renewal: National Strategy Action Plan*, London: Cabinet Office.

SEU (2003a) *Mental health and social exclusion: Consultation document*, London: ODPM.

SEU (2003b) *Action on mental health – A guide to promoting social inclusion*, London: ODPM.

SEU (2004) *Mental health and social exclusion: Social exclusion*, London: ODPM.

Smith, C.A., Smith, C.J., Kearns, R.A. and Abbott, M.W. (1993) 'Housing stressors, social support and psychological distress', *Social Science and Medicine*, vol 37, pp 603-12.

Townsend, P., Davidson, N. and Whitehead, M. (1982) *Inequalities in health: The Black Report and the health divide*, Harmondsworth: Penguin.

Tulle-Winton, E. (1997) 'Happy in Castlemilk? Deprivation and depression in an urban area', *Health and Place*, vol 3, pp 161-70.

Viinamäki, H., Kontula, O., Niskanen, L. and Koskela, K. (1995) 'The association between economic and social factors and mental health in Finland', *Acta Psychiatrica Scandinavica*, vol 3, pp 208-13.

Walker, D. (2001) 'Turnout drops to lowest since 1918: state of the parties so far', *The Guardian*, Friday 8 June (www.guardian.co.uk/Archive/Article/0,4273,4200583,00.html).

Weich, S. and Lewis, G. (1998a) 'Poverty, unemployment and common mental disorders: population based cohort study', *British Medical Journal*, vol 317, pp 115-19.

Weich, S. and Lewis, G. (1998b) 'Material standard of living, social class and the prevalence of the common mental disorders in Britain', *Journal of Epidemiology and Community Health*, vol 52, pp 8-14.

Weich, S., Lewis, G. and Jenkins, S.P. (2001) 'Income inequality and the prevalence of common mental disorders in Britain', *British Journal of Psychiatry*, vol 178, pp 222-7.

West, R. (1995) 'Psychosocial health', in Health and Lifestyles Project, *A survey of the UK population*, London: Health Education Authority.

Whiteside, N. (1988) 'Unemployment and health: an historical perspective', *Journal of Social Policy*, vol 17, pp 177-94.

Whitley, E., Gunnell, D., Dorling, D. and Smith, G.D. (1999) 'Ecological study of social fragmentation, poverty and suicide', *British Medical Journal*, vol 319, pp 1034-7.

WHO (World Health Organisation) (1999) *The World Health report: Making a difference*, Geneva: WHO.

Wilkinson, R.G. (1996) *Unhealthy societies: The afflictions of inequality*, London: Routledge.

Wilkinson, R.G. (2001) 'Social status, inequality and health', in T. Heller, R. Muston, M. Sidell and C. Lloyd (eds) *Working for health*, London: Open University Press and Sage Publications.

Wilson, S.H. and Walker, G.M. (1993) 'Unemployment and health: a review', *Public Health*, vol 107, pp 153-62.

Yen, I.H. and Kaplan, G.A. (1999) 'Poverty area residence and changes in depression and perceived health status: evidence from the Almada County Study', *International Journal of Epidemiology*, vol 28, pp 90-4.

Part Three:
People

ELEVEN

Children, poverty and social exclusion

Eva Lloyd

Introduction

Conducted at the approach of the new millennium, the 1999 Poverty and Social Exclusion (PSE) Survey built on the methodology of the previous Breadline Britain Surveys (Mack and Lansley, 1985; Gordon and Pantazis, 1997), and the Small Fortunes Study (Middleton et al, 1997). While child poverty and social exclusion had featured strongly in both, the PSE Survey adds a new dimension to the exploration of children's experience of poverty and social exclusion by directly measuring their access within households to necessities of life, both items and activities, rather than focusing primarily on the household level. In all, data from 1,046 children aged 0-16 were included, allowing separate analyses to be undertaken. Almost half of all households surveyed included one or more children.

Around the same time that the PSE Survey was being finalised, the Prime Minister Tony Blair (1999) used the 1998 Beveridge lecture to announce the government's intention to eradicate child poverty within a generation: "… our historic aim will be for ours to be the first generation to end child poverty, and it will take a generation. It is a 20-year mission but I believe it can be done" (p 7). Made after the United Nations had declared the period 1997-2006 as the International Decade for the Eradication of Poverty, this announcement not only placed children centre-stage in the government's anti-poverty strategy, but it was also accompanied by the rolling out of a range of policies and strategies aimed at tackling both the causes and consequences of child poverty. Indeed Platt (2005) has gone as far as to speak of the 'rediscovery' of child poverty during this recent period.

A flurry of studies subsequently appeared from governmental (DWP, 2003) and academic bodies (Adelman et al, 2003), providing qualitative and quantitative analyses of progress made in achieving the aim of eradicating child poverty within less than a quarter of a century. The findings of some of these studies are discussed further below. However, among recent poverty studies the PSE Survey remains unique in several respects. First, the PSE, through the earlier Omnibus Survey, sets out specifically to find out the views of parents on the necessities of life in modern Britain for children (Gordon et al, 2000a). Second, the Survey attempts to measure child poverty directly by assessing the extent to which children are deprived of material and social necessities. The PSE Survey also examines children's experiences of exclusion, for example, in terms of their lack of access to services. It is against this information that the accuracy and appropriateness of the current official anti-poverty strategies can and should be measured.

The PSE's quantitative information is complemented by a range of recent qualitative studies reflecting the daily-lived experience of children growing up in poverty (Shropshire and Middleton, 1999; Bradshaw, 2001; Ridge, 2002). Some of these explored children's own views on living in poverty (Shropshire and Middleton, 1999; Ridge, 2002). This is an important development, as most studies (including the PSE Survey), irrespective of whether quantitative, qualitative or mixed methodologies are employed, only use parents and carers as the main informants on their children's lives (Barnes, 2001).

At the time of writing this chapter[1], the seventh analysis of government poverty statistics from the New Policy Institute has just appeared. The Monitoring Poverty and Social Exclusion Survey confirms that overall poverty statistics have improved substantially for families with children, with some 700,000 children having been lifted out of poverty since 1998/99 (Palmer and Kenway, 2004). Their findings suggest that the government is on target to reduce child poverty by a quarter by the end of 2004, although the latest analysis from the Institute for Fiscal Studies (Brewer et al, 2005) concludes that child poverty is declining only marginally, despite the generosity of the new payments to families, including the child tax credits. Warnings have already been sounded, too, that further reductions may be increasingly hard to achieve, that poverty continues to affect minority ethnic groups, large families, and families in which parents have a disability, differently, and that the challenge of ending poverty more generally still needs addressing (Sutherland et al, 2003; Dornan, 2004).

Indeed, some key indicators directly pertinent to child poverty have worsened significantly since the late 1990s. These include a doubling of the number of households in temporary accommodation since 1997, and an increase of a quarter since 2000 in the number of English households accepted as 'homeless' by local authorities, of which one third are families with dependent children. No change occurred in the worryingly high percentage, a quarter, of 11-year-olds in England failing to reach Key Stage 2 in English and Maths. Such worsening indicators suggest that gains already made in terms of children's likely healthy development and life chances risk being lost.

Moreover, the primary causes of poverty today seem to have reverted at least in part to those prevalent 100 years ago, with low wages being a crucial factor, rather than unemployment. Despite the change in causes, consequences and definitions of poverty in the last century, Seebohm Rowntree's observation rings almost as true today as it did at the turn of the previous century:

> That in this land of abounding wealth, during a time of perhaps unexampled prosperity, probably more than one fourth of the population are living in poverty, is a fact that may well cause great searchings of heart. There is surely need for a greater concentration of thought by the nation upon the well-being of its own people…. (Rowntree, 1901, p 304, quoted in Glennerster et al, 2004, p 169)

This is the social, economic and physical context and environment in which British children are currently growing up. It affects not only their present quality of life, but may also affect every aspect of their later development (Duncan et al, 1994; Gregg et al, 1999; Bradshaw, 2001; Ermish et al, 2001). It leaves no room for complacency as regards the need to continue the fight against poverty in general and child poverty in particular (Hirsh, 2004).

The present discussion focuses primarily on issues affecting children aged 16 and under (Chapter Twelve deals with the poverty and social exclusion of young people aged 16 and upward). An analysis of the 1999 PSE data on the nature and extent of child poverty in Britain may provide pointers towards optimal policies and successful strategies that need consolidation or development (Kemp et al, 2004). Indeed, it may help identify which policies and strategies impact on which dimensions of child poverty. The next section highlights monitoring systems measuring the impact on child poverty of the 1997 and 2001 Labour government's anti-poverty policies and strategies.

Policy developments since 1997

Having recognised the complex and multi-dimensional nature of child poverty and social exclusion, these have been addressed by the present government across a wide front (HM Treasury, 1999a, 1999, 2001). Key elements of its anti-poverty strategy focus on welfare reforms and public service changes, including area-based and universal public services that contribute to improving poor children's life chances and breaking cycles of deprivation (HM Treasury, 2004, para 1.19).

For a while it looked as if the term, and the concept of, 'social exclusion' was set to become a substitute for the term 'poverty'. In 1997 the government established the Social Exclusion Unit (SEU) to contribute to coordinated anti-poverty strategy formation, yet the concept of poverty was retained in the official discourse surrounding children and poverty. The Unit's main report on children and young people (2000) did indeed employ the term, while focusing on problems associated with poverty.

However, HM Treasury retained the official lead on child poverty. In its 2000 Spending Review, the commitment to reduce the number of children in poverty by at least a quarter by the end of 2004 was translated into a Public Service Agreement (PSA) target for 2004, to be held jointly by HM Treasury and the then Department of Social Security. Efforts towards achieving this target were intensified in 2003 with the addition of several more general anti-poverty targets, while the overall project was subjected to an extensive progress review in 2004 (HM Treasury, 2004). As discussed above this target is about to be met according to the latest Monitoring Poverty and Social Exclusion Survey (Palmer and Kenway, 2004).

The monitoring system for the different components specific to the anti-child poverty programme was incorporated by the government in 1998 in an annual review aimed also at assessing progress with their more general anti-poverty strategies (DSS, 1999). For six years now, this annual review *Opportunity for All* has been reporting on progress in eradicating poverty (see also Chapter Five in this volume). Since the 2001 Census, these reviews have been complemented by reports from the Office for National Statistics focusing on social inequalities in the six key areas of education, work, income, living standards, health and social participation (Drever et al, 2000; Babb et al, 2004).

By 2004 (DWP, 2004) the format of this review reflected several developments since baseline data were first collected in 1997. Out of a total of 54 indicators of progress, 15 specific indicators are used to measure child poverty. The government selected this core set of indicators after an extensive consultation exercise, the 2002 Child Poverty Review (DWP, 2003). Among these, a core set of three interrelated indicators (tiers) capture different aspects implicated in child poverty. These indicators relate to low income and 'consistent poverty':

- Absolute low income – to measure whether the poorest children are seeing their families' incomes rise in real terms, that is before housing costs;
- Relative low income – to measure whether the poorest families are keeping pace with the growth of incomes in the economy as a whole; and
- Material deprivation and low income combined – to provide a wider measure of children's living standards. (DWP, 2003, p 12; 2004, para 1.13)

Using this core set of indicators, a reduction in child poverty is indicated by progress on all three indicators. It is worth noting that the measures of material deprivation first developed for the PSE Survey are now included in the annual Family Resources Survey undertaken by the Office for National Statistics on behalf of the Department for Work and Pensions (for further discussion see Chapter One, this volume).

This Review was followed in April 2004 by the Report by the House of Commons Work and Pensions Select Committee on *Child poverty in the UK* (2004). Noting that child poverty notably affects children in different sections of the population, the Committee recommended concerted action to help four categories in particular. These were: families with children, families/parents with disabilities and families/parents of children with disabilities, as well as minority ethnic and lone-parent families. The Committee also drew attention to the anomalies in the tax credit system as far as large families are concerned.

In the light of this evidence, the 2004 Spending Review announced an adjusted child poverty PSA target: to halve the number of children in relative low-income households between 1998/99 and 2010/11, on the way to eradicating child poverty by 2020 (DWP, 2004, p 11).

Both the Child Poverty Review's conclusions and the 2004 Spending Review were directly informed by the publication of the 1999 PSE findings (Gordon et al, 2000a), which highlighted the need for a long-term poverty measure focusing on living standards, rather than one focusing exclusively on income levels (see Chapter One for a discussion on the impact of the PSE Survey).

Snapshots of household income levels, also known as the 'black box' approach to measuring family poverty (Gordon et al, 2000a, p 35), would not pick up on trends over time, or on different experiences within households, as the 1999 PSE Survey did. Such trends confirmed by the 1999 PSE Survey in respect of child poverty, include:

- there may be considerable family income mobility year on year leading to continuous financial insecurity;
- low income and child necessity deprivation do not correlate exactly;
- poverty rates, defined in terms of material and social deprivation, are highest for children, particularly children under the age of 11; and
- poverty rates are higher for large families and lone-parent households.

These trends echo findings reported by Kemp et al (2004) in the research review forming part of the Joseph Rowntree Foundation sponsored programme of research into ladders out of poverty. Research by Hill and Jenkins (2001), Adelman et al (2003), Piachaud (2001), Piachaud and Sutherland (2001), and Sefton (2004) in particular, demonstrate similar outcomes for children. While public spending on children has increased substantially since 1997, and has been skewed towards poor children, much remains to be done at a national level to improve their access to services (Sefton, 2004).

Although the 1999 PSE Survey principally intends to make a contribution to the national investigation of poverty and social exclusion and their inter-relationship, it also seeks to add to the international poverty debate by measuring absolute and overall poverty, as agreed at the 1995 World Summit for Social Development in Copenhagen (UN, 1995). We will therefore first situate the PSE Survey within an international context, before turning to a more detailed exploration of its findings on children, poverty and social exclusion at the national level.

Child poverty and the international context

Subsequent to the 1995 Copenhagen Summit, Britain and 116 other countries agreed to adopt a two-tier approach to the measure of 'absolute' and 'overall' poverty as regards prevailing economic conditions in their countries. They also committed to eradicating the former and reducing the latter. Absolute poverty is defined in terms of severe deprivation of basic human needs, whereas overall poverty relates to lack of access to basics as well as lack of participation in decision-making and in civil, social and cultural life (UN, 1995; see also Chapter Three in this volume).

Apart from inheriting the commitment to overall poverty reduction made in 1995 by the previous administration, the present Labour government also aspires to realise the right of British children under the 1989 United Nations Convention on the Rights of the Child, ratified by the UK in 1991. Article 27, part 1, stipulates the right of every child to a standard of living adequate for the child's physical, mental, spiritual, moral and social development. Monitoring progress under the Convention, as well as under national legislation, requires an appropriate institutional framework. Finally, member states also pursue anti-poverty strategies within a European Union (EU) framework (Ruxton and Bennett, 2001).

Barnes (2001) sets out the institutional frameworks and main mechanisms by which other countries monitor the well being of their children, including poverty levels. While the UK is by no means the only country which remains without overall coordination in this area, progress has been made recently, with the establishment of the *Opportunity for All* Surveys, the creation of the post of Minister for Children in 2003 and the appointment of children's commissioners in Wales in 2001, in Northern Ireland in 2003, in Scotland in 2004, and in England in 2005.

The government has itself acknowledged (HM Treasury, 2004, p 15) that its anti-poverty drive has been informed and influenced not only by emerging national poverty data, but also by Britain's ranking in terms of relative poverty among industrialised nations. For example, the Luxembourg Income Study confirms that in the late 1990s, Britain's child poverty rates were only marginally better than those in Ireland, Italy and Canada, with the US coming out worst of all (Hills, 2004a, Table 3.6). Furthermore, in the middle of that decade, the UK ranked third from the bottom in an international comparison in terms of relative child poverty rates between 26 industrialised countries, even when these rates were adjusted for level of general living standards in the countries in question (UNICEF, 2000). Moreover, OECD (Organisation for Economic Cooperation and Development) research cited by Hills (2004b, p 144) confirmed that persistent poverty was a feature of British poverty rates, setting it apart in this respect from other industrialised nations.

This fact proved directly related to a small number of characteristics distinguishing the British situation from that in other OECD countries and highly pertinent to child poverty. These included high rates of workless households with children (Gregg and Wadsworth, 2001), low-pay households (Hills, 2004b), and low employment levels and rates of pay among its relatively high percentage of lone-parent households

(Stewart, 2005a). The PSE findings confirm how crucial these features remained in respect of child poverty at the end of the 20th century.

However, Britain's ranking has recently been improving, at least in some respects and within both the EU and OECD context. Whereas up to 1997 Britain had the worst relative child poverty rates in the EU, it had progressed from 15th to 10th position by 2001 (Hills and Stewart, 2005). Not only that, but most other European countries had experienced relative child poverty rate rises during this same period (Stewart, 2005b). Among 27 OECD countries for which relative poverty data were available, Britain now occupies the 20th place, at a time when the proportion of children in poverty has risen in the majority of 'rich' nations. Britain is commended in the latest UNICEF child poverty report for its concerted strategies to reduce its "exceptionally high child poverty rate" (UNICEF, 2005, p 04). This again suggests that some of New Labour's policies and strategies are having an impact, notably the introduction of the National Minimum Wage, child benefit packages and tax credit reforms, and despite increases in median income at the same time (Hills, 2004b, p 144). As far as inequalities in health are concerned, however, the latest evidence suggests less progress than intended (Shaw et al, 2005).

The government is addressing all three work–related poverty issues identified above with reference to OECD and EU comparisons. As far as parents of young children are concerned, this notably includes the National Childcare Strategy, as well as the more general Welfare to Work Strategy which, among other things, seeks to meet a target of getting 70% of lone parents into employment by 2010. The content and rationale of and for these strategies as well as their success, continue to be the subject of lively debate and considerable criticism from within the UK (Sutherland, 2002; Skinner; 2003; Kemp et al, 2004; NAO, 2004; Penn, 2004; see also Chapter Fourteen on lone mothers). Similarly, the format and impact of recent changes to the tax and benefit system have been critically examined and found wanting (Brewer et al, 2002, 2003).

Taking an international perspective, the present government's anti-poverty drive appears beset by similar challenges as facing other industrialised nations (Cornia and Danziger, 1997) and particularly those engaged in the US 'War on Poverty' begun in the 1960s (Huston et al, 1994; Seccombe, 2000). US poverty researchers identified major challenges arising from the complex, multi-dimensional nature of child poverty within robust economies, and its strong associations with gender and ethnicity. Similar factors of gender, ethnicity and disability characterise poverty in Britain.

Having located the 1999 PSE Survey within its international, including EU, context, should serve to improve our understanding of the implications of the actual findings on children, poverty and social exclusion in Britain.

The necessities of life for children

As a first step to measuring the extent of child poverty, respondents in the June 1999 Omnibus Survey were asked about the necessities of life relating to a number of activities and items (see also Chapter Four in this volume for a discussion about adult items and activities). Building on work undertaken in the 1990s (Middleton et al, 1994, 1997), the PSE Survey included a list of 30 items and activities for children. Respondents were asked to say whether a child item or activity was necessary, which no child should have to go without through lack of money. Table 11.1 shows that there was high support for almost all

Table 11.1: Percentage of respondents perceiving child item and activity as necessary

Children's items and activities	Necessary	Desirable	Don't know
A warm waterproof coat	95	5	1
New, properly fitted shoes	94	6	1
Bed/bedding to her/himself	93	6	1
Fresh fruit/vegetables daily	93	6	1
Celebrations on special occasions	92	7	1
Three meals daily	90	9	1
A hobby or leisure activity	90	10	1
Books of her/his own	89	10	1
Play group for pre-school aged children	88	11	1
All school uniform required	88	12	1
Toys (eg dolls, teddies)	83	15	2
Educational games	83	16	2
At least seven pairs of underpants	83	16	2
Enough bedrooms for every child	78	21	1
Meat/fish/vegetarian twice daily	77	22	2
Swimming at least monthly	75	23	2
A school trip at least once a term	74	24	2
At least four pairs of jumpers	73	25	2
A holiday away from home	71	27	2
Some new, not second-hand clothes	70	28	2
At least four pairs of trousers	69	29	3
A garden to play in	68	31	1
A carpet in the children's bedroom	67	31	2
Construction toys (eg Lego)	62	36	2
Leisure equipment	60	38	2
Friends round for tea/snack	59	37	4
A bike, new or second hand for children	54	43	3
At least 50p a week for sweets	49	48	3
Computer suitable for school work	41	55	3
Computer games	18	78	4

Note: Individual weight used for this analysis; analysis excludes those who refused to answer question.

children's items and activities. Out of 30 items and activities, only three attracted less than 50% support from the whole population. Items attracting the highest levels of support include clothing (for example, a warm waterproof coat), housing (for example, bed/bedding), food (for example, fresh fruit and vegetables on a daily basis), as well as social activities (for example, celebrations on special occasions). As with the adult items and activities, the population regards a wide range of material items and social activities for children as necessary.

Children's items and activities were included in the previous 1983 Poor Britain and 1990 Breadline Britain Surveys, and so it is possible to measure changes in attitudes towards children's items and activities over time (Figure 11.1). In contrast to some adult groups of items and activities (see Chapter Four in this volume), the data show increasing support among the population, as a whole, for children's necessities.

Differences in opinion between parents and non-parents might be expected in relation to the children's activities and items. But, in fact, there appears to be a close agreement (Figure 11.2, see also the Appendix to this chapter). Parents are more likely to see the importance of visits to school as a necessary activity (91% compared to 79%), collecting children from school (83% compared to 74%), as well as carpets in the children's bedroom (75% compared to 66%). But friends round for tea/snack and a holiday away from home are both more likely to be seen as essential by non-parents.

Figure 11.1: Changing perceptions of necessities relating to children

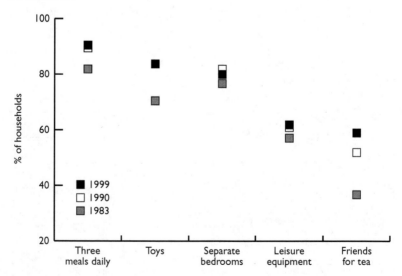

Figure 11.2: Perception of necessities: comparing parents and non-parents

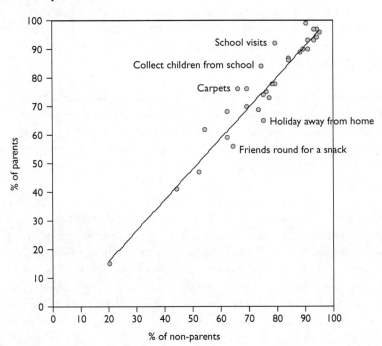

Parents = −5.32 + 1.07 × Non-parents
$R^2 = 0.92$

What the findings from the PSE Survey demonstrate is that the population increasingly supports a wide range of material items and social activities for children. Almost all the items and activities included in the questionnaire are regarded as necessities by both parents and non-parents alike, indicating that a social consensus exists on the necessities of life for children.

The extent and nature of child poverty

The PSE Survey adds a great deal to the knowledge that has been derived from other child poverty research. However, one of the benefits of the survey is that by examining the extent to which children go without necessities it provides a systematic and direct measure of child poverty[2]. As regards the daily experience of children in Britain, its findings confirm that, during the 20th century's last decade, poverty had become more widespread to the extent that:

> A third of British children go without at least one of the
> things they need, like three meals a day, toys, out of school
> activities or adequate clothing. Eighteen percent of children
> go without two or more items or activities defined as
> necessities by the majority of the population. (Gordon et al,
> 2000a, p 68)

What does this mean in practice for children and their families?
Table 11.2 demonstrates which items and activities, as defined by
parents, their children lack in their daily lives because they cannot be
afforded. This particular range of material items and everyday life
experiences would appear extremely modest in comparison to what
is potentially available for British children today.

The table illustrates the alarming extent of deprivation experienced
by a substantial proportion of children in Britain. For instance, among
children lacking at least two of the necessary items and activities,
documented in the third column, 9% go without daily fruit or
vegetables, 11% go without a warm, waterproof coat, 18% rely on
second-hand clothes, 20% miss out on celebrations of special occasions,
68% go without any holiday away from home, 10% share a bedroom
with a sibling of a different gender and among the relevant age group
18% of parents lack the money to buy their child a new or second-
hand bike. Such deprivation poses a serious risk to children's healthy
development and life chances, as outlined in Bradshaw (2001).

In which households do children go without necessities in the way
described in the previous section? Table 11.3 lists predisposing
household characteristics linked to poverty. The impact of household
employment on child poverty is particularly illuminating. While it is
evident that children in jobless households are much more likely to
be deprived of one or more necessity (63%) and two or more necessities
(42%), these findings also demonstrate that 'making work pay' for adults
is a different matter altogether. Poverty rates are still shockingly high
in households with workers; 37% of children in households with one
full-time worker and 32% in households with two full-time workers
are deprived of at least one item.

The table also documents that the percentage of children lacking
necessities is higher for lone-parent households than it is for couple
households. More than half of children in lone-parent households
lack at least one item and one in three lack two or more. Other key
findings, demanding urgent policy responses, relate to children's age
and the number of their siblings. Younger children, those aged two to
four years, are significantly more likely to lack two or more items than

Table 11.2: The extent of 'necessities deprivation' among children

	% of children who lack item because their parents cannot afford it		
	All children	**Children who lack at least one of the 27 necessary items**	**Children who lack at least two of the 27 necessary items**
Food			
Fresh fruit/vegetables daily	2	5	9
Three meals a day	(1)	(3)	(5)
Meat/fish/vegetarian twice daily	4	11	21
Clothes			
New, properly fitted shoes	2	7	12
Warm, waterproof coat	2	6	11
School uniform[a]	2	6	12
Seven plus pairs of underpants	2	6	11
Four plus pairs of trousers	3	9	18
More than four jumpers/cardigans	3	8	16
New, not second-hand, clothes	3	9	18
Participation and activities			
Celebrations on special occasions	4	10	20
Hobby/leisure activity[a]	3	9	18
School trip at least once a term[a]	2	5	(10)
Swimming at least once a month	7	21	34
Holiday away from home	22	64	68
Leisure equipment[a]	3	9	17
Friends round for tea/snack[a]	4	11	21
Developmental			
Books of own	(0)	0	(1)
Play group (pre-school age children)[a]	(1)	(4)	(7)
Educational games	4	12	21
Toys (eg dolls, play figures)[a]	(1)	(1)	(3)
Construction toys	3	10	19
Bike: new/second-hand[a]	3	10	18
Environmental			
Bed and bedding to self	(1)	(2)	(3)
Bedrooms for every child of different sexes[a]	3	10	10
Carpet in bedroom	(1)	(4)	(5)
Garden in which to play	4	10	8
Base	792	273	139

Notes: Figures in brackets indicate less than 20 unweighted cases
[a] age-related items.
Source: Adapted from Gordon et al (2000a, Table 9)

children in the other age groups, including infants. Similarly, children of all ages in households with three or more children are more likely to suffer deprivation than those in smaller households. In summary,

Table 11.3: Characteristics of poor children

	% of children lacking one or more item/activity	% of children lacking two or more items/activities
Employment status of the household[a]		
2 full-time/more than 2 workers	32	15
1 full-time worker, 1 part-time	19	6
1 full-time	37	19
1 or more part-time	52	30
No workers	63	42
Household type[a]		
Couple	29	11
Lone parent	52	33
Other	39	13
Income quintile group[a]		
4 and 5 (richest)	(13)	(4)
3	28	(7)
2	27	14
1 (poorest)	67	37
Age of child		
0-1	36	(16)
2-4	37	23
5-10	37	17
11-16	29	15
Number of children in the household[a]		
1	29	13
2	25	11
3	42	25
4+	68	39
Respondent has a long-standing illness[a]		
No	32	16
Yes	41	24
Ethnicity[a]		
White	30	14
Non-white	54	35
Tenure[a]		
Own	24	11
Local authority rented	69	41
Other rented	57	34
Household member receiving IS/JSA[a]		
No	28	12
Yes	66	43
Total	34	18

Notes: Figures in brackets indicate less than 20 unweighted cases.

[a] Significant differences between all groups on both deprivation measures ($p<0.05$).

[b] Significant difference between this group and others on two or more item deprivation measures ($p<0.05$).

IS = Income Support, JSA = Jobseeker's Allowance.

Source: Adapted from Gordon et al (2000a, pp 38-9)

large families, parents with young children and lone-parent families suffer greater risks of poverty.

Table 11.3 illustrates another factor, illness in the family, as playing a substantial role in the generation of child poverty. Parental long-standing illness is more likely to result in deprivation than long standing illness of a child; 41% of children lack at least one necessity in households where the respondent has health problems of this kind. Similar findings were reported from the OPCS Disability Surveys in the mid-1980s (see Gordon et al, 2000b, p 75).

The table confirms that ethnicity is a key factor predisposing children and their families to poverty. Over one third of minority ethnic children in the PSE Survey are deprived of two or more necessities and over one half of at least one. Moreover, it has also been reported elsewhere that if members of minority ethnic households are employed, their income is more likely to be on the lowest income quintile (HM Treasury, 1999c).

There are also marked risks for children living in social rented housing and this may reflect the process of residualisation which has been taking place in social housing since the 1980s, such that social housing is used as a safety net for the poorest and most vulnerable of individuals and families (Forrest and Murie, 1990).

Finally, the table confirms that children living in households in receipt of benefits face significantly higher risks of poverty. Two in every three children living in such households lack at least one necessity and 43% lack two or more. The benefit system is clearly failing to protect families from falling into poverty.

The distribution of poverty within households with children

Previous research by Middleton and her colleagues (1997) provided evidence for the notion of parental sacrifice whereby children are protected from poverty through the sacrifices their parents make. In this section, we explore the extent to which poverty occurs within the household by comparing the experiences of going without by parents and children. The composite picture presented by Table 11.4 and Figure 11.3 demonstrates that it is parents more than children who are likely to go without certain necessities when poverty is unequally distributed across the household. For instance, whereas 30% of parents go without new clothes, 18% properly fitting shoes and 4% without adequate food, their children did not (Table 11.4). This information complements the finding that spending in poor families on children is proportionally higher than in richer families (Middleton et al, 1997). It should also be understood in the context of the PSE

Table 11.4: Proportions of parents and children lacking items[3]

	% neither lacking	% both lacking	% parent goes without, child does not	% child goes without, parent does not
Clothes	68	(2)	30	(0)
Shoes	80	(2)	18	(1)
Food	96	(0)	4	0
A hobby or sport	80	3	15	(2)
A holiday	60	19	18	(2)

Note: Figures in brackets indicate less than 20 unweighted cases.

Source: Adelman et al (2000, Table 3.7)

Figure 11.3: Comparison of parents and children going without

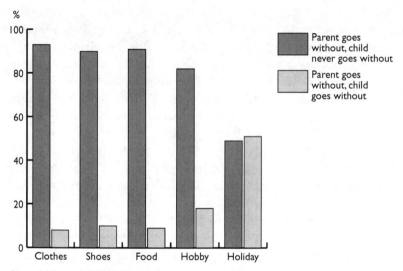

Source: Adelman et al (2000, Figure 3.4).

Survey finding that households without children are far less likely to go without.

The table confirms that parents bear the brunt of necessities deprivation when there is not enough money for necessities for all members of the family. Apart from the case of holidays and a hobby or sport, the numbers of families where both parents and children were missing out on necessities were too small to draw firm conclusions. It is worth reminding ourselves that the public, as surveyed by the PSE Survey, does now see these activities as necessities for children.

Moreover, Figure 11.3 shows households with children where at least one family member went without a selected number of items and activities in the last year because of shortage of money. As regards four out of the five items, over 80% of children do not go without, even if their parents do. Holidays are the most likely activity that both parents and their children go without. Yet over half the children in these households still have holidays. Certainly, the lack of access to activities, such as a holiday, does set children apart from their peers, as will be explored in more depth below in the section dealing with children and social exclusion.

In the light of this evidence of parental sacrifice for the benefit of their children, Adelman et al (2000) conclude that household poverty need not be severe for parents to be forced to go without certain necessary items, but that for parents to allow this to impact on their children, the household is likely to be suffering from severe poverty.

Despite the restrictions imposed by the PSE's quantitative nature, on the interpretations it allows regarding children's lived experience of poverty and social exclusion, there is at least one subset of data that touches on likely dynamics within households with children living in poverty. This concerns parents' worries about their children, which the Survey also explored.

Parents' worries about their children

Assuming a linear relationship between levels of material deprivation and social exclusion and parental worries about their children would appear reasonable, in the light of the environmental stresses on poor families documented in qualitative and quantitative poverty research (Middleton et al, 1994; Adelman et al, 2003). This is not to say that there may not also be high levels of parental worries among the materially better-off, for instance related to drug use and educational failure, but the environment is likely to be more positive for better-off children. The picture presented by the PSE Survey is more complex, however.

Perhaps surprisingly, whereas 34% of all parents in the PSE Survey admit to being 'very' or 'fairly' worried about problems with their children, this only increases to 37% for parents living in poverty. Slightly more poor parents, 41%, are 'not at all worried' about their children than those not poor, 36%. On the other hand, well over half of parents who had experienced poverty 'often' or 'most of the time' in the past acknowledge worries about their children, compared to around a quarter of parents who had 'never', 'rarely' or 'occasionally' been poor in the past.

Household type does not appear to unduly influence the degree to which parents harbour worries about their children. Percentages range from 31% being worried among households consisting of two adults and two children to 45% for households containing two adults and three or more children, and 41% for lone-parent households.

Possible relationships between worries and the occupational status of the parent interviewed, measured by means of the National Statistics Socio-economic Classification (NS-SEC) of occupations, are not immediately transparent from the data. Whereas two thirds of parents who had never worked or had been long-term unemployed acknowledge such worries, the next highest percentages, 55% and 45% respectively, are among parents in lower supervisory/technical occupations and those in higher managerial and professional occupations.

Children's age is predictably relevant, with all parents most worried about the age group 11-15. However, such worries never pre-occupy more than half of all parents in the Survey. While fathers and mothers are about equally worried about their children, a breakdown by parental gender and child age group reveals that more mothers than fathers are worried about their children in the 11-15 age group.

These findings raise questions as to the nature of these worries for different groups. The specific issues giving rise to parental concern are explored in more depth by Christina Pantazis in Chapter Nine in this volume. In the section on children and social exclusion below, data on worries related to school will be revisited. Overall, however, the counterintuitive conclusion is justified on the basis of the available data in the PSE Survey that poverty does not significantly affect levels of parental worry about their children.

However, it may be that parental worries relating to living conditions are not translated by them into specific worries about their children, but are seen as challenges for the whole family. Such concerns may have covered service exclusion and exclusion from community activities and family celebrations, for instance. We now turn to social exclusion as it affects children in Britain today.

Children and social exclusion

Townsend's (1979) ground-breaking redefinition of poverty in terms of relative deprivation precluding individuals' full participation in the customary activities of their society has contributed to the gradual recognition of the concept of social exclusion by practitioners, policy makers and politicians. The PSE data on socially perceived necessities suggest that this is also increasingly recognised by the general public. This definition was accepted by campaigning organisations such as the Child Poverty Action Group, and, more recently, the End Child Poverty Coalition.

Grounded in these developments (Levitas, 1999), the PSE Survey operationalised social exclusion into four dimensions: impoverishment or exclusion due to a lack of income and resources, labour market exclusion, service exclusion and exclusion from social relations (for further discussion see Chapter Five in this volume). The Survey provides evidence of children's social exclusion from services and social participation, as well as from education. The information on the extent of social relations and social participation among adults and children, in particular, constitutes a unique feature of this Survey, while the data on the extent to which families experienced service exclusion are absolutely crucial.

As already discussed in relation to necessities deprivation, adult exclusion from services and social relations may not correspond exactly with children's social exclusion, although the two are intimately connected, especially in the case of younger children. For instance, the PSE Survey shows that households with children are less likely than other types of households to participate in social activities considered essential, such as hobby and leisure activities or celebrations on special occasions, although they report social contacts with family and friends on a par with other types of household (Gordon et al, 2000a, p 63). The most frequently cited reason for non-participation in common social activities is lack of money, across household type (participation in social activities is discussed in further detail in Chapter Five in this volume).

It may be reasonable to assume that children stand to benefit from their parents' social contacts, such as with grandparents, or even from their parents' contacts with adult friends. For instance, parental contacts may include those with neighbours or friends with children. Social activities constitute evidence of some social contacts per se, but the experience of social support involves stronger relationships. Social support is explored in the PSE Survey in terms of the respondents' feeling that they potentially have people to turn to for informal caring support, advice or help with heavy household jobs, among other things.

A reassuring finding for households with children is that the majority report that they feel they have access to good levels of overall social support (Gordon et al, 2000a, p 64). Social support is clearly implicated in general health and well being, including mental health, of families with children (Wiggins et al, 2004). Again, children may benefit indirectly from the increased well being of their parents, due to adequate levels of social support available to the household. Where adults suffer from long-term illness or have a disability, children in the role of their parents' carers may become the main form of social support, but there are insufficient PSE data available to explore this specific situation further.

Children's well being may not only be affected by a lack of general household participation in social activities and access to social relations and social support (Attoe, in press), but they can also be directly deprived in terms of their exclusion from social activities and services aimed at their own age group. The rate at which children are deprived from age-related items and activities was shown in Table 11.2.

Participation rates in a subset of age-adjusted social activities considered essential by parents are shown in Table 11.5. This table provides additional information to that included in Table 11.2, confirming that, with the exception of the play group, more than two thirds of children are able to participate in the activities listed. However, according to parents, significant minorities of children are unable to engage in them for financial reasons. Most significantly this relates to an annual holiday away from home at least (18%), but also 6% of parents report that their children are excluded from monthly visits to the swimming pool because of financial constraints. Given the likely impact on children's quality of life coupled with the potential for long-term developmental effects, such forms of exclusion need addressing as a matter of urgency.

It is clear that in poor households with children, children not only risk going without necessities such as a warm, waterproof coat and fresh fruit or vegetables once a day, but also without activities like monthly trips to the swimming pool, or having friends round fortnightly for tea or a snack. This risk is cumulative, meaning that if a child is deprived of one necessary item or activity, the chance of lacking any specific necessity is about three times the average; it doubles again if the deprivation threshold is set at two items or activities (Gordon

Table 11.5: Participation and exclusion from children's activities

	Do	Don't do, don't want to	Don't do, can't afford to	Not applicable
Hobby or leisure activity	82	6	5	7
Celebrations on special occasions	96	(1)	(3)	0
Swimming at least once a month	67	22	6	5
Play group (pre-school children)	39	29	(3)	30
Holiday away from home at least one week a year	78	(3)	18	(1)
School trip at least once a term	77	10	(2)	(1)
Friends round for tea/snack fortnightly	74	16	(4)	6

Note: Figures in brackets indicate less than 20 unweighted cases.

et al, 2000a, p 35). Children's social development would seem undeniably at risk under such circumstances.

Service exclusion in households with children

Service exclusion is another dimension of social exclusion whose effect on children may either be mediated by their parents, or felt more directly by children themselves as well as by their parents. Exclusion from, or restricted access to, basic services such as utilities or public transport is a crucial aspect of deprivation and may equally affect the quality of life of the whole household.

The PSE Survey reveals that among households with children, 7% have experienced utility disconnection and 15% have restricted their consumption of gas, water, electricity or the telephone because of affordability. This alarming finding may well be an underestimate, as there is evidence that lack of affordability may be under-reported, or disguised by respondents through describing it as unavailability (Gordon et al, 2000a, p 57).

Additionally, lack of affordability prevents 45% of households with children accessing one or more essential public or private services such as public sports facilities or cinemas. Lack of affordability is defined as 'individual exclusion' by Gordon et al (2000a, p 56), whereas 'collective exclusion' refers to unavailability of services. Lack of availability proved the main barrier to use of one or more public or private services, which is reported by 46% of the overall PSE sample.

Because of the importance of access to financial services, the PSE Survey asked a separate question about households having a bank or building society account and inferred that 5% of the population was without such access. This not only means that parents may have more difficulty in demonstrating the use of such facilities in management of household budgets to their children, but also throws doubt on their ability to help children learn to save and promote their understanding of the economic world (Shropshire and Middleton, 1999). Moreover, the likelihood of parents resorting to other means of getting credit, usually characterised by extortionate interest rates, is greater under these circumstances. If so, this would add to the family's financial burdens.

As far as services aimed primarily or directly at children are concerned, making sense of the relationship between essential service participation and poverty levels is not entirely straightforward. The proportion of children excluded from, for instance, public transport to school, or from playgroup, is very small and therefore not amenable to further analysis. However, exclusion from play facilities, after-school clubs and youth clubs is definitely related to five characteristics of households as follows (Adelman et al, 2003):

- households with no one in employment
- households containing single parents or adults in addition to parents
- households in the lowest income quintile
- households in local authority or housing association accommodation
- households in receipt of Income Support (IS) or Jobseeker's Allowance (JSA).

Again, affected children belong to similar household categories as were identified as prone to necessities deprivation in Table 11.4. A discussion of the extent to which poor children's education may be affected deserves a separate section in this chapter.

Social exclusion and children's education

Another form of service exclusion with immediate consequences for quality of life and potentially major implications for children's life chances is suspension or exclusion from school (Smith et al, 1995; McGlone, 2001). This issue is explored with parents as part of the PSE's questions on worries about children's problems, including problems at school in the previous 12 months. The 6% of children who had experienced suspension are more likely to come from unemployed or lone-parent households, from households in the bottom income quintile, or those in receipt of IS/JSA (Adelman et al, 2003).

By means of a logistic regression analysis PSE parental claims about their children being bullied or ever having been accused of being bullies were investigated. Parents reported a substantial level of bullying: it had occurred to 41% of children (Adelman et al, 2003). However, this finding may be related to the method of entering the pertinent survey data, for if parents reported a child as having been bullied, this was noted down as applying to all children in the family. Nearly three quarters of the chance of being bullied turned out to be predictable and strongly related to a range of family and household characteristics associated with deprivation. This would appear to contradict earlier findings (for example, Middleton et al, 1994), suggesting that children's personal characteristics and failure to conform to peer group dress or behaviour norms are important factors in being bullied. However, it could be argued that such factors may be related to family and household characteristics associated with deprivation.

For instance, children in households in receipt of benefit are three times more likely to be bullied than those not in such households, while children in households containing an adult with a long-standing illness are over twice as likely to be bullied than others. Findings predicting the chance of being a bully are less clear-cut and figures were mostly too low to permit a meaningful analysis.

Special educational needs, too, irrespective of whether these were supported by a statement of such needs, appear to be strongly related to household circumstances. This confirms previous research that has shown that poor families are more likely to have disabled children (Gordon et al, 2000b).

The subjective experience of poverty and social exclusion

Exploring the association between poverty and other experiences, including social exclusion, is one of the main aims of the PSE Survey. Therefore adult attitudes, perceptions of the causes of poverty and subjective personal experience, such as impact on well being, are also surveyed. This yields interesting and at times surprising results.

According to their own subjective assessment, at least a third of households with children report that they consider their actual income to be lower than the amount they need to keep out of absolute, overall and general poverty. Regarding general poverty, percentages range from 29% of households containing a couple and one child, to 62% of lone-parent households with two children (Gordon et al, 2000a, p 31).

Such subjective and experiential PSE data, however, are not available for younger children themselves (although for young people they have been analysed in some depth by Fahmy in Chapter Twelve in this volume and by Adelman et al, 2003). PSE data from the households containing children allow us no more than speculation about, for instance, the impact on children's well being of parental experiences of poverty, or about their exact circumstances. To know more requires longitudinal and qualitative studies.

Among poor adults, 76% report feeling isolated as a result of lack of money, 70% report feeling depressed, 48% are very dissatisfied with the area they live in and 39% expect that the next two years will bring even greater reductions in their standard of living. Further analyses of the PSE data on emotional well being by Adelman et al (2003, Table 12.6) confirmed that the more severe child and parental poverty, the more highly parents scored on the General Health Questionnaire

(GHQ), which measures aspects of anxiety and depression (for further discussion on mental health see Chapter Ten in this volume).

Such findings leave no room for complacency about risks posed by high levels of deprivation for children's development and well being both in the short and longer term. For instance, some aspects of rising levels of mental health problems among children and young people in Britain since the Second World War may well be associated with poverty, mediated through factors such as household structure and parental stress (Quilgars, 2001). Where parents succumb to depression and other stress-related mental or physical health problems, their ability to care appropriately for their children may be jeopardised. In the case of infants in particular, maternal depression has been clearly related to the risk of adverse outcomes for children, with the effects in the disadvantaged population often being particularly severe (Murray et al, 1999, 2001). Alternatively, under these circumstances older children may be forced into caring roles, with the additional fear of being separated from parents as a result. These poverty-related conditions may put their well being and healthy development further at risk.

These findings can be used in assessing the likely impact and effectiveness of policies and strategies being employed in the fight against child poverty in Britain and, if necessary, inform their modification.

Conclusions

First and foremost, these PSE findings provide evidence of the extent of poverty among up to a third of British children at the millennium. Among these children, those from minority ethnic households, jobless households, lone-parent households, low-income households, and households in the social rented sector are disproportionately represented. Moreover, households with young children are confirmed to be at greater risk of poverty than households with older children, as are those households with more than two children.

For the first time, the PSE Survey allows the extent of necessities deprivation among British children to be transparently documented, using criteria for minimum levels of access to services, material goods and activities, recognised as relevant by a representative sample of the population. Children's experience of poverty and social exclusion is thereby clearly located within its wider context.

We recognise that at the time the PSE Survey was conducted, the impact of the present government's anti-poverty drive could hardly have been detected as yet. However, the PSE findings about the conditions under which poverty occur nevertheless continue to provide a useful resource for informing anti-poverty initiatives.

While gains have been made since 1999 in lifting children out of poverty, the most recent official statistics confirm that the challenges identified here remain considerable. The inequality that characterises the conditions under which children grow up is unjustifiable in present-day British society.

The PSE Survey demonstrates that even under conditions of full employment, child poverty and social exclusion would not simply disappear (Gordon et al, 2000a, p 71). Adequate welfare benefits will be needed to supplement or replace parental earned income under certain conditions, as well as high quality and accessible health, education, family support and social services. At the same time, we recognise that the present government's focus on employment and low pay issues is right in the light of PSE information, but on its own it is not sufficient. In an era that has witnessed the disappearance of the family wage, an over-reliance on paid work as a route out of poverty for households with children may eventually become counterproductive in achieving the government's aim of eradicating child poverty within a generation.

The evidence for children's necessities deprivation in households suffering low income, even where at least one adult may be in full- or part-time work, emphasises the need to address this issue across a broad policy front. Whereas two parents in paid employment may be sufficient to keep the household above the poverty threshold, lower levels of parental employment give no guarantee against child poverty, or indeed against children's social exclusion, notably service exclusion.

The informative findings on children's social exclusion and its links with poverty also confirm the value of the PSE's multi-dimensional approach to measuring this concept among adults as well as children within their families. The evidence for children's social exclusion produced by the PSE Survey is by no means exhaustive, however, and other potential manifestations remain to be explored. In future studies of this kind, communicating directly with children about their day-to-day experiences is highly recommended.

These findings also highlight the urgent need to explore the different dimensions of child poverty and social exclusion by means of longitudinal studies. Yet the PSE Survey offers sufficient cross-sectional data on children, poverty and social exclusion to inform a preliminary evaluation of the appropriateness of current anti-poverty policies and strategies. As far as the methodology of child poverty studies is concerned, incorporating the deprivation of necessities method into a longitudinal design would better allow the proper evaluation of their impact on children. Evidence from PSE analyses of the distribution of poverty within households, for example, that households with younger children are at greater risk of poverty than those containing older children, suggests that it would be useful to revisit equivalence scales (Adelman et al, 2000; see also Chapter Two in this volume). Since those data were collected, the present government has indeed started to utilise OECD equivalence scales.

All the evidence reviewed in this chapter suggests that a continuing clear focus is needed both on changing socio-economic structures and on providing social safety nets in order to reduce and eventually eradicate child poverty. The inequalities that still characterise many children's quality of life and life chances in Britain are truly intolerable in the 21st century.

Notes

[1] Much of the analysis presented in this chapter is drawn from Adelman et al (2000) and Adelman et al (2003). The author would like to thank Laura Adelman and her colleagues for comments on a previous version of the chapter.

[2] The PSE Survey restricted itself to an analysis of socially perceived necessities for children as determined by their parents, rather than by all adults.

[3] Only those items and activities considered as necessities have been included in this analysis. Other items such as pocket money were not included.

References

Adelman, A., Middleton, S. and Ashworth, K. (2000) *Intra-household distribution of poverty and social exclusion: Evidence from the 1999 PSE Survey of Britain*, Working Paper No 23, Loughborough: Centre for Research in Social Policy.

Adelman, L., Middleton, S. and Ashworth, K. (2003) *Britain's poorest children: Severe and persistent poverty and social exclusion*, London: Centre for Research in Social Policy for Save the Children.

Attoe, P. (in press) 'The social costs of child poverty: a systematic review of the qualitative evidence', *Children in Society, 2005*.

Babb, P., Martin, J. and Haezewindt, P. (2004) *Focus on social inequalities*, London: The Stationery Office (www.statistics.gov.uk/focuson/socialinequalities).

Barnes, H. (2001) 'How other countries monitor the well-being of their children', in J. Bradshaw (ed) *Poverty: The outcomes for children*, ESRC Occasional Paper 26, London: Family Policy Studies Centre.

Blair, T. (1999) 'Beveridge revisited: a welfare state for the twenty-first century', in R. Walker (ed) *Ending child poverty*, Bristol: The Policy Press.

Bradshaw, J. (ed) (2001) *Poverty: The outcomes for children*, ESRC Occasional Paper 26, London: Family Policy Studies Centre.

Brewer, M., Clark, T. and Goodman, A. (2002) *The government's child poverty target: How much progress has been made?*, Commentary 87, London: Institute for Fiscal Studies.

Brewer, M., Goodman, A. and Shephard, A. (2003) *How has child poverty changed under the Labour government? An update*, Briefing Note 32, London: Institute for Fiscal Studies (www.ifs.org.uk/bnx/nm32.pdf).

Brewer, M., Goodman, A., Shaw, J. and Shephard, A. (2005) *Poverty and inequality in Britain: 2005*, London: Institute for Fiscal Studies.

Cornia, G.A. and Danziger, S. (1997) *Child poverty and deprivation in industrialised countries 1945-1995*, Oxford: Clarendon Press.

Dornan, P. (ed) (2004) *Ending child poverty by 2020: The first five years*, London: Child Poverty Action Group.

Drever, F., Fisher, K. Brown, J. and Clark, J. (2000) *Social inequalities*, London: The Stationery Office.

DSS (Department of Social Security) (1999) *Opportunity for All: 1st annual report*, London: The Stationery Office.

Duncan, G.J., Brooks-Gunn, J. and Klebanov, P.K. (1994) 'Economic deprivation and early childhood development', *Child Development*, vol 65, pp 296-318.

DWP (Department for Work and Pensions) (2003) *Measuring child poverty*, London: The Stationery Office.

DWP (2004) *Opportunity for All: 6th annual report*, London: The Stationery Office.

Ermish, J., Francesconi, M. and Pevalin, D.J. (2001) *Outcomes for children of poverty*, DWP Research Report No 158, Leeds: Corporate Document Services.

Forrest, R. and Murie, A. (1990) *Residualisation and council housing: A statistical update*, Bristol: School for Advanced Urban Studies.

Glennerster, H., Hills, J., Piachaud, D. and Webb, J. (2004) *One hundred years of poverty and policy*, York: Joseph Rowntree Foundation.

Gordon, D. and Pantazis, C. (1997) *Breadline Britain in the 1990s*, Aldershot: Ashgate.

Gordon, D., Adelman, L., Ashworth, K., Bradshaw, J., Levitas, R., Middleton, S., Pantazis, C., Patsios, D. Payne, S., Townsend, P. and Williams, J. (2000a) *Poverty and social exclusion in Britain*, York: Joseph Rowntree Foundation.

Gordon, D., Parker, R. and Loughran, F., with Heslop, P. (2000b) *Disabled children in Britain: A reanalysis of the OPCS Disability Surveys*, London, The Stationery Office.

Gregg, P. and Wadsworth, J. (2001) 'Everything you always wanted to ask about measuring worklessness and polarization at the household level but were afraid to ask', *Oxford Bulletin of Economics and Statistics*, vol 63 (special issue), pp 777-806.

Gregg, P., Harkness, S. and Machin, S. (1999) *Child development and family income*, York: Joseph Rowntree Foundation.

Hill, M.S. and Jenkins, S.P. (2001) 'Poverty among British children: chronic or transitory?', in B. Bradbury, J. Micklewright and S. Jenkins (eds) *Falling in, climbing out: The dynamics of child poverty in industrialised countries*. New York, NY: UNICEF.

Hills, J. (2004a) *Inequality and the state*, Oxford: Oxford University Press.

Hills, J. (2004b) 'Poverty challenges and dilemmas for the next 20 years', in H. Glennerster, J. Hills, D. Piachaud and J. Webb (eds) *One hundred years of poverty and policy*, York: Joseph Rowntree Foundation.

Hills, J. and Stewart, K. (2005) 'A tide turned but mountains yet to climb?', in J. Hills and K. Stewart (eds) *A more equal society? New Labour, poverty, inequality and exclusion*, Bristol: The Policy Press.

Hirsh, D. (2004) *Strategies against poverty: A shared road map*, York: Joseph Rowntree Foundation.

HM Treasury (1999a) *The modernization of Britain's tax and benefit system Number 5: Supporting children through the tax and benefit system*, London: The Stationery Office.

HM Treasury (1999b) *Tackling poverty and extending opportunity*, London: The Stationery Office.

HM Treasury (1999c) *Supporting children through the tax and benefits system*, *5*, London: The Stationery Office.

HM Treasury (2001) *Tackling child poverty: Giving every child the best possible start in life*, London: The Stationery Office.

HM Treasury (2004) *Child poverty review*, London: The Stationery Office.

Huston, A.C., McLoyd, V.C. and Coll, C.G. (1994) 'Children and poverty: issues in contemporary research', *Child Development*, vol 65, pp 275-83.

Kemp, P., Bradshaw, J., Dornan, P., Finch, N. and Mayhew, E. (2004) *Routes out of poverty: A research review*, York: Joseph Rowntree Foundation.

Levitas, R. (1999) 'Defining and measuring social exclusion: a critical overview of current proposals', *Radical Statistics* 71 (www.radstats.org.uk/n0071/articles.htm).

Mack, J. and Lansley, S. (1985) *Poor Britain*, London: Allen and Unwin.

McGlone, F. (2001) 'School exclusions', in J. Bradshaw (ed) *Poverty: The outcomes for children*, ESRC Occasional Paper 26, London: Family Policy Studies Centre.

Middleton, S., Ashworth, K. and Walker, R. (1994) *Family fortunes: Pressures on parents and children in the 1990s*, London: Child Poverty Action Group.

Middleton, S., Ashworth, K. and Braithwaite, R. (1997) *Small fortunes: Spending on children, childhood poverty and parental sacrifice*, York: Joseph Rowntree Foundation.

Murray, L., Cooper, P.J. and Hipwell, A. (2001) 'Cognitive vulnerability to depression in 5-year old children of depressed mothers', *Journal of Child Psychology and Psychiatry*, vol 42, no 7, 891-9.

Murray, L., Sinclair, P., Cooper, P. and Ducournau, P. (1999) 'The socioemotional development of 5-year old children of postnatally depressed mothers', *Journal of Child Psychology and Psychiatry*, vol 40, no 8, pp 1259-71.

NAO (National Audit Office) (2004) *Early years: Progress in developing high quality childcare and early education accessible to all*, London: The Stationery Office.

Palmer, G. and Kenway, P. (2004) *Monitoring poverty and social exclusion 2004*, York: Joseph Rowntree Foundation (www.npi.org.uk/reports/mpse2004.pdf).

Penn, H. (2004) *Childcare and early childhood development programmes and policies – Their relationship to eradicating child poverty*, Childhood Poverty Research and Policy Centre report No 8 (www.childhoodpoverty.org/index).

Piachaud, D. (2001) *Child poverty, opportunities and quality of life*, London: The Political Quarterly Publishing Company Ltd.

Piachaud, D. and Sutherland, H. (2001) 'Child poverty in Britain and the New Labour Government', *Journal of Social Policy*, vol 30, no 1, pp 95-118.

Platt, L. (2005) *Discovering child poverty: The creation of a policy agenda from 1800 to the present*, Bristol: The Policy Press.

Quilgars, D. (2001) 'Mental health', in J. Bradshaw (ed) *Poverty: The outcomes for children*, ESRC Occasional Paper 26, London: Family Policy Studies Centre.

Ridge, T. (2002) *Childhood and social exclusion: From a child's perspective*, Bristol: The Policy Press.

Rowntree, B.S. (1901) *Poverty: A study of town life*, London: Macmillan & Co (reissued by The Policy Press in 2000).

Ruxton, S. and Bennett, F. (2001) *Including children? Developing a coherent approach to child poverty and social exclusion across Europe*, Brussels: Euronet.

Seccombe, K. (2000) 'Families in poverty in the 1990s: trends, causes, consequences and lessons learned', *Journal of Marriage and the Family*, vol 62, pp 1094-13.

Sefton, T. (2004) *A fair share of welfare: Public spending on children in England*, CASE report 25, London: Centre for Analysis of Social Exclusion with Save the Children.

SEU (Social Exclusion Unit) (2000) *National Strategy for Neighbourhood Renewal: Report of Policy Action Team 12: Young people*, London: Cabinet Office.

Shaw, M., Davey Smith, G. and Dorling, D. (2005) 'Health inequalities and New Labour: how the promises compare with real progress', *British Medical Journal*, vol 330, pp 1016-21.

Shropshire, J. and Middleton, S. (1999) *Small expectations: Learning to be poor*, York: Joseph Rowntree Foundation.

Skinner, C. (2003) *Running around in circles: Coordinating childcare, education and work*, Bristol/York: The Policy Press/Joseph Rowntree Foundation.

Smith, T., Noble, M., Barlow, J., Sharland, E. and Smith, G. (1995) *Education divides: Poverty and schooling in the 1992*, London: Child Poverty Action Group.

Stewart, K. (2005a) 'Changes in poverty and inequality in the UK in an international context', in J. Hills and K. Stewart (eds) *A more equal society? New Labour, poverty, inequality and exclusion*, Bristol: The Policy Press.

Stewart, K. (2005b) 'Towards an equal start? Addressing childhood poverty and deprivation', in J. Hills and K. Stewart (eds) *A more equal society? New Labour, poverty, inequality and exclusion*, Bristol: The Policy Press.

Sutherland, H. (2002) *One parent families, poverty and Labour policy*, London: National Council for One-Parent Families.

Sutherland, H., Sefton, T. and Piachaud, D. (2003) *Poverty in Britain: The impact of government policy since 1997*, York: Joseph Rowntree Foundation.

Townsend, P. (1979) *Poverty in the United Kingdom*, Harmondsworth: Penguin.

UN (United Nations) (1995) *The Copenhagen Declaration and Programme of Action*, World Summit for Social Development, 6-12 March, New York, NY: UN Department of Publications.

UNICEF (2000) *A league table of child poverty in rich nations*, Report Card No 1, Florence: Innocenti Research Centre.

UNICEF (2005) *Child poverty in rich countries*, Report Card No 6, Florence: Innocenti Research Centre.

Wiggins, M., Oakley, A., Roberts, I., Turner, H., Rajan, L., Austerberry, H., Mujica, R. and Mugford, M. (2004) 'The social support and family health study: a randomised controlled trial and economic evaluation of two alternative forms of postnatal support for mothers living in disadvantaged inner-city areas', *Health Technology Assessment*, vol 8, no 32 (www.ncchta.org/project.asp?PjtId=1060).

Work and Pensions Select Committee (2004) *Child poverty in the UK*, vol 1, London: The Stationery Office.

Appendix

Table A11.1: Perception of necessities by whether respondent is a parent (%)

	Parent (n=471)	Non-parent (n=1,264)
Three meals a day	92	91
Toys	86	84
Leisure equipment	58	62
Enough bedrooms	77	79
Computer games	14	20
Waterproof coat	95	95
Books of his/her own	98	90
New bike	61	54
Construction toys	67	62
Educational games	85	84
New shoes	96	94
At least seven pairs of underpants	85	84
At least four jumpers, cardigans	73	75
All school uniform	88	88
At least four pairs of trousers	75	69
At least 50p per week pocket money	46	52
Meath/fish/vegetarian equivalent twice a day	77	78
Computer suitable for school work	40	44
Fresh fruit/vegetables every day	93	94
A garden to play in	69	69
Some new, not second-hand clothes	68	73
A carpet in their bedroom	75	66
A bed and bedding to him/herself	96	93
A hobby or leisure activity	89	91
Celebrations on special occasions	92	93
Swimming at least once a month	72	77
Play group for pre-school aged children	89	89
A holiday away from home	64	75
A school trip once a month	74	76
Friends round for tea/snacks	55	64
Collect children from school	83	74
Visits to school	91	79

Note: Individual weight used for this analysis; analysis excludes don't know/refused/not asked.

TWELVE

Youth, poverty and social exclusion

Eldin Fahmy

Introduction

As part of the government's evolving strategy tackling poverty and social exclusion there has been an especial emphasis on young people in recent years. The overall focus of government policy in relation to youth and social inclusion is outlined within the *Opportunity for All* reports (for example, DWP, 2004), and by the National Strategy Action Plan on Social Inclusion (DWP, 2003). The emphasis here has generally been on the outcomes of processes of social exclusion in terms of, for example, educational under-achievement and labour market non-participation, rather than on the root causes of disadvantage. Indicators of success in addressing poverty and social exclusion among young people have therefore often focused on tackling 'inappropriate' behaviours (for example, teenage pregnancies, young people not in education or training, truancies and exclusions, and so on) (for example, DSS, 1999; SEU, 1999; DWP, 2004).

The development of government policy in this area is summarised in the Social Exclusion Unit's (SEU) *Policy Action Team Report 12* (PAT12) as part of the development of the government's Neighbourhood Renewal Strategy (SEU, 2000a). PAT12 specifies a wide range of measures in relation to young people. Again, however, the focus of policy development has been in relation to specific 'problem groups' through, for example, proposals for the introduction of Drugs Action Teams, Youth Offending Teams, and the development of an integrated support service ('Connexions') catering primarily for young people not in education, employment or training (Watts, 2001). Similarly, the focus on 'excluded youth' is also evident in the policy emphasis on improving the prospects for young people not in education, employment or training (for example, SEU, 1999).

These policy developments undoubtedly reflect the deepening of social inequalities in the UK in the 1980s and 1990s. A host of studies document the dramatic increase in poverty over this period among the UK population as a whole (for example, Mack and Lansley, 1985; Gordon and Pantazis, 1997; see also Chapter One in this volume). In relation to young people, the erosion of social citizenship rights and the economic marginalisation of youth as a result of economic restructuring during the 1980s have both contributed to the social exclusion of increasing numbers of young people over this period (Williamson, 1993; France, 1997). Increasing levels of homelessness among young people, labour market withdrawal, and educational under-achievement have all been areas of academic and policy-focused attention in recent years. Youth research in the 1990s has identified some of the debilitating effects of these trends for young people's increasingly hazardous transitions to adulthood (Istance et al, 1994; Craine, 1997; Dean, 1997; Smith, 1999).

However, as with much current policy development in the area of social exclusion, empirical research has tended to focus on specific problems or indicators in the absence of conceptual clarity about what social exclusion itself denotes. By focusing on only the most extreme forms of social marginalisation and disadvantage this approach tends to obscure the extent of social and economic exclusion among the UK population as a whole, and the factors which obstruct participation in social life. For example, despite the recent emphasis on socially excluded youth, much less attention has been given to levels of income poverty, and material and social deprivation among young people. Indeed, despite very welcome and long-overdue policy interventions in this area, there is a tendency for youth to 'fall between the gaps' in policy development where young people's needs are simultaneously considered alongside children (those aged under 19) and adults of working age (those aged 19+). This approach does not address the distinctiveness of youth as a stage in the lifecourse and the unique challenges faced by young people in the transition to adulthood. This chapter seeks to begin to redress this imbalance by presenting findings from the 1999 Poverty and Social Exclusion (PSE) Survey of Britain relating to the extent and dynamics of poverty and social exclusion among young people in Britain at the millennium.

Defining youth

The analyses presented in this chapter reflect the views and circumstances of the 'young' PSE respondents (aged 16-25) (a detailed social and demographic profile of PSE respondents is given in the

Appendix to this chapter). There is of course no universally agreed definition of 'youth'. Legal definitions of childhood, youth and adulthood present a complex, chaotic, and essentially arbitrary array of definitions (see Coles, 1995). Rather than pursuing a chronological definition, youth is better viewed as a period of transition, or set of transitions, between the dependency of childhood and the social and economic independence of adulthood. However, as Gillis (1974) shows, the emergence of youth as a social category was also closely tied to socio-economic, cultural and political changes initiated by industrialisation and the development of compulsory mass education. Youth as a life phase thus describes a period of constant flux which is subject to complex processes of negotiation and re-negotiation between young people, their families and peers, and the institutions of the wider society, notably the state through its social and labour market policies (Jones and Wallace, 1992). As such youth represents a period of 'quasi-citizenship' in which young people's rights and entitlements change in response to changes in social and economic circumstances.

Most youth researchers agree that youth transitions at the millennium are more protracted, more complex, and in some cases more hazardous, than for previous generations. Coles (1995), for example, refers to *extended* and *fractured* transitions in which young people's economic dependency on their parents continues longer, and status transitions produce uncertain and often unsatisfactory results. The contraction of the youth labour market, together with the erosion of young people's social entitlements, is central to these accounts, extending the transition to independent adult status into the early to mid twenties in most cases. The 1988 Social Security Act initiated this process by removing 16- and 17-year-olds' benefit entitlements and introducing a lower rate of benefits for 18- to 24-year-olds. Although recent government guidance seeks to ease the effects of some of these restrictions by making it easier for 16- and 17-year-olds to demonstrate 'estrangement' from parents/guardians and thus claim benefits, the reinstatement of a right to benefits for 16- and 17-year-olds is not on the government's agenda (HM Treasury, 2004). In the context of the virtual collapse of the youth labour market in the 1980s these reforms had the effect of frustrating many young people's efforts to achieve financial independence. For the most vulnerable, the consequences in terms of persistent unemployment and the risk of homelessness are well documented (for example, Craine, 1997; Jones, 1997; Williamson, 1997; Johnston et al, 2000; Webster et al, 2004). For example, recent estimates suggest there could be as many as 11,600 homeless young people aged between 16 and 17 years (Pleace and Fitzpatrick, 2004). As we shall see, young people's exclusion from the rights and entitlements of full adulthood has been similarly reinforced in relation to National Minimum Wage legislation.

Young people living in poverty

Income poverty

Research into poverty and inequality typically concentrates on income as a measure of economic well being, usually by classifying households with an income below a certain proportion of the mean or median household income as poor. There are a number of problems associated with this approach to measuring income poverty (see Chapter Two for further discussion). The appropriateness of the equivalence scales used to adjust income to need, the contribution of housing costs in determining income levels, and whether mean or median income should be measured are all open to question, as is the choice of income threshold (see, for example, Townsend and Gordon, 1992; Townsend, 1996).

However, and notwithstanding these difficulties, the PSE Survey reveals a moderate age effect in terms of measures of income inequality whether using the Organisation for Economic Cooperation and Development (OECD), Households Below Average Income (HBAI), or PSE equivalisation scales. Table 12.1 presents three different measures of inequality in net weekly equivalised household income based on the OECD, HBAI, and PSE income equivalisation scales which adjust income to need. The extent of income inequality varies somewhat according to the indicator used, with the PSE scale recording the largest proportion (26%) of households below 50% of mean income. In all three cases, however, a greater proportion of young people (aged under 25) reported significantly below average incomes than among the sample as a whole, with estimates ranging from 20% to 26%.

The 2002 Budget extended the principle of Minimum Income Guarantees (MIG) in the form of a Working Tax Credit to all those

Table 12.1: Income inequality age group (%)

	Age group (%)			
	Under 25	25-34 years	35+ years	All
Below 60% median OECD	20	11	16	16
Below 50% mean HBAI	24	15	24	22
Below 50% mean PSE	26	15	25	23
Below MIG threshold	17	12	25	21

aged 25 and over in full-time employment, set at a rate of £154 for single people and £183 for couples with effect from April 2003. However, until October 2004 neither this nor any other similar principle was applied to young people in work in order to safeguard their incomes. Following the recent review of Minimum Wage protection for young workers (for example, HM Treasury, 2004; Low Pay Commission, 2004), the youth Development Rate has been extended to include 16- and 17-year-old workers, albeit at a still lower rate than that applicable to 18- to 24-year-olds. Nonetheless, there is no reason to suppose that someone aged under 25 needs less income to meet their basic material and social needs than older citizens, although this has been the underlying premise of social security payments since 1988. As with the social security changes introduced in 1988, the exclusion of young people from the MIG represents a further erosion of young people's social rights and entitlements as citizens that urgently need to be addressed.

As Table 12.1 shows, applying these MIG standards to the PSE household income data reveals that among young people aged under 25 one sixth (17%) of the PSE sample has household incomes below the MIG thresholds outlined above. Moreover these data also reveal a very substantial gender effect, especially among young PSE respondents, with more than four times as many young women (29%) reporting incomes below the MIG thresholds compared with young men (7%) (see Figure 12.1). Indeed these data suggest that gender differences in levels of poverty *among* young people may be at least as significant as differences in levels of poverty and deprivation *between* younger and older age groups (the gendered dimensions of poverty and social

Figure 12.1: Respondents with household incomes below MIG threshold (%)

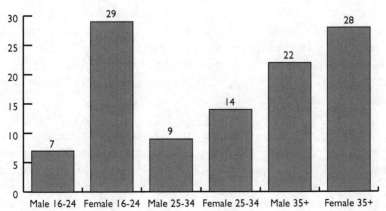

exclusion are explored in greater depth in Chapter Thirteen in this volume).

Using a budget standard approach reveals a rather similar gendered picture of poverty among young people. Based on data derived from the Family Expenditure Survey (FES) and other sources, Morris and colleagues estimated that at April 1999 prices £131.86 per week constituted a minimum income for healthy living for young men under 30 (Morris et al, 2000). Applying this standard to PSE net weekly household income data suggests that 7% of young men under 30 lack sufficient income for healthy living. However, and although this budget standard is designed for young men, applying this threshold to the PSE data for women under 30 suggests that this affects twice the proportion of women (14%).

These analyses support earlier work by the European Commission, which show the risk of income poverty to be higher for young people (and especially young women) aged 16-24 than for the adult population as a whole both in the UK, as well as across EU15 member states (CEC, 2003). Comparative analysis of poverty within the 15 EU member states (EU15) reveals a broadly similar picture, with higher levels of income poverty among young Europeans (aged 16-24) compared to all EU15 citizens, and higher levels of poverty among young women compared with young men. Based on Eurostat's 'official' poverty rates derived from the European Community Household Panel (ECHP), in 2000 20% of young male UK citizens were officially poor compared with 23% of young female UK citizens, and 14% of young male EU15 citizens compared with 16% of young women (CEC, 2003). Indeed, as Figure 12.2 shows, the poverty rate for young UK citizens is consistently higher both than young EU15 citizens and overall poverty rates for the UK and the EU15, based on ECHP data for 1998-2000.

While research into poverty and inequality usually focuses on income, inequalities in wealth are also an important issue. Notwithstanding the difficulties in measuring wealth among the very wealthy (see Scott, 1994), analysis of data from the 1995/96 Family Resources Survey (FRS) confirms the close relationship between the ownership of wealth and individuals' positions within the lifecourse. Single people aged under 35, and especially those aged 18-24 and young single parents, were on average very poor in terms both of income and especially wealth, although there are also considerable inequalities of wealth and income within these age groups (Rowlinson et al, 1999). However, in themselves income-based measures are a fairly crude indicator of levels of poverty and deprivation. In particular there is a substantial mismatch

Figure 12.2: EU poverty rate in the UK and EU15 by age group, 1998-2000

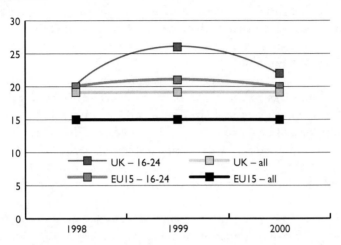

Source: ECHP 1998-2000 (CEC, 2003)

between poverty measured *indirectly* as low income and poverty measured *directly* as observed deprivation (Hallerod, 1998). As Gordon and Townsend (1990) argue, individuals and households are most adequately described as *poor* when they have both a low standard of living and a low income relative to societal norms (see also Gordon, 2001). The measurement of poverty adopted within the 1999 PSE Survey reflects this thinking. Establishing a poverty threshold thus involves consideration of both income and standard of living (defined in terms of an individual's material and social living conditions and their participation in the social life of the country; see Chapter Two for a fuller discussion of the PSE measure).

Lack of socially perceived necessities

The optimal 'fit' between low income and deprivation for PSE respondents is described by the level of net household equivilised income at which households lack two or more of the social and material necessities of life, as defined by Office for National Statistics (ONS) Omnibus Survey respondents. The proportion of PSE respondents who lack two or more of the social and material necessities of life varies both with age and with gender. In total, over one quarter (27%) of PSE respondents were deprivation-poor according to this measure. Material and social deprivation is also gendered, with a greater proportion of women (30%) lacking two or more socially perceived necessities than men (24%). However, as Figure 12.3 shows, among young respondents aged under 25 well over one third (36%) lack two or more of the social or material necessities of life, and, as with income poverty, social and material deprivation is again strongly gendered, with 43% of young women experiencing deprivation in comparison with 28% of young men.

However, the approach to poverty measurement adopted throughout this volume seeks to maximise the differences between 'poor' and 'non-poor' in relation to *both* income and deprivation simultaneously – 'PSE poverty' (see Chapter Two in this volume). The consequences of adopting this more multi-dimensional approach to the measurement of poverty are illustrated in Figure 12.3. Two features of the social distribution of PSE poverty are particularly noteworthy here. First, levels of poverty are considerably higher among young people than among the older respondents. Although rates of PSE poverty are highest among the 25-34 age group (35%), as Figure 12.3 shows, youth remains a powerful predictor of poverty with one third (33%) of young people living in poverty compared with one fifth (21%) of respondents aged 35+. Second, as might be expected, gender is a significant factor in shaping levels of poverty both for young people and for the wider sample as a whole. Among PSE respondents aged under 25, more than two fifths (42%) of young women were experiencing poverty compared with less than one quarter (24%) of young men.

These data also illustrate the lack of correspondence between income and deprivation measures of poverty. While the household incomes of young people are, on average, considerably lower than among the 25-34 age group, levels of deprivation among young people are only slightly lower. Housing is one of the most significant costs which

Figure 12.3: PSE poverty, by age group and gender (%)

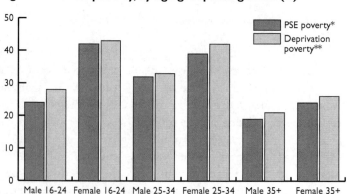

Notes: * Deprived of two or more necessities and on a low income.
** Deprived of two or more necessities.

distinguishes young people from the adult population as a whole. A majority (60%) of the young respondents in the PSE sample live with their parents or guardians and this is likely to have a significant effect on their access both to material necessities (via their parents) and social necessities (since their housing costs are usually considerably lower). Thus although young people's incomes are low, a similar proportion of those living with parents are poor (23%) compared with the sample as a whole (25%). However, among those young people living independently or sharing with other non-relatives nearly half (46%) are income poor.

Moving out of the parental home and living independently is usually considered a key dimension of the transition to adulthood (for example, Coles, 1995; Jones, 1995). However, as White (1994) argues, housing transitions are influenced by economic and political factors. Arguably the contraction of the youth labour market, the concentration of young people in usually low-paid service sector employment, and the erosion of young people's entitlements to Housing Benefit and Income Support have all undermined young people's capacity to effect early housing and domestic transitions. As a result these processes have also re-defined 'youth' by making youth transitions increasingly protracted.

Subjective poverty

The PSE Survey also used a subjectively assessed measure of poverty to estimate how much money respondents consider necessary to avoid *absolute* and *overall poverty* as defined by the 1995 United Nations World Summit for Social Development (UN, 1995; see also Chapter Three in this volume). Respondents were asked to estimate the average weekly income needed to keep a household like theirs out of each of these forms of poverty. In addition, respondents were asked to determine whether their income was 'below the level of income you think is necessary to keep a household such as yours out of poverty' (described as 'general' poverty).

As Table 12.2 shows, younger respondents' perceptions of the 'poverty line' are somewhat higher than those of older respondents. Among young people, estimates of the various poverty thresholds are between 10% and 14% higher than for those aged 35+. This may reflect generational differences in respondents' expectations and aspirations. Older people may sometimes underestimate the effects of inflation when making financial decisions and this is likely to influence their perceptions of an appropriate poverty threshold. Similarly, it could be argued that younger people are more likely to be influenced by a

Table 12.2: Weekly income needed to keep people above the poverty line, by age group (%)

	Age group (%)			
	Under 25	**25-34 years**	**35+ years**	**All**
General poverty threshold				
Estimated income needed (£)	239	242	218	224
A little/lot above	60	59	69	66
About the same	18	17	13	14
A little/lot below	22	24	18	20
Absolute poverty threshold				
Estimated income needed (£)	200	203	181	187
A little/lot above	69	69	78	76
About the same	15	10	7	8
A little/lot below	15	20	16	17
Overall poverty threshold				
Estimated income needed (£)	281	267	247	253
A little/lot above	55	63	68	66
About the same	17	6	8	8
A little/lot below	29	31	24	26

climate of affluence and material consumption even where these obviously clash with their own personal circumstances.

As Table 12.2 illustrates, one in five respondents (20%) believe that their household income is below that necessary to avoid poverty (general poverty), and one in six (17%) also feel that their income is insufficient to meet the very basic needs defined by the absolute poverty threshold. These findings are even more striking when the effects of age differences in responses are considered. Taking a broader view of poverty which includes an inability to participate in social and cultural life due to a lack of resources (overall poverty), well over a quarter (29%) of young people feel their incomes falls below such a threshold, as shown in Table 12.2.

The overall correspondence between respondents' subjective assessments of their overall poverty status and the objective measurement of poverty used in the PSE Survey is also striking. An almost identical proportion of respondents (26%) consider their incomes to be below that necessary to avoid overall poverty compared with that used in the Survey to describe 'objective' poverty (25%). However, there is a greater divergence between subjective perceptions of overall poverty and the PSE measure in relation to age differences. In particular it appears that young respondents underestimate somewhat their own poverty. Thus, 29% of young people, and 31% of the 25-34 age group, consider themselves to be in overall poverty compared with 34% of young people, and 37% of the 25-34 age group defined as objectively poor by the PSE measure.

This may reflect differing perceptions of the necessities of life in contemporary Britain. Table 12.3 illustrates the extent of age differences in perceptions of those items or activities considered to be necessities of life in the June 1999 ONS Omnibus Survey (see also Chapter Four in this volume). As this table shows, in most cases fewer young people considered these items to be essentials of modern life in Britain compared with the sample as a whole. In most cases the relationship between age group and perceptions of necessities was linear so the variation between, for example, young people and older people in their perceptions of the necessities of life is even more striking.

As Table 12.3 illustrates, in most cases young people were less likely to perceive 'material' items (such as a television, telephone, or dictionary) as necessities compared with older age groups. Many of these items also, or primarily, fulfil a *social* function. However, since a greater proportion of young people do not consider these to be essential compared with older age groups it is perhaps unsurprising that young people also underestimate the extent of their own poverty in comparison with the more objective PSE poverty measure.

Table 12.3: Perceptions of the necessities of life in Britain in 1999, by age group

	18-24 years	All	Difference
Two pairs of all-weather shoes	40	66	−26
A television	43	57	−14
Telephone	58	72	−14
Fresh fruit and vegetables daily	75	86	−11
Money to spend on self weekly	49	60	−11
A dictionary	45	55	−10
A warm waterproof coat	76	86	−10
A holiday away from home	45	55	−10
Presents for friends/family yearly	48	57	−9
A washing machine	67	76	−9
Collect children from school	82	73	+9

Young people and social exclusion

Exclusion from the labour market

Contemporary approaches to social exclusion frequently cite labour market withdrawal as a key component of social exclusion (see Chapters Five and Six in this volume). Within European policy discourse, tackling the problem of long-term unemployment and labour market non-participation has long been viewed as central to addressing social exclusion (for example, CEC, 1994a, 1994b). In the UK, this emphasis is reflected in the work of the government's SEU, especially in relation to young people. Addressing the 'problem' of young people not in employment, education or training has been a major focus of policy in this area. At the end of 1998 173,000 16- to 18-year-olds (9%) were not in employment, education or training across England and Wales according to Department for Education and Employment estimates (DfEE, 1999). The SEU report *Bridging the gap* has been central in the development of government policy in this area, outlining initiatives designed to increase post-compulsory education and training, for example, through the development of the new 'Connexions' service (SEU, 1999).

However, as Colley and Hodkinson (2001) argue, underlying the SEU's approach is an individualised and moral account which focuses on young people's own deficiencies and shortcomings. The report rarely refers to the structural changes which have undermined young people's labour market position and made the transition to adult increasingly precarious for disadvantaged young people (see, for example, Bates and Riseborough, 1994; Ball et al, 2000). In particular, it fails to acknowledge the effects of the collapse of the youth labour market, and the 'warehousing' function (Roberts, 1995) increasingly played by post-compulsory education and training since the 1980s.

Paid employment is declared in *Bridging the gap* to be, in the words of Tony Blair, "the best defence against social exclusion" (SEU, 1999, p 6). However, young people are far more likely than older workers to be in low-paid jobs. More than 40% of those aged under 21 earned less than the adult National Minimum Wage of £3.50 per hour in 1998, compared with just 10% of those aged over 21 (Low Pay Commission, 1998). Two thirds (67%) of 16- and 17-year-olds, and well over one third of 18- to 20-year-olds in employment were within the lowest paid decile of the UK working population (Low Pay Commission, 1998, p 76). These trends are illustrated in Figure 12.4.

Although more recent analyses suggest some narrowing of the pay gap between adults and young people as a result of Minimum Wage protection and up-rating (for example, Low Pay Commission, 2003, pp 113-14), for those within the lowest income decile at age 18 earnings potential is unlikely to increase significantly with age but rather tend to level off from as early as 20 or 21 (Low Pay Commission, 1998; Webster et al, 2004). Indeed, in the period between 1979 and 2001, young people's pay fell dramatically as a proportion of adults' pay. For 18- to 20-year-olds, wages fell during the same period (1979-96)

Figure 12.4: The low paid as a percentage of all employees, by age

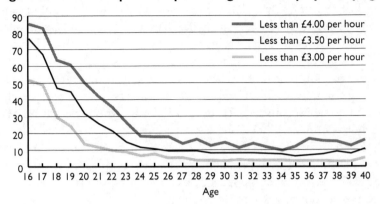

Source: Labour Force Survey, autumn 1997/Low Pay Commission (1998)

from 62% to 47% for men, and from 77% to 57% for women (Low Pay Commission, 1998, p 37). These findings are also reflected in the PSE sample data. Of those in employment and prepared to divulge their earnings, mean net weekly earnings among those aged under 25 are just 62% of those for the sample as a whole.

These trends partly reflect the effects of labour market policies since the 1980s, for example through the removal of Wages Council protection for young people in 1986. There are currently no plans to re-introduce such protection and young people under 18 are also excluded from protection under Minimum Wage legislation, although recent government proposals (for example, HM Treasury, 2004) provide for the extension of Minimum Wage protection to 16- and 17-year-olds at a reduced Development Rate with effect from October 2005. For those aged under 22 Minimum Wage rates are set below those for working adults (£4.10 and £4.85 respectively, with effect from October 2004). Furthermore, as mentioned above young people's exclusion from the MIG legislation reinforces the erosion of young people's social citizenship status initiated in the 1980s. As was argued above these developments also represent a significant re-definition of youth transitions.

Service exclusion

Most people regard easy access to essential services as important. The 1999 British Social Attitudes Survey, for example, revealed that a majority of the 6,000 people surveyed believed that basic services (such as doctors, corner shops, and primary schools) should be within a 15-minute walk of home (Stratford, 2000). Similarly, a majority of the PSE Survey respondents consider a wide range of public and private services to be essential (rather than just desirable) (see Chapter Eight for a more detailed discussion of services and service exclusion). On the whole, age differences in respondents' perceptions of the importance of these services were insubstantial. As might be expected the most significant age effects relate to services associated with specific phases in the lifecourse. As Table 12.4 indicates, young people are less likely to consider services for older people (that is, transport for the aged, home helps, and meals on wheels) to be essential compared with the sample as a whole, and more likely to consider services relating to children and young people (that is, school transport, youth clubs, and pre-school playgroups) as essential.

Some services (such as GPs, post offices, chemists, supermarkets, bank/building societies, dentists, and hospitals) are used almost universally by all households in the sample and hence no significant age differences are evident. As Table 12.5 illustrates, age differences in patterns of usage of other social amenities largely reflect anticipated age differences in patterns in leisure. Hence young people are more

Table 12.4: Respondents regarding selected local services as essential, by age group (%)

	18-24 years	All	Difference
Transport for the aged	19	41	−22
Home help	18	36	−18
Meals on wheels	18	35	−17
Public transport to school	38	26	+12
Play groups	39	28	+11
Youth clubs	29	19	+10
Medium to large supermarkets	70	61	+9
Petrol stations	86	78	+8
Public sports facilities	75	68	+7
Nurseries	34	27	+7

Table 12.5: Respondents using selected local services, by age group (%)

	18-24 years	All	Difference
Museums and galleries	15	33	−18
Place of worship	14	31	−17
Cinema	68	52	+16
Optician	66	81	−15
Bus services	67	53	+14
Public sports facilities	59	46	+13
Village/community halls	21	34	−13
Pub	71	58	+13
Petrol station	66	77	−11

likely to use cinemas, pubs and public sports facilities, and less likely to use museums, galleries, and places of worship, compared with the sample as a whole.

While age differences in respondents' perceptions of the importance of services and amenities, and in patterns of actual usage were often not significant, substantial age differences did emerge in relation to respondents' assessments of the adequacy of services in meeting their needs. It is useful to distinguish here between *social amenities* which fulfil a primarily social or leisure function (libraries, sports facilities, museums, community halls, pubs, cinemas, evening classes and places of worship), and *community services* which address more basic, material needs (GPs, hospitals, dentists, opticians, post offices, buses, trains, chemists, supermarkets and banks). Figure 12.5 illustrates the proportion of respondents who are dissatisfied with at least one of the services they use in these categories. First, a greater proportion of respondents are dissatisfied with *community services* (19%) compared with social and leisure amenities (7%).

Second, in both cases young respondents are less satisfied with these services compared with older age groups and the sample as a whole. This is especially so in relation to key public and private sector services such as health services, transport and finance described by the *community services* scale. As Figure 12.5 shows, almost one third (30%) of young respondents were dissatisfied with these services compared with less than one fifth (19%) of the sample as a whole. These data broadly confirm the age profile of public satisfaction with local services presented in recent research by the SEU (SEU, 2000b). Using a multivariate CHAID approach this study suggests that the main age effect occurs at the other end of the age spectrum with those aged over 55 expressing greater satisfaction with a range of public services

Figure 12.5: Dissatisfaction with amenities and community services, by age group (%)

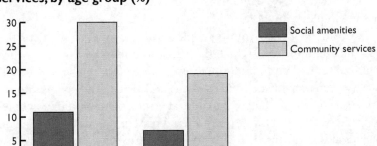

(GPs, libraries, councils, police, benefits agencies) compared with younger age groups.

Young people's dissatisfaction with many of the key public and private services outlined above at least partly reflects their inadequacy in addressing the needs of young people. Until recently young people have been largely neglected in terms of policy and research in comparison with adults and children (Dennehy et al, 1997). A failure to address young people's needs and concerns in the provision of key services has been one legacy of this trend, and is belatedly encouraging a greater awareness of the need to involve young people in the planning and delivery of key public services (for example, CYPU, 2001). The importance of services in raising the standard of living of households living on low incomes should not be underestimated. Gordon and Townsend (2000), for example, find that over half the income of the poorest 10% of households is in the form of 'benefits-in-kind'. However, the allocation of public spending on mainstream services to address disadvantage among young people is an especial problem. Similar problems are also evident in relation to the provision of public services for vulnerable young people (see, for example, Howarth and Street, 2000).

Exclusion from social relations

The inability to participate in a range of common social activities due to a lack of resources is central in most definitions of relative deprivation (for example, Townsend, 1979). PSE respondents were asked about a range of items considered by respondents in the Omnibus Survey to be necessities[1]. Analysis of those unable to afford to engage in these activities reveals few significant age differences. The main exception, however, is in relation to holidays away from home at least once a year. More than one third (36%) of respondents aged under 25 are unable to afford to take a holiday once a year compared with one sixth (17%) of the sample as a whole.

The ways in which young people relate to wider social networks and the community in which they live has important effects on their well being. Coleman (1988), for example, refers to the extent and quality of an individual's contacts with family and friends as constituting their 'social capital'. Table 12.6 illustrates the extent of young people's social networks and the reasons offered by respondents for not seeing friends and family more frequently in comparison with the sample as a whole. Both in relation to friends and to family young people appear to be less socially isolated compared with all adults, with 7% having

Table 12.6: Respondents' social contact, by age group (%)

	16-24 years	All	Difference
Contact with family member(s): less than weekly	7	10	−3
Contact with friends/neighbours: less than weekly	1	7	−6
Reasons for not seeing friends/family more often:			
Do not want to	24	29	−5
Cannot afford to	9	5	+4
Lack of time due to paid work	12	19	−7
Caring responsibilities	10	10	0
No vehicle/poor public transport	17	7	+10
Too far away	15	19	−4
Other	12	11	+1

infrequent contact with family, and just 1% seeing friends less than weekly. The reasons offered for not maintaining more frequent social contact also differ somewhat from the sample as a whole with more young people citing a lack of available transport and fewer citing insufficient time due to work commitments.

Civic engagement and community participation

Recent years have witnessed renewed concerns about the apparent withdrawal of young people from civic engagement in the UK. Anxiety has focused in particular on declining levels of electoral participation by young people, and more generally on their apparent disengagement from conventional politics. Underlying such fears, however, is a deeper concern with possible changes in young people's social consciousness and the development of more 'individualised' social outlooks and identities which militate against involvement in a diverse range of 'collective' community organisations (for example, Wilkinson and Mulgan, 1995; Furlong and Cartmel. 1997).

The data presented in Table 12.7 certainly demonstrate that overall young people are somewhat less likely to participate in a range of social, community and political organisations than older age groups. More than half (52%) of respondents aged under 25 have not taken part in any of the activities listed compared with 41% of those aged 35+, and 43% of the sample as a whole. However, with the exception of faith-based organisations and tenants' and residents' associations, the differences are not substantial. Whether these data reflect lower levels of social participation per se, or simply a predisposition towards engagement in the types of relatively unstructured, informal and community-based activities which are more difficult to measure using survey methods is open to question. Thus, although young respondents

Table 12.7: Respondents' social and community participation, by age group

	16-24 years	All	Difference	Significance
Sports club	29	18	+11	<0.01
Voluntary service group	9	8	+1	ns
Other community or civic group	4	3	+1	<0.05
Political party	2	2	0	<0.05
Any other group or organisation	10	11	−1	<0.01
Women's Institute or similar guild	0	1	−1	<0.05
Trade union	8	10	−2	Ns
Environmental group	1	3	−2	Ns
Women's group or organisation	1	3	−2	<0.01
Other pressure group	0	2	−2	<0.01
Social or working men's club	6	9	−3	Ns
Parents or school association	1	6	−5	<0.01
Religious group or organisation	4	12	−8	<0.01
Tenants or residents association, etc	0	9	−9	<0.01
None	**52**	**43**	**+9**	**<0.05**

report lower levels of formal social and community involvement compared with the sample as a whole, other data reveal that young people are nevertheless often highly committed in a range of 'collective' voluntary and campaigning settings (see, for example, BYC, 1998; Roker et al, 1999).

Similar issues are pertinent in the investigation of young people's civic engagement and political participation. Measures of political participation are often scaled in order to more reliably measure their social and spatial distribution. Table 12.8 details a range of measures which seek to tap different dimensions of a citizen's engagement with the political process. The items listed below describe a range of 'formal' modes of participation in politics and as such exclude the types of unstructured and informal participation often favoured by marginalised groups (Lister, 1990, 1997). However, as a measure of formal engagement with the political process this scale displays a high degree

Table 12.8: Reliability analysis of civic engagement index

	Item-total correlation	Alpha if deleted
Presented my views to a local councillor	0.41	0.65
Written a letter to an editor	0.31	0.68
Urged someone outside my family to vote	0.38	0.66
Urged someone to get in touch with a local councillor or MP	0.47	0.64
Made a speech before an organised group	0.46	0.65
Been an officer of an organisation of club	0.38	0.66
Taken an active part in a political campaign	0.28	0.68
Helped on fund raising drives	0.41	0.66

Cronbach's Coefficient Alpha = 0.690

of internal consistency. As Table 12.8 shows, the reliability coefficient for this scale is 0.69 suggesting a close correlation between this index and other similar indices.

This index reveals a clear relationship between age and levels of engagement in the formal representative process, as Figure 12.6 shows. Among young people aged less than 25 only one in ten (10%) had participated in two or more of the activities measured by this scale compared with 29% of the sample as a whole. Even more strikingly, half of the sample as a whole and two thirds (68%) of those respondents aged under 25 had not participated in any of the measures described by this scale.

Social exclusion can be conceptualised as a state of incomplete citizenship arising from a range of exclusionary mechanisms including but not limited to processes of economic marginalisation (Gore, 1995). Analysis of the PSE data certainly demonstrates a clear association between poverty and social participation among the PSE sample as a whole, with those respondents classified as poor using the PSE measure being less likely to participate both in civic life and social and community organisations (Bradshaw and Williams, 2000). However, in addition to material resources, young people's civic engagement is also shaped by their access to the types of personal networks, resources and skills which facilitate active engagement. Indeed, young people's differential access to this 'cultural capital' (Bourdieu and Passeron, 1976) is among the most fundamental of obstacles to the effective exercise of political citizenship faced by disadvantaged young people.

As a consequence of their position of dependence and subordination within the lifecourse, young people, and especially disadvantaged young people, are unlikely to benefit from the types of social and professional connections, or to participate in the types of organised civil associations,

Figure 12.6: Civic engagement scale, by age group (%)

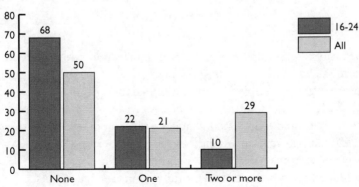

which facilitate political participation. In addition to their relatively weak position vis-à-vis the personal resources which encourage involvement, young people are also remote from the types of collective resources and networks which might encourage them to engage with formal political institutions. Young people's lack of access to these types of individual and collective resources constitute real barriers to their exercise of political citizenship and in the process serve to exclude young people, especially disadvantaged young people, from exercising genuine influence on the policy-making process.

As a result of growing concerns about young people's social and civic participation, a renewed policy focus on encouraging young people's participation is evident both within the UK and especially at the European level, for example as outlined within the 2001 European youth White Paper (CEC, 2001). However, until recently this agenda has given rather less consideration to the socio-economic factors which restrict young people's choices and capacity for autonomous action. As the European Youth Forum suggest (EYF, 2004), facilitating young people's social and civic participation thus involves treating young people as full citizens through:

- according greater consideration to youth concerns across the policy spectrum;
- providing free access to education at all levels;
- developing youth employment policies which effectively tackle low income and poor working conditions;
- introducing a secure social protection system with a right to social security for all young people;
- improving provision of subsidised housing and transport for young people; and
- better dissemination of information on young people's rights and social entitlements.

Conclusion

The analyses presented in this chapter demonstrate the prevalence of income poverty among young people in the UK at the millennium. However, young people are not a homogenous group. Demographic and structural inequalities of gender, social class origin, educational achievement, and ethnicity all shape the terrain of youth transitions in the UK, and more than any other group the social position of young people is also characterised by considerable fluidity. A much larger sample would be necessary to fully explore the effects of such distinctions on young people's material and social circumstances using a survey approach. The consequences of poverty for young people's experiences of the transition to adulthood is also an area which requires much further work building on existing research in this area (for example, Dennehy et al, 1997; Roker, 1998). Nonetheless these data demonstrate the centrality of both gender and young people's domestic arrangements as determinants of material and social well being, with young women and those living independently being more likely to experience poverty.

Poverty among young people is also much more widespread than might be suggested by the focus of government concerns with 'disaffected' and 'excluded' youth. The emphasis of current youth policy on 'problem' groups obscures both the underlying structural processes of economic and social marginalisation, as well as the widespread nature of poverty and social exclusion among young people in Britain today. As Craig (2000, pp 17-18) observes of New Labour:

> The government appears to remain convinced that redistribution of income is an inappropriate policy response to poverty and that strategies for including disaffected young people should be based on structural reform and work-related initiatives. The issue ... of replacing benefits for 16- to 17-year olds appears not to be on the agenda.

In the process responsibility for the predicament of disadvantaged young people is shifted to young people themselves. Such a perspective rarely acknowledges, for example, the effects of the contraction of the youth labour market, low pay, and the consequences of housing policies which undermine young people's domestic transitions to adult independence.

Social policy developments in the 1980s and 1990s exacerbated these trends through the erosion of young people's social entitlements. Changes in social benefit regulations and the deregulation of the labour and housing markets have resulted in increasingly protracted and precarious transitions for many young people. While the introduction of Minimum Wage legislation and Working Tax Credits signal a shift away from the divisive social policies of the 1980s and 1990s, young people have often been excluded from this legislation. The development of more inclusive social policies thus requires that young people be treated on more equal terms, for example, in relation to the framing of Minimum Income legislation. However, underlying current policy is an implicit assumption that young people should continue to live with their parents and stay on in tertiary education. For many disadvantaged young people this is unlikely to be a realistic option in the foreseeable future unless more fundamental structural inequalities are addressed. For some young people the effects of such assumptions are potentially disastrous. Addressing poverty and social exclusion among young people therefore requires the development of a more inclusive approach to social and economic policy which restores young people's social entitlements, and in the process offers greater support for young people's transition to independent adult status.

Note

[1] These were: participation in a hobby or leisure activity; one week's holiday away from home without relatives; celebrations on special occasions; having friends or family round for a meal or snack; visiting friends or family; attending weddings or funerals; and visiting friends or family in hospital.

References

Ball, S., Maguire, M. and Macrae, S. (2000) *Choice, pathways and transitions post-16*, London: Routledge Falmer.

Bates, I. and Riseborough, G. (1994) *Youth and inequality*, Buckingham: Open University Press.

Bourdieu, P. and Passeron, J.C. (1976) *Reproduction in education, society and culture*, London: Sage Publications (translated by R. Nice).

Bradshaw, J. and Williams, J. (2000) 'Active citizenship, social exclusion and social norms', PSE Working Paper Number 13 (available at www.bris.ac.uk/poverty/pse).

BYC (British Youth Council) (1998) *State of the Young Nation Survey*, London: BYC.

CEC (Commission of the European Communities) (1994a) *European social policy: A way forward for the Union*, Brussels: European Commission.

CEC (1994b) *Growth, competitiveness, employment: The challenges and ways forward in the 21st century*, Brussels: European Commission.

CEC (2001) *A new impetus for European youth*, COM(2001)681, Brussels: European Commission.

CEC (2003) *Joint report on social inclusion: Summarising the results of the examination of the national action plans for social inclusion*, COM(2003)773, Brussels: CEC.

Coleman, J.S. (1988) 'Social capital in the creation of human capital', *American Journal of Sociology*, vol 94, pp S95-S120.

Coles, B. (1995) *Youth, youth transitions and social policy*, London: UCL Press.

Colley, K. and Hodkinson, P. (2001) 'Problems with *Bridging the gap*: the reversal of structure and agency in addressing social exclusion', *Critical Social Policy*, vol 21, no 3, pp 335-59.

Craig, C. with Kelsey, S. (2000) *Reaching disaffected youth*, Working Papers in Social Sciences and Policy No 2, Hull: University of Hull.

Craine, S. (1997) 'The "Black Magic Roundabout": cyclical transitions, social exclusion and alternative careers', in R. MacDonald (ed) *Youth, the 'underclass' and social exclusion*, London: Routledge.

CYPU (Children and Young People's Unit) (2001) *Learning to listen: Core principles for the involvement of children and young people*, London: DfEE.

Dean, H. (1997) 'Underclassed or undermined? Young people and social citizenship', in R. MacDonald (ed) *Youth, the 'underclass' and social exclusion*, London: Routledge.

Dennehy, A., Harker, P. and Smith, L. (1997) *Not to be ignored: Young people, poverty and health*, London: Child Poverty Action Group.

DfEE (Department for Education and Employment) (1999) *Education and labour market status of young people in England aged 16-18, 1992 to 1998*, DfEE Statistical Bulletin, 11/99.

DSS (Department of Social Security) (1999) *Opportunity for All: Tackling poverty and social exclusion. Indicators of success – Definitions, data and baseline information*, London: The Stationery Office.

DWP (Department for Work and Pensions) (2003) *National strategy action plan on social inclusion*, London: DWP.

DWP (2004) *Opportunity for All: Sixth annual report*, Cm 6239, London: The Stationery Office.

EYF (European Youth Forum) (2004) *Policy paper on youth autonomy*, COMEM0052-04, Brussels: EYF.

France, A. (1997) 'Youth and citizenship in the 1990s', *Youth and policy*, vol 16, pp 28-43.

Furlong, A. and Cartmel, F. (1997) *Young people and social change: Individualisation and risk in late modernity*, Buckingham: Open University Press.

Gillis, J.R. (1974) *Youth and history: Tradition and change in European age relations, 1770-present*, New York, NY: Academic Press.

Gordon, D. and Townsend, P. (eds) (2000) *Breadline Europe: The measurement of poverty*, Bristol: The Policy Press.

Gordon, D. (2001) 'Measuring absolute and overall poverty', in D. Gordon, and P. Townsend (eds) *Breadline Europe: The measurement of poverty*, Bristol: The Policy Press.

Gordon, D. and Pantazis, C. (1997) *Breadline Britain in the 1990s*, Aldershot: Ashgate.

Gordon, D. and Townsend, P. (1990) 'Measuring the poverty line', *Radical Statistics*, vol 47, pp 5-12.

Gore, C. (1995) 'Markets, exclusion and citizenship', in G. Rodgers, C. Gore and J.B. Figueiredo (eds) *Social exclusion: Rhetoric, reality, responses*, Geneva: International Labour Organization.

Halleröd, B. (1998) 'Poor Swedes, poor Britons: a comparative analysis of relative deprivation', in H.-J. Andreß (ed) *Empirical poverty research in a comparative perspective*, Aldershot: Ashgate.

HM Treasury (2004) *Supporting young people to achieve: Towards a new Deal for Skills*, London: HMSO.

Howarth, C. and Street, C. (2000) *Sidelined: Young people's access to services*, London: New Policy Institute.

Istance, D., Rees, G. and Williamson, H. (1994) *Young people not in education, Training or employment in South Glamorgan*, Cardiff: South Glamorgan TEC/University of Wales.

Johnston, L., MacDonald, R., Mason, P., Ridley, L. and Webster, C. (2000) *Snakes and ladders: Young people, transitions and social exclusion*, Bristol/York: The Policy Press/Joseph Rowntree Foundation.

Jones, G. (1995) *Leaving home*, Buckingham: Open University Press.

Jones, G. (1997) 'Youth homelessness and the "underclass"', in R. MacDonald (ed) *Youth, the 'underclass' and social exclusion*, London: Routledge.

Jones, G. and Wallace, C. (1992) *Youth, family and citizenship*, Buckingham: Open University Press.

Lister, R. (1990) *The exclusive society: Citizenship and the poor*, London: Child Poverty Action Group.

Lister, R. (1997) *Citizenship: Feminist perspective*, Basingstoke: Macmillan.

Low Pay Commission (1998) *The National Minimum Wage. First Report of the Low Pay Commission*, Cm 3976, London: The Stationery Office.

Low Pay Commission (2003) *The National Minimum Wage: Building on success. Fourth Report of the Low Pay Commission*, London: The Stationery Office.

Low Pay Commission (2004) *Protecting young workers: The National Minimum Wage. Low Pay Commission Report 2004*, Cm 6152, London: The Stationery Office.

Mack, J. and Lansley, S. (1985) *Poor Britain*, London: Allen Unwin.

Morris, J.N., Donkin, A.J.M., Wonderling, D., Wilkinson, P. and Dowler, E.A. (2000) 'A minimum income for healthy living', *Journal of Epidemiology and Community Health*, vol 54, no 12, pp 885-9.

Nunnally, J.C. (1978) *Psychometric theory*, New Delhi: Tate McGraw-Hill.

Pleace, N. and Fitzpatrick, S. (2004). *Centrepoint youth homelessness index: An estimate of youth homelessness in England*, York: Centre for Housing Policy, University of York.

Roberts, K. (1995) *Youth and employment in modern Britain*, Milton Keynes: Open University Press.

Roker, D. (1998) *Worth more than this: Young people growing up in family poverty*, Brighton: Trust for the Study of Adolescence.

Roker, D., Player, K. and Coleman, J. (1999) *Challenging the image: Young people as volunteers and campaigners*, Leicester: National Youth Agency.

Rowlinson, K., Whyley, C. and Warren, T. (1999) *Wealth in Britain: A lifecycle perspective*, London: Policy Studies Institute/Joseph Rowntree Foundation.

Scott, J. (1994) *Poverty and wealth: Citizenship, deprivation and privilege*, Harlow: Longman.

SEU (Social Exclusion Unit) (1999) *Bridging the gap: New opportunities for 16-18 year olds not in education, employment or training*, London: The Stationery Office.

SEU (2000a) *Policy Action Team Report 12: Young people*, London: The Stationery Office.

SEU (2000b) *Attitudes to public services in deprived areas – Final report. People's panel analysis*, London: SEU/MORI.

Smith, J. (1999) 'Youth homelessness in the UK. A European perspective', *Habitat International*, vol 23, no 1, pp 63-77.

Stratford, N. (2000) *Rural and urban views on the countryside: Findings from the British Social Attitudes Survey 1999*, Report to the Countryside Agency, London: National Centre for Social Research.

Townsend, P. (1979) *Poverty in the UK*, Harmondsworth: Penguin.

Townsend, P. (1996) 'The struggle for independent statistics on poverty', in R. Levitas and W. Guy (eds) *Interpreting official statistics*, London: Routledge.

Townsend, P. and Gordon, D. (1992) *Unfinished statistical business on low income?*, Statistical Monitoring Unit Report No 3, Bristol: University of Bristol.

UN (United Nations) (1995) *Copenhagen Declaration and Programme of Action*, World Summit for Social Development, 6 March, New York, NY: UN Department of Publications.

Watts, A.G. (2001) 'Career guidance and social exclusion: a cautionary tale', *British Journal of Guidance and Counselling*, vol 29, no 2, pp 157-76.

Webster, C., Simpson, D., MacDonald, R., Abbas, A., Cieslik, M., Shildrick, T. and Simpson, M. (2004) *Poor transitions: Social exclusion and young adults*, York: Joseph Rowntree Foundation.

White, L. (1994) 'Co-residence and leaving home: Young adults and their parents', *Annual Review of Sociology*, vol 20, pp 81-102.

Wilkinson, H. and Mulgan, G. (1995) *Freedom's children: Work, relationships and politics for 18-34 year olds in Britain today*, London: Demos.

Williamson, H. (1993) 'Youth policy in the United Kingdom and the marginalisation of young people', *Youth and Policy*, vol 40, pp 33-49.

Williamson, H. (1997) 'Status zero youth and the underclass', in R. MacDonald (ed) *Youth, the 'underclass' and social exclusion*, London: Routledge.

Appendix

Table A12.1: Sample characteristics of young respondents

	Under 25	25–34 years	All
Gender			
Male	50	52	**48**
Female	50	48	**52**
Marital status			
Never married	96	40	**20**
Married/living with spouse	4	50	**58**
Divorced/separated	–	10	**12**
Widowed	–	–	**9**
Household type			
I adult, no children	10	14	**18**
I adult with I+ child	6	6	**3**
2 adults, no children	10	24	**36**
2 adults with I+ children	12	44	**21**
3+ adults, no children	40	6	**16**
3+ adults, I+ child	24	6	**7**
Economic status			
Working	57	83	**57**
Unemployed	13	4	**3**
Permanently unable to work	2	1	**5**
Retired	–	–	**24**
Keeping house	6	10	**7**
Student	22	3	**3**
Other inactive	1	<1	**2**
Valid *n*	**126**	**285**	**1,529**

THIRTEEN

Gender, poverty and social exclusion

Christina Pantazis and Elisabetta Ruspini

Introduction

Poverty has always been a gendered experience. At the start of the last century, 61% of adults on all forms of poor relief were women (Lewis and Piachaud, 1987, pp 27-30), and women continued to be consistently poorer than men throughout the century. This unequal vulnerability reflects gendered access to resources and women's dependency on the family, principally on fathers or husbands. In the early 20th century fewer women than today were in paid employment, earnings often fell below subsistence needs, and state provision was less generous and access to it more restricted (Glendinning and Millar, 1991). In spite of major changes in the social and economic roles of women, poverty remains a gendered experience at the start of 21st century with women more vulnerable to poverty. Women are not only more likely than men to experience deprivation, but they experience it in different ways: specific risk factors affect women in particular; women's poverty spells are longer; and women are particularly exposed to economic fluctuations, since they have much lower and more unstable family and individual incomes (see, among others, Daly, 1989; Millar, 2000; Ruspini, 2000). For example, female-headed households, with or without dependent children, are far more vulnerable to poverty than households where an adult male is present. Lone motherhood has indeed become one of the key groups for the analysis of gender and poverty. As Levitas et al show in Chapter Fourteen, women without children and without access to a male wage also have increased risks of poverty. Some men, however, also face greater risks of poverty as a consequence of de-industrialisation (see, for example, Convery, 1997).

Social exclusion is also a gendered experience. It has been described as a phenomenon in which one or more of the social sub-systems is functioning inadequately: the economic system, leading to exclusion from the labour market; the social system, including a welfare state whose failure leads to impoverishment; family and community systems, leading to exclusion from social relations; and the power distribution system (Ministry of Health and Social Affairs, 2000). Dominant models of social exclusion concentrate disproportionately on exclusion from the labour market, and perhaps in consequence, as Millar (2003, p 186) has observed, "there has been little explicit analysis of social exclusion from a gender perspective". Millar suggests that Room's (1999) approach, which sees social exclusion as multi-dimensional, dynamic, local and relational, has the potential to highlight the differential resources between men and women but also key issues such as autonomy and dependency. Similarly, the Poverty and Social Exclusion (PSE) Survey's multi-dimensional approach and its emphasis on social relations enable exploration of the interaction of social exclusion and gendered processes in the distribution of resources (Ruspini, 2000).

The gendered experience of poverty and social exclusion

The risk of poverty varies among women and over women's lifecourses. It is linked to their responsibility for caring and domestic work: women draw income from men, the labour market and the welfare state in different proportions, according to the burden of caring responsibilities, time constraints, life chances and choices (see, among others, Lewis, 1993; Scheiwe, 1994). Power within marriage and the family is directly related to the control of financial resources and to the degree of participation in the labour market. Generally speaking, husbands have more power than wives in the control of family resources (see, for example, Pahl, 1989) because of their stronger relationship with the labour market and greater earning power. Women have much weaker bargaining power than men in the economy and in the home. Their access to economic resources and to information, capacities and opportunities are often mediated and limited by men and by domestic responsibilities.

Social changes over the 20th century have diversified poverty risks, especially for women (Ruspini, 2002). Increasing trends towards delayed marriage, higher divorce and separation, and lone motherhood, result in men contributing less to the income of women and children. Women are increasingly dependent on their own market earnings, which remain lower than men's, both because of segregation and discrimination in the labour market, and because women commonly curtail their employment during child-rearing years. Changing family patterns and population ageing result in new and more complex relationships of obligation and exchange across and between generations and households, which can affect the caring capacity of women and families (Millar, 1998). Furthermore, current welfare restructuring policies, which shift a greater responsibility for the care of elderly people onto relatives, disproportionately affect women (Hills, 1993). Working-class women are doubly disadvantaged by being more likely to have to provide care to elderly parents at an earlier age, when it conflicts with employment, and by having poorer financial resources to ease this caring burden (Arber and Ginn, 1993).

Young carers are particularly vulnerable to social exclusion (Howard, 2001). Some miss school and may fail to gain even basic qualifications. Consequently caring at a young age can have a significant effect on later earnings and risk of poverty. More young carers are girls, and although young boys also carry out caring work where parents need help, gender plays a complex role in expectations of care from each sex (Olsen, 1996; Payne, 2001).

Family responsibilities thus still shape women's lives, in terms of their employment patterns, the type of occupation they work in, their earnings and their social security benefits. There is a time conflict between paid and unpaid work, and women's responsibilities for reproductive labour *limit* the range of paid economic activities they can undertake. This includes limits on their geographic mobility. 'Flexible' employment may help in reconciling caring responsibilities and work needs, but the consequent low pay and insecurity may also be a route into poverty. Furthermore, women who face the triple burden of full-time work, housework and caring find it particularly difficult to find time to socialise outside work (Martin and Wallace, 1984; Russell, 1999). Some research suggests that women's pattern of labour market participation is less conducive to constructing social networks that are resistant to unemployment: while women have fewer but more intimate social contacts, men usually have a wider range of friendships based on joint activities rather than intimacy (Russell, 1999).

The inequalities that women experience in paid work are mirrored in their different access to, and levels of, income replacement benefits (Glendinning and Millar, 1991) from both private occupational and public sources. In most welfare states rights to benefits are still linked to occupational welfare and those who are unable to enter the labour market are also denied many welfare rights. Women's right to welfare is often a function of their dependence on a male breadwinner (Lewis and Ostner, 1994). This treatment of women as economic dependants contributes to women's poverty (Lee, 1999) both immediately and in later life. A period of financial dependency to bring up children or care for ageing parents has consequences for both state and occupational pension rights, thus increasing the likelihood of poverty in old age (Arber and Ginn, 1995; Arber, 1998; Land, 2000).

Financial institutions such as insurance companies and mutual societies – as well as families, labour markets and the welfare state – provide mechanisms for distributing resources between women and men, and between generations. Access to credit, as well as financial markets, is highly gendered. In particular, gender discrimination is a key element to understand gender dimensions of financial exclusion, as women's poverty is directly related to the lack of access to economic resources, such as credit, land ownership and inheritance. However, the assumptions on which financial markets operate – especially with regard to access to credit and to mortgages – have not yet been subject to the detailed scrutiny to which labour markets have been subjected (Land, 2000).

Thus the gendered character of poverty results from the gendered mechanisms of social integration and exclusion more broadly. Female poverty is the result of a complex interaction of factors: sociodemographic change; the work women do within the non-monetary economy; gender divisions in the field of work and employment; and the fact that social policy tends to assume that women will be dependent on a male partner. Where men take on caring roles, this is more likely to be through choice – often caring for a dependent spouse – while women more frequently take on caring roles through feelings of obligation, particularly cross-generational caring, and this difference in motivation is associated with the costs of caring work for those involved (Finch and Groves, 1983; Graham, 1983; Ungerson, 1987; Payne, 2001).

Men, on the other hand, are more vulnerable (compared to women) to critical work-related events. De-industrialisation destroyed a large number of skilled manual jobs and contributed to increasing unemployment, and to the growth of marginal forms of employment. A study on the dynamics of poverty in Germany and Britain showed that the largest causes of movement into poverty for men were unemployment or movement from full-time to part-time or marginal employment, and illness (Ruspini, 1998). Family breakdown may also leave single men highly vulnerable, particularly where they have limited networks of social support (Baden, 1999; and Levitas, Chapter Five in this volume). Previous empirical findings (Hearn et al, 2000) show that the social exclusion of men links not only with unemployment, but also with men's isolation within and separation from families, and associated social and health problems.

Problems and challenges in researching the gendered experience of poverty and social exclusion

The gendered nature of poverty cannot be 'captured' by an absence of a gender-sensitive methodology. The visibility of women's and men's poverty depends heavily on the choices made in conceptualising and measuring poverty itself. Income measures pose particular problems in this regard (Ruspini, 2000), both in terms of where to draw the line, and in conceptualising and measuring income and money resources (Daly, 1992). Moreover, resources other than income, such as gifts, services or benefits in kind, and savings produced through women's domestic labour, can profoundly affect people's standard of living. Both the extent and distribution of resources from hidden transfers and home production are hard to estimate (Ruggles, 1990). Equivalence scales are also problematic, since not only household size, but age, gender and health impinge on the satisfaction of needs and on consumption (see Gordon, Chapter Two in this volume). Income-based 'poverty lines' are inherently gender-blind.

In this respect, the PSE Survey, which uses direct measures of deprivation of both material and social necessities in a range of fields, goes some way to addressing these problems. However, the PSE approach continues to pose some difficulties for gender poverty researchers. The PSE measure of poverty is based on both deprivation and low income (see Chapter Two in this volume, for further discussion) and allows for comparisons in risks of poverty between different household formations. It still suffers from the usual problems affecting all aggregate studies of poverty (whether based on income, expenditure or consumption) in that it is unable to shed light on intra-household poverty. A 'black box approach' to the family or household underestimates, or undervalues, differences in power within it – between women and men, or between younger members and older members – and the consequences for differential standards of living within the household. Previous research has shown resource inequalities between husband and wife and sometimes deprivation on the part of the wife and children (see, for example, Brannen, 1987; Pahl, 1989). Where women are in paid employment, their pay is typically spent on household necessities, and only rarely and in smaller amounts on women's own needs. For each pound entering the household economy through the mother, more is spent on the family than for each pound brought in by the father. As a consequence, women go without more often than men: some women are denied access to resources and some go without voluntarily to increase that available for their partners and children (Brannen and Wilson, 1987; Glendinning and Millar, 1987; see also Chapter Eleven in this volume, on children). Moreover, as Payne suggests (1991), some facilities are apparently bought jointly, but consumption is not shared equally: the family car, heating for the home, hot water, for example. Women and men often hold different views over necessary expenditure, and the ways in which money can be saved (Charles and Kerr, 1987; Graham, 1987; Wilson, 1987), and this pattern of consumption in low income-households makes women's task of making ends meet more difficult.

Payne and Pantazis (1997, p 99) acknowledged some of the limitations with the 1990 Breadline Britain Survey, the PSE's forerunner: "the respondents' answers were treated as representative of the household as a whole, so we do not know the extent to which resources, and the experience of poverty, were shared amongst household members". The same methodological difficulty applies to the PSE Survey. It did not collect information on every individual in the household, which would have allowed for a detailed analysis of socially perceived necessities deprivation at the intra-household level.

However, it does allow some *limited* analysis of intra-household poverty. It includes a small subset of questions asking respondents whether they and/or their partners personally went without certain items or activities in the previous year due to a lack of money, so potential differences between men and women can be explored on this group of items and activities[1]. The PSE Survey also asked respondents to estimate how much money would be needed to avoid absolute and overall poverty as defined by the Copenhagen Summit (see Townsend et al, Chapter Three in this volume), to see whether their own income exceeds these levels. This therefore allows for a gendered analysis of subjective understandings of poverty, as well as more 'objective' measures such as deprivation level. Finally, the Survey looks directly at different dimensions of social exclusion (labour market, service exclusion and exclusion from social relations) which have significant gendered underpinnings.

The remainder of the chapter is divided into two sections, looking first at poverty and then at social exclusion through a gendered lens. A lifecourse approach is used, sensitive to the fact that critical life events have important impacts on the extent, severity and nature of poverty among men and women[2]. As we have seen, family events, such as birth, separation, divorce or widowhood, have been found to be critically important in explaining the position of women, while for men labour market detachment and the onset of illness are more significant (Ruspini, 1999; Joshi and Davies, 2002).

In order to explore variations across the lifecourse, we have constructed a variable which includes gender, age, and the presence of dependent children in the household[3]. Lifecourse *changes* are best explored through longitudinal data (Ruspini and Dale, 2002), which disentangle age and cohort effects in a way that cross-sectional surveys such as the PSE cannot, but it is still possible to look at *variations* between those at different stages of the lifecourse at a particular point in time. Table 13.1 illustrates the distribution of respondents across the lifecourse. Some of the groups are small in size (that is, less than *n*=50) and, therefore, interpretation of results relating to these groups needs to be treated with caution. The variable does not of course include all critical life events such as marriage, divorce, separation or widowhood, or loss of employment: to do so would result in numbers so small they would be wholly unreliable.

Table 13.1: Distribution of respondents, by gender, age and presence of children in the household

	Women	Men
16-24, no children	4[a]	6[a]
16-24, dependent children	4[a]	3[a]
25-34, no children	6[a]	11
25-34, dependent children	11	10
35-54, no children	18	17
35-54, dependent children	18	14
55 to pensionable age[b]	8	19
Pensionable age to 74	20	12
75+	11	9

Notes: [a] Less than 50 cases.

[b] Pensionable age for women is 60 and for men 65.

Gender and poverty through the lifecourse

Lack of socially perceived necessities

We have argued above that women are more likely to be poor than men, and that women and men experience poverty differently. The 1990 Breadline Britain Survey demonstrated that 24% of women lacked three or more socially perceived necessities compared with only 17% of men, with lone mothers and single elderly women most affected (Payne and Pantazis, 1997). Nine years later the PSE findings show a similar discrepancy between men and women, with 28% of women lacking two or more necessities compared with 22% of men.

Table 13.2 shows that poverty is greatest among those groups with dependent children. The highest risks of poverty are among 25- to 34-year-olds, where the presence of at least one dependent child increases the proportion living in deprived households from 17% to 56% in the case of women and from 17% to 47% in the case of men. Younger women (16-24) with dependent children also have very high risks of poverty (48%). Women's withdrawal, either wholly or in part from the labour market to concentrate on early years child rearing, is an important factor to consider when understanding why poverty risks are especially high for these groups; in addition, there are financial costs in raising children, which further increase the risks of poverty for households with children (Middleton et al, 1994). The presence of children, however, does not continue to affect poverty risks indefinitely. Between the ages of 35 and 54, women's poverty risks are only marginally affected by the presence of children while for men they are slightly reduced. Women in this age group are likely to see increased earnings as they begin to re-enter the labour market (Joshi and Davies, 2002), whereas men are likely to see their incomes rise as they progress with their careers (Hutton, 1994). Table 13.2 also demonstrates stark *inequalities* in poverty risks between men and women. The greatest gender discrepancies are among those aged over 75, where women are twice as likely as men to be living in poverty. These older women are likely to be widowed and living alone. They are more likely to be reliant solely on the state pension, and these pensions may be lower than those of men due to incomplete national insurance contributions (Ginn and Arber, 1999; Bardasi and Jenkins, 2002) and failure to claim means-tested supplements (for further discussion of pensioner poverty, see Chapter Fifteen in this volume).

Table 13.2: Percentage of respondents living in poverty (PSE measure)

	Women	**Men**
16-24, no children	33	30
16-24, dependent children	48	23
25-34, no children	17	17
25-34, dependent children	56	47
35-54, no children	23	23
35-54, dependent children	25	18
55 to pensionable age	16	19
Pensionable age to 74	24	17
75+	28	13
Total	**28**	**22**

Intra-household poverty – going without items and activities

In an attempt to open the 'black box' of the household, the PSE Survey asked respondents whether they and/or their partner went without certain items and activities in the previous year due to lack of money. In the majority of couples neither partner goes without items such as food, heating and telephoning friends and family, but relatively larger proportions of couples are deprived of participating in social activities such as having a hobby or going to the pub because of a lack of money (Adelman et al, 2000). However, in a small percentage of couples there are differences between items and activities that partners say they lacked. In these couples, females are more likely to say that they went without clothes, shoes, food, heating, telephoning friends and family, and going out, whereas men are more likely to cite going without visits to the pub, having a hobby or taking a holiday because of a lack of money (Adelman et al, 2000). Overall, slightly more women say they go without than their partners (21% compared to 17%), confirming previous research by Cantillon and Nolan (1998). Women are particularly likely to go without when resources are limited (Table 13.3). For example, in poor-income households 27% of female respondents say that their partners lack fewer items than they do.

Pahl (1989) argues that consumption patterns are affected by the control of household finances. In the PSE Survey, just over half of couple households (54%) say that they manage their finances jointly; in one quarter (24%) the female partner looks after the household money except for their partner's spending money. Only 12% of male partners look after the household money in the same way (Adelman et al, 2000). Vogler (1994) found similar proportions using the 'joint pool' method in which household finances are shared and managed

**Table 13.3: Differences between the extent to which poor[a]
respondents and partners go without, by gender**

	Column %		
	Male respondent	Female respondent	All respondents
Respondent and partner not lacking any items	52	46	49
Respondent and partner lacking one item	(9)	(7)	8
Respondent and partner lacking over two, equal number of items	17	(20)	18
Partner lacks less items than respondent	11	27	17
Partner lacks more items than respondent	(11)	(1)	(7)

Note: Figures in brackets indicate less than 20 unweighted cases; [a] defined in terms of household income being 50% below the median.

Source: Adelman et al (2000, Table 3.4)

jointly. However, when pressed as to who had the ultimate responsibility for organising household money and bills, respondents often named one partner, indicating that "the general 'pool' category masks three analytically different forms of pool – the male, the female pool, and the jointly managed pool" (Vogler, 1994, p 214, cited in Adelman et al, 2000). We cannot assume that PSE respondents who say that they manage their finances jointly ultimately share this management. This has important implications for consumption patterns. Under the pooled system, 17% of males and 23% of females felt that they went without items more than their partner (Adelman et al, 2000). Under the system where the female is given a housekeeping allowance and the male controls the rest of the money, there were no male respondents reporting that either they or their partner went without items. However, 18% of females in households with the same types of financial management thought that they were going without more than their partners. This finding raises important issues with respect to the extent to which women's lack of financial autonomy is related to their reduced patterns of consumption compared with men, as well as the degree to which women's deprivation can remain hidden from view when men are largely in control of the household finances.

Subjective poverty

We were also interested in gathering information based on people's own subjective accounts of poverty, to see how well their own perceptions matched the PSE Survey's socially perceived necessities measure of poverty discussed earlier. Respondents were offered three definitions of poverty – general, absolute, and overall poverty – and asked, 'how many pounds, after tax, do you think are necessary to keep a household, such as the one you live in, out of general, absolute and overall poverty?'. Table 13.4 reports the proportions of men and women, at different stages of the lifecourse, with actual incomes below the mean income perceived by the sample, as a whole, as necessary to avoid poverty.

The data confirm that men's and women's experiences of poverty vary. Women as a group are consistently more likely, compared with men, to have insufficient income. When we examine whether household income is inadequate to cover the basic necessities of life (that is, to keep them out of absolute poverty), 6% more women than men have an income below that level (18% compared to 12%). There are also significant variations across different lifecourse groups. Almost one in three women aged 16-24 and living with at least one dependent

Table 13.4: Percentage of respondents whose actual income is below what is needed to keep their household out of absolute, general and overall poverty

	Women			Men		
	Absolute	General	Overall	Absolute	General	Overall
16-24, no children	16	23	27	5	10	39
16-24, dependent children	30	33	43	4	14	9
25-34, no children	14	7	14	6	12	7
25-34, dependent children	26	24	26	19	33	29
35-54, no children	12	19	21	10	14	21
35-54, dependent children	14	17	23	9	16	26
55 to pensionable age	19	17	20	15	19	21
Pensionable age to 74	16	25	22	10	22	22
75+	22	30	33	25	31	36
Total	**18**	**21**	**24**	**12**	**19**	**23**

child have an income which is insufficient to keep them and their household out of absolute poverty, while 43% have an insufficient income to keep them out of overall poverty. Thus, we have a picture emerging that this group is highly vulnerable to the risk of poverty, particularly poverty of the absolute kind, which involves an income which is inadequate to cover even the barest necessities of life such as an adequate diet, housing, heating, clothing, water and prescription costs.

Gender and social exclusion through the lifecourse

The remaining section of this chapter considers the relationship between gender and different dimensions of social exclusion (that is, labour market exclusion, service exclusion, exclusion from social relations, and confinement) used in the PSE Survey.

Labour market exclusion

Labour market detachment has been at the forefront of social exclusion debates (see Chapters Five and Six in this volume). Where gender has been interrogated, the focus has largely been on men, for example, in the context of youth unemployment (for example, SEU, 1999; see also Chapter Twelve in this volume). At times these debates have drifted into a moralising discourse about the apparent existence of an underclass which is made up of criminally inclined unemployed men and unmarried mothers living off the state (for a discussion, see Levitas, 2005). Women have featured less prominently in academic and policy debates about social exclusion in the context of labour market detachment. Of course there are some exceptions to this (see, for example, Smith, 1997), and one group which has been the target of government labour market policy, in particular, is lone mothers. Getting lone mothers off welfare benefits and into the world of paid work through the New Deal (see Chapter Fourteen in this volume) is part of New Labour's attempt to stave off what it regards as the intergenerational transmission of deprivation (Deacon, 2002).

Although the numbers in the PSE Survey are too small to present an analysis of the lifecourse variable by single status, the data does confirm that men, throughout each stage of the lifecourse, are generally more likely to be in paid work than women (Table 13.5). Men are especially likely to be in paid employment when children are present in the household (for example, employment rates reach 90% in each case for men in the 25-34 and 35-54 age groups). In contrast, women living with children have lower rates of paid employment and this is especially marked for the two youngest groups. The data are, therefore, suggestive of men occupying a breadwinning role to support their partners who may have temporarily or permanently withdrawn from the labour market to care for children. This form of privatisation of family care must be understood not only as an active choice by women, but as one made in the context of a lack of publicly funded childcare (Joshi and Davies, 2002).

The data also reveal that in the period before retirement, people are less likely to be in paid work. Female labour force participation rates for those women aged from 55 to retirement (aged 60) are a mere 52%. Reduced rates of paid employment are also evident among men aged between 55 and 64 (47%), confirming other studies (for example, Bardasi and Jenkins, 2002) on the premature detachment of this group

Table 13.5: Percentage of women and men in the paid labour market

	Women			Men		
	Works	Un-employed	Inactive	Works	Un-employed	Inactive
16-24, no children	55	9	36	61	22	17
16-24, dependent children	52	14	35	59	5	36
25-34, no children	88	4	8	88	3	10
25-34, dependent children	67	5	28	93	4	3
35-54, no children	76	8	17	83	6	11
35-54, dependent children	74	1	25	94	1	5
55 to pensionable age	52	2	46	53	3	44
Pensionable age to 74	10	0	90	23	0	77
75+	0	0	100	0	0	100
Total	**50**	**3**	**47**	**63**	**4**	**33**

of men from the labour market. Men of this age are more likely to be economically inactive than unemployed (44% compared to 3%), and of those economically inactive 47% described themselves as 'sick, injured or disabled' while 39% say that they are retired. The notion of 'early retirement' which tends to be advanced to explain men's low participation rates in pre-formal retirement tends to mask the extent to which men are actually without paid work because they are too ill to work or because there are simply no available jobs for them.

Women of all ages are less likely to be in work, but also more likely to be categorised as economically inactive rather than unemployed. Many women who are economically inactive are performing unpaid work by caring for children or elderly relatives. Much caring is, however, performed by women in employment, thus creating a *triple* burden of work for some women, consisting of paid work, unpaid domestic work, and unpaid caring responsibilities (Arber and Ginn, 1995).

Table 13.6 shows that women, as a group, are only marginally more likely than men to be living in households with no paid workers. But some groups of women, such as 16- to 24-year-olds with dependent children, are particularly at risk from living in jobless households. Similarly, almost one quarter of women aged between the ages of 55 to 60 are living in these types of households. However, a higher proportion of men aged 55 to retirement age are in jobless households (31%), partly because the retirement age for men is 65. Davies et al's (1994) study showed that women may be reluctant to take on a job where the husband is unemployed for fear of damaging his pride as the breadwinner. In this context, women's pay from employment may be seen by both as taking away *his* entitlement to state benefits with the result that women may withdraw from the labour market.

Table 13.6: Percentage of women and men in jobless households

	Women		Men	
	No workers	Workers	No workers	Workers
16-24, no children	15	85	17	83
16-24, dependent children	30	70	9	91
25-34, no children	10	90	8	92
25-34, dependent children	18	82	7	93
35-54, no children	14	86	11	89
35-54, dependent children	10	90	4	96
55 to pensionable age	24	74	31	69
Pensionable age to 74	14	18	13	21
75+	2	1	2	0
Total	**14**	**62**	**13**	**70**

Service exclusion

There has been more limited research on the relationship between service exclusion and gender although we know that service exclusion does affect women and men differentially – including those sharing the same home (Payne, 1991). Respondents in the PSE Survey were asked a range of questions which attempted to capture their exclusion from utilities within the home, as well as public and private services outside the home (see Chapter Eight in this volume for further detail on service exclusion outside the home).

Disconnections and restricted consumption

Respondents were asked both whether they had ever been disconnected or used less than they needed to of gas, electricity or the telephone because of affordability. Overall 6% of the sample had experienced disconnection of any one of these basic utilities, but as expected, a higher proportion (11%) had reduced their consumption because of costs. The vast majority of disconnections related to the telephone. Marginally more women than men report that they had been disconnected from the telephone (6% compared to 4%). Risks are particularly high for both men and women with children. For example, among women living with dependent children 19% of 16- to 24-year-olds and 14% of those aged between 25 and 34 years report that they had been disconnected because of lack of affordability. Men aged 25-34 living with dependent children, however, have the highest risk of being disconnected (21%).

More women report restricted consumption compared to men (13% compared to 8%) and this confirms Payne's (1991) view that women are more likely to cut back on heating and other services within the home, with the exception of water, where very few of either women or men report using less because of affordability. Women use less gas (7% compared to 4%), electricity (8% compared to 4%) and the telephone (9% compared to 4%). Restricted consumption is inversely affected by age so that under-usage increases as the age of the respondent falls, although a higher rate of under-usage is also generally related to the presence of children. Women between the ages of 25 and 34 and the ages of 35 and 54 with dependent children report particularly high rates of restricted use of gas, 11% and 10% respectively. Women with dependent children are again more likely to use the telephone less often because of affordability, with 16% reporting restricted use in the case of 16- to 24-year-olds and 15% in that of 25- to 34-year-olds. The highest rates of restricted use of electricity are among women aged 35-54 (13%) and men aged 25-34 (8%). Among men restricted consumption is greatest for those aged between 55 and retirement; they are twice as likely to use less gas (8%) and almost twice as likely to use the telephone less often as other men (7%).

Local services

For public services consumed outside the home, the data show women to fare slightly worse than men with regards to individual service exclusion (that is, exclusion due to affordability). But there are wide variations within these groups. For example, although only 6% of women have been categorised as 'individually excluded' in relation to public services, these risks of exclusion are double for certain categories, such as women under the age of 35 living with dependent children and also women in the immediate post-retirement group (Table 13.7). There is evidence of a much higher degree of collective exclusion (defined as unavailable or inadequate services), but there do not appear to be strong patterns of association with gender or with the presence of dependent children. High rates of individual exclusion do not appear to be related to collective exclusion.

As expected, there are higher rates of individual exclusion from private services among both men and women, although women fare slightly worse (Table 13.8). Particularly affected are men and women aged between 25 and 34 with dependent children – with over one quarter in each category reporting that they cannot afford at least one private service such as the dentist, chemist and so on. Women are

Table 13.7: Percentage of women and men individually and collectively excluded from public services

	Individual		Collective	
	Women	**Men**	**Women**	**Men**
16-24, no children	3	1	47	44
16-24, dependent children	11	0	48	55
25-34, no children	1	1	43	63
25-34, dependent children	9	5	57	46
35-54, no children	4	3	68	54
35-54, dependent children	6	6	44	47
55 to pensionable age	5	5	37	47
Pensionable age to 74	9	5	43	36
75+	1	2	45	41
Total	**6**	**4**	**49**	**48**

Table 13.8: Percentage of women and men individually and collectively excluded from private services

	Individual		Collective	
	Women	**Men**	**Women**	**Men**
16-24, no children	9	1	53	69
16-24, dependent children	17	7	40	51
25-34, no children	3	1	47	40
25-34, dependent children	27	28	48	51
35-54, no children	5	3	67	60
35-54, dependent children	7	1	46	40
55 to pensionable age	5	3	46	47
Pensionable age to 74	8	6	60	47
75+	4	3	60	59
Total	**8**	**5**	**53**	**50**

slightly more likely to say that they are collectively excluded from at least one private service because of unavailability or inadequacy of the service, with women aged between 35 and 54 and without children being particularly affected.

Exclusion from social relations

Participation in common social activities

Differences in the use of leisure are strongly related to traditional gender roles (Russell, 1999). Women's caring responsibilities and unequal burden of housework restrict their leisure time (Green et al., 1990), whilst their use of such time is further hampered by their lower access to personal spending money (Millar and Glendinning, 1989; Vogler and Pahl, 1993), the absence of safe transport, and limited childcare facilities (Russell, 1999). Consequently, women's activities are much more home-centred than the activities of men (Morris, 1988; Green et al, 1990, pp 58-67).

PSE Survey respondents were asked which factors prevent their participation in common social activities such as 'going to the pub' and 'visiting friends or family'. After 'lack of interest', 'lack of money' is the most common factor affecting people's participation rates. Overall only slightly more women than men report that affordability prevents their participation in common social activities. But the presence of children within the household has a huge impact on both women's and men's participation rates, with the highest rates of non-participation as a result of money affecting women aged 25-34 (45%) and men in the corresponding category (33%), as well as women between the ages of 16 and 24 (36%). 'Lack of time due to childcare responsibilities' is also an important factor and this affects more women than men in households with dependent children. Women are also much more likely than men to cite 'lack of time due to paid work'. This reflects the competing demands placed on women as they try to combine paid work in the labour market and unpaid work at home while also trying to find time for leisure for themselves and their families. As expected, the most common factors affecting the participation of those over 75 are 'lack of interest' and 'health': one in five responses in the case of women and more than one in 10 in the case of men cite health problems.

Social isolation

The extent of social contact also varies by gender. Wilmott's (1987) survey-based study found that women were in more contact with family members than their male partners although there were no gender differences in the number of friends or frequency of contact. Allan's (1989) work suggests that women have fewer but more intimate friendships and have closer kin relationships than men, while men are thought to have a wider range of friendships based on joint activities rather than intimacy.

The PSE Survey shows that overall women are more likely than men to see or speak to family members on both a daily and weekly basis. There are significant differences among men and women, particularly with regards to daily contact (see Table 13.9). While only one third of women are without daily contact, this increases to about one half in the case of men. The largest gender differences relate to

Table 13:9: Percentage of women and men seeing or speaking to family members (non-household) on a daily basis

	See or speak to family daily		See or speak to family weekly	
	Women	**Men**	**Women**	**Men**
16-24, no children	79	83	100	95
16-24, children	70	39	94	67
25-34, no children	62	36	88	96
25-34, children	74	59	93	99
35-54, no children	66	44	95	81
35-54, children	66	31	94	77
55 to pensionable age	79	63	99	91
Pensionable age to 74	67	57	91	91
75 +	52	52	88	95
Total	**67**	**51**	**93**	**88**

those aged 35-54 and living with children: women are more than twice as likely as men to be in daily contact with family members (66% compared to 31%). However, the differences between men and women are lower for older groups: by the age of 75 women and men are equally likely to speak to or see family members on a daily basis. Men fare slightly better on weekly contact, but there are still high proportions of men, particularly those aged 16-24 and with children and those in middle years (35-54), without weekly contact with family members.

While contact rates are generally higher for friends and neighbours than they are for family, women are again more likely than men to see or speak to others – both on a daily and weekly basis (Table 13.10). Some of the explanation for this may be found in studies which show that women have much closer ties with their local communities than men. Bell and Ribbons (1994) found a strong pattern of social exchange between mothers of young children within the local community, for example (cited in Russell, 1999). Table 13.10 also shows that both men's and women's social contact declines with age although much more obviously for women in retirement.

In response to the follow-up question about factors preventing contact with family and friends, 'lack of time due to paid work' was most frequently cited, followed by 'lack of time due to childcare responsibilities' (see Chapters Three and Six in this volume for further discussion on the impact of paid work on social relations).

Table 13.10: Percentage of women and men seeing or speaking to friends or neighbours (non-household) on a daily basis

	See or speak to friends/ neighbours daily		See or speak to friends/ neighbours weekly	
	Women	**Men**	**Women**	**Men**
16-24, no children	96	99	96	100
16-24, children	88	97	98	100
25-34, no children	98	61	100	90
25-34, children	83	70	100	96
35-54, no children	72	69	93	90
35-54, children	79	67	97	87
55 to pensionable age	73	71	90	92
Pensionable age to 74	68	55	90	86
75+	65	63	88	89
Total	**76**	**69**	**94**	**91**

Social support

Women and men differ in their access to social support. Morris found a high level of social support between female neighbours, which was "rooted more in their shared domestic role than in differences deriving from the labour market" (1995, p 49). Russell (1999) found that women were more likely than men to have someone outside the home whom they could rely on for emotional support if they were feeling depressed, but were less likely to have someone who could provide them with help to find a job. Russell also suggested that women were better able to sustain social support during unemployment.

PSE Survey respondents were asked several questions relating to expectations of practical and emotional support across a range of different situations, including needing help around the house in times of illness or needing to talk to someone when going through a difficult period. As Table 13.11 shows, women have higher levels of good emotional support than men (78% compared to 66%). These levels are particularly high for women aged between 16 and 24 with children (97%) and women between the ages of 25 and 34 without children (98%). The general pattern is that good emotional support declines with age for both men and women, but particularly for women over 75 years of age (57%). Almost one in five women in this age group say that they have poor emotional support.

On the other hand, Table 13.12 shows that overall women have slightly lower levels of good practical support in comparison to men (61% compared to 64%). The general trend is again for good support to decline with age, such that levels of good practical support drop significantly to only 50% for women aged 75 and over.

Table 13.11: Percentage of female and male respondents experiencing different levels of emotional support

	Women			Men		
	Good	Reasonable	Poor	Good	Reasonable	Poor
16-24, no children	90	10	0	82	18	0
16-24, children	97	3	0	61	39	0
25-34, no children	98	2	0	65	29	6
25-34, children	78	15	7	66	34	0
35-54, no children	71	23	6	64	29	7
35-54, children	85	13	2	62	34	4
55 to pensionable age	70	23	7	63	33	4
Pensionable age to 74	69	27	4	66	28	7
75+	57	26	18	70	25	5
Total	**78**	**19**	**5**	**66**	**30**	**4**

Table 13.12: Percentage of female and male respondents experiencing different levels of practical support

	Women			Men		
	Good	Reasonable	Poor	Good	Reasonable	Poor
16-24, no children	75	21	4	75	19	6
16-24, children	64	35	1	30	63	7
25-34, no children	66	32	2	75	20	5
25-34, children	64	29	7	66	33	1
35-54, no children	57	38	5	53	43	3
35-54, children	75	22	3	82	15	3
55 to pensionable age	60	33	7	63	34	3
Pensionable age to 74	54	40	6	57	36	7
75+	50	36	15	59	35	7
Total	**61**	**33**	**6**	**64**	**32**	**4**

Civil and political engagement

There is an abundant literature showing that men and women do not equally participate in the political process (see, for example, Russell, 2002). Women remain seriously unrepresented in parliaments, governments and public bodies. In the UK women make up only 18% of Members of Parliament, 35% of all Ministers and Junior Ministers and only 27% of local councillors. Norris and Lovenduski's (1995) study found that issues of gender, ethnicity and class affected legislative recruitment, although some political parties (for example, Labour and the Green Party) showed greater social diversity. Stacey and Price (1981) use the concept of public and private domains to explain the obstacles women encounter in achieving politically powerful positions.

Women in the UK are, however, as likely as men to vote in elections (Hills, 1981), and are often actively involved in local community schemes (Campbell, 1993) if less involved in formal politics. The PSE Survey questions on civic engagement incorporated a range of activities covering different dimensions of the political process and civic life, showing some interesting gender differences. Women are more likely than men to have been involved in a range of civil and political activities over the last three years (54% compared to 47%), almost equally likely to be currently involved in political organisations (55% compared to 57%), and marginally more likely to have voted in either the last General Election or the local election (78% compared to 75%). Thus, the PSE data undermine common assumptions that women are less involved in politics. However, the data also confirm young people's disaffection from the political process, upon which there has been considerable commentary (see Chapter Twelve in this volume).

Confinement

The final dimension of exclusion from social relations which this chapter considers is confinement. Recent debates on social exclusion have focused on its connection with crime and, in particular, the effects of crime on people's ability to go about their daily activities (see Chapter Nine in this volume). One specific focus has been on the extent to which 'fear of crime' impacts negatively on individual and community participation. Some groups have been found to be more fearful: women, in particular (Warr, 1984), older people (Pain, 1995), and poor people (Pantazis and Gordon, 1997), and Pantazis (2000) explains these higher rates of insecurity in terms of social, economic and physical vulnerability.

The PSE Survey confirms that women generally feel less safe than men. Over 40% of women feel unsafe when out in the streets after dark compared to 17% of men (Table 13.13). This increases to 63% for women aged 16-24 with dependent children. Similarly, women are likely to feel more unsafe within the home than men. Fifteen per cent say they feel unsafe when alone in their own home. Again the group to feel most unsafe is women aged 16-24 with dependent children.

However, the PSE Survey's follow-up questions on what factors prevent respondents from participating in common social activities and meeting up with family more often reveal that few people cite crime as a factor. While feeling unsafe may have negative consequences for both men's and women's well-being, the data from the PSE Survey demonstrate that 'fear of crime' does not restrict people's ability to participate in common social activities although it may affect how and when they do so.

Table 13.13: Percentage of men and women feeling unsafe

	In streets		At home	
	Women	**Men**	**Women**	**Men**
16-24, no children	36	12	25	2
16-24, dependent children	63	18	33	4
25-34, no children	44	14	14	0
25-34, dependent children	30	24	13	17
35-54, no children	43	7	18	5
35-54, dependent children	36	10	12	2
55 to pensionable age	33	23	13	1
Pensionable age to 74	47	19	18	7
75+	52	28	7	3
Total	**42**	**17**	**15**	**4**

Conclusion

Using a multi-dimensional, social exclusion approach seems to be an appropriate way to tackle the problem of poverty with a gender-sensitive perspective and to adequately understand its nature and causes. This view of social exclusion that regards deprivation as not solely based on poverty or income or access to resources but also on social relations, is a potentially useful framework for analysing gender (Millar, 2000).

Our findings confirm that poverty and social exclusion are gendered experiences. Whichever measure of poverty is used, women are consistently more likely to be impoverished than men. If, on the one hand, inequalities between men and women are greatest among those in the older retirement group, on the other hand, younger women with children have higher poverty risks and are also more likely to be without paid work and to live in jobless households. Although paid work is expected to help lift people out of poverty, the reality of women's work is that it pays less well than men's work, and is often casualised, unskilled, low paid and requiring long hours. As Chapters Five and Six show, participation in paid work may also impact negatively on other aspects of social participation. It may hamper people's opportunities for social contact and ability to maintain or form close friendships. Our findings show that women as a category manifest greater contact with friends and family, and have higher confidence in the availability of emotional support. The friendship networks that provide this are frequently developed while taking time out of employment to care for their children. Older women who are no longer actively participating in caring or working roles may, however, find themselves not only financially impoverished but also lacking contact with family and friends and unable to rely on the availability of emotional and practical support.

Men are more vulnerable than women to critical work-related events. However, they report lower levels of: poverty; unemployment (especially where there are children in the household); and individual and collective exclusion from public and private services. However, they may experience higher rates of exclusion from some dimensions of social relations. In particular, men display weaker social contacts with friends and family and are also less able to rely on having potential practical and emotional support in times of need. Further research is required, which considers the exact relationship between social contact and social support among men, and how those two critical social dimensions of exclusion interact with exclusion from the labour market.

Despite the evident gendered nature of poverty and social exclusion, the:

> ... gendered dimension in the Government's anti-poverty strategy is largely implicit and indirect rather than direct.... Tackling gender inequality in poverty does not appear to be an explicit objective or outcome to be achieved. It is unlikely that targets to, for example, eradicate child poverty or provide older people with security in retirement will be achieved unless gender is full addressed within those policies. (Bradshaw et al, 2003, p v-vi)

The gender-blindness of most poverty programmes reveals the weak links between gender and poverty in both analysis and social policy. Although gender is a key determinant of social inequality, poverty programmes have not ordinarily incorporated gender as an important dimension: they rarely ask what effect they are likely to have on poor women or poor men. And gender programmes have not done well in focusing on poverty. In attempting to 'mainstream' their issues, poverty programmes and gender programmes have often neglected the intersection between them (UNDP, 2000, chapter 9 especially). The lack of gender awareness by researchers, policy makers and planners has resulted in gender bias, which often results in a set of priorities and financial commitments that do not reflect the differences in the life experiences between women and men. This problem can only be resolved through the development of 'gender-sensitive' policies that acknowledge the current gendered character of inequality and seek to reduce inequalities between women and men.

Focusing on the gender dimension of poverty is far more than simply producing statistics on the situation of men and, especially, on women. The structural causes of female and male poverty and social exclusion are to be found in the complex interaction between social change, changing gender identities and gendered processes in the labour market, welfare systems and households. A crucial methodological challenge for women's poverty and social exclusion research remains how to open the 'black box'. Possibilities include combining different poverty measures, and collecting data for both households and individuals, and designing variables to capture the processes involved in the acquisition, control and expenditure of assets, cash and non-cash resources within households. Thus, the gender dimension of poverty and social exclusion can only be understood in the light of an accurate analysis of the interaction between the gendered processes in the distribution of resources.

Notes

[1] The questions also relate to children going without in the past year. See Chapter Eleven in this volume for the analysis of intra-household poverty between parents and children.

[2] Past studies have referred to the 'lifecycle of inequality' to reveal the differential outcomes for women across a range of areas including income, employment and education (EOC, 2001), but this chapter uses the term 'lifecourse', in preference, to capture the fluid, rather than fixed, stages of the lifecourse.

[3] The construction of such a variable provides a means by which increased risks of poverty and social exclusion can be exposed when critical life events occur. It is not to imply that women's and men's lives will model these stages in exact ways.

References

Adelman, L., Ashworth, K. and Middleton, S. (2000) 'Intra household distribution of poverty and social exclusion' (www.bris.ac.uk/poverty/pse/work_pap.htm).

Allan, G. (1989) *Friendship: Developing a sociological perspective*, Hemel Hempstead: Harvester Wheatsheaf.

Arber, S. (1998) 'Health, ageing and older women' in L. Doyal (ed) *Women and health services: An agenda for change*, Buckingham: Open University Press.

Arber, S. and Ginn, J. (1993) 'Gender differences in informal caring', *Health and Social Care in the Community*, vol 3, no 1, pp 19-31.

Arber, S. and Ginn, J. (1995) 'Gender differences in the relationship between paid employment and informal care', *Work Employment and Society*, vol 9, no 3, pp 445-71, September.

Baden, S. (1999) 'Gender, governance and the "feminisation of poverty"', Background Paper No 2, Meeting on 'Women and Political Participation: 21st Century Challenges', United Nations Development Programme, 24-26 March, New Delhi, India.

Bardasi, E. and Jenkins, S. (2002) *Income in later life: Work history matters*, Bristol/York: The Policy Press/Joseph Rowntree Foundation.

Bell, L. and Ribbens, J. (1994) 'Isolated housewives and complex maternal worlds: the significance of social contacts between women with young children in industrial societies', *The Sociological Review*, vol 42, no 2, pp 227-62.

Bradshaw, J., Finch, N., Kemp, P., Mayhew, E. and Williams, J. (2003) *Gender and poverty in Britain*, London: EOC.

Brannen, J. (1987) *Taking maternity leave: The employment decisions of women with young children*, London: Thomas Coram Research Unit.

Brannen, J. and Wilson, C. (1987) 'Introduction', in J. Brannen and C. Wilson (eds) *Give and take in families. Studies in resource distribution*, London: Allen & Unwin, pp 1-17.

Campbell, B. (1993) *Goliath: Britain's dangerous places*, London: Methuen.

Cantillon, S. and Nolan, S. (1998) 'Are married women more deprived than their husbands?', *Journal of Social Policy*, vol 27, no 2, pp 151-71.

Charles, N. and Kerr, M. (1987) 'Just the way it is: gender and age differences in family food consumption', in J. Brannen and G. Wilson (eds) *Give and take in families*, London: Allen & Unwin, pp 155-74.

Convery, P. (1997) 'Unemployment', in A. Walker and C. Walker (eds) *Britain divided: The growth of social exclusion in the 1980s and 1990s*, London: Child Poverty Action Group.

Daly, M. (1989) *Women and poverty*, Dublin: Attic Press.

Daly, M. (1992) 'Europe's poor women? Gender in research on poverty', *European Sociological Review*, vol 8, no 1, pp 1-12.

Davies, R., Elias, P. and Penn, R. (1994) 'The relationship between a husband's unemployment and his wife's participation in the labour force', in D. Gaillie, C. Marsh and C. Vogler (eds) *Social change and the experience of unemployment*, Oxford: Oxford University Press.

Deacon, A. (2002) 'Echoes of Sir Keith? New Labour and the cycle of disadvantage', *Benefits – A Journal of Social Security Research, Policy and Practice*, vol 10, no 3, pp 179-84.

EOC (Equal Opportunities Commission) (2001) *Women and men in Britain: The lifecycle of inequality*, London: EOC.

Finch, J. and Groves, D. (1983) (eds) *A labour of love*, London: Routledge & Kegan Paul.

Ginn, S. and Arber, S. (1999) 'Changing patterns of pension inequality: the shift from state to private pensions', *Ageing and Society*, vol 19, pp 319-42, May.

Glendinning, C. and Millar, J. (eds) (1987) *Women and poverty in Britain*, Hemel Hempstead: Harvester Wheatsheaf.

Glendinning, C. and Millar, J. (1991) 'Poverty: the forgotten Englishwoman', in M. MacLean and D. Groves (eds) *Women's issues in social policy*, London: Routledge.

Graham, H. (1983) 'Caring: a labour of love', in J. Finch and D. Groves (eds) *A labour of love*, London: Routledge & Kegan Paul.

Graham, H. (1987) 'Women's poverty and caring', in C. Glendinning and J. Millar (eds) *Women and poverty in Britain*, Hemel Hempstead: Harvester Wheatsheaf.

Green, E., Hebron, S. and Woodward, D. (1990) *Women's leisure, what leisure?*, London: MacMillan.

Hearn, J., Müller, U., Oleksy, E., Pringle, K., Chernova, J., Ferguson, H., Gullvåg Holter, Ø., Kolga, V., Novikova, I., Ventimiglia, C., Lattu, E., Tallberg, T., Olsvik, E. with McIlroy, D. and Niemi, H. (2000) 'The social problem of men', article for The European Research Network on Men in Europe project, 'The social problem and societal problematisation of men and masculinities', HPSE-CT-1999-0008 (www.cromenet.org).

Hills, J. (1981) 'Britain', in J. Lovenduski and J. Hills (eds) *The politics of the second electorate: Women and public participation*, London: Routledge.

Hills, J. (1993) *The future of welfare. A guide to the debate*, York: Joseph Rowntree Foundation.

Howard, M. (2001) *Paying the price: Carers, poverty and social exclusion*, London: Child Poverty Action Group.

Hutton, S. (1994) 'Men's and women's incomes: evidence from survey data', *Journal of Social Policy*, vol 23, no 1, pp 21-40.

Joshi, H. and Davies, H. (2002) 'Women's incomes over a synthetic lifetime', in E. Ruspini and A. Dale (eds), *The gender dimension of social change: The contribution of dynamic research to the study of women's life courses*, Bristol: The Policy Press, pp 111-31.

Land, H. (2000) 'La ricostruzione della dipendenza delle donne', in F. Bimbi and E. Ruspini (eds) *Povertà delle donne e trasformazione dei rapporti di genere*, Inchiesta, no 128, April-June, pp 85-90.

Lee, A. (1999) 'Income distribution within households and women's poverty', Paper prepared for APEC Study Centre Consortium 1999 Conference 'Towards APEC's Second Decade: Challenges, Opportunities and Priorities', Auckland, New Zealand, 31 May-2 June.

Levitas, R. (2005) *The inclusive society* (2nd edn), London: Macmillan.

Lewis J. (1993) 'Introduction: women, work, family and social policies in Europe', in J. Lewis (ed) *Women and social policies in Europe: Work, family and the state*, Aldershot: Edward Elgar, pp 1-24.

Lewis, J. and Ostner, I. (1994) *Gender and the evolution of European social policies*, ZeS-Arbeitspapiere no 4, Bremen: Centre for Social Policy Research (ZES), University of Bremen.

Lewis, J. and Piachaud, D. (1987) 'Women and poverty in the twentieth century', in C. Glendinning and J. Millar (eds) *Women and poverty in Britain*, Hemel Hempstead: Harvester Wheatsheaf, pp 28-52.

Martin, R. and Wallace, J. (1984) *Working women in recession: Employment, redundancy, and unemployment*, Oxford: Oxford University Press.

Middleton, S., Ashworth, K. and Walker, R. (1994) *Family fortunes: Pressures on parents and children in the 1990s*, London: Child Poverty Action Group.

Millar, J. (1998) 'Policy and changing family forms: placing lone parenthood in context', Paper presented at the Seminar 'Current European Research on Lone Mothers', Gothenburg University, Sweden, April.

Millar, J. (2000) 'Genere, povertà e esclusione sociale', in F. Bimbi and E. Ruspini (eds) *Povertà delle donne e trasformazione dei rapporti di genere*, Inchiesta, no 128, April-June, pp 9-13.

Millar, J. (2003) 'Gender, poverty and social exclusion', *Social Policy and Society*, vols 2-3, pp 181-8.

Millar, J. and Glendinning, C. (1989) 'Gender and poverty', *Journal of Social Policy*, vol 18, no 3, pp 363-81.

Ministry of Health and Social Affairs (2000) 'Defining poverty and ways of measuring it', (http://pre20031103.stm.fi/english/tao/publicat/poverty/definit.htm).

Morris, L. (1988) 'Employment, the household and social networks', in D. Gaille (ed) *Employment in Britain*, Oxford: Basil Blackwell.

Morris, L. (1995) *Social divisions: Economic decline and social structural change*, London: UCL Press.

Norris, P. and Lovenduski, J. (1995) *Political recruitment: Gender, race and class in the British Parliament*, Cambridge: Cambridge University Press.

Olsen, R. (1996) 'Young carers: challenging the facts and politics of research into children and caring', *Disability and Society*, vol 11, no 1, pp 41-54.

Pahl, J. (1989) *Money and marriage,* London: Macmillan.

Pain, R. (1995) 'Elderly women and fear of violent crime: the least likely victims? A reconsideration of the extent and nature of risk', *British Journal of Criminology*, vol 35, no 4, pp 584-97.

Pantazis, C. (2000) 'Fear of crime, vulnerability and poverty', *British Journal of Criminology*, vol 40, pp 414-36.

Pantazis, C. and Gordon, D. (1997) 'Poverty and crime', in D. Gordon and C. Pantazis (eds) *Breadline Britain in 1990s*, Aldershot: Ashgate.

Payne, S. (1991) *Women, health and poverty. An introduction*, Hemel Hempstead: Harvester Wheatsheaf.

Payne, S. (2001) 'Illness and women's social roles: the relationship between economic dependency, caring responsibilities and poverty', in C. Facchini and E. Ruspini (eds) *Salute e disuguaglianze di genere, condizioni sociali e corso di vita*, Milan: Franco Angeli, pp 177-207.

Payne, S. and Pantazis, C. (1997) 'Gender and poverty', in D. Gordon and C. Pantazis (eds) *Breadline Britain in the 1990s*, Aldershot: Ashgate.

Room, G. (1999) 'Social exclusion, solidarity and the challenge of globalisation', *International Journal of Social Welfare*, vol 8, pp 166-74.

Ruggles, P. (1990) *Drawing the line: Alternative poverty measures and their implications for public policy*, Washington, DC: The Urban Institute Press.

Ruspini, E. (1998) 'Women and poverty dynamics: the case of Germany and Great Britain', *Journal of European Social Policy*, vol 8, no 4, pp 291-316.

Ruspini, E. (1999) 'Women and poverty: a new research methodology, monitoring poverty and the influence of past and current policies', Developing Poverty Measures: Research in Europe ESRC Seminar Series, Budapest, 21-22 May.

Ruspini, E. (2000) 'Poverty and the gendered distribution of resources within households', *Issue of Radical Statistics on Money and Finance*, no 75, Autumn, pp 25-37.

Ruspini, E. (2002) 'Women and social change', in E. Ruspini and A. Dale (eds), *The gender dimension of social change: The contribution of dynamic research to the study of women's life courses*, Bristol: The Policy Press, pp 11-26.

Ruspini, E, and Dale, A. (2002) *The gender dimension of social change: The contribution of dynamic research to the study of women's life courses*, Bristol: The Policy Press.

Russell, H. (1999) 'Friends in low places: gender, unemployment and sociability', *Work, Employment and Society*, vol 13, no 2, pp 205-24.

Russell, M. (2002) *Women's political participation in the UK*, London: British Council.

Scheiwe, K. (1994) 'Labour market, welfare state and family institutions: the links to mothers' poverty risks. A comparison between Belgium, Germany and the United Kingdom', *Journal of European Social Policy*, vol 4, no 3, pp 201-24.

SEU (Social Exclusion Unit) (1999) *Bridging the gap: New opportunities for 16-18 year olds*, London: The Stationery Office.

Smith, Y. (1997) The household, women's employment and social exclusion, *Urban Studies*, vol 34, no 8, pp 1159-77.

Stacey, M. and Price, M. (1981) *Women, power and politics*, London: Tavistock.

UNDP (United Nations Development Programme) (2000) *Overcoming human poverty: UNDP Poverty Report 2000*, New York, NY: UNDP.

Ungerson, C. (1987) *Policy is personal: Sex, gender and informal care*, London: Tavistock.

Vogler, C. (1994) 'Money in the household', in A. Anderson, F. Bechhofer and J. Gershuny (eds) *The social and political economy of the household*, Oxford: Oxford University Press.

Vogler, C. and Pahl, J. (1993) 'Social and economic change and the organisation of money in marriage', *Work, Employment and Society*, vol 7, no 1, pp 71-95.

Warr, M. (1984) 'Fear of victimisation: Why are women and the elderly more afraid?', *Social Science Quarterly*, vol 65, pp 681-702.

Wilmott, P. (1987) *Social networks and social support*, London: Policy Studies Institute.

Wilson, G. (1987) 'Money: pattern of responsibility and irresponsibility', in J. Brannen, C. Wilson (eds) *Give and take in families. Studies in resource distribution*, London: Allen & Unwin, pp 136-54.

Women and Equality Unit (2003) *Women in the UK: Key facts and figures*, Gender Briefing, February, London: Department of Trade and Industry.

FOURTEEN

Lone mothers, poverty and social exclusion

Ruth Levitas, Emma Head and Naomi Finch[1]

Introduction

Lone parenthood has had an increasingly high profile as the focus of research and policy over the last 40 years. This is partly because lone parenthood has been increasing, and has continued to do so in recent years. Between 1991 and 1998, the proportion of all families headed by a lone parent rose from 18% to 26% (Marsh and Perry, 2003). Between 30% and 40% of all children in Britain will spend part of their life in a lone-parent family (Rowlingson and McKay, 2002; Marsh and Perry, 2003). The degree of public, political and academic attention that lone-parent families have attracted presumes that they have both a special and a common status, based either on an assumption that they *have* distinctive problems, or that they *constitute* a distinctive problem for social policy. In this chapter, we focus on the situation of lone mothers, compared with that of mothers in two-parent families, and with that of women of working age living alone without children[2]. Data from the Poverty and Social Exclusion (PSE) Survey is set in the context of wider research on lone parents, especially the large new government data set, Families and Children in Britain (FACS). The PSE Survey findings underline the extent of material deprivation among lone parents, and demonstrate that benefit rates in 1999/2000 were inadequate to prevent poverty and social exclusion. The PSE data also look at a range of forms of social exclusion, including exclusion from the labour market, from access to services and from social relations. It raises questions about the extent to which the social exclusion that lone parents face, particularly from common social activities, is to be understood as the product of poverty or of worklessness – and thus whether labour market participation, the government's solution of choice, is an appropriate one, or whether other measures need to be taken to raise lone mothers out of poverty by amendments to the benefits regime. In comparing the situation of lone mothers with other mothers and with solo women, it also suggests that gender and class, rather than lone motherhood per se, may be the principal drivers of lone mothers' poverty (Millar, 1989; Standing, 1999; Rowlingson, 2001; Rowlingson and Millar, 2001; Rowlingson and McKay, 2002).

Empirical studies since the 1960s (Marsden, 1969) have repeatedly shown that households headed by lone parents are materially disadvantaged (Millar, 1989; Bradshaw and Millar, 1991). The extent of lone parents' deprivation, together with difficulties resulting from the conflicting demands of labour market activity and childcare, means that they have properly been a focus of social policy and research. This includes a wide range of academic research in both British and, increasingly, international contexts (for example, Millar, 1989; Lewis, 1997; Duncan and Edwards, 1997, 1999; Kiernan et al, 1998; Land, 1999; Kilkey, 2000; Lewis, 2000; Marsh 2001; Millar and Rowlingson, 2001). Official government research has generated a range of surveys, such as the cohort study of lone parents through the 1990s conducted by the Department of Social Security (DSS) and Policy Studies Institute (PSI) as part of the Programme of Research into Low Income Families (PRILIF) (Marsh and McKay, 1993; Ford et al, 1995; Marsh et al, 1998; Finlayson et al, 2000), as well as the more recent SOLIF (Survey of Low Income Families) or FACS Surveys instigated in 1999 and discussed below (McKay, 2002; Marsh and Rowlingson, 2002; Vegeris and McKay, 2002; Marsh and Perry, 2003; Barnes and Willitts, 2004).

Much public attention to lone parenthood has been of a different kind, and has involved something of a moral panic about lone *mothers* who constitute over 90% of lone parents. In the 1990s lone mothers were, as Kiernan et al (1998) demonstrate, presented as a social threat and a social problem. Charles Murray (1990, 1994) suggested that rising numbers of lone mothers were indicative of a growing underclass presaging moral and social breakdown. He also saw lone mothers as the cause of this decay, as their sons were potential criminals, and their daughters likely to be morally lax and themselves become lone mothers. Murray complained about a benefit structure that encouraged lone motherhood by financing it. Government ministers and media stories complained of a 'culture of dependency' and specifically of young women getting pregnant in order to be allocated council housing. Rather than *having* problems as a result of their poverty, lone mothers were regarded as *being* a problem (Roseneil and Mann, 1996; Levitas, 1998a, 1998b).

Murray's strictures were intended to apply particularly to young, never-married mothers, who were or are often assumed to be the 'typical' lone parent, despite constituting less than a quarter of all lone parents in 1999. When New Labour came to power in 1997, it rejected the demonisation of lone parents that had characterised the Thatcher and Major governments. Nevertheless, its policies reflected a mix of concerns. By the mid-1990s, over two thirds of lone-parent households were dependent on Income Support, compared with less than 10% in 1971. The dependency of lone parents on welfare benefits was represented as the reason for their poverty and an indicator of their social exclusion. It was also an unwelcome element in public expenditure. Comparative evidence shows that the UK has one of the lowest levels of labour market participation among lone parents in OECD countries, and one of the biggest gaps between the participation rates of married/cohabiting mothers and lone mothers (Bradshaw et al, 1996; OECD, 1998). But 'workless households' – that is, households without an adult in paid work – are a moral as well as a practical concern for New Labour. As Blair argued in one pre-election television broadcast in 1997, such households, whether or not headed by a lone parent, failed to instil by example an appropriate work ethic in their children. The policy for reducing poverty among lone-parent families, reducing benefit dependency and overcoming their social exclusion, is primarily a labour market solution. The Blair government's target is to achieve 70% of lone parents in paid work by 2010, up from 44% in 1999. The New Deal for Lone Parents (NDLP) is designed to encourage or enforce labour market participation. This policy is backed up by the National Minimum Wage, the Working Families Tax Credit, Child Tax Credits (replaced by Working and Child Tax Credits from April 2003), and a National Childcare Strategy, as well as legislation aimed at increasing the payment of Child Support by fathers. There are other elements of New Labour policy that impinge on some lone parents, including the Teenage Pregnancy Strategy, set up after the publication of the Social Exclusion Unit's (SEU) report on the subject (SEU, 1999), which aims to cut the number of conceptions among under 18s and thus the number of young single mothers; and Sure Start, which is the flagship policy of the National Plan for Social Inclusion, produced in response to the European Union (EU) strategy to combat social exclusion. Sure Start was initially concerned with pre-school education for disadvantaged children and with supporting parenting, but now has as part of its remit reducing the number of workless households.

The NDLP was initially introduced as a wholly voluntary scheme, with personal advisers available to give a 'one-stop' package of advice on job search, training and childcare, to encourage lone parents back into paid work. But there were sticks as well as carrots. In 1997, as part of the incentive structure to encourage lone parents into paid work, Lone Parent Benefit was abolished (Levitas, 1998a; Smith, 1999) – leaving lone parents worse off at least until subsequent general increases in benefits for children were instituted. The overall thrust of Labour's policy is clear: the route out of poverty and social exclusion for lone parents and their children is through paid work. Against Murray's image of the 'bad' lone mother, New Labour counterpose the 'good' lone parent, who, whatever their route into this situation, is able to combine paid work and parenthood, and instil a proper work ethic into their children (Carabine, 2001; Head, 2004). This has, however, been combined with substantial rises in Child Benefit benefiting all children, including those in lone-parent households, together with a commitment to ending child poverty altogether, although accounts of progress on this have been mixed (for example, Sutherland et al, 2003).

The distinction between lone parents and lone mothers reminds us that lone parents are not all alike. Before the 1970s, when lone parents became an administrative category within the benefits system, even the general category of lone mother was not in general use. Women were distinguished by their route into lone parenthood – bereavement, separation or divorce, or unmarried motherhood; and lone fathers were barely considered. These different groups are known to vary in their age, number of children, propensity to be in paid employment and risk of poverty. Not only are there variations between lone parents, but the boundaries of the category are fluid and uncertain. Lone parents do not necessarily think of themselves as such, but may have a variety of different (and shifting) relationships with partners or ex-partners living elsewhere (Head, 2004). And lone parenthood is a transitional status, with many lone parents (re)partnering within a few years (Millar and Ridge, 2001). The PRILIF Surveys showed that half of the 1991 sample respondents were no longer lone parents by 1998. Studies also differ in whether they focus on lone-parent *families* (who may live in households with other adults, such as the lone parent's own parents) or lone-parent *households* (made up of a lone adult with dependent children), although of course there is a very large overlap between these. There is no commonly agreed definition even between government surveys, with the FACS Survey preferring the former approach, and the General Household Survey (GHS) and Households Below Average Income (HBAI) series adopting the latter.

The PSE Survey

The main purpose of the DSS/PSI studies in the 1990s and of the more recent FACS Surveys is to investigate the factors, including Income Support measures such as Family Credit and the Working Families Tax Credit, impacting on the work and well being of families with dependent children. The PSE Survey has a different brief: to assess the degree of material hardship relative to publicly agreed standards of necessity, and to explore directly different aspects of social exclusion rather than inferring such exclusion from poverty or joblessness. In this chapter, the focus of analysis is a comparison of the poverty and social exclusion of lone mothers compared with mothers in two-parent families, and compared to solo women of working age who do not have dependent children living with them. We look at poverty in terms of income deprivation and the deprivation of necessities; labour market exclusion; and exclusion from social relations[3]. As the situation of children is discussed in Chapter Eleven, the focus here is on the situation of lone mothers themselves compared to partnered mothers and solo women. All three of these groups are relatively disadvantaged: women are worse off than men, and households with children are also often worse off than other sections of the population. Marsh and McKay (1993) suggest that, although there are similarities between poor lone-parent and poor two-parent families, there are also differences in their disadvantage[4].

The characteristics of lone mothers and partnered mothers in the PSE sample endorse existing knowledge about such families. Lone mothers are more likely to have only one child, and they are younger than partnered mothers. Nevertheless, lone mothers are not predominantly young and unmarried as stereotypes tend to suggest. Although 16% are under 25, nearly half (48%) are over 35; among partnered mothers, 7% are under 25 and 56% over 35. Less than half the lone mothers (43%) are never-married, and more than half (57%) divorced, widowed or separated. In this respect, they resemble the solo women (45% never married, 55% divorced, widowed or separated) more than the partnered mothers, 84% of whom are married to their current partner. Lone mothers are more likely to suffer pain and/or limiting long-standing illness than partnered mothers, although the risk is even higher for solo women. For partnered mothers, limiting long-standing illness is not particularly associated with poverty; for those dependent on their own resources, both lone mothers and solo women, there is a closer association between such illness and poverty.

Poverty and deprivation

The relative poverty of lone mothers and their families is indisputable. The PSE Survey confirms this poverty. As Table 14.1 shows, lone mothers are more likely to be poor according to the PSE measure than are mothers in two-parent families[5]. But even mothers with partners are a relatively disadvantaged group compared to the population as a whole, as are solo women. Lone mothers suffer a double disadvantage, first by being mothers, and second by mothering alone and not having access to a male wage.

Respondents were asked whether they regarded themselves as poor. The replies to this question suggest that people are likely to slightly understate their poverty, but otherwise map well on to the PSE measure. The closeness of this relationship suggests that the responses to a question about lifetime poverty may also be treated as reasonably accurate. And, as Tables 14.2 and 14.3 show, solo women and lone mothers again contrast markedly with partnered mothers, notwithstanding the extreme circumstances of the lone mothers. Over two thirds of lone mothers describe themselves as always or 'sometimes' poor, compared with around half of solo women and just over one in five mothers in two-parent families. And both lone parents and solo women are more likely to have experienced poverty frequently or for much of their lives, although it is notable that solo women are the

Table 14.1: Levels of poverty of lone mothers, solo women and partnered mothers (%)

	Lone mothers	Solo women	Partnered mothers	Total sample
Poor	67	42	29	26
Rising	2	7	3	2
Vulnerable	13	10	5	13
Not poor	18	42	63	60
Total	100	100*	100	100*

Note: * Figures do not add up to 100% due to rounding.

Table 14.2: Perceived poverty of lone mothers, solo women and partnered mothers (%)

Current perception of poverty	Lone mothers	Solo women	Partnered mothers	Total sample
All the time	20	17	4	7
Sometimes	50	32	19	20
Never	31	51	77	73
Total	100*	100	100	100

Note: * Figure does not add up to 100% due to rounding.

Table 14.3: Persistent poverty of lone mothers, solo women and partnered mothers (%)

Experience of lifetime poverty	Lone mothers	Solo women	Partnered mothers	Total sample
Never	40	54	62	59
Rarely	16	8	13	13
Occasionally	30	23	13	19
Often	9	15	10	7
Most of the time	5	0	2	2
Total	100	100	100	100

most likely to have experienced a lifetime of poverty. This is particularly striking, given that the social class profile of the solo women closely resembles that of the partnered mothers, with about 30% being in managerial or professional occupations, and only 7% in routine occupations, while the occupations of lone mothers are classified as professional or managerial for only 11%, and for 25% as routine.

One of the strengths of the PSE Survey is its capacity to translate raw figures about poverty into images of substantive material deprivation. This is reflected both in data about housing, and the deprivation of material and social necessities, summarised in the Appendix to this chapter. Lone mothers have worse housing than either solo women or partnered mothers. Almost two thirds of lone mothers are in rented social sector accommodation, compared to 30% of solo women and 11% of partnered mothers. Lone mothers report more problems with accommodation than do partnered mothers. While both groups may suffer from lack of space (unlike solo women), the quality of space occupied by lone mothers and their children is markedly worse than that of two-parent families. This group is much more likely to suffer from housing problems such as damp, rot and mould; to lack light; and to lack space to sit outside. Although solo women are less likely to be owner-occupiers than partnered mothers and more likely to be living in social housing, they are the least likely to report problems with their accommodation. They are, however, the group most likely to lack outside space.

Asked about individual necessities, however, the picture changes. The necessities index contains seven items relating to the state of the home: a damp-free house, adequate heating to living areas, carpets in living rooms and bedrooms, adequate beds and bedding, enough money to keep the home in a decent state of decoration, to replace worn-out furniture, and to repair or replace household appliances. Partnered mothers are as or more likely than the general population to have each of these items, although even so 10% lack a damp-free house, and over a third lack enough money to replace worn-out furniture. Lone mothers are not only more likely to suffer from damp housing (19%), but only a minority can afford to replace worn-out furniture (29%), repair appliances (42%) or keep the home in a decent state of decoration (61%). What is most striking, however, is that solo women are also far less likely than partnered mothers to have these necessities. And although on most items they score better than the lone parents, in some instances they are the worst off: they are the least likely to have carpets, adequate bedding, adequate heating and decent decoration. A similar pattern emerges for household appliances and consumer durables. Partnered mothers are more likely than the population as a whole to have access to a car and to own each item on a list of appliances including washing machine, dishwasher and home computer. Lone mothers are far less likely to own any individual item, with less than 40% having access to a car compared with 94% of partnered mothers, and 7% lacking a washing machine. Again, solo women as a group are worse off than partnered mothers, but also less likely to own a range of appliances than are the lone parents. Lone mothers are less likely to possess adequate clothing than partnered mothers, who are themselves marginally less well off in this respect than the population as a whole. Over a quarter of lone mothers do not own two pairs of weatherproof shoes, and bought second-hand, rather than new, clothes. Partnered mothers also eat better than lone mothers. Like the population as a whole, 11% of mothers in couples do not have fresh fruit or vegetables daily, but this is true of 18% of lone mothers. Solo women, however, are the most deprived of the food items: 13% do not regularly have two meals a day and 22% lack fruit and vegetables.

Levels of deprivation can be assessed not just by the individual items, but also by the number of material and social necessities lacked by the different groups. Again, all three groups are worse off than the general population, with lone parents showing the greatest depth of poverty. As Table 14.4 shows, over 70% of lone parents lack two or more necessities, compared with 49% of solo women, 32% of partnered mothers, and 28% of the population as a whole. Over half of lone parents lack five or more necessities, compared with 31% of solo women, 16% of partnered mothers, and 14% of the whole population.

Deprivation is also signalled by the disconnection or restricted use of utilities. A quarter of all lone mothers have experienced utility disconnection of some kind (chiefly telephone disconnection), nearly five times the level in the general population and four times that for partnered mothers and over three times that for solo women. However, far higher proportions have restricted their use of the telephone, of

Table 14.4: Proportion of lone mothers, solo women and partnered mothers lacking different numbers of perceived necessities (%)

Number of necessities	Lone mothers	Solo women	Partnered mothers	Total sample
None	20	39	54	59
One	9	13	15	14
Two to four	18	18	16	14
Five or more	53	31	16	14

fuel and even of water below the level they need because of cost. Here, as Table 14.5 shows, partnered women are again in a better situation, while solo women and lone parents are both more severely deprived.

These patterns of deprivation suggest that while the absence of a male wage accounts for the difference in living standards between partnered and lone mothers, it also impacts on solo women. Thus the poverty of lone mothers is attributable to gender, as well as to motherhood.

Table 14.5: Proportion of lone mothers, solo women and partnered mothers restricting use of utilities because of cost (%)

Utility whose use is restricted	Lone mothers	Solo women	Partnered mothers	Total sample
None	59	68	89	89
Water	9	2	1	1
Gas	27	17	6	6
Electricity	20	21	5	6
Telephone	27	18	9	6

Labour market exclusion

The relationship between paid work and social exclusion is contested. Government policy is directed to raising labour force participation rates on the assumption that this is a route out of poverty. Paid work is also seen as inclusionary as a form of social participation in its own right. At the extreme, social inclusion and labour force participation may be treated as synonymous (Hutton, 1995; Levitas, 1998a). The PSE data provide evidence on labour force participation. Whether non-participation constitutes exclusion, however, is less clear.

Table 14.6 shows that over half of all lone mothers in the sample are either in paid work or unemployed, leaving some 40% without current attachment to the labour market, although none of them have never worked[6]. Slightly more are in part-time than in full-time employment.

Table 14.6: Labour market activity of lone mothers, solo women and partnered mothers (%)

Individual labour market activity	Lone mothers	Solo women	Partnered mothers	Total sample
Full-time work	21	51	27	40
Part-time work	27	8	49	16
Unemployed	9	15	2	3
Permanently unable to work	2	20	2	5
Other 'inactive'	41	6	21	36
Total	100	100	100	100

Notably, the levels of paid work and unemployment combined for lone mothers are quite close to those for the general population, for well over 40% of the adult population are not in paid work; however, as we have seen, lone mothers are more vulnerable to poverty and deprivation. Partnered mothers are more likely to be in employment, with a labour force participation rate of 78% including a tiny number of unemployed, but their work is predominantly part-time rather than full-time. They are far less likely to describe themselves as unemployed, and about half as likely to have no labour market attachment. They are also more likely to be in paid work than solo women, whose labour force participation rate is 74% including 15% unemployment. One in five solo women describe themselves as permanently unable to work, but those in work are overwhelmingly likely to work full time.

However, when we look at household relations to the labour market, the differences are starker. Only 5% of partnered mothers live in a household with no paid workers, and over two thirds (68%) are in a household with two or more people in paid work, compared with 41% for the total sample. Their household access to income from wages and salaries is thus significantly greater than for the population as a whole. In this respect, too, lone mothers are more like solo women. While 53% of lone mothers are in jobless households, a surprising 44% of single, working-age women living alone also have no paid work, compared to a third of the total sample.

To describe this situation as labour market exclusion constructs labour market participation as the norm, with government policies focusing on supply-side measures to boost participation. Prior to the 1997 Election and the institution of the NDLP, Labour's campaigning literature insisted that 'most lone parents want to work' – ignoring the fact that the research on which this claim was based only demonstrated that most lone parents wanted and expected to engage in paid work at some time in the future, not immediately. Marsh and Perry (2003, p 147) argue that the reason most commonly given by lone parents for not being in paid work is that they do not want to spend more time away from their children. This, together with the cost of childcare, is also the primary reason given in the 2004 FACS Survey (Barnes and Willitts, 2004). Other researchers have suggested that the willingness to move into work is governed by gendered moral rationalities and local discourses, meaning that the views of many mothers, lone or partnered, about employment are bound up with views of the obligations and responsibilities of motherhood (Duncan and Edwards, 1999; Barlow and Duncan, 2000; Millar and Ridge, 2001). Less attention has been given to demand-side factors, such as the availability of employment that is compatible with childcare responsibilities in terms of time and location, and which is sufficiently well paid to outweigh the time costs. The original aims of the NDLP referred explicitly to the sustainability of paid work, as well as the transition into it, but in practice it has been wholly focused on the latter (Hasluck, 2000; see also Millar, 2000). Thus the emphasis on paid work has remained an issue of debate.

However, the presumption that paid work, even when available and sustainable, is necessarily a route out of poverty is not borne out by the PSE data. Very few if any of our three groups of women who are in workless households are not poor, but in all cases a substantial proportion of those households with paid work remain poor. This risk is highest for the lone mothers, nearly half of whom remain poor even when in paid work, including about two thirds of those in part-time work, and about a quarter of those in full-time work. About a third of solo women in paid work are in poverty, as are just over a quarter of partnered mothers. This is partly attributable to the kinds of paid work that lone mothers do, the vast majority being in low-skilled manual or non-manual work, or work in personal services.

Exclusion from social relations

Lone mothers suffer exclusion from common social activities such as socialising with friends and family (see the Appendix at the end of this chapter). Overwhelmingly they attribute this limitation on their social lives to lack of money rather than choice. Just over a quarter are able to participate in all the listed activities, compared with over half the partnered mothers and solo women. Two thirds of lone mothers are excluded from two or more activities, compared with around one third of each of the other two groups (Table 14.7). Less than half of lone mothers have a week's holiday away from home each year; they are far less likely than other groups to holiday abroad. They are also

Table 14.7: Number of common social activities participated in by lone mothers, solo women and partnered mothers (%)

	Lone mothers	Solo women	Partnered mothers	Total sample
Participates in all common social activities	27	53	53	63
Lacks one activity	7	15	9	11
Lacks two or more activities	67	33	38	27
Total	100*	100*	100	100*

Note: * Figures do not add up to 100% due to rounding.

much less likely to have an occasional meal out, or to have a hobby or leisure activity. Only 9% travel by coach or train to visit friends or family, with nearly half of lone mothers unable to afford such contact.

All three groups are disadvantaged overall compared with the population as a whole. Nevertheless, there are some differences between the groups in the patterns of exclusion. Both lone mothers and solo women are more likely than partnered mothers to have an evening out or to go to the pub once a fortnight, presumably reflecting their common need for adult company outside the home, and are less likely to have family or friends round for a meal, snack or drink (which may be connected with the relatively poor state of their accommodation, as well as direct cost). Solo women, however, are least likely to engage in some forms of socialising that may reflect close bonds or the needs of children, such as having celebrations on special occasions, visiting friends and family, attending weddings and funerals, or visiting friends and family in hospital.

The main shuffle-card question gave women who did not participate in each individual activity the options of don't do/don't want and don't do/can't afford. Lone-parent respondents overwhelmingly opted for the can't afford option on most items. However, there is evidence that other factors, notably shortage of time, also curtail participation in common social activities. When women were asked the general question of which factors are important in limiting participation, and allowed to list more than one, time proved crucial for both sets of mothers, although not for the solo women (Table 14.8).

The 'time-crunch' calculation shows, unsurprisingly, that all mothers are much more likely to experience moderate or extreme time stress than are other groups in the population. Poverty also increases vulnerability to time stress for all groups – although less so for lone mothers than for partnered mothers. Paid work is likely to increase time stress for lone parents, without necessarily lifting them out of poverty, and thus constrain rather than promote social participation.

Table 14.8: Main factors inhibiting social participation by lone mothers, solo women and partnered mothers (%)

	Lone mothers	Solo women	Partnered mothers	Total sample
Cost	100	89	61	50
Lack of interest	25	29	23	44
Lack of time due to childcare	55	6	50	18
Lack of time due to other caring responsibilities	8	2	2	4
Lack of time due to paid work	5	8	20	14
No vehicle/poor public transport	16	17	3	5
No one to go out with	8	22	0	6

Although lack of money and lack of time curtail social interaction, we cannot infer that lone mothers are socially isolated. It is notable that they are barely more likely than the sample as a whole to cite 'no one to go out with' as a reason for non-participation. Again, it is solo women for whom this was an issue. For both these groups, not having a car and poor provision of public transport are a constraint. And while more than a third of all three groups feel unsafe walking alone in the dark, the figure is higher for solo women and highest of all for the lone mothers, over 43% of whom experience fear.

The confining effects of fear and poor transport exacerbate problems of time and money. But in terms of social networks and social support, lone motherhood does not seem to lead to exclusion from social relations. Levels of reported contact with family and friends are higher for all three groups of women than for the population as a whole, and almost all have contact with family and friends at least weekly. Lone mothers are the most likely to have daily contact (81%), and the most likely to have at least weekly contact (95%) with a family member outside the home. Only 2% do not speak to family or friends daily, compared with 13% of the population as a whole. These networks are relied on for financial survival. Unlike partnered mothers, who are hardly more likely than the general population to 'borrow to make ends meet', a large number of the lone mothers (42%) had done so, overwhelmingly from family (26%) or friends (17%). Most lone mothers also report good levels of emotional support, indeed better than those reported by partnered mothers (Table 14.9). The levels of practical support available to lone mothers are, however, lower than for those in couples. Again, this suggests that the problems lone mothers face are primarily practical, rather than constituting exclusion from social relations. Solo women are worse off on every indicator of social support than either group of mothers, and worse off than the general population[7].

Table 14.9: Proportion of lone mothers, solo women and partnered mothers with no or not much support in specified situations (%)

Type of support	Lone mothers	Solo women	Partnered mothers	Total sample
Help around home when ill	16	20	18	9
Help with heavy tasks	16	18	14	13
Help with informal caring	13	46	8	29
Looking after possessions	14	13	11	11
Advice	5	15	8	13
Talking to if depressed	5	13	7	11
Help with relationship problems	12	21	11	23

The findings of the PSE Survey in relation to lone mothers are clear. Their problems are primarily practical and material. The poverty of lone mothers impinges on their social participation. They need more resources in order to have the material and social necessities endorsed by the population as a whole. And they need access to these without an intensification of the time pressure they already experience.

Are things getting better?

The PSE Survey was carried out in 1999, before New Labour's policies for increasing labour market participation and supporting the incomes of families had time to take effect. It provides a base-line for future studies of poverty and social exclusion, and a comparison with substantive deprivation in earlier Breadline Britain Surveys (Mack and Lansley, 1985; Gordon and Pantazis, 1997), but cannot in itself tell us whether recent policies have reduced the hardship of lone mothers and their children. HBAI figures suggest that the relative income poverty of lone-parent households has declined slightly, although even this is susceptible to differences in measurement. In 1999/2000 57% of lone-parent households had incomes less than half the contemporary mean, compared with 20% of couples with children; the proportions with incomes below 60% of the contemporary median were almost identical, at 58% and 20% respectively (DWP, 2001). The 60% median has subsequently been adopted as a common measure across the EU. By 2001/02, the proportion of lone parents below this level had dropped to 53%, with the risk for couples with children remaining constant at 20%. However, the proportion of lone parents below 50% of mean household incomes had changed hardly at all, at 56%, while the proportion of couples with children in this economic category had risen to 21% (DWP, 2003). By 2002/03, there was a slight improvement, with 53% of lone-parent households below 50% of mean incomes, and 20% of two-parent families; 51% of lone-parent households were below 60% of the median (DWP, 2004)[8].

The best sources of data on changes since 1999 are the SOLIF/ FACS Surveys. These postdate the PSE Survey, with the first sweep being carried out in 1999, and the second and third in 2000 and 2001[9]. Their principal objectives are to analyse the effectiveness of work incentive measures (especially the Working Families Tax Credit) and the effects of welfare policy on families' living standards. They use a variation of the Breadline Britain/PSE methodology to collect data on material circumstances and to compile a hardship index, as well as income data, routes into and out of lone parenthood, routes into and out of paid work, and information on attitudes and morale. They have the advantage of being a large enough data set to look at differences among lone parents, having over 2,000 lone-parent families in each sweep[10]. However FACS collects little information about social exclusion (and does not use the term); the presentation of the data is strongly influenced by policy concerns with the effects of paid work; and the sole focus on families with children obscures their general deprivation relative to the population as a whole, and the crucial role played by gender. And although the data set would allow for comparisons in material hardship over time, the latest published results (Marsh and Perry, 2003; Barnes and Willitts, 2004) do not report the data in this form.

In terms of the government's own strategies, Marsh and Perry (2003) report some evidence of success. Lone parents increased their labour market participation. The proportion of lone parents in paid work for 16 hours or more a week rose from 38% to 48% over a period of 27 months, while 29% of those working between 16 and 29 hours a week in 1999 were working over 30 hours by 2001. Consequently, the proportion receiving in-work benefits rose from 18% to 28% – although an alarming 8% of lone parents and 24% of low/moderate-income couples with children were eligible for but not receiving Working Families Tax Credit. By 2002, 34% of lone parents were in receipt of Working Families Tax Credit, although the published data do not indicate whether this is a result of greater eligibility or better take-up; however, the proportion working 16 or more hours a week was unchanged at 48%. Payment of Child Support is more common where the lone mother is in work, and there is a close association between the payment of such support and contact between child(ren) and non-resident fathers. However, FACS – in common with almost all official statistics – does not analyse these results by social class. It does endorse the suggestion that much of this is an age effect, with younger, single mothers less likely to be in paid work or to receive Child Support. Moving onto Working Families Tax Credit ostensibly makes the family less poor, as the rates are more generous than Income Support. However, the fact that 'welfare to work' means, for most lone mothers 'welfare to work plus welfare' is underlined by the fact that in 2001 only 10% of all lone parents (including lone fathers) earned enough to be ineligible for benefits of some kind, while in 2002, 66% of lone parents working more than 16 hours a week received Working Families Tax Credit. Moreover, without the direct measures of hardship based on the PSE approach, it is impossible to know what the increased income means in practice, once in-work costs are taken into account. And increased labour market participation is likely to produce greater time poverty for lone parents.

Longitudinal analysis of the first two years of the FACS Surveys is not encouraging: Vegeris and McKay (2002) show that two thirds of lone-parent families experience hardship, compared with less than half of couples with dependent children. While 44% of lone parents were better off in 2000 than in 1999, 32% were actually worse off. The proportion of lone parents *not* experiencing hardship rose only slightly from 32% to 36%, despite the substantial increase in labour market participation[11]. Nevertheless, they give a qualified endorsement to inducing lone parents into work, implying a kind of lag effect between improved income and the reduction of hardship. FACS, they say, provides:

> ... more evidence to back the importance of a full-time earner to better living standards and equally the importance of job retention for avoiding family hardship. By far, non-working families (the biggest single group being lone parent families) were the most deprived of material goods and social participation and experienced the highest incidence of hardship. Efforts to help these families find jobs should take account of the hardship carried through into work which is sometimes slow to respond to additional income. (Vegeris and McKay, 2002, p 93)

'Making work pay' has resulted in a situation where lone mothers (and others) who remain on Income Support suffer severe hardship, as shown both by the PSE Survey and by FACS. In 2001, nearly half of all lone parents were dependent on Income Support. For most, this was clearly a transitional dependency: nearly a third of recipients had been receiving the benefit for less than two years, and over half for less than four. Some women cease to be classified as lone mothers simply because their children have grown up and cease to be officially classified as dependent. A substantial proportion leave lone parenthood for cohabitation or marriage, and, historically, this has been the main way out of poverty for lone mothers (Kiernan et al, 1998). Estimates of the mean duration of lone parenthood vary from three to six years. It is shorter for single lone mothers than for those who are separated or divorced, partly because they are younger (Kiernan et al, 1998; Rowlingson and McKay, 2002), but there is some evidence that it is rising (Marsh and Perry, 2003). Consequently, many lone parents remain poor for extended periods of time. In 2002, 35% of all lone parents (as well as 30% of two-parent family claimants) had been dependent on Income Support for over six years (Barnes and Willitts, 2004). More non-earning families in 2000 reported running out of money each week than in 1999. They were four times as likely to experience severe hardship as families with a wage earner (Vegeris and McKay, 2002). Applying the principle of 'less eligibility' contradicts the promise of 'work for those who can, security for those who cannot'. Vegeris and McKay accept that paid employment may not be an option for some families because of the ill health of parents and children, and may be inappropriate or indeed unavailable at some times for others. If they still treat workforce participation as the ultimate goal, Vegeris and McKay properly do not treat the hardship experienced by such families as necessary and natural, and see it as an artefact of the benefit system that needs to be addressed. Especially in the light of explicit policy goals to eradicate child poverty, they argue that "welfare policy needs to adequately support out-of-work families towards a more optimal time for workforce participation, if at all possible" (Vegeris and McKay, 2002, p 93).

This, like the PSE Survey findings, would point towards a more redistributive policy based on need rather than labour market participation. However, the political possibility of this has been undermined rather than furthered in recent years. The general legitimacy of lone parenthood has increased together with a reduced emphasis on the importance of marriage and traditional family forms and roles. At the same time, social attitudes, at least among families with children, have become more rather than less hostile to supporting lone mothers as full-time carers (Marsh and Perry, 2003)[12]. The British Social Attitudes Survey also suggests that attitudes have hardened against redistribution. These attitudinal shifts may themselves be partly the result of government rhetoric and policy. But they also act against the government's own goals. FACS also shows that morale and self-esteem are undermined by hardship and by ill health, both of which are disproportionately suffered by lone parents. Higher morale is associated with entry to paid work, and may well also be relevant to the possibility of (re)partnering; (re)partnering is also more common among lone mothers who are better off financially[13]. More importantly, levels of morale are crucial to quality of life.

Conclusion

The combination of widening general inequality (Marsh, 2001) with persistent gender inequality in the distribution of paid and unpaid work (Millar, 1989; Kiernan et al, 1998; Millar and Ridge, 2001), places lone parents in a particularly vulnerable position. The PSE Survey documents the consequences of this in terms of material and social deprivation. It shows that lone mothers remain one of the poorest groups in society, and that this poverty constrains their own lives and social participation as well as the opportunities they are able to offer their children. Paid work will not necessarily solve their problems: they are likely to remain materially deprived and may suffer increased time poverty. And whether or not they are in paid employment, lone mothers are undoubtedly all working long hours in an unpaid capacity caring for so many of the country's children.

Notes

[1] Thanks also to Paula Surridge, who suggested the comparison with solo women; to Dave Gordon, for repeated data runs; and to Jonathan Bradshaw for contributions to an earlier working paper on this topic.

[2] We have chosen this comparison for two reasons. One is that the number of lone fathers in our sample was very small, and the situation of lone fathers is often different from that of lone mothers because they stand in a different relationship to the labour market. The other is that mothers generally are a relatively disadvantaged group, partly but not only because households with children are on average less well off than those without. In two-parent families, in the 50% of cases where the informant was the mother, higher rates of poverty were reported than when the informant was the father. Although this means that the information we have about couples is not strictly comparable with the Families and Children in Britain (FACS) Survey, it is closer than it would be if the PSE (Poverty and Social Exclusion) Survey households where the father was the informant were included, as by design over 99% of the FACS respondents in couples were mothers (Marsh and Perry, 2003, p 26). The data in the current analysis defines a lone mother

as a woman living alone with children aged 16 or under. The comparator groups are women of working age (under 60) living alone, and mothers in two-parent families with children aged 16 or under. The sample sizes are 115, 72 and 130 respectively, weighted to 45, 41 and 195 in a total sample size of 1,536.

[3] Service exclusion is the subject of Chapter Eight (in this volume) and civic participation is discussed in the working paper by Bradshaw and Williams (2000) (see www.bris.ac.uk/poverty/pse/work_pap).

[4] The experience of lone mothers may also vary with ethnicity. In the PSE sample about 11% of the lone mothers and 4% of the partnered mothers in the sample were from a minority ethnic group. These numbers are too small for further analysis, although it is worthy of note that all the minority ethnic lone mothers in the sample were poor. Given the incidence of poverty among minority ethnic groups as a whole, this is unsurprising but disturbing. Recent work on minority ethnic lone parents includes Pettigrew (2003) and Reynolds (2001).

[5] See Chapter Two, in this volume, for definitions.

[6] They would officially be defined as 'economically inactive'. However, this definition ignores the economic importance of unpaid and caring work, so the term will not be used here.

[7] The PSE Survey explores social support through asking respondents about the level of support they have in each of seven situations. Four items relate to practical support: needing help around the home when in bed with the flu; help with heavy household and gardening jobs; help with caring responsibilities for children or elderly or disabled adults; having someone to look after the home or possessions when away. Three are related to emotional support: needing advice about an important life change; someone to talk to if depressed; and someone to talk to about problems with a spouse or partner.

[8] All figures here are for incomes After Housing Costs (AHC). Notably, the 2004 FACS Survey gives only Before Housing Costs (BHC) figures, which suggest that 26% of lone parents (and 12% of couples) are below 60% of the median. These figures are lower than those in the 2004 HBAI, where the corresponding figure is 31%. This discrepancy is probably the result of differences between FACS/HBAI in definitions of lone-parent families/ lone-parent households.

[9] These surveys are designed to generate both cross-sectional and longitudinal data on the circumstances of families with children. The first two sweeps include lone-parent families at all income levels, and couples with children with low and moderate incomes; the third (and later) sweeps include better-off couples with dependent children, to produce a representative sample.

[10] Of these, in 2001, 4% were headed by lone fathers; 41% by women separated or divorced from marriage; and 28% separated from cohabitation. Only 2% of lone parents were widows, and the remaining 24% were women defined as single. By single, the Department for Work and Pensions mean never married to or cohabiting with the father of their dependent children, although they may have been divorced or separated from an earlier relationship. 'Single' thus refers to current living arrangements, rather than marital status.

[11] These analyses are not repeated in the 2004 FACS report.

[12] Because FACS only collects data from families with dependent children, and collects it almost entirely from mothers, this may reflect the fact that mothers in couples, as well as lone mothers, are under increasing pressure to undertake paid work even while their children are very young.

[13] While (re)partnering remains a significant route out of poverty, it cannot be assumed that this is always an unequivocally positive outcome for mothers or child(ren).

References

Barlow, A. and Duncan, S. (2000) 'Supporting families? New Labour's communitarianism and the "rationality mistake": Part 1', *Journal of Social Welfare and Family Law*, vol 22, no 1, pp 23-42.

Barnes, M. and Willitts, M. with Anderson, T., Chaplin, J., Collins, D., Groben, S., Morris, S., Noble, J., Phillips, M. and Sneade, I. (2004) *Families and children in Britain: Findings from the 2002 Families and Children Study (FACS)*, DWP Research Report 206, Leeds: Corporate Document Services.

Bradshaw, J. and Millar, J. (1991) *Lone parent families in the UK*, DSS Research Report 6, London: HMSO.

Bradshaw, J., et al (1996) *Policy and the employment of lone parents in 20 countries*, Observatory on National Family Policies, York: University of York/EU.

Carabine, J. (2001) 'Constituting sexuality through social policy: the case of lone motherhood 1834 and today', *Social and Legal Studies*, vol 10, no 3, pp 291-314.

Duncan, S. and Edwards, R. (1997) *Single mothers in an international context: Mothers or workers?*, London: UCL Press.

Duncan, S. and Edwards, R. (1999) *Lone mothers, paid work and gendered moral rationalities*, London: Macmillan.

DWP (Department for Work and Pensions) (2001) *Households below average income 1994/95-1999/2000*, DWP, Leeds: Corporate Document Services.

DWP (2003) *Households below average income 1994/95-2001/02*, DWP, Leeds: Corporate Document Services.

DWP (2004) *Households below average income 1994/95-2002/03*, DWP, Leeds: Corporate Document Services.

Finlayson, L., Ford, R., Marsh, A., McKay, S. and Mukherjee, A. (2000) *The British lone parent cohort 1991 to 1998*, DWP Research Report 128, Leeds: Corporate Document Services.

Ford, R., Marsh, A. and McKay, S. (1995) *Changes in lone parenthood 1989-1993*, DSS Research Report 40, London: HMSO.

Gordon, D. and Pantazis, C. (eds) (1997) *Breadline Britain in the 1990s*, Bristol: Department of Social Policy and Planning, University of Bristol.

Hasluck, C. (2000) *Evaluation of the New Deal for Lone Parents*, DSS Research Report 110, Leeds: Corporate Document Services.

Head, E. (2004) 'Caring and paid work in the lives of lone mothers', PhD Thesis, Bristol: University of Bristol.

Hutton, W. (1995) *The state we're in*, London: Jonathan Cape.

Kiernan, K., Land, H. and Lewis, J. (1998) *Lone motherhood in twentieth century Britain: From footnote to front page*, Oxford: Clarendon Press.

Kilkey, M. (2000) *Lone mothers between paid work and care: The policy regime in twenty countries*, Aldershot: Ashgate.

Land, H. (1999) 'New Labour, new families?', *Social Policy Review 11*.

Levitas, R. (1998a) *The inclusive society? Social exclusion and New Labour*, Basingstoke: Macmillan (2nd edn, Palgrave Macmillan, 2005).

Levitas, R. (1998b) 'Social inclusion and the politics of New Labour: welfare, work and lone parent families' in V. Ferriera, T. Tavares and S. Portugal, *Shifting bonds, shifting bounds: Women, mobility and citizenship in Europe*, Oeiras: Celta Editora.

Lewis, J. (ed) (1997) *Lone mothers in European welfare regimes: Shifting policy logics*, London: Jessica Kingsley.

Lewis, J. (2000) 'Work and care', *Social Policy Review 12*.

McKay, S. (2002) *Low/moderate-income families in Britain: Work, working families' tax credit and childcare in 2000*, DWP Research Report 161, Leeds: Corporate Document Services.

Mack, J. and Lansley, S. (1985) *Poor Britain*, George Allen and Unwin: London.

Marsden, D. (1969) *Mothers alone: Poverty and the fatherless family*, London: Allen Lane/Penguin Press.

Marsh, A. (2001) 'Helping British lone parents get and keep paid work', in J. Millar and K. Rowlingson (eds) *Lone parents, employment and social policy: Cross-national comparisons*, Bristol: The Policy Press.

Marsh, A. and McKay, S. (1993) *Families, work and benefits*, London: Policy Studies Institute.

Marsh, A. and Perry, J. (2003) *Family change 1999-2001*, DWP Research Report 180, Leeds: Corporate Document Services.

Marsh, A. and Rowlingson, K. (2002) *Low/moderate-income families in Britain: Changes in 1999-2000*, DWP Research Report 165, Leeds: Corporate Document Services.

Marsh, A., Ford, R. and Finlayson, L. (1998) *What happens to lone parents*, DSS Research Report 77, London: The Stationery Office.

Millar, J. (1989) *Poverty and the lone parent family: The challenge to social policy*, Aldershot: Avebury.

Millar, J. (2000) 'Lone parents and the New Deal', *Policy Studies*, vol 21, no 4, pp 333-45.

Millar, J. and Ridge, T. (2001) *Families, poverty, work and care: A review of literature on lone parents and low income families*, DWP Research Report 153, Leeds: Corporate Document Services.

Millar, J. and Rowlingson K. (eds) (2001) *Lone parents, employment and social policy: Cross-national comparisons*, Bristol: The Policy Press.

Murray, C. (1990) *The Emerging British Underclass*, London: Institute for Economic Affairs.

Murray, C. (1994) *Underclass: The crisis deepens*, London: Institute for Economic Affairs.

OECD (1998) *Employment outlook*, June, Paris: OECD.

Pettigrew, N. (2003) *Experiences of lone parents from minority ethnic communities*, DWP Research Report 187, Leeds: Corporate Document Services.

Reynolds, T. (2001) 'Black mothering, paid work and identity', *Ethnic and Racial Studies*, vol 24, no 6, pp 1046-64.

Roseneil, S. and Mann, K. (1996) 'Unpalatable choices and inadequate families. Lone mothers and the underclass debate', in E. Silva (ed) *Good enough mothering? Feminist perspectives on lone motherhood*, London: Routledge.

Rowlingson, K. (2001) 'The social, economic and demographic profile of lone parents', in J. Millar and K. Rowlingson (eds) *Lone parents, employment and social policy: Cross-national comparisons*, Bristol: The Policy Press.

Rowlingson, K. and McKay, S. (2002) *Lone parent families: Gender, class and state*, Harlow: Pearson.

Rowlingson, K. and Millar, J. (2001) 'Supporting employment: emerging policy and practice', in J. Millar and K. Rowlingson (eds) *Lone parents, employment and social policy: Cross-national comparisons*, Bristol: The Policy Press.

SEU (Social Exclusion Unit) (1999) *Teenage pregnancy*, London: SEU.

Smith, R. (1999) 'Arguing against the cuts in lone parent benefits: reclaiming the desert ground in the UK', *Critical Social Policy*, vol 19, no 3, pp 313-34.

Standing, K. (1999) '"Parental" involvement; a contradiction in policy?', *Journal of Social Policy*, vol 28, no 3, pp 479-95.

Sutherland, H., Sefton, T. and Piachaud, D. (2003) *Poverty in Britain: The impact of government policy since 1997*, York: Joseph Rowntree Foundation.

Vegeris, S. and McKay, S. (2002) *Low/moderate-income families in Britain: Changes in living standards*, DWP Research Report 164, Leeds: Corporate Document Services.

Appendix 14.1

Table A14.1: Material and social necessities and standard of accommodation enjoyed by lone mothers, solo women and partnered mothers (% in each category who have item/do activity)

Item	Lone mothers	Solo women	Partnered mothers	Total sample
Accommodation problems				
No accommodation problems	40	58	51	57
Two or more problems with accommodation	31	15	16	18
Shortage of space	31	15	30	21
Not enough light	11	5	2	5
Inadequate heating facilities	7	5	8	6
Leaky roof	2	0	7	4
Damp walls/ floors/ foundations etc	16	8	8	8
Rot in window frames/ floors	11	10	6	11
Mould	13	10	6	6
No outside space	11	13	3	6
Household necessities				
Damp-free house	81	85	90	90
Adequate heating to living areas	93	90	99	97
Carpets in living rooms and bedrooms	98	78	95	95
Adequate bedding	98	90	100	99
Money to keep home in decent state of decoration	61	60	82	83
Money to replace worn-out furniture	29	44	64	64
Money to repair/replace appliances	42	60	83	78
Contents insurance	51	73	93	85
Consumer durables				
Car	39	59	94	76
Fridge	95	90	99	97
Freezer	91	88	100	95
Washing machine	93	85	100	96
Tumble dryer	47	46	67	58
Dishwasher	9	17	43	30
Microwave	79	75	91	81
TV	95	100	100	99
Video	88	88	98	90
Satellite TV	25	15	35	31
Phone	86	95	97	98
Mobile phone	43	43	66	44
Home computer	32	20	59	39
Internet access	10	28	36	26
CD player	88	70	94	75
Food				
Two meals/day	93	87	94	96
Fresh fruit/veg daily	82	78	89	89
Meat/fish/equiv daily	82	77	98	94
Roast joint/equiv weekly	77	64	91	85

(continued)

Table A14.1: (continued)

Item	Lone mothers	Solo women	Partnered mothers	Total sample
Clothes				
Two pairs all-weather shoes	74	85	88	90
Warm waterproof coat	81	83	89	94
New, not second-hand, clothes	74	83	91	91
Dressing-gown	86	85	95	87
Outfit for special occasions	81	83	90	92
Outfit for job interviews	71	75	87	76
Miscellaneous				
Dictionary	80	90	95	92
Presents for family/friends	85	87	99	96
Savings for rainy day or retirement	33	53	72	66
Daily newspaper	35	53	48	58
Small amount to spend on self	44	71	71	83
Money for all prescribed medicines	93	83	92	91
Activities				
Hobby or leisure activity	62	85	77	79
Evening out once a fortnight	53	55	47	59
Meal out once a month	36	58	55	59
Visit to pub once a fortnight	44	43	30	45
Week's holiday a year	42	65	69	67
Annual holiday abroad	18	49	41	46
Celebrations on special occasions	93	85	100	96
Friends/family round for meal, snack or drink	76	80	85	83
Visits to friends/family	96	88	99	94
Coach/train fares to visit family/friends	9	25	19	25
Attending weddings/ funerals	91	83	96	93
Visiting friends/family in hospital	80	66	87	84
Attending church, synagogue, mosque etc	21	30	35	30
Collecting children from school	65	13	77	31
Visits to school sports day/ parents evening	81	13	87	37

FIFTEEN

Pensioners, poverty and social exclusion

Demi Patsios

Introduction

Over the past five years, the aim of tackling of poverty and social exclusion has driven some of the major policy initiatives of the UK government (DSS, 1999). Until very recently, however, the emphasis was on children and young families and those of working age detached from the labour market. Less attention was paid to the plight of those people in retirement or at the latter stages of the lifecourse. According to Howarth et al (1999), this has been because of the perceived absence of adequate data on the nature of poverty and social exclusion experienced by older people, although a recent Social Exclusion Unit (SEU) report draws on a range of data to discuss issues affecting older people including poverty, social isolation and exclusion from services (ODPM, 2005). The Poverty and Social Exclusion (PSE) Survey offers considerable scope for expanding not only our understanding of the material and social hardships faced by some older people but also informing policy which addresses their circumstances and needs.

The relative merits of different approaches to understanding and measuring poverty and social exclusion have been thoroughly addressed in earlier chapters (see Part 1: Principles). This chapter focuses specifically on the prevalence and incidence of poverty and social exclusion among people of pensionable age. In particular, it examines the extent to which some pensioner groups are more vulnerable to material and social deprivations than others.

At present, there are around 11 million pensioners in the UK: 4 million men and 7 million women. Pensioners make up around 18% of the population. The pensioner population is rising, mainly because people are living longer (ONS, 1999). Not only are older people living longer and healthier lives, the position of pensioners, on average, has been improving relative to the rest of society. In the 1980s and

1990s, pensioner incomes grew by two thirds in real terms (DSS, 2000). These changes have resulted in improvements in the economic status of a number of older people, enabling many more of them to lead lives of greater independence. Not all pensioners, however, have benefited equally from these real rises in pensioner income. Those better-off pensioners benefited more than the worse-off pensioners in terms of real income (DSS, 1999). Thus, the stereotype that most pensioners are living on low incomes and struggling to make ends meet is only partially correct (SCSS, 2000). Nevertheless, many pensioners continue to live at or near poverty levels. This is particularly true for widowed and single pensioners, especially older women.

Much of the literature on social exclusion, particularly at European level, focuses on attachment to the labour market. Older people reaching retirement age are required to withdraw from paid employment and they may, therefore, be more susceptible to both poverty and some forms of social exclusion. The imposition of a statutory retirement age causes a 'structured dependency' and focusing on employment does not adequately address the social processes of the exclusion of older people (Townsend, 1981; Walker, 2000). Social exclusion should be seen in terms of a loss of access to all life chances society has to offer. It should be understood in respect of one's ability to participate in the mainstream life of society.

Pensioner poverty: findings from the PSE Survey

Income poverty

Income has long been used as an indicator of pensioner poverty (cf Townsend and Wedderburn, 1965). Table 15.1 presents a summary of four different measures of income poverty:

- percentage below 50% mean of McClements (HBAI [Households Below Average Income]) net weekly equivalised income;
- percentage below 50% mean of PSE net weekly equivalised income;
- percentage below 60% median of modified OECD (Organisation of Economic and Cooperative Development) net weekly equivalised income; and
- percentage below Minimum Income Guarantee (MIG) threshold (as at April 2001).

Table 15.1: Net weekly household income and percentage of pensioner households falling 'below' selected measures of income poverty (Before Housing Costs [BHC]) in the PSE Survey

	Younger pensioner couple	Older pensioner couple	Younger single pensioner	Older single pensioner	All pensioner households
PSE net weekly income (not equivalised)	£284	£249	£150	£122	£218
50% mean McClements (HBAI)	33	58	43	55	41
50% mean (PSE)	32	60	50	62	43
60% median (OECD)	32	58	49	59	43
MIG[a] (April 2001)	7	46	21	46	19
Total (n)	143	22	103	33	301

Notes: Younger pensioner couple: two adults, female 60 to 79 years of age, male 65 to 79 years of age (one or both), living together.

Older pensioner couple: two adults, male and female 80 years of age and older (one or both), living together.

Younger single pensioner: one adult, female 60 to 79 years of age or male 65 to 79 years of age, living alone.

Older single pensioner: one adult, male or female 80 years of age and older, living alone.

[a] MIG: Minimum Income Guarantee threshold calculated using April 2001 level (£78.45 a week for a single person, £86.05 for those aged 80 or over, £121.95 for a couple, £131.05 for those aged 80 or over).

Table 15.1 shows that the prevalence of income poverty can depend on the measurement used. For older pensioners (looking at both singles and couples), estimates of income deprivation range from 46% to 62%, whereas for younger pensioners they range from 7% to 50%. However, there are relatively small differences in the poverty rates based on the three equivalisation scales and income thresholds (HBAI, PSE and modified OECD). The significant differences are between these three income poverty measures and the MIG rates, which are considerably lower, and so a much smaller percentage of pensioners have incomes below MIG levels. Table 15.1 also shows that older pensioners are relatively more likely than their younger counterparts (singles and couples alike) to be income poor.

The PSE findings also reveal that income deprivation is not equally distributed between older men and women. Figure 15.1 shows that women – particularly those living alone – are more likely than men

Figure 15.1: Gender differences in measurements of poverty within pensioner households (% below, BHC)

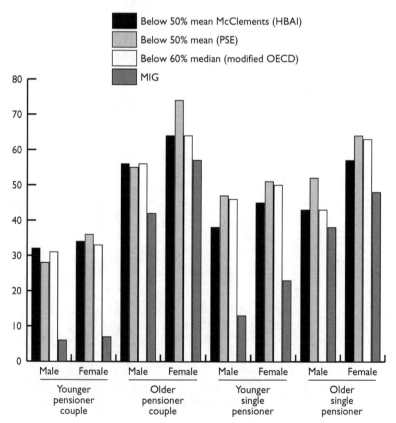

434

to be income poor irrespective of which measure is used (see also Chapter Thirteen on the relationship between gender and poverty).

To sum up, older pensioners, particularly those living in single pensioner households and older women, are most likely to be 'at risk of poverty' due to low income. Two in five pensioner households fall below the 'blunt' measures which are often used by the government and statisticians as indicators of poverty. This confirms past findings that not all pensioners have benefited equally from real rises in pensioner income and that pensioners lower down on the income distribution have gained less in terms of average income growth since the 1980s (DSS, 2000).

However, a major limitation of using income or benefits as a proxy measure (or indicator) of poverty is that many low-income households do not claim the benefits to which they are entitled. This problem is particularly acute among households comprised of older people (DWP, 2002). Between 22% and 36% of these eligible households do not claim Income Support (DWP, 2002). However, there are also other benefits going unclaimed by eligible pensioners, including Housing Benefit, Council Tax Benefit and Attendance Allowance. While it can be argued that priority should be given to those missing out on Income Support, it is important to realise that pensioners not claiming their entitlement to help with housing costs or the cost of their own or their spouse's disability could well end up with disposable income (after housing and the costs of disability) below MIG levels.

Lack of socially perceived necessities

Unlike measures of income poverty which rely solely on net equivalised household income, the PSE Survey method establishes the proportion of respondents who are not able to afford two or more items and/or activities which 50% or more of the general population consider as necessities and who also have a low net equivalised income (see Chapter Two in this volume for further explanation of the PSE measure).

Table 15.2 presents the percentage and risk (odds ratio) of different pensioner households being poor according to the PSE Survey method. According to this measure, 22% of all pensioner households are likely to be poor – they suffer from both low income and multiple deprivation. This is a slightly lower proportion than the rate for non-pensioners (25%). Furthermore, when pensioners living in different types of households are compared, pensioner couples have relatively low rates of poverty (15%) and single pensioners have average poverty levels

Table 15.2: Percentage and risk (odds ratio) of being poor using the PSE measure

	Poor (%)	Odds ratio
Younger pensioner couple	17	0.6
Older pensioner couple	13	0.5
Younger single pensioner	30	2.1
Older single pensioner	19	0.9
All pensioner households	22	1.0

(25%). Younger single pensioners are *relatively* most likely to be poor. Older single pensioners are somewhat less likely and pensioner couples half as likely to be poor.

Subjective poverty

The use of either household income as a proxy or risk 'indicator' or the PSE Survey method as a 'measure' of poverty is problematic as both methods assume that there is an equal sharing of resources among all household members. Neither really takes account of differences in lifestyles nor the tastes and preferences of different pensioner groups or individuals within the household. Older people – because of the period in which they grew up (the 1930s depression and the Second World War) – typically do not exhibit the same consumption and expenditure patterns as their younger counterparts. Understandably, there will also be differences between those living in single pensioner households versus pensioner couple households and so on. Nor does either method tell us very much about how much income pensioners say they need to prevent living in poverty and being excluded from a 'minimum standard of living'.

One way to establish the level of income needed for a minimum standard of living is simply to ask pensioners. It could reasonably be argued that it is they who are in the best position to determine how much income is needed to keep a household like theirs out of poverty. Establishing subjective poverty thresholds was done by asking respondents whether they were poor or not using *absolute* and *overall* definitions of poverty adopted by the United Nations World Summit for Social Development in Copenhagen in 1995. Respondents estimated the average weekly income needed to keep a household like theirs out of each of these different subjective levels of poverty (see Chapter Three in this volume, for further discussion of these measures).

Table 15.3 summarises respondents' views in 1999 on the level of income needed to keep their type of household above each of the

Table 15.3: Subjective assessments of 'general', 'absolute' and 'overall' poverty and income needed each week to surmount poverty (%)

	Younger pensioner couple	Older pensioner couple	Younger single pensioner	Older single pensioner	All pensioner households
MIG (2001)	£122	£131	£78	£86	
Absolute poverty					
Mean estimated weekly income	£138	£172	£110	£94	£126
Above	83	65	62	67	73
Below	15	12	25	14	18
About the same	3	23	14	19	9
Total (n)	131	16	92	26	266
General poverty					
Mean estimated weekly income	£186	£175	£118	£106	£154
Above	63	59	54	58	59
Below	19	18	29	11	21
About the same	18	23	17	31	19
Total (n)	135	15	95	26	271
Overall poverty					
Mean estimated weekly income	£186	£231	£142	£118	£167
Above	68	47	48	59	59
Below	21	31	38	24	27
About the same	11	22	14	17	13
Total (n)	130	16	87	25	257

Notes: Numbers represent average pounds per week/column percentages.

Missing values and Don't knows excluded from calculation of percentages. Errors are due to rounding.

Outlier value of £9,996/week (n=1) excluded from calculation of mean estimated income to surmount 'absolute poverty'.

Outlier value of £3,000/week (n=1) excluded from calculation of mean estimated income to surmount 'overall poverty'.

poverty lines and the extent to which their household income fell below or above these subjective poverty thresholds. The MIG rates in April 2001 are shown for comparison; they are significantly lower for all types of pensioner households than the subjective absolute poverty threshold.

Eighteen per cent of pensioners report that their incomes are insufficient to avoid absolute poverty. Similarly, 21% say their incomes are below the general poverty threshold and 27% of pensioners have incomes below the overall poverty threshold level. The 'objective' PSE poverty rate of 22% for pensioners is effectively identical to the 'subjective' general poverty rate of 21% reported by pensioners and both these rates are higher than the percentage of pensioners (19%) with incomes below the MIG levels, indicating that the MIG levels are set too low to avoid both objective and subjective poverty.

Figure 15.2 shows that poor pensioners have an average household income higher than the MIG rates, indicating that the MIG rates are at least £10-£40 per week too low to prevent poverty. Non-poor pensioner households have average weekly net incomes which are considerably higher than the MIG rates.

Other researchers have attempted to establish the actual level of income needed to meet 'minimum' and 'adequate' standards of living based on people's actual living circumstances. Parker (1999) estimated the net income required for those 65-74 years of age to reach a Low

Figure 15.2: Average difference between actual net weekly household income and the MIG, by PSE measure

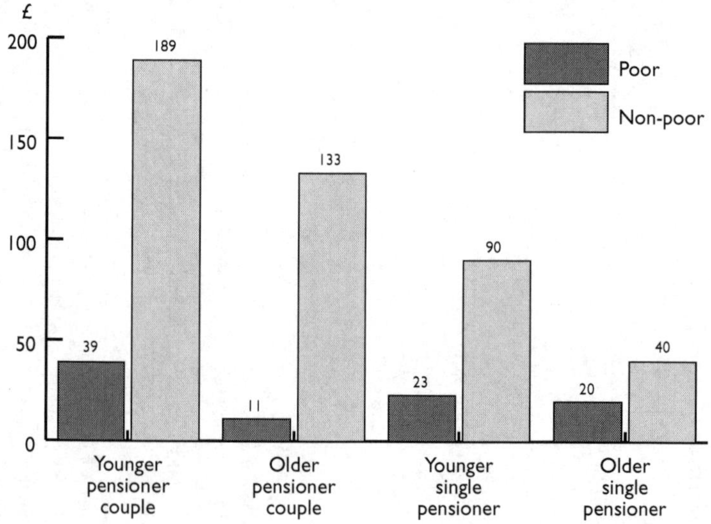

Cost but Acceptable (LCA) standard of living (and to live healthily). Her LCA approach used budget standards methodology and showed that incomes needed to cover basic living costs varied according to age, gender, household composition, heating system, availability of public transport and other variables. It presented actual preferred spending patterns of low-income older people and the income levels needed to avoid poverty. As the author pointed out, however, these were not intended to represent the amounts that all pensioners in these age groups needed to achieve a certain living standard. Circumstances, needs and expectations varied, and although some households may be able to manage on the LCA, others may need more.

Surveys in Britain (for example, Family Resources Survey, Pensioner Income Series), including the PSE Survey, have consistently shown that older pensioners have significantly lower incomes than younger pensioners. Part of the reason for this is that by this stage in life some older people have exhausted their savings and have seen the real value of their pensions eroded, since the upratings link with earnings was abolished in 1980. Equally important, a significant number of today's pensioners were unable to build up good second pensions during their working lives because of low wages, caring responsibilities, or long periods of unemployment. In short, they had little opportunity to save for a comfortable retirement and many older pensioners now find that the pension which was adequate when they retired is no longer sufficient to maintain a minimum standard of living (Hirsh, 2003). The government has acknowledged some of these problems and has introduced measures to help alleviate income poverty. For example, it provides the over-75s with a free television licence and has boosted Winter Fuel Payments for the over-80s. According to Sutherland et al (2003), despite minor changes to the tax and benefits system and improving benefit take-up, these policy changes were not sufficient to make up for the upward movement in the income poverty line[1]. However, pensioners often have lower housing costs than younger households (particularly owner-occupiers), so income poverty lines which do not take account of housing costs (such as the UK government's and European Union's [EU] preferred methods used in this study) often overestimate the extent of pensioner income poverty.

To further combat pensioner poverty, the government introduced the MIG in April 2001, in the belief that the levels set could lift almost all single pensioners and pensioner couples living in rented accommodation above the key 'half average income' threshold (HBAI). Although this represented a significant step towards eradicating pensioner poverty, the reality is that there is still a problem due to lack of take-up and the insufficient levels at which the MIG/Pensioner Credit were set. Approximately 2.5 million older people who are entitled to claim the MIG (now known as the Guarantee Credit) because their income is so low do not claim it. Some find the means test which assesses the financial circumstances of the pensioner and their spouse quite invasive and stigmatising. Eligible non-claimants of benefits should be a major concern for the government, which has gone some way by simplifying forms, running promotional campaigns and reducing the number of times pensioners are means tested, but clearly more needs to be done to ensure benefits reach those entitled to them. However, it must also be said that some pensioners, regardless of their circumstances, will choose not to undergo such an 'investigation' nor receive assistance from the state.

Additionally, some older people on lower incomes do not save for retirement because they could lose means-tested state benefits which would otherwise be available under Income Support, leaving them no better off. Thus, the most effective way forward was seen to be an improved basic state pension which acts as a foundation on which to build up savings. An increased basic state pension would also reach the large group of pensioners who are not in receipt of Income Support, who fail to claim means-tested assistance and who are thus living at incomes below the MIG level (SCSS, 2000).

To this end, the Government replaced the MIG with the Pensions Credit in October 2003. It has two parts, both of which are assessed jointly for couples: the *Guarantee Credit* (GC), based on the MIG but with some relaxation of rules, and the *Savings Credit* (SC), which is an additional top-up for those with modest incomes above the MIG and/or basic pension level. The Pension Credit seeks to mitigate the problem whereby individuals who have saved for retirement find that they lose benefits that would have been available under the MIG if that saving had not been made. In short, it attempts not to penalise pensioners who have built up their savings for retirement, thereby avoiding the problem of the 'savings/poverty trap'.

Although little is known about what to expect in relation to take-up of the new tax credits, Sutherland et al's (2003, p 36) policy simulations estimates of poverty suggest that these policy changes may result in a poverty rate reduction of three percentage points from 21% to 18% between the policy regimes of 2000/01 and 2003/04 on a BHC basis. The reduction on an AHC basis was much greater – 11 percentage points from 26% to 15%. It is difficult to compare the current findings with these simulations as Sutherland et al simply counted the number of pensioners living in households with income below the poverty line, that is, below 60% of contemporary median equivalised income, without trying to distinguish by family type or the characteristics of other family members.

Pensioners and social exclusion: findings from the PSE Survey

The PSE Survey framework distinguished four dimensions of exclusion: impoverishment, or exclusion from adequate income or resources; labour market exclusion; service exclusion; and exclusion from social relations. The first of these aspects, poverty (objective and subjective), was covered in the previous section. The following sections set out the main findings of the Survey in relation to the other three dimensions, with particular emphasis on service exclusion and exclusion from social relations.

Exclusion from the labour market

The labour market provides an important arena for social contact and interaction. For those active in the labour market, employment is a major route to adequate income. However, given the statutory retirement age in Britain, 93% of pensioners in the Survey are unsurprisingly 'labour market inactive'. Interestingly, however, nearly one in nine younger pensioners (single and couples) are still working. Using most contemporary definitions of social exclusion which rely heavily on attachment to the labour market, almost all pensioners would be considered socially excluded. Living in a jobless household has also been used as an indicator of social exclusion (Gordon et al, 2000). One quarter of younger pensioner households and just over one half of younger single pensioners live in households with one or more workers. Using this measure, six out of 10 younger pensioners and all older pensioners are 'excluded'. As discussed elsewhere (Chapters Five and Six by Levitas and by Bailey, in this volume), we should be cautious about treating labour market inactivity in itself as social exclusion, since it affects a very high proportion of the population, especially pensioners (Gordon et al, 2000).

The 'structured dependency' (Townsend, 1981) created by statutory retirement[2] prevents many pensioners from working their way out of poverty. The cost of providing state pensions is also increasing because people are living longer after they stop working. The government has phased in retirement at 65 for women born after the 1950s, which would bring Britain in line with an EU directive outlawing discrimination regarding retirement on the basis of age. It is also considering further increases to the retirement age for workers as part of its plans to reduce the cost of funding pensions, as well as offering attractive incentives to those who choose to defer the state pension for five years[3]. Although the government has made some positive steps in the right direction – outlawing discrimination in employment and vocational training on the grounds of age and allowing older people to combine occupational pension income with earnings – it is still presented with various policy challenges in terms of supporting working after state pension age. Among these are: devising campaigns to challenge negative attitudes towards older workers; changes in the law to abolish statutory retirement and give older workers the right to ask for more flexible hours; financial strategies to increase income and provide incentives for employers and older people; and more help and advice for people approaching retirement (Barnes et al, 2004). The government's strategy in response to these challenges, outlined in *Opportunity age* (DWP, 2005), which includes additional employment rights and financial incentives, should serve to reinforce the government's commitment to end age discrimination as well as having broader benefits to pensioners suffering various social and economic disadvantages.

Service exclusion

Another key component of social exclusion is lack of access to basic services, whether in the home (basic domestic services such as power and water supplies) or outside the home (common public and private services such as transport, shopping facilities and financial services).

Utility disconnection, restricted use and borrowing money

PSE Survey respondents were asked if any of their utilities had ever been disconnected or if they had ever used less than they needed. They were also asked if they ever had to borrow money in order to pay for their day-to-day needs. Although there was some evidence that a few younger single pensioners have problems with their telephone being disconnected (2%), overall there was little evidence that pensioners have problems generally with utilities being disconnected. The winter moratorium banning the disconnection of elderly consumers between October and March every year probably accounts for the low rates of disconnections for gas or electricity, but there may also be a general reluctance on the part of fuel companies to disconnect 'vulnerable' customers during other times of the year. Although rates of disconnections among older groups are low, the PSE Survey provides evidence that many pensioners – particularly poorer and younger pensioners – restrict their use of certain utilities. Overall, 7% of pensioners restrict their use of such services as gas, electricity and the telephone.

Using the PSE poverty measure, Figure 15.3 shows the percentage of poor compared to non-poor pensioners reporting restricted use of at least one utility. Roughly one in five (couples) and one in four (singles) poor younger pensioners report restricted use. However, restricted use of utilities is much less common among older pensioners.

Relatively fewer poor older pensioners – although they may have low incomes – report restricted utility use. This may be because they are more likely than younger pensioners to rent in the social sector, where properties typically have high-energy efficiency according to the government's Standard Assessment Procedure (SAP) for home energy ratings (DTI/DEFRA, 2001). The results also indicate that very few older pensioners (poor and not poor) had to borrow money in the last year to pay for their day-to-day needs but that one in 10 poorer younger pensioners 'had to' borrow money from their families to pay for their day-to-day needs.

Figure 15.3: Percentage of poor and non-poor pensioners reporting restricted use of at least one 'domestic' utility

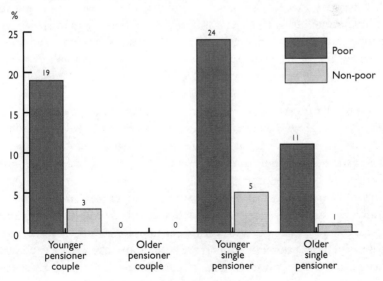

Use of public and private services

An older person's ability to remain independent in the community depends on access to a range of public and private services as well as those provided to meet personal care needs, so if services such as public transport are not available, they are more likely to be affected (DSS, 1999). In this instance, it is helpful to draw on the distinction Powell et al (2001) made between 'people poverty' and 'place poverty'. Older people may not have lower incomes but, by virtue of where they live, they are excluded from mainstream society because necessary public and private services simply are not present or adequate to meet their material and social needs. Scharf et al's (2002) study[4] is of some relevance here, having found that the impact of social exclusion on older people has a more serious effect on those living in deprived areas. This distinction is not dissimilar to Gordon et al's notions of 'individual exclusion' and 'collective exclusion' (2000) where the former relates to services being unaffordable and the latter relates to services simply not being available or being unsuitable.

In the PSE Survey, respondents were asked about access to a range of public services (libraries, hospitals), private services (places of worship, public transport) and services for the elderly and/or disabled (home help, meals-on-wheels); see also Fisher and Bramley, Chapter Eight in this volume. Table 15.4 provides a summary of the three service areas (public, private and elderly/disabled services) plus a combined public/private service category in terms of availability, affordability and both. The results show that availability ('collective' exclusion) rather than affordability ('individual' exclusion) is the major problem for accessing public and private services for pensioners, whereas for elderly/disabled services, the opposite is true. Being unable to afford public/private services affects single pensioners more than pensioner couples (young and older alike). Roughly one in three single pensioners cannot afford or do not have available in their area at least two public and/or private services. Moreover, older single pensioners are least likely to be able to afford or have available at least one elderly/disabled service. Roughly 7% of single pensioners cannot afford use of special transportation for those with mobility problems.

Further analyses revealed that poverty is integrally related to service exclusion among pensioners. When individual (affordability) and collective (availability) exclusion are combined for each major service type, in general, poorer pensioners are much more likely to be excluded than non-poor pensioners. This is particularly the case for private services.

Table 15.4: Individual and collective exclusion from two or more public/private services and from one or more elderly/disabled persons' services

	Younger pensioner couple	Older pensioner couple	Younger single pensioner	Older single pensioner	All pensioner households
Public services					
Cannot afford	1	0	3	0	1
Unavailable	6	0	7	7	6
Cannot afford/unavailable	8	0	11	7	8
Private services					
Cannot afford	3	0	3	0	3
Unavailable	9	14	14	23	13
Cannot afford/unavailable	13	14	19	23	16
Public/private					
Cannot afford	4	0	7	0	4
Unavailable	19	14	25	31	22
Cannot afford/unavailable	26	14	32	31	28
Elderly/disabled services[a]					
Cannot afford	3	6	9	13	6
Unavailable	1	0	2	5	2
Cannot afford/unavailable	4	6	10	17	7

Notes: Numbers represent column percentages.

[a] Questions about services for older people were only asked if the respondent was over 64 years of age or had a long-standing illness or disability. Three elderly/disabled services were asked about : home help, meals-on-wheels, and special transport for those with mobility problems. For comparative purposes, one or more elderly/disabled persons' services have been used as the threshold.

Activity and service use restricted due to health or disability

It is important to note that factors other than affordability and availability can result in exclusion from services. Older people can feel that they are isolated from or prevented from engaging in the normal activities of society due to a health problem or disability. The PSE Survey looked at the presence and severity of pain, long-standing illness, disability or infirmity and the extent to which these health and disability conditions affect participation in activities or use of services. The proportion of respondents reporting pain or discomfort varied somewhat between different pensioner groups – single pensioners are slightly more likely (10% in each case) than pensioner couples (6% in each case) to report severe pain or discomfort. Notwithstanding differences in the experience of pain or discomfort, similar proportions of younger and older pensioners report the presence of a long-standing limiting illness (roughly 60% in each case) and whether or not this illness limits their activities generally (roughly 30% in each case). Moreover, poorer pensioners are relatively more likely than non-poor pensioners to report that they have 'severe pain' or a long-standing illness, and one which limits their activities.

There are differences between pensioners when they were asked about specific activities and services which they cannot participate in due to their limiting illness. Older pensioners (single and couples) are more likely than younger pensioners to report that their health problem/disability prevents participation in the following activities: going shopping (approximately 25%), going to the cinema or theatre (approximately 20%), and going to the library or museum (approximately 19%). A significant minority of disabled pensioners are therefore excluded from using many services due to inadequate levels of access. It is to be hoped that this discriminatory situation may change as the provisions of the 1995 Disability Discrimination Act become more fully implemented. Pensioners living in poverty are also more likely than those not living in poverty to report that a health problem or disability prevents them from participating in these specific activities and services.

Specific difficulties with activity/service use

Those people reporting a long-standing illness, disability or infirmity and at least one problem with participating in the activities and/or using the services were then asked to specify the exact nature of the difficulty. Overall, two thirds of pensioners specified at least one problem.

Single pensioners (young and older alike) are more likely than pensioner couples to report difficulty getting to the venue (56% compared with roughly 35%), whereas pensioner couples are more likely to report difficulty getting to the venue and getting around once inside (35% of younger pensioners) or other problems (26% of older pensioners).

Although there have been considerable improvements in disability-free life expectancy between 1980 and 1994/95 for both men and women aged 65 and over (ONS, 1999), poorer pensioners do not appear to have shared equally in these improvements in health (Acheson, 1998; Gordon et al, 1999). The PSE findings confirm that poorer pensioners are more likely to report health problems or disabilities, and ones that limit their participation in common activities/services generally. Participation in activities rather than use of services is more problematic for older pensioners. Many poorer older pensioners are prevented from doing such things as going shopping, or going to the cinema or library, as well as using a bank or building society or using a public telephone because of their health or disability. These same pensioners confirm that they do not engage in activities because they have difficulties getting to the venue, getting into the place and moving around once inside.

The PSE Survey has shown that many poorer older pensioners have greater health problems, and as such, are excluded from participating in activities due to both a lack of income and consequent mobility problems. Some poor pensioners cannot afford special transport which confirms once more the great importance of mobility to engagement in society and the concomitant need for government intervention. Although the government does provide concessionary bus fares (50%) for all over-60s in England, it continues to deny mobility payments to those disabled over the age of 65. There is greater scope for ensuring that pensioners who have mobility problems are not excluded from fully participating in social life.

Exclusion from social relations

Engagement in social interaction with family and friends or normal social activities is a key component of social exclusion (Burchardt et al, 1999), and has recently been acknowledged as key aspect of social exclusion affecting the lives of older people (ODPM, 2005). In the PSE Survey, exclusion from social relations was operationalised in five ways: non-participation in common social activities; isolation; lack of support; disengagement; and confinement (for further discussion see Chapter Five in this volume).

Non-participation in common social activities

The PSE Survey allows us to calculate the extent to which people participate in a range of common social activities and the proportion excluded due to lack of money (affordability). One in five pensioners (19%) cannot afford to participate in at least one common social activity[5].Younger single pensioners are most likely to cite affordability as a problem (26%) and older pensioner couples least likely (6%). Lack of money is a primary cause of social activity exclusion: three quarters of poor younger pensioner couples cite affordability as a problem (compared with only 4% of non-poor pensioners).

Social isolation

Social isolation refers to the integration of individuals (and groups) into the wider social environment (Victor et al, 2002). A key component of social isolation is contact with social networks (Wenger et al, 1996), which have been shown to be instrumental to the health and well-being of older people (Rubinstein et al, 1994; ODPM, 2005). As people get older, however, their support networks often shrink and change as friends and relatives die or move, and this can result in adverse consequences for their health and well being (Choi and Wodarski, 1996). A recent survey commissioned by Age Concern (NOP, 2004) highlighted the extent of isolation among older people when it revealed that one in five people over 65 are alone for more than 12 hours a day and that more than a quarter of people over 65 do not have a best friend, which is higher than any other age group. These people are more at risk of depression and ill health caused by social isolation and loneliness (NOP, 2004).

Respondents in the PSE Survey were asked to report the frequency with which they saw or spoke to family and friends or neighbours (other than those they lived with, for example, their spouse). Compared with non-pensioners, pensioners are less likely to have at least daily contact with their social network (80% versus 88%). When pensioner households are compared, we find that single pensioners are more likely than pensioner couples to have at least daily contact with friends and neighbours (75% compared with 55% of pensioner couples), as well as weekly contact with family and friends (roughly 86% versus roughly 75% of pensioner couples). Additionally, differences are found between poor and non-poor pensioners in terms of contact with their social network. For example, two thirds of poor younger pensioner couples compared with three quarters of their non-poor counterparts report seeing family members and/or friends daily.

Respondents were also asked what prevents them contacting or seeing their family members and friends 'more often'. Almost one half of all pensioners are able to see their family and friends as often as they wish. Slightly fewer older pensioner couples (40%) see them as often as they wish. Younger pensioner couples are more likely to report living too far away (33%), whereas the other pensioner groups are more likely to report no vehicle (roughly 14% in each case) or being too ill, sick or disabled (roughly 12% in each case). Very few poorer older pensioners (single and couples alike) are not able to see their family and friends more often because they cannot afford to. Poorer older pensioner couples are more likely to give reasons such as problems with physical access or being too ill, sick or disabled (50% in each case), or that they lack a vehicle and that public transport is poor (22% in each case), whereas poorer older single pensioners are more likely to report being too old (20%). In contrast, reasons why younger pensioners do not see their family and friends are more often related to living in poverty. Roughly one in seven poor younger pensioners (single and couples alike) do not see family or friends more often because they cannot afford to.

Lack of social support

For many people, when times are hard or when help is needed, family and friends will be the first line of support (Shanas, 1979; Wenger, 1989, 1994). One indicator of a properly functioning social network is the amount of practical and emotional care and support available in times of need. In the PSE Survey, respondents were asked how much support they would 'expect' to get in seven situations (see Chapter Five in this volume for further discussion of social support), including support from members of the household, other family and friends and any other source of support. Single pensioners (younger and older) are more likely than their couple counterparts to report poor levels of practical and emotional support. One in five single pensioners compared with one in ten pensioner couples report poor levels of practical/emotional support. Poverty also appears to be related to poor levels of combined practical and emotional support. Figure 15.4 shows that poorer pensioners are more likely than non-poor pensioners to report lower levels of potential support for both types of assistance.

A consistent picture has emerged from this analysis; it is clear that for pensioners poverty is associated with greater social isolation and

Figure 15.4: Percentage of poor and non-poor pensioners reporting lower levels of combined practical and emotional potential support

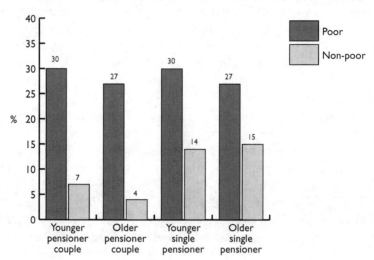

reduced social support, particularly in poorer younger pensioner households.

Civil and political disengagement

Another important indicator of social exclusion is engagement in community or civic affairs (for example, club membership and voting). Respondents were asked about a range of civic activities undertaken in the last three years as well as any current involvement. Overall, 13% of pensioners are not involved in any activities. Older pensioners are least likely to be involved in civic affairs during the last three years (26% of singles and 16% of couples). Older pensioners – especially single pensioners – are less likely than younger pensioners to have: presented their views to a local councillor; urged someone outside their family to vote; urged someone to get in touch with a local councillor; or been an officer of an organisation or club. However, no major differences exist between poor and non-poor pensioners in terms of past civic engagement.

In terms of current civic engagement, older single pensioners are least likely to be involved (53% cited none of the activities). They are less likely than other pensioners to be a member of: a religious group or church (13%); a tenants' or residents' association (5%); a voluntary service group (2%); a sports club (1%); and any other group or organisation (5%). However, it was also found that, compared with non-poor single pensioners, poor single pensioners are more likely to be members of a social club (15%) or a tenants'/residents' association (12%). Therefore pensioner poverty is not associated with a lack of civic engagement. However, civic engagement tends to decline with increasing age.

Confinement

Some pensioners are prevented from participating in common social activities because they are either unable to get out of the home, they lack transport or they have another problem which prevents them from going out. Respondents were asked to identify factors for not participating in each of the 15 common social activities. When all factors for not participating were combined, we found that four out of five pensioners cite at least one factor which prevents them from participating in the PSE Survey activities. Younger pensioners are more likely than older pensioners to cite affordability as a factor (17% compared with 7% of older pensioners), whereas older pensioners are more likely to cite being too old, ill, sick or disabled (roughly 19%) as a key factor for non-participation. Single pensioners (younger and older) are unsurprisingly more likely than pensioner couples to report that they have no one to go out with (roughly 5%). Not surprisingly, poorer pensioners are more likely than non-poor pensioners to report lack of money as the main problem for not participating in each of the activities (roughly 31% of younger pensioners and 23% of older pensioners). However, the findings also show that poorer pensioners – particularly older pensioner couples – are generally more likely than non-poor pensioners to report being too old, ill, sick or disabled to participate in the activities (23%) and that they have problems with physical access (that is, getting into the venue) (15%).

Another form of confinement is concern for personal safety (cf DETR, 1998; Home Office, 1998). A survey carried out by Age Concern in 2002 found that one in three older people felt that fear of crime affected their quality of life and made them feel lonely and isolated (Age Concern, 2003). Although the PSE Survey found that older people (65+) are more afraid than younger people (aged 16-24) when walking around in their local area after dark, the Survey also showed that very few pensioners (roughly 1%) are confined due to their fear of crime. The evidence, from the PSE Survey, therefore, is that fear of crime does not restrict older people's involvement in activities. However, the Survey results do not allow us comment on the extent to which older people restrict when and how they engage in social activities.

Many pensioners – particularly poorer, older and single ones – are excluded from social relations because they cannot afford to participate in common social activities, are socially isolated, they lack potential social support, do not engage in civic affairs, or are socially confined. Although affordability (ability to pay) will always play a major role in the ability of older people to participate in some common social activities, it alone cannot ensure pensioner engagement. In addition, older people's social networks can contract due to death of a spouse, close relatives or friends, as well as adult children and friends moving away. The impact of exclusion from social relations may be felt most by single, older pensioners whose diminishing social networks affect not only their opportunity for social participation but also the support provided to them in times of need. Arguably, exclusion from social relations may have the greatest impact on pensioners given their stage in the lifecourse.

Poverty is clearly a major cause of pensioner exclusion – it is associated with restricted utility service use, increased debts, inability to access elderly services (home helps, meals-on-wheels, etc), inability to participate in common social activities and increased confinement, social isolation and a lack of social support. However, poverty is not a cause of reduced civic engagement among pensioners, and nor is it a direct cause of exclusion from some public and private services.

Given that informal social networks are the major source of support and care provided to frail elderly people living in the community (Wenger, 1989, 1994), it is disconcerting that many pensioners, particularly single poorer ones, do not feel that they have practical and emotional support in times of need. As such, there is a need to develop policies that not only facilitate such relationships, but sustain them as well (Scharf et al, 2002). Furthermore, some thought could also be given to allowing paid leave for workers who need to care for a parent or close relative for a short period of time. In situations where it is not possible to build up an older person's social network, the government needs to ensure that formal mechanisms can be called on in times of need. To a certain degree, programmes like meals-on-wheels and home help substitute for informal support networks, by providing a service to older people who need some help in order to remain independent in the community. The *Opportunity for All* report (DWP, 2004) does indicate that there has been an increase in the proportion of older people being helped to live independently in terms of receipt of intensive home care and receipt of community-based services between the baseline years 1998/99 and 2002/03. This is an encouraging social advance, which should help to improve the quality of life and independence of vulnerable older people by supporting them to live in their own homes wherever possible.

Given the interplay and importance of affordability, personal circumstances, social networks and personal health in determining social participation and integration, it would be difficult to suggest an all-encompassing policy for helping poorer or isolated pensioners enter into supportive and fulfilling social relationships. However, there is one group of pensioners which should be the focus of any comprehensive policy aimed at alleviating social hardships: poor single pensioners who are not able to participate because they lack a social network and/or are in poor health. Arguably, among pensioners, these are the most socially deprived and excluded.

Conclusion

This chapter has focused on the prevalence of poverty and social exclusion among people of pensionable age in Britain. A fuller picture of the extent to which income, deprivation and social exclusion affect pensioners has been provided using the PSE Survey framework. The preceding analyses have shown not only that many pensioners clearly suffer from poverty and are excluded from participating in the mainstream life of society but also that poverty, deprivation and social exclusion are inextricably linked. It has confirmed that there are many ways in which pensioners can become cut off from society and impoverished (Townsend, 1979, 1987). Poverty should be viewed as both material deprivation and the exclusion from social opportunities that makes it possible for many older people to take part in the activities that are deemed customary and 'necessary' in their community.

The picture which emerges is of two very distinct groups of pensioners, each varying in the degree to which they experience poverty and social exclusion: a 'better-off' group, made up mostly of younger pensioners living in pensioner couple households, who experience low levels of poverty and social exclusion, and a 'worse-off' group, who are often female pensioners living alone, experiencing much higher levels of poverty and social exclusion. Single pensioners are more likely to be poor than pensioner couples, irrespective of age. However, a complex picture of the nature of pensioner poverty and social exclusion has been furnished by the PSE data. Like previous, more limited research, the PSE Survey found that if only low income is examined then older pensioners are much more likely to be poor than younger pensioners – reported income decreases with age. However, almost all other measures of poverty, deprivation and exclusion show that the older the pensioner the less likely they are to be poor – reported deprivation also decreases with age. Older pensioners are less likely to be deprived of necessities due to a lack of money, less likely to have had to borrow money, less likely to have restricted utility use and less likely to be 'subjectively' poor. By contrast, older pensioners are more likely to report that they cannot afford to pay for elderly services (home helps, etc) and they also have lower levels of participation in civic activities. Poverty and exclusion are highest among single women pensioners, the majority of whom are older. However, younger single women pensioners are the poorest and most excluded group. Being widowed young has a profound impact on poverty, exclusion and well being. Government policy tends to provide increasing financial help with increasing age. However, the PSE Survey results would indicate that larger pensions and greater financial help for younger widows are needed.

These analyses have provided only a 'snap-shot' of pensioner poverty and social exclusion at the close of the millennium. To get a clearer picture of *process* versus *state*, particularly as regards poverty and social exclusion among pensioners, subsequent analyses will need to examine the extent to which there have been changes in each of the components of the main PSE framework and whether or not more pensioner-specific measures need to be incorporated.

The PSE Survey provides rich and adequate data on the experience of poverty and social exclusion of pensioners. Because the components of poverty and social exclusion are so closely tied to each other, it is very difficult to be definitive regarding policy interventions which embrace all the challenges faced by deprived and excluded older people. However, it is clear that the levels of both the state pension and the MIG/Pensioner Credit are too low to prevent pensioner poverty. Stakeholder pensions have not been a success and mis-selling of private pensions and the closure of many final salary occupational pension schemes by employers has seriously eroded the security and value of private sector pension provision. The private sector is incapable of providing an answer to pensioner poverty, particularly given that the PSE Survey found that 9% of poor respondents reported being mis-sold a "financial service such as a personal pension or an endowment mortgage" (see Pantazis, Chapter Nine in this volume). Possible solutions suggested by Townsend (1999) include widening entitlement to the basic state retirement pension and restoring the link with earnings. Means testing should be reduced by treating the basic state retirement pension as the MIG and raising it in value to a level sufficient to avoid poverty. The state pension scheme should consist of two tiers – with the lower tier being a defined minimum but *adequate* income, financed by collective provision through weekly individual 'working investments' as a percentage of earnings. A second tier based on a revised and updated SERPs model is needed as is legislation and stronger regulation to prevent further closures of final salary occupational pension schemes by employers.

Notes

[1] Based on 60% of contemporary median equivalised income.

[2] The state pension is based on national insurance contributions and is paid to people who have reached pension age (currently 60 for women, 65 for men) and who have met the qualifying conditions. Those reaching state pension age who do not have enough contributions for a full pension may get a reduced pension or may not get one at all. People can also choose to put off claiming their state pension and can earn extra state pension by doing so. At present, those in receipt of state pension are entitled to work but this is governed by the employer – employers (in their company policy) set the mandatory age of retirement for their employees. Workers who continue to work beyond state pension age have the same rights/entitlements as other workers (holidays/holiday pay, statutory notice etc) except that they do not qualify for redundancy payments and they cannot take their case before a tribunal for unfair dismissal. Many of the current provisions are likely to change in December 2006 when the government introduces its new age discrimination legislation. This will do away with compulsory retirement below the age of 65 (except where this can be objectively justified) and provides for a national default retirement age of 65 which employers can choose to adopt. However, the default age is not a compulsory retirement age. Employees will be able to work beyond that age whenever they and their employers agree. Employees who want to continue to work beyond the default retirement age or their employer's own justified retirement age will have the right to have their request considered seriously by their employer (DWP, 2005).

[3] The government appointed the Turner Commission to review the state of pensions in Britain and to produce a set of recommendations in 2005.

[4] The study interviewed adults 60+ (*n*=600) in Liverpool, Manchester and the London Borough of Newham. They used 11 of out the 20 listed PSE

Survey public and private local services. However, the Keele Study asked about frequency of use (for example, last week, last month, etc), whereas the PSE Survey asked about reasons for non-use of local services (for example, whether they were used and inadequate, or not used because they were unavailable).

[5] Calculation excludes activities which were not considered necessities by the majority (50%) of the population.

References

Acheson, D. (1998) *Independent inquiry into inequalities in health*, London: The Stationery Office.

Age Concern (2003) *The fear factor: Older people and fear of street crime – A survey of views, experiences and impact on quality of life*, London: Age Concern, March.

Barnes, H., Parry, J. and Taylor, R. (2004) *Working after state pension age: Qualitative research*, DWP Research Report No. 208, London: The Stationery Office.

Burchardt, T., Le Grand, J. and Piachaud, D. (1999) 'Social exclusion in Britain 1991-1995', *Social Policy and Administration,* vol 33, no 3, pp 227-44.

Choi, N.G. and Wodarski, J.S. (1996) 'The relationship between social support and health status of elderly people: does social support slow down physical and functional deterioration?', *Social Work Research*, vol 20, no 1, pp 52-63.

DETR (Department of the Environment, Transport and the Regions) (1998) *English House Condition Survey 1996*, London: The Stationery Office.

DSS (Department of Social Security) (1999) *Opportunity for All: Tackling poverty and social exclusion*, London: The Stationery Office.

DSS (2000) *The Pensioner's Income Series, 1997-98*, London: DSS Analytical Services Division.

DTI (Department of Trade and Industry)/DEFRA (Department of the Environment, Fisheries and Rural Affairs) (2001) *The UK fuel poverty strategy*, London: DTI/DEFRA.

DWP (Department for Work and Pensions) (2002) *Income related benefits estimates of take-up in 1999/2000*, London: The Stationery Office.

DWP (2004) *Opportunity for All: Sixth Annual Report 2004*, London: The Stationery Office.

DWP (2005) *Opportunity age*, London: The Stationery Office, March.

Gordon, D., Davey Smith, G., Dorling, D. and Shaw, M. (eds) (1999) *Inequalities in health: The evidence presented to the Independent Inquiry into Inequalities in Health*, Bristol: The Policy Press.

Gordon, D., Adelman, L., Ashworth, K., Bradshaw, J., Levitas, R., Middleton, S., Pantazis, C., Patsios, D., Payne, S., Townsend, P. and Williams, J. (2000) *Poverty and social exclusion in Britain*, York: Joseph Rowntree Foundation, September.

Hirsh, D. (2003) 'Simplicity, security and choice: work and saving for retirement', Response to Green Paper by Joseph Rowntree Foundation (www.jrf.org.uk/knowledge/responses/docs/simplicitysecurityandchoice.asp), March.

Home Office (1998) *British Crime Survey*, London: Government Statistical Service.

Howarth, C., Kenway, P., Palmer, G. and Miorelli, R. (1999) *Monitoring poverty and social exclusion 1999*, York: Joseph Rowntree Foundation, December.

NOP (National Opinion Polls) (2004) *'Generation' Survey*, New York, NY: NOP, December.

ODPM (Office of the Deputy Prime Minister) (2005) *Excluded older people*, SEU Interim Report, London: ODPM.

ONS (Office for National Statistics) (1999) *Social focus on older people*, London: The Stationery Office.

Parker, H. (ed) (1999) *Low Cost but Acceptable incomes for older people: A minimum income standard for households aged 65-74 in the UK*, Bristol: The Policy Press.

Powell, M., Boyne, G. and Ashworth, K. (2001) 'Towards a geography of people poverty and place poverty', *Policy and Politics*, vol 29, no 3, pp 243-54.

Rubinstein, R., Lubben, J. and Mintzer, J. (1994) 'Social isolation and social support: an applied perspective', *Journal of Applied Gerontology*, vol 13, no 1, pp 58-72.

Scharf, T., Phillipson, C., Smith, A. and Kingston, P. (2002) *Growing older in socially deprived areas: Social exclusion in later life*, London: Help the Aged.

SCSS (Select Committee on Social Security) (2000) *House of Commons Social Security Committee – Seventh Report, Session 1999-2000. Pensioner Poverty, HC-606*, London: The Stationery Office, August.

Shanas, E. (1979) 'The family as social support system in old age', *Gerontologist*, vol 19, pp 169-74.

Sutherland, H., Sefton, T. and Piachaud, D. (2003) *Poverty in Britain: The impact of government policy since 1997*, York: Joseph Rowntree Foundation.

Townsend P. (1979) *Poverty in the United Kingdom*, Harmondsworth: Penguin.

Townsend, P. (1981) 'The structured dependency of the elderly: the creation of policy in the twentieth century', *Ageing and Society*, vol 1, no 1, pp 5-28.

Townsend, P. (1987) 'Deprivation', *Journal of Social Policy*, vol 16, no 2, pp 125-46.

Townsend, P. (1999) *New pensions for old: The key to welfare reform*, Bristol: Townsend Centre for International Poverty Research, University of Bristol (www.bris.ac.uk/poverty/Background_files/townsend%20publications%2048-03.doc).

Townsend, P. and Wedderburn, D. (1965) *The aged in the welfare state*, London: G. Bell and Sons.

Victor, C.R., Scambler, S., Bond, J. and Bowling, A. (2002) Loneliness in later life: preliminary findings from the Growing Older project', *Quality in Ageing – Policy, Practice and Research*, vol 3, no 1, March.

Walker, A. (2000) 'Poverty and equality in old age', in J. Bond, P. Coleman and S. Peace (eds) *Ageing in society: An introduction to social gerontology* (2nd edn), London: Sage Publications.

Wenger, G.C. (1989) 'Support networks in old age: constructing a typology', in M. Jefferys (ed) *Growing old in the twentieth century*, London: Routledge.

Wenger, G.C. (1994) *Understanding support networks and community care: Network assessment for elderly people*, Aldershot: Avebury.

Wenger, G.C., Davies, R., Shahtahmasebi, S. and Scott, A. (1996) 'Social isolation and loneliness in old age: review and model refinement', *Ageing and Society*, vol 16, no 3, pp 333-58.

SIXTEEN

Conclusion

The range of topics covered in the chapters of this volume illustrates the extent and richness of the data gathered by the Poverty and Social Exclusion (PSE) Survey. Other researchers are increasingly working with the archived data set[1], but this book will remain the core summary of its methodology and findings. The conclusions of this analysis are theoretical, methodological and empirical – and, in the end, political, since there are some crucial messages that should inform social policy and the anti-poverty agenda.

The defining characteristics of the PSE Survey in its approach to poverty are twofold. First, it is based on a consensual measure, a minimum standard of living supported by a majority of the population. Second, that standard of living is conceived in concrete rather than abstract terms, and specified in terms of agreed necessities. This entails the *direct* measurement of deprivation in terms of the lack of material and social necessities, rather than *indirect* assessment on the basis of income alone.

The PSE Survey method of scientifically measuring poverty in terms of both low income and deprivation of necessities generates alarming figures for the numbers and proportion of the population living in want at the beginning of the new millennium. About one in every four people, nearly 25% of the population of Britain, were living in poverty by this measure. What this means in terms of the millions of adults and children forced to go without adequate housing, food and clothing is set out at the start of the Introduction, and elaborated throughout the book. The importance of direct deprivation measures has been accepted by the government and incorporated into its new measure of child poverty, but not as yet in relation to adults.

No headline figures comparable with those for poverty can be given for those suffering social exclusion. The PSE Survey's unique approach looks at social exclusion across a series of different dimensions – impoverishment, lack of labour market participation, service exclusion and exclusion from social relations. The last dimension is itself assessed across several facets: participation in common social activities, social networks, social support, civic participation and confinement. A key finding of the PSE Survey is that these different elements of social exclusion do not coincide with each other in a straightforward way. In the absence of such coincidence, and in the absence of either an academic or a social consensus about the meaning of social exclusion, it makes no sense to offer a headline figure of the numbers or proportion of the population socially included or excluded. What we can say, however, is that substantial proportions of the population suffer exclusion of one kind or another, and that impoverishment is a major risk factor for other forms of exclusion. While levels of social participation vary by age, gender, household type and employment status, poverty has the strongest negative effect on social participation of any of these variables.

Thus:

- Almost 10 million adults and 1 million children are too poor to be able to engage in common social activities such as visiting friends and family, having celebrations on special occasions or attending weddings and funerals.
- Nine per cent of the population have no family member outside the household who they see or speak to at least weekly. Just over 1%, or more than half a million people, have neither a friend nor a family member with whom they are in contact at least weekly.
- Nine per cent perceive themselves as unlikely to have much emotional or practical support available in times of need.
- Eighteen per cent of the population have no civic engagement at all, and that rises to 30% if voting is excluded.

The close relationship between poverty and many aspects of social exclusion is also illustrated by the discussion in Chapter Three of absolute and overall poverty. The analysis of PSE Survey data shows that these concepts, as elaborated by the United Nations, are meaningful in a British context. Not only were respondents able to say how much money would be needed to be free from absolute and overall poverty, but there was a strong relationship between responses to this question, actual levels of deprivation of necessities, and actual net household income. Thus, although subjective measures mean that "the elucidation of opinion takes precedence over the elucidation of behaviour" (p 81), the empirical evidence shows that these judgements are in practice "quite close to objective measures of ... needs" (p 82). The PSE Survey demonstrates, therefore, that absolute and overall poverty can be operationalised in nationally specific and socially meaningful ways in rich as well as poor countries, opening the way to better cross-national comparisons.

However, the scope of 'overall poverty', and especially its inclusion of needs to 'keep up with your family and social duties and relationships', and to 'feel part of your village or local community', begs questions about the separability of poverty and social exclusion. As Chapter Four shows, public assessment of necessities in 1999 holds some social activities of equal or greater importance than some material goods. There is strong public acknowledgement that the fulfilment of social roles, relationships and activities qualify as necessities of life. Indeed, there is greater consensus about the minimum acceptable standard of living than there is common experience of that standard. And there is surprisingly little variation between different social groups, apart from the divergence – and harsher judgements – of the young age group.

The Breadline Britain methodology was devised originally to counter two objections to Townsend's Poverty in the UK Survey: the need for a consensual definition of necessities, and the argument that non-possession of specified items might be a matter of choice rather than a lack of resources. Chapter Three raises some crucial issues about the limits to both consensual poverty lines and subjective measures of poverty, while both Chapters Four and Five provide decisive evidence about the role of choice and preference. In particular, both subjective measures of poverty and consensual poverty lines prioritise opinion over behaviour, activity or inactivity that might reveal need, even if that need is not articulated. The issue of choice is incorporated into the PSE Survey, as into the earlier Surveys, through asking whether particular items lacked are unwanted or unaffordable. Recent critiques have suggested that despite claims of unaffordability, the deprivation revealed in the PSE Survey reveals preference rather than poverty – that is, it is a matter of choice. This new variant of a traditional 'secondary poverty' thesis is important, especially in a political climate where customer and consumer choice are given a high priority. The analyses in Part 1 of this volume, however, demonstrate that this argument is simply wrong, and neither material nor social deprivation is chosen. Where exclusion from common social activities is concerned, the objective effect of poverty is stronger, rather than weaker, than subjective claims of unaffordability would suggest.

The second section of this book is concerned with the *processes* which result in poverty and social exclusion. Both the UK government and the European Union (EU) place considerable emphasis on the importance of unemployment and the lack of paid work as a cause of poverty and exclusion and the importance of active labour market policies as a primary policy means to tackle these problems. Chapter

Six directly addresses these arguments and provides new insights into the question 'does work pay?'. The answers are complex, with the overall picture being positive: work is associated with significantly lower levels of poverty on both objective and subjective measures, and higher levels of support, particularly emotional support. Women appear to gain more from employment in financial terms than traditional measures and income statistics would suggest.

However, the impacts of employment on poverty are far greater than on exclusion, casting doubt on the UK government's view that work is 'necessary' for inclusion. The results clearly show that more work is not always better, particularly in relation to social relationship inclusion. Part-time work is associated with greater social support, better contact with family and friends and significantly lower levels of exclusion than is either no work or full-time work. Longer hours often result in not just diminishing but negative returns. A clear policy conclusion is that part-time working for many people should be viewed as preferable and should be rewarded accordingly – and the incentives or pressures to work full time should be reduced. This issue will become increasingly important as the government seeks to extend its definition of who 'ought to work' to include a range of groups previously considered outwith the labour market – the long-term sick in receipt of Incapacity Benefits or lone parents, for example. If these groups are to be 're-connected' to the labour market, it is most likely to be on a part-time basis. Work brings some benefits in financial and social terms, but there also remain very large numbers of in-work poor and excluded.

The PSE Survey provides uniquely rich data on debt and financial exclusion, particularly in relation to wider questions of poverty and social exclusion. It allows debt and financial exclusion not only to be examined separately, but also looks at the overlaps and interactions between them. Debt is virtually non-existent among older pensioners whereas financial exclusion affects both the young and old alike. Both financial exclusion and getting into debt are unsurprisingly strongly associated with both objective and subjective poverty and low income.

Debt is a key cause of stress and poor mental health. A significant increased risk of poor mental health is found among those reporting social exclusion, not only those who are socially excluded from labour market activity but also those excluded from other activities. Particular aspects of deprivation are also associated with higher risks of common mental disorders – poor housing conditions and area deprivation, for example. The risks appear to differ for men and women, and for those who are parents. Nonetheless, the PSE Survey data suggest that all who experience poverty and exclusion are at an increased risk of suffering from poor mental health and over half of the poor have a significant risk of suffering from mental disorders.

The relationship between social exclusion and mental health suggests that policies aiming to reduce exclusion by labour market inclusion may fail to address the difficulties experienced by many of those who are in paid work. Control over one's life, both material and social, is a mediating factor between the experience of poverty or exclusion and the experience of mental ill health. Policy needs to address ways of returning that sense of control to poor and excluded men and women. The lack of control that results from poverty and exclusion has many negative manifestations, including significantly greater risks of social harm, fear of crime and victimisation. Living in poverty is both hazardous and stressful. Poverty exposes people to many forms of harm including illness, fear and debt and places enormous stress on people's social relationships especially with children, parents or partners, as well as others such as neighbours and work colleagues. Government policies that seek to protect people from the impact of crime and 'disorder' will constantly fall short if they fail to tackle the underlying cause of people's insecurity, that is, poverty.

Income redistribution both in cash but also in kind through the provision of high-quality, accessible and universally available services is the most effective method of reducing poverty and social exclusion. Unfortunately, the PSE Survey shows that many public services open to all have tended to display a decline in usage over the 1990s, and this is associated with a reduction in the proportion of people regarding these services as essential. This retreat from universalism, which partly reflects the wider range of alternatives (greater choice), may pose problems for maintaining political and financial support for such provision.

A pro-rich bias is evident in the usage of leisure and information services (libraries, museums, evening classes, etc) over the 1990s, and in many cases this bias has increased. Bus services remain pro-poor in their distribution of usage. Children's services display a mixed picture, with some shift in favour of higher incomes in the case of childcare. Services for older people show a generally pro-poor pattern, although this lessened somewhat for home care over the 1990s. For the wider group of private and public services considered in 1999, most are either neutral or pro-rich in their distribution. Only corner shops and post offices show a slight bias in favour of the poor, suggesting that these more 'local' services are important for this group.

The services for which constraints of inadequacy, unavailability or unaffordability are most widely cited are play facilities, school meals, youth clubs, and public transport for children. Unavailability/unsuitability is the dominant type of constraint, rather than affordability. These services are clearly priority targets for improvements in supply and quality, and families with children are the key group affected. Poor households face poorer quality services, and deprivation reinforces constraints on service usage. They are much more likely to report problems of local environmental quality, lack of open space, housing disrepair and crime, patterns which have persisted throughout the 1990s.

The analyses presented in Part 3 of this volume focused on *people* and confirm that the extent and impact of poverty and social exclusion are not experienced uniformly across society. The groups most affected by poverty are those who are outside the paid labour market or in a subordinated position within it. This applies both to women because of gender segregation in the labour market and also to certain minority ethnic groups not discussed in detail in the PSE Survey because of concerns about reliability associated with small samples.

Among the most vulnerable of groups are children, with their opportunities and outcomes in later life often being rooted in their experiences in early stages of the lifecourse. The impact of poverty on outcomes for children across a whole range of indicators has, of course, been recognised by government and it is why it has set itself the ambitious target of eradicating child poverty within a generation. The enormity of the task is confirmed by the PSE Survey findings that as many as one in three British children are going without at least one thing they need, such as three meals a day, toys, out-of-school activities or adequate clothing, while one in five children are worse off, lacking at least two items and activities defined as life's necessities by the majority of parents[2]. Yet, these findings are, if anything, an underestimate of the extent and degree of poverty that takes place in households and families. The PSE Survey, through its exploration of intra-household experiences of deprivation, reveals that parents are significantly more likely to go without certain material goods and activities than their children, thereby providing further empirical support for the notion of parental sacrifice. Mothers, in particular, are more likely to go without essential items such as clothes and food because of their centrality in performing caring roles and greater share of other domestic responsibilities. This finding has significant implications for anti-poverty policy.

The PSE Survey also provides evidence on the extent of poverty and impact of social exclusion on young adults. It confirms that many young people aged between 16 and 24 face distinct and challenging difficulties in making the transition into adulthood. Poverty rates for young people tend to be higher compared to older groups, with young women being at a particular disadvantage. Young people's experiences are also marred by a dissatisfaction with a range of local services, but especially community services, and young people are also much more likely to be disengaged from social, community and political participation. Although paid work is often emphasised as the best route out poverty and social exclusion, young people are often locked into work which is low paid – a situation which is reinforced and exacerbated by the exclusion of under 18-year-olds from the Minimum Wage legislation, the lower National Minimum Wage rates for those aged between 18 and 21, and young people's exclusion from the Minimum Income Guarantee (MIG).

Young women (16-24 years) living with dependent children are repeatedly much more likely to be poor on all measures. Almost one in two experience necessities deprivation and this closely mirrors their subjective assessments of overall poverty. More worrying perhaps is the finding that one in three report that their income is insufficient to keep a household like theirs out of absolute poverty. In comparison, this group of young women is more likely to be unemployed and living in jobless households, and to experience exclusion from public services due to affordability. Despite these women living in what are clearly very difficult circumstances, the PSE Survey finds that they have, however, a comparative advantage in terms of social contact and access to potential support, especially emotional support.

The PSE Survey revealed further differential impacts of poverty and social exclusion on gender. Differences exist between men and women, and there are also discrepancies within these groups. Although the government's policies on tackling poverty and social exclusion currently lack a distinctly gendered focus, the PSE findings demonstrate that women as a group are more likely than men to experience impoverishment, joblessness, service exclusion, and to have weaker practical support, although they do not experience the same extent of social isolation as men. These experiences vary by age and family status and clear patterns emerge for distinct groups.

The Survey found that many older pensionable women have precarious lives. Although poverty rates for this group are not as high as they are for younger women, they face the greatest gender inequalities. They are twice as likely as comparable men to live in a state of material and social deprivation. And although they do not experience labour market exclusion, they do experience higher than average levels of exclusion from local services, and rates of social isolation. Almost half go without speaking to family daily and more than a third go without daily contact with friends. One in ten lack weekly contact with either friends or family. This group of women, more than any other, has the poorest emotional and practical support; nearly one in five do not feel that they can rely on emotional support, while nearly one in seven lacks practical support.

Compared to partnered women with children, lone mothers and solo women have higher poverty risks and are more socially excluded, although the situation for lone mothers is dramatically worse. More than two thirds of lone mothers experience necessities deprivation (compared to 42% of solo women, and 29% of partnered women) although they often have strong support networks and good levels of emotional support. Thus, although lone motherhood often results in poverty it does not lead to exclusion from social relations. By contrast, solo women have both higher than average risks of poverty and exclusion from social relations, especially inadequate social support. This group of women not only lacks the benefits of having access to a male wage but also lacks the support that often comes from living with others.

Lack of access to a male wage plays a significant contribution to poverty risks for some groups of women but also for men. The PSE Survey finds significant reductions in paid employment exist among men in the period immediately pre-retirement (between the ages of 55 and 64). Men in this age group are more likely to be 'economically inactive' than unemployed and nearly half of those 'economically inactive' suffer from poor health. This group will soon be the target of the government's attempts to reduce Incapacity Benefit in a further drive to move people off benefits and into work. Yet the TUC (2004) claims that the vast majority of the 1.5 million who receive Invalidity Benefit "are either too ill to work ... or want to work but cannot find a job, often due to employer prejudice". The government's efforts to reduce labour market 'exclusion' (for this group of men) may increase their exclusion if the work available is full time and poorly paid.

So far these findings have generally related to non-retired groups. Chapter Fifteen reveals a complex set of findings concerning pensioner households. Although income for pensioner households declines with age, as a group pensioners experience a slightly lower rate of necessities deprivation than non-pensioners, and single pensioners – especially women – are significantly more likely to be poor. Furthermore, nearly one in five pensioners report that their incomes are insufficient to avoid absolute poverty, and the MIG rates are significantly lower for all types of pensioner households than the subjective absolute poverty threshold.

Younger single pensioners are also more likely than other retired groups to experience either individual or collective exclusion from public local services, although older single pensioners report higher similar forms of exclusion from private services, as well as exclusion from services such as home help and meals-on-wheels. Both single groups are more likely to have low levels of practical and emotional support.

Policy implications

Work isn't working

The results of the PSE Survey suggest that not only child poverty and pensioner poverty but the poverty of working-age adults needs to be at the centre of policy concerns. At the moment the policy focus on this group is almost entirely on raising labour force participation rates in the expectation that paid work will overcome poverty. The PSE Survey demonstrates that this not the case. Many of those in paid work do not earn enough to lift them out of poverty. In-work benefits may supplement income but do not address the social exclusion that results from pressure on time, especially for those with caring responsibilities. Encouraging people to work longer hours is clearly not the answer to the problems of poverty and social exclusion. Longer hours are not associated with a significant reduction in poverty and often result in social exclusion, particularly from social relations. For many, part-time work may be the optimum solution to reducing both poverty and social exclusion and maintaining control over their lives, but only if the financial rewards of part-time work are improved.

More eligibility

The policy of 'making work pay' is in fact a policy of less eligibility – that is, deliberately ensuring that those who are outside the labour market are worse off than those in paid work. This is the primary cause of poverty and social exclusion in Britain, particularly among lone parents, pensioners, the sick and disabled, and jobless households. The only solution is an increase in cash benefits and improved availability and higher quality of universal public services, free at the point of use.

Environment matters

It is not just lack of resources which results in deprivation and stress for poor people. It is also the quality of the environment in which they are forced to live. Inadequate and sub-standard housing conditions, unavailable or unsatisfactory services, run-down and dirty neighbourhoods, and crime-ridden estates result in stress and reduce people's ability to participate in social life. However, the current emphasis on area inequalities fails to address the widespread need for more investment and better social housing, and ignores the needs of the substantial proportions of the poor who do not live in poor areas (see also Pantazis and Gordon, 2000; Levitas, 2005).

Poor law

The current focus on crime and 'disorder' does not address the main problems affecting poor people such as debts and relationship difficulties. Thus the harms experienced by people living in poverty extend beyond the problems related to crime and 'disorder'. The government's current preoccupation with draconian criminalisation policies is serving to increase the very exclusion it is seeking to tackle.

The problem of riches

At the beginning of the 21st century, the UK is one of the most unequal societies in Europe. The policies pursued by Conservative and Labour governments since 1979 have resulted in a major redistribution of resources from the poor to the rich, increasing inequalities in both income and health outcomes. In order to reduce poverty and social exclusion requires that the government reverse this redistribution to the rich, and, at a minimum, return to the levels of inequality in income and power that existed in the mid-1970s. This would see poverty and social exclusion reduced by at least half. The only way to end child poverty, in particular, and poverty in general, within a generation would be to embark on a serious policy of redistribution.

Notes

[1] www.data-archive.ac.uk/findingData/snDescription.asp?sn =4349

[2] Indeed, analysis comparing the views of parents and non-parents revealed a remarkable consistency on which items constitute necessities, with both

material goods and social activities receiving strong support, thereby indicating a societal consensus on the necessities of life for children.

References

Levitas, R. (2005) *The inclusive society ? Social exclusion and New Labour* (2nd edn), Hampshire: Macmillan Palgrave.

Pantazis, C. and Gordon, D. (2000) *Tackling inequalities: Where are we now and what can be done?*, Bristol: The Policy Press.

TUC (Trade Union Congress) (2004) 'Welfare cuts would hurt genuine claimants' (www.tuc.org.uk/economy/tuc-8755-f0.cfm).

Index

Page references for figures and tables are in *italics*; those for notes are followed by n